The Economy as an Evolving Complex System III

Santa Fe Institute
Studies in the Sciences of Complexity

Lecture Notes Volume

Author	Title
Eric Bonabeau, Marco Dorigo, and Guy Theraulaz	Swarm Intelligence: From Natural to Artificial Systems
Mark E. J. Newman and Richard Palmer	Modeling Extinction

Proceedings Volumes

Editor	Title
James H. Brown and Geoffrey B. West	Scaling in Biology
Timothy A. Kohler and George J. Gumerman	Dynamics in Human and Primate Societies
Lee A. Segel and Irun Cohen	Design Principles for the Immune System and Other Distributed Autonomous Systems
H. Randy Gimblett	Integrating Geographic Information Systems and Agent-Based Modeling Techniques
James P. Crutchfield and Peter Schuster	Evolutionary Dynamics: Exploring the Interplay of Selection, Accident, Neutrality, and Function
David Griffeath and Cristopher Moore	New Constructions in Cellular Automata
Murray Gell-Mann and Constantino Tsallis	Nonextensive Entropy—Interdisciplinary Applications
Lashon Booker, Stephanie Forrest, Melanie Mitchell, and Rick Riolo	Perspectives on Adaptation in Natural and Artificial Systems
Erica Jen	Robust Design: A Repertoire of Biological, Ecological, and Engineering Case Studies
Kihong Park and Walter Willinger	The Internet as a Large-Scale, Complex System
Lawrence E. Blume and Steven N. Durlauf	The Economy as an Evolving Complex System III

The Economy as an Evolving Complex System, III

Current Perspectives and Future Directions

Editors

Lawrence E. Blume
Cornell University

Steven N. Durlauf
University of Wisconsin

Santa Fe Institute
Studies in the Sciences of Complexity

OXFORD
UNIVERSITY PRESS

2006

OXFORD
UNIVERSITY PRESS

Oxford University Press, Inc., publishes works that further
Oxford University's objective of excellence
in research, scholarship, and education.

Oxford   New York
Auckland   Cape Town   Dar es Salaam   Hong Kong   Karachi
Kuala Lumpur   Madrid   Melbourne   Mexico City   Nairobi
New Delhi   Shanghai   Taipei   Toronto

With offices in
Argentina   Austria   Brazil   Chile   Czech Republic   France   Greece
Guatemala   Hungary   Italy   Japan   Poland   Portugal   Singapore
South Korea   Switzerland   Thailand   Turkey   Ukraine   Vietnam

Library of Congress Cataloging-in-Publication Data
The economy as an evolving complex system, III : current perspectives and future directions
/ editors Lawrence E. Blume, Steven N. Durlauf.
p. cm. — (Santa Fe Institute studies in the sciences of complexity)
Papers associated with a conference of same name held at the Santa Fe Institute 2001.
Includes bibliographical references and index.
ISBN-13 978-0-19-516258-5; 978-0-19-516259-2 (pbk.)
ISBN 0-19-516258-7; 0-19-516259-5 (pbk.)
1. Evolutionary economics—Congresses. 2. Rational expectations (Economic theory)—
Congresses. 3. Economics—Congresses. I. Title: Economy as an evolving complex
system 3. II. Title: Economy as an evolving complex system three. III. Blume, Lawrence.
IV. Durlauf, Steven N. V. Proceedings volume in the Santa Fe Institute studies in the
sciences of complexity.
HB97.3.E2643 2005
330—dc22   2004054700

9 8 7 6 5 4 3 2 1

Printed in the United States of America
on acid-free paper

About the Santa Fe Institute

The *Santa Fe Institute* (SFI) is a private, independent, multidisciplinary research and education center, founded in 1984. Since its founding, SFI has devoted itself to creating a new kind of scientific research community, pursuing emerging science. Operating as a small, visiting institution, SFI seeks to catalyze new collaborative, multidisciplinary projects that break down the barriers between the traditional disciplines, to spread its ideas and methodologies to other individuals, and to encourage the practical applications of its results.

All titles from the *Santa Fe Institute Studies in the Sciences of Complexity* series carry this imprint which is based on a Mimbres pottery design (circa A.D. 950–1150), drawn by Betsy Jones. The design was selected because the radiating feathers are evocative of the outreach of the Santa Fe Institute Program to many disciplines and institutions.

Contributors List

Lawrence E. Blume, *Cornell University, Department of Economics, 430 Uris Hall, Ithaca, NY 14853, and Santa Fe Institute, 1399 Hyde Park Road, Santa Fe, NM 87501; e-mail: lbl9@cornell.edu*

Samuel Bowles, *Santa Fe Institute, 1399 Hyde Park Road, Santa Fe, NM 87505; e-mail: bowles@santafe.edu*

William A. Brock, *University of Wisconsin, Department of Economics, 1180 Observatory Drive, Madison, WI 53706; e-mail: wbrock@ssc.wisc.edu*

Christopher D. Carroll, *John Hopkins University, Department of Economics, 440 Mergenthaler Hall, Baltimore, MD 21218-2685; e-mail: ccarroll@jhu.edu*

Timothy G. Conley, *Northwestern University, Department of Economics, Evanston, IL 60208-2600; e-mail: tconley@nwu.edu*

Steven N. Durlauf, *University of Wisconsin, Department of Economics, 1180 Observatory Drive, Madison, WI 53706-1393; e-mail: sdurlauf@ssc.wisc.edu*

Marcus G. Daniels, *Santa Fe Institute, 1399 Hyde Park Road, Santa Fe, NM 87505; e-mail: mgd@santafe.edu*

David Easley, *Cornell University, Department of Economics, Uris Hall, Ithaca, NY 14853; e-mail: dae3@cornell.edu*

J. Doyne Farmer, *Santa Fe Institute, 1399 Hyde Park Road, Santa Fe, NM 87505; e-mail: jdf@santafe.edu*

Xavier Gabaix, *Economics Department, MIT, Cambridge, MA 02149; e-mail: xgabaix@mit.edu*

László Gillemot, *Santa Fe Institute, 1399 Hyde Park Road, Santa Fe, NM 87505; e-mail: laci@santafe.edu*

Herbert Gintis, *15 Forbes Avenue, Northampton, MA 01060; e-mail: hgintis@comcast.net*

Parameswaran Gopikrishnan, *Boston University, Center Polymer Studies and Department of Physics, 590 Commonwealth Avenue, Boston, MA 02215; e-mail: gopi@buphy.bu.edu*

Supriya Krishnamurthy, *Swedish Institute of Computer Science, Box 1263, SE-16429 Kista, Sweden; e-mail: supriya.krishnamurthy@sics.se*

Moshe Levy, *Hebrew University, Jerusalem Business School, Jerusalem 91905, Israel; e-mail: mslm@mscc.huji.ac.il*

Giulia Iori, *King's College London, Mathematics, Strand, London WC2R 2LS, United Kindgom; e-mail: giulia.iori@kcl.ac.uk*

Charles F. Manski, *Northwestern University, Department of Economics, 2003 Sheridan Road, #307, Evanston, IL 60208–2600*

Joel Mokyr, *Department of Economics and Hisotry, Northwestern University, 2003 Sheridan Rd., Evanston, IL 60208 and Gitan Beglas School of Economics, University of Tel Aviv; e-mail: j-mokyr@northwestern.edu*

Stephen Morris, *Yale University, Department of Economics, New Haven, CT 06520; e-mail: stephen.morris@yale.edu*

Vasiliki Plerou, *Boston University, Center for Polymer Studies and Department of Physics, Boston, MA 02215; e-mail: plerou@bu.edu*

Larry Samuelson, *University of Wisconsin, Department of Economics, 1180 Observatory Drive, Madison, WI 53706-1320; e-mail: LarrySam@ssc.wisc.edu*

Hyun Song Shin, *London School of Economics, Department of Finance and Accounting, London WC2A 2AE, United Kingdom; e-mail: h.s.shin@lse.ac.uk*

Eric Smith, *Santa Fe Institute, 1399 Hyde Park Road, Santa Fe, NM 87505; e-mail: desmith@santafe.edu*

H. Eugene Stanley, *Boston University, Department of Physics, Center for Polymer Studies, 590 Commonwealth Ave., Boston, MA 02215; e-mail: hes@bu.edu*

Giorgio Topa, *Domestic Resesarch Function, Federal Reserve Bank of New York, 33 Liberty Street, New York, NY 10045; e-mail: giorgio.topa@ny.frb.org*

H. Peyton Young, *The Johns Hopkins University, Department of Economics, Baltimore, MD 21218-2685; e-mail: pyoung@jhu.edu*

Contents

Introduction
  Lawrence E. Blume and Steven N. Durlauf   1

The Epidemiology of Macroeconomic Expectations
  Christopher D. Carroll   5

Social Learning and the Adoption of Knowledge
  Charles F. Manski   31

Rationality and Selection in Asset Markets
  Lawrence E. Blume and David Easley   49

Statistical Physics and Economic Fluctuations
  H. Eugene Stanley, Xavier Gabaix, Parameswaran
  Gopikrishnan, and Vasiliki Plerou   67

Market Efficiency, the Pareto Wealth Distribution, and the Lévy
Distribution of Stock Returns
  Moshe Levy   101

A Random Order Placement Model of Price Formation in the
Continuous Double Auction
  J. Doyne Farmer, László Gillemot, Giulia Iori, Supriya
  Krishnamurthy, D. Eric Smith, and Marcus G. Daniels   133

Multinomial Choice with Social Interactions
  William A. Brock and Steven N. Durlauf   175

Heterogeneity and Uniqueness in Interaction Games
  Stephen Morris and Hyun Song Shin   207

Perspectives on the Economy as an Evolving Complex System
  Larry Samuelson   243

The Diffusion of Innovations in Social Networks
  H. Peyton Young   267

Dynamic Properties of Local Interaction Models
  Timothy G. Conley and Giorgio Topa   283

Useful Knowledge as an Evolving System: The View from Economic
History
  Joel Mokyr   309

Prosocial Emotions
  Samuel Bowles and Herbert Gintis   337

Index   367

Introduction

Lawrence E. Blume
Steven N. Durlauf

The chapters in this volume are derived from work done at the conference The Economy as an Evolving Complex System III, held at the Santa Fe Institute in November 2001. As the third such book of this type, this volume provides a snapshot of the evolution of the research associated with the Santa Fe Institute Economics Program.

The Economy as and Evolving Complex System I, published in 1988, is largely speculative in that it describes the possibilities associated with the application of complex systems ideas to economics. *The Economy as an Evolving System II*, published in 1997, presents some of the successes of the research program that was only dimly visible in 1987. The current volume, based on nearly 15 years of a functioning Economics Program, in turn reflects work in economics and complexity as a mature research program.

How do the accomplishments of the Economics Program compare to the aspirations of the 1985 meeting? On some levels, there has been great success. Much of the original motivation for the Economics Program revolved around the belief that economic research could benefit from an injection of new mathe-

The Economy as an Evolving Complex System III,
edited by Lawrence E. Blume and Steven N. Durlauf, Oxford University Press

1

matical models and new substantive perspectives on human behavior. One sees exactly these features in the work presented here. Statistical mechanics methods in physics, for example, have proven useful in modeling populations of economic agents. Similarly, evolutionary perspectives on the development of humans have proven valuable in broadening the ways in which the motivations and beliefs of economic actors are described.

At the same time, this volume reflects some of the ways in which, at least informally, some of the early aspirations were not met. The models presented here do not represent any sort of rejection of neoclassical economics. One reason for this is related to the misunderstanding of many non-economists about the nature of economic theory; simply put, the theory was able to absorb SFI-type advances without changing its fundamental nature. Put differently, economic theory has an immense number of strengths that have been complemented and thereby enriched by the SFI approach. Hence, relative to the halcyon period of the 1980s, this SFI volume is more modest in its claims, but we think much stronger in its achievements.

The chapters in this volume indicate those areas where the promise of 1988 has at least partly been fulfilled. One important theme since the beginning of the program concerns the nature of learning. Many of the chapters in The *Economy as an Evolving System III* reflect this theme and, in turn, present new insights. In "The Epidemiology of Macroeconomic Expectations," Christopher Carroll considers a model in which individual actors learn about properties of the macroeconomic via the diffusion of forecasts by a small set of agents, interpreted as professional forecasters. This type of expectational structure is shown to successfully replicate observed patterns of unemployment and inflation expectations as measured in survey data. In "Social Learning and the Adoption of Knowledge," Charles Manski studies the evolution of technological innovations when agents face "fundamental" learning limits; these limits derive from the idea that certain features of the environment in which innovations are evaluated may not be statistically identified, forcing agents to make decisions in the face of ambiguity; Manski assumes agents are rational decisionmakers, but places the agents in a context in which alternative perspectives on the environment are observationally equivalent. Manski shows that this environment can lead to complex innovation dynamics and can replicate the classical S-shaped pattern of innovation adoption. Blume and Easley's chapter "Rationality and Selection in Asset markets" examines the implications of trader rationality for the price behavior of financial assets. They argue that rationality imposes few constraints on asset prices. Nonetheless, the market as a whole may in effect learn by transferring wealth across traders with different beliefs, and this market learning may have long-run asset price implications. This finding complements the contribution of Farmer et al. by arguing that it is the interaction mechanism rather than specific agent behaviors that drive the general features of asset price processes.

A second theme in this book concerns the identification and analysis of patterns in individual and aggregate data, primarily in financial markets. Within the econophysics literature, which represents the forays of natural scientists into economics, a primary concern has been the identification of "stylized facts" that characterize data in various markets as well as formal models to explain these stylized facts. This empirical work has placed particular emphasis on the identification of various scaling laws in financial data. Interest in scaling laws derives from their ubiquity in interacting physical systems, which has rendered physicists well equipped to identify such phenomena. H. Eugene Stanley, Parameswaran Gopikrishnan, and Vasiliki Plerou, in "Statistical Physics and Economic Fluctuations," review this now immense body of empirical work. A complementary analysis is conducted by Moshe Levy in "Market Efficiency, the Pareto Wealth Distribution, and the Levy Distribution of Stock Returns." This analysis shows how one popular power law in the econophysics literature concerning the distribution of wealth may be causally related to another widely asserted finding concerning the distribution of stock prices. The sorts of facts developed by Stanley et al. and Levy motivate J. Doyne Farmer et al.'s contribution, "A Random Order Placement Model of Price Formation in the Continuous Double Auction." They develop a model of a double auction trading mechanism in which "zero intelligence" agents interact in order to see what sorts of price and trading patterns emerge; interestingly, patterns appear to be empirically sensible. Farmer's work suggests that a number of regularities in asset markets may not depend on the particular rationality assumptions of the actors, and are thus, in this sense, universal, a finding that is consistent with physical models of interactions.

A third theme the origins of which cannot be traced to the 1987 meeting but which developed in the period around the 1995 meeting, concerns the analysis of social interactions. Generally speaking, social interactions refer to dependence between individual actors that are not mediated by markets. Examples of social interactions include peer group effects in schools and role model influences in communities; these examples reflect the common application of social interaction models to the study of individual outcomes such as teen pregnancy or cigarette smoking. In "A Multinomial Choice Model of Social Interactions," William Brock and Steven Durlauf show how to develop an analysis of social interactions that builds the interdependencies that characterize complex systems into a framework consistent with individual decision making. The chapter characterizes both the theoretical implications of these interdependences and describes how to implement the model econometrically. In "Heterogeneity and Uniqueness in Interaction Games," Stephen Morris and Hyun Shin observe that models of social interaction are a special case of a more general game-theoretic model wherein players respond to the distribution of their opponents' actions. This general class includes local interaction games, random matching games and games of incomplete information. They use this analogy to explore important analytical issues common to all three frameworks, including the uniqueness of Nash equilibrium and multiplier effects in the presence of strategic complementarities. The microfoundations of social interactions are explored by Larry Samuelson in "Perspectives on the Economy as an Evolving Complex System." Samuelson attempts to address an important lacuna in the theory of social interactions: namely, the absence of a theory as to why social interactions exist (as opposed to their implications). Samuelson argues that one way to understand social interactions is that they arise as a consequence of informational or competitive pressures. In particular, he shows how these factors can produce consumption interdependences in equilibrium. "The Diffusion of Innovations in Social Networks" by H. Peyton Young examines the effects of network topology on the diffusion of behaviors. A key empirical question is, what is the expected length of time for a network to "switch over" from the old behavior to the new? Young uncovers conditions on network topology the decision process that, surprisingly, bound the expected waiting time for diffusion to occur from above, independently of the size of the network. Social interactions also underlie the analysis in "Dynamic Properties of Local Interactions Models" by Timothy Conley and Giorgio Topa. Conley and Topa develop a model in which individual employment probabilities are determined by the employment status of an individual's neighbors. Such a dependence arises naturally when information about jobs diffuses locally. Conley and Topa demonstrate that this framework can capture important aspects of observed spatial interdependences across Chicago neighborhoods.

A fourth conference theme concerns efforts to use insights from evolutionary theory to understand aspects of individual and social cognition. Joel Mokyr develops an evolutionary approach to the process of technological innovation in "Useful Knowledge as an Evolving System: The View from Economic History." He shows us how a theory of knowledge evolution can be executed in a manner analogous to Darwinian models of evolution in living systems. He warns us that while much can be learned from this analogy, there are important differences. In "Prosocial Emotions," Samuel Bowles and Herbert Gintis argue that one can understand the evolution of emotions such as guilt and shame as mechanisms that facilitate social cooperation. As such, they argue that emotions evolved because of their reproductive value to groups and hence their individual members. The Bowles and Gintis study is part of a new wave of social science research at SFI and so, likely represents a bridge to the next Economy as an Evolving Complex System conference.

Kenneth Arrow has served as the intellectual leader of the SFI Economics Program ever since its inception. Whatever successes the program can claim very much derive from the brilliance and the wisdom he has provided. With equally large amounts of affection, appreciation, and respect, this book is dedicated to him.

The Epidemiology of Macroeconomic Expectations

Christopher D. Carroll

Macroeconomists have long emphasized the importance of expectations in determining macroeconomic outcomes, and an enormous theoretical literature has developed examining many models of expectations formation. This chapter proposes a new approach, based on epidemiological models, in which only a small set of agents (professional forecasters) formulate their own expectations, which then spread through the population via the news media in a manner analogous to the spread of a disease. The chapter shows that the very simplest epidemiological model, called the "common source" model, does a good job of explaining the dynamics of inflation and unemployment expectations, and more complicated epidemiological models produce dynamics similar to those that emerge from the common source model.

This chapter was written in connection with the conference "The Economy as an Evolving Complex System III" at the Santa Fe Institute in November of 2001, in honor of Kenneth Arrow's contributions to the Santa Fe Institute and

The Economy as an Evolving Complex System III,
edited by Lawrence E. Blume and Steven N. Durlauf, Oxford University Press

5

to economics. A companion paper [9] presents empirical work that was part of an earlier draft of this chapter.

1   INTRODUCTION

Economists have long understood that macroeconomic outcomes depend critically upon agents' expectations. Keynes [13] believed that economies could experience booms and busts that reflected movements in "animal spirits" (a view that has some appeal at the current moment of dot-com hangover), but the basis for most of today's macro models is the rational expectations approach pioneered in the 1970s by Lucas, Sargent, Barro, and others. This approach makes a set of assumptions that are much stronger than rationality alone. In particular, the framework assumes that all agents in the economy are not merely rational, but also share identical (correct) beliefs about the structure of the economy, and have instantaneous and costless access to all the latest economic data. Each agent processes these data using the true macroeconomic model to obtain a forecast for the future path of the economy, on the assumption that all other agents have identical beliefs and information (and therefore forecasts).

This set of assumptions has turned out to be a powerful vehicle for macroeconomic modeling, but has never been free from the criticism that it does not resemble the real world of conflicting opinions and forecasts, workers (and even some business leaders) who may not pay much attention to macroeconomic matters, and information that can sometimes be costly to obtain and process. Rational expectations models also have problems explaining some robust stylized facts, such as the apparent inexorability of the tradeoff between inflation and unemployment rate (see Ball [4] or Mankiw [15]). Partly in response to these problems, an emerging literature has been exploring models based on an assumption that agents engage in some form of data-based learning process to form their expectations; for surveys, see Sargent [22] or Evans and Honkapohja [11]. But the rational expectations framework remains the dominant approach, partly because it tends to be mathematically more tractable than many proposed alternatives.

This chapter proposes a tractable alternative framework for the formation of a typical person's expectations. Rather than having their own macroeconomic model and constantly feeding it the latest statistics, typical people are assumed to obtain their views about the future path of the economy from the news media, directly or indirectly. Furthermore (and importantly), not every person pays close attention to all macroeconomic news; instead, people are assumed to absorb the economic content of news reports probabilistically, in a way that resembles the spread of disease in a population, so that it may take quite some time for news of changed macroeconomic circumstances to penetrate to all agents in the economy.

Roberts [19] and Mankiw and Reis [16, 17] have recently proposed aggregate expectations equations that are mathematically very similar to aggregate implications of the baseline epidemiological model of expectations proposed here.

Roberts' work was motivated by his separate findings in Roberts [20, 21] that empirical macro models perform better in a variety of dimensions when survey-based inflation expectations are used in place of constructed model-consistent rational expectations. Mankiw and Reis [16, 17] obtain similar findings, and particularly emphasize the point that these models can explain the inexorability of an inflation-unemployment tradeoff much better than the standard model with rational expectations does.

However, neither Roberts [19] nor Mankiw and Reis [16, 17] devote much effort to explaining *why* the dynamics of aggregate expectations should evolve as they proposed (though Roberts does suggest that his equation might result from the diffusion of press reports). Mankiw and Reis motivate their model by suggesting that there are costs either of obtaining or of processing inflation every time an agent updates; however, they do not provide an explicit information-costs or processing-costs microfoundation.

This chapter provides an explicit microfoundation for a simple aggregate expectations equation, based on simple models of the spread of disease. Rather than tracking the spread of a disease through a population, the model tracks the spread of a piece of information (specifically, the latest rational forecast of inflation).

A companion paper, Carroll [9], estimates the baseline model and finds that it does a good job of capturing the dynamics of household survey expectations about both inflation and unemployment. Furthermore, that paper shows that household inflation expectations are closer to the expectations of professional forecasters during periods when there is more news coverage of inflation, and that the speed with which household expectations adjust to professional expectations is faster when there is more news coverage.

After providing the epidemiological foundation for the model estimated in Carroll [9] and summarizing the basic empirical results from that paper, this chapter explores the implications of several extensions to the model, using the kinds of "agent-based" simulation techniques pioneered at the Santa Fe Institute and at the Center for Social and Economic Dynamics (CSED) at the Brookings Institution.

The first extension is to allow heterogeneity in the extent to which people in different households pay attention to macroeconomic news. This version of the model is capable of generating demographic differences in macroeconomic expectations like those documented in Souleles [23], which are very hard to rationalize in a rational expectations model. Both this extension and the baseline version of the model are then simulated in order to derive implications for the standard deviation of inflation expectations across agents. When the simulated data are compared to the empirical data, the results are mixed. On one hand, the patterns over time of the empirical and the simulated standard deviations bear a strong resemblance, rising sharply in the late 1970s and early 1980s and then gradually falling off again. On the other hand, the *level* of the standard deviation in the empirical data is much higher than in the simulated data; however, I show that adding simple forms of memory error can make the model and the data match up reasonably well.

The next extension examines what happens when the model is generalized to a more standard epidemiological context: A "random mixing" framework in which people can be "infected" with updated inflation expectations by conversations with random other individuals in the population. It turns out that when the baseline framework that assumes infection only from news sources is estimated on simulated data from the random mixing model, the baseline framework does an excellent job of capturing the dynamics of mean inflation expectations; this suggests that the "common source" simplification is probably not too problematic.

The final extension is to a context in which people communicate only with near "neighbors" in some social sense, rather than with random other individuals in the population. Simulation and estimation of the baseline model on this population find that the baseline model again does a good job of capturing expectational dynamics; however, in one particular respect the results in this framework are a better match for the empirical results than is the baseline model.

The chapter concludes with some general lessons and ideas for future research.

2   THE EPIDEMIOLOGY OF EXPECTATIONS

2.1   THE *SIR* MODEL

Epidemiologists have developed a rich set of models for the transmission of disease in a population. The general framework consists of a set of assumptions about who is susceptible to the disease, who among the susceptible becomes infected, and whether and how individuals recover from the infection (leading to the framework's designation as the "SIR" model).

The standard assumption is that a susceptible individual who is exposed to the disease in a given period has a fixed probability p of catching the disease. Designating the set of newly infected individuals in period t as N_t and the set of susceptible individuals as S_t,

$$N_t = pS_t \,. \tag{1}$$

The next step is to determine susceptibility. The usual assumption is that in order to be susceptible, a healthy individual must have contact with an already-infected person. In a population in which each individual has an equal probability of encountering any other person in the population (a "well-mixed" population), the growth rate of the disease will depend upon the fraction of the population already infected; if very few individuals are currently infected, the small population of diseased people can infect only a small absolute number of new victims.

However, there is a special case that is even simpler. This occurs when the disease is not spread person-to-person, but through contact with a "common source" of infection. The classic example is Legionnaire's disease, which was transmitted to a group of hotel guests via a contaminated air-conditioning system (see Fraser et al. [12] for a description from the epidemiological literature). Another application is to illness caused by common exposure to an environmental factor such as air pollution. In these cases, the transmission model is extremely simple: Any healthy individual is simply assumed to have a constant probability per period of becoming infected from the common source. This is the case we will examine, since below we will assume that news reports represent a "common source" of information available to all members of the population.

One further assumption is needed to complete the model: the probability that someone who is infected will recover from the disease. The simplest possible assumption (which we will use) is that infected individuals never recover.

Under this set of assumptions, the dynamics of the disease are as follows. In the first period, proportion p of the population catches the disease, leaving $(1 - p)$ uninfected. In period 2, proportion p of these people catch the disease, leading to a new infection rate of $p(1 - p)$ and to a fraction $p + p(1 - p)$ of the population being infected. Spinning this process out, it is easy to see that starting from period 0 at the beginning of which nobody is infected, the total proportion infected at the end of t periods is

$$\text{Fraction Sick} = p + p(1 - p) + p(1 - p)^2 \ldots + p(1 - p)^t \qquad (2)$$

$$= p \sum_{s=0}^{t} (1 - p)^s \qquad (3)$$

whose limit as $t \to \infty$ is $p/p = 1$, implying that (since there is no recovery) everyone will eventually become infected. In the case where "infection" is interpreted as reflecting an agent's knowledge of a piece of information, this simply says that eventually everyone in the economy will learn a given piece of news.

2.2   THE EPIDEMIOLOGY OF INFLATION EXPECTATIONS

Now consider a world in which most people form their expectations about future inflation by reading newspaper articles. Imagine for the moment that every newspaper inflation article contains a complete forecast of the inflation rate for all future quarters, and suppose (again momentarily) that any person who reads such an article can subsequently recall the entire forecast. Finally, suppose that at any point in time t all newspaper articles print identical forecasts.[1]

Assume that not everybody reads every newspaper article on inflation. Instead, reading an article on inflation is like becoming infected with a common-source disease: In any given period each individual faces a constant probability λ of becoming "infected" with the latest forecast by reading an article.

---

[1]This subsection is largely drawn from Carroll [9]; however, that paper does not discuss the epidemiological interpretation of the derivations, as this derivation does.

Individuals who do not encounter an inflation article simply continue to believe the last forecast they read.[2]

Call π_{t+1} the inflation rate between quarter t and quarter $t + 1$,

$$\pi_{t+1} = \log(p_{t+1}) - \log(p_t), \qquad (4)$$

where p_t is the aggregate price index in period t. If we define M_t as the operator that yields the population-mean value of inflation expectations at time t and denote the newspaper forecast printed in quarter t for inflation in quarter $s \geq t$ as $N_t[\pi_s]$, by analogy with equation (2) we have that

$$M_t[\pi_{t+1}] = \lambda N_t[\pi_{t+1}] + (1 - \lambda) \{\lambda N_{t-1}[\pi_{t+1}] + (1 - \lambda)(\lambda N_{t-2}[\pi_{t+1}] + \ldots)\}. \qquad (5)$$

The derivation of this equation is as follows. In period t a fraction λ of the population will have been "infected" with the current-period newspaper forecast of the inflation rate next quarter, $N_t[\pi_{t+1}]$. Fraction $(1 - \lambda)$ of the population retains the views that they held in period $t - 1$ of period $t + 1$'s inflation rate. Those period $t - 1$ views in turn can be decomposed into a fraction λ of people who encountered an article in period $t - 1$ and obtained the newspaper forecast of period $t + 1$'s forecast, $N_{t-1}[\pi_{t+1}]$, and a fraction $(1 - \lambda)$ who retained their period-$t - 2$ views about the inflation forecast in period $t + 1$. Recursion leads to the remainder of the equation.

This expression for inflation expectations is identical to the one proposed by Mankiw and Reis [16, 17], except that in their model the updating agents construct their own rational forecast of the future course of the macroeconomy rather than learning about the experts' forecast from the news media. The equation is also similar to a formulation estimated by Roberts [20], except that Roberts uses past realizations of the inflation rate on the right side rather than past forecasts.

Mankiw and Reis loosely motivate the equation by arguing that developing a full-blown inflation forecast is a costly activity, which people might, therefore, engage in only occasionally. It is undoubtedly true that developing a reasonably rational quarter-by-quarter forecast of the inflation rate arbitrarily far into the future would be a very costly enterprise for a typical person. If this were really what people were doing, one might expect them to make forecasts only very rarely indeed. However, reading a newspaper article about inflation, or hearing a news story on television or the radio, is not costly in either time or money. There is no reason to suppose that people need to make forecasts themselves if news reports provide such forecasts essentially for free. Thus the epidemiological derivation of this equation seems considerably more attractive than the loose calculation-costs motivation provided by Mankiw and Reis, both because this is a fully specified model and because it delivers further testable implications (for

---

[2]This is mathematically very similar to the Calvo [8] model in which firms change their prices with probability p.

example, if there is empirical evidence that people with higher levels of education are more likely to pay attention to news, the model implies that their inflation forecasts will, on average, be closer to the rational forecast; see below for more discussion of possible variation in λ across population groups).

Of course, real newspaper articles do not contain quarter-by-quarter forecasts of the inflation rate into the infinite future as assumed in the derivation of eq. (5), and even if they did, it is very unlikely that a typical person would be able to remember the detailed pattern of inflation rates far into the future. In order to relax these unrealistic assumptions, it turns out to be necessary to impose some structure on implicit views about the inflation process.

Suppose people believe that at any given time the economy has an under-lying "fundamental" inflation rate. Furthermore, suppose people believe that future changes in the fundamental rate are unforecastable; that is, after the next period the fundamental rate follows a random walk. Finally, suppose the person believes that the actual inflation rate in a given quarter is equal to that period's fundamental rate plus an error term ϵ_t which reflects unforecastable transitory inflation shocks (reflected in the "special factors" that newspaper inflation stories often emphasize). Thus, the person believes that the inflation process is captured by

$$\pi_t = \pi_t^f + \epsilon_t \tag{6}$$

$$\pi_{t+1}^f = \pi_t^f + \eta_{t+1}, \tag{7}$$

$$\vdots \qquad \vdots$$

where ϵ_t is a transitory shock to the inflation rate in period t while η_t is the permanent innovation in the fundamental inflation rate in period t. We further assume that consumers believe that values of η beyond period $t+1$, and values of ϵ beyond period t, are unforecastable white noise variables; that is, future changes in the fundamental inflation rate are unforecastable, and transitory shocks are expected to go away.[3]

Before proceeding, it is worth considering whether this is a plausible view of the inflation process; we would not want to build a model on an assumption that people believe something patently absurd. Certainly, it would not be plausible to suppose that people always and everywhere believe that the inflation rate is characterized by eqs. (6)–(7); for example, Ball [3] shows that in the U.S. from 1879–1914 the inflation rate was not persistent, while in other countries there have been episodes of hyperinflation (and rapid disinflation) in which views like eqs. (6)–(7) would have been nonsense.

However, the relevant question for the purposes of this chapter is whether this view of the inflation process is plausible for the period for which I have inflation

---

[3] Note that we are allowing people to have some idea about how next quarter's fundamental rate may differ from the current quarter's rate, because we did not impose that consumers' expectations of η_{t+1} must equal zero.

TABLE 1   Dickey-Fuller and augmented Dickey-Fuller tests for a unit root in inflation.

Lags	Degrees of Freedom	ADF Test Statistic
0	166	2.59***
1	165	2.84*
2	164	2.28

This table presents results of standard Dickey-Fuller and augmented Dickey-Fuller tests for the presence of a unit root in the core rate of inflation (results are similar for CPI inflation). The column labelled "Lags" indicates how many lags of the change in the inflation rate are included in the regression. With zero lags, the test is the original Dickey-Fuller test; with multiple lags, the test is an Augmented Dickey Fuller test. In both cases a constant term is permitted in the regression equation. The sample is from 1959q3 to 2001q2. (Quarterly data from my DRI database begin in 1959q1. In order to have the same sample for all three tests, the sample must be restricted to 1959q3 and after.) One, two, and three stars indicate rejections of a unit root at the 10 percent, 5 percent, and 1 percent thresholds. RATS code generating these and all other empirical results is available at the author's website.

expectations data. Perhaps the best way to examine this is to ask whether the univariate statistical process for the inflation rate implied by eqs. (6) and (7) is strongly at odds with the actual univariate inflation process. In other words, after allowing for transitory shocks, does the inflation rate approximately follow a random walk?

The appropriate statistical test is an augmented Dickey-Fuller test. Table 1 presents the results from such a test. The second row shows that even with more than 160 quarters of data it is not possible to reject at a 5 percent significance level the proposition that the core inflation rate follows a random walk with a one-period transitory component—that is, it is not possible to reject the process defined by eqs. (6)–(7).[4] When the transitory shock is allowed to have effects that last for two quarters rather than one, it is not possible to reject a random walk in the fundamental component even at the 10 percent level of significance (the last row in the table).

Note that the unit root (or near unit root) in inflation does not imply that future inflation rates are totally unpredictable, only that the history of inflation by itself is not very useful in forecasting future inflation *changes* (beyond the disappearance of the transitory component of the current period's shock). This does not exclude the possibility that current and lagged values of other variables might have predictive power. Thus, this view of the inflation rate is not necessarily in conflict with the vast and venerable literature showing that other variables (most notably the unemployment rate) do have considerable predictive power for the inflation rate (see Staiger, Stock, and Watson [25] for a recent treatment).

---

[4]The near-unit-root feature of the inflation rate in the post-1959 period is well known to inflation researchers; some authors find that a unit root can be rejected for some measures of inflation over some time periods, but it seems fair to say that the conventional wisdom is that at least since the late 1950s, inflation is "close" to a unit root process. See Barsky [6] for a more complete analysis, or Ball [3] for a more recent treatment.

Suppose now that rather than containing a forecast for the entire quarter-by-quarter future of the inflation rate, newspaper articles simply contain a forecast of the inflation rate over the next year. The next step is to figure out how such a one-year forecast for inflation can be integrated into some modified version of eq. (5). To capture this, we must introduce a bit more notation. Define $\pi_{s,t}$ as the inflation rate between periods s and t, converted to an annual rate. Thus, for example, in quarterly data we can define the inflation rate for quarter $t+1$ at an annual rate as

$$\pi_{t,t+1} = 4(\log p_{t+1} - \log p_t) \tag{8}$$
$$= 4\pi_{t+1} \tag{9}$$

where the factor of four is required to convert the quarterly price change to an annual rate.

Under this set of assumptions, Carroll [9] shows that the process for inflation expectations can be rewritten as

$$M_t[\pi_{t,t+4}] = \lambda N_t[\pi_{t,t+4}] + (1 - \lambda)M_{t-1}[\pi_{t-1,t+3}]. \tag{10}$$

That is, mean measured inflation expectations for the next year should be a weighted average between the current newspaper forecast and last period's mean measured inflation expectations. This equation is, therefore, directly estimable, assuming an appropriate proxy for newspaper expectations can be constructed.[5]

2.3 ESTIMATES

Estimating empirically requires the identification of empirical counterparts for household-level inflation expectations and newspaper inflation forecasts (10). Conveniently, the University of Michigan's Survey Research Center has been asking people in households about their inflation expectations for well over thirty years. To be precise, survey participants are first asked:

> During the next 12 months, do you think that prices in general will go up, or go down, or stay where they are right now?

and then those who say "go up" (the vast majority) are asked

> By about what percent do you expect prices to go up, on the average, during the next 12 months?

The Survey Research Center uses the answers to these questions to construct an index of mean inflation expectations, which is an almost exact counterpart

---

[5]This equation is basically the same as eq. (5) in Roberts [19], except that Roberts proposes that the forecast toward which household expectations are moving is the "mathematically rational" forecast (and he simply proposes the equation without examining the underlying logic that might produce it).

TABLE 2   Estimating and testing the baseline model.

Estimating equation $M_t[\bullet_{t,t+4}] = \alpha_0 + \alpha_1 S_t[\bullet_{t,t+4}] + \alpha_2 M_{t-1}[\bullet_{t-1,t+3}] + \epsilon_t$							
Eqn	α_0	α_1	α_2	$\bar{R}^2$	Watson	StdErr	Test p-value
Estimating Baseline Model on Inflation Expectations							
Memo:	4.34			0.00	0.29	0.88	$\alpha_0 = 0$
	$(0.19)^{***}$						0.000
1		0.36	0.66	0.76	1.97	0.43	$\alpha_1 + \alpha_2 = 1$
		$(0.09)^{***}$	$(0.08)^{***}$				0.178
2		0.27	0.73	0.76	2.12	0.43	$\alpha_1 = 0.25$
		$(0.07)^{***}$	$(0.07)^{***}$				0.724
3	1.22	0.51	0.26	0.84	1.74	0.35	$\alpha_0 = 0$
	$(0.20)^{***}$	$(0.08)^{***}$	$(0.09)^{***}$				0.000
Estimating Baseline Model on Unemployment Expectations							
Memo:	6.27			0.00	0.07	1.25	$\alpha_0 = 0$
	$(0.31)^{***}$						0.000
1		0.30	0.69	0.95	1.59	0.28	$\alpha_1 + \alpha_2 = 1$
		$(0.07)^{***}$	$(0.07)^{***}$				0.036
2		0.30	0.70	0.94	1.50	0.29	$\alpha_1 = 0.25$
		$(0.07)^{***}$	$(0.07)^{***}$				0.476
3	-0.03	0.30	0.69	0.95	1.60	0.29	$\alpha_0 = 0$
	(0.19)	$(0.08)^{***}$	$(0.07)^{***}$				0.890

$M_t[\bullet_{t,t+4}]$ is the Michigan household survey measure of mean inflation expectations or projected unemployment expectations in quarter t, $S_t[\bullet_{t,t+4}]$ is the Survey of Professional Forecasters mean inflation or unemployment forecast over the next year. Inflation equations are estimated over the period 1981q3 to 2000q2 for which both Michigan and SPF inflation forecasts are available; Unemployment equations are estimated over the period 1978q1 to 2000q2 for which both Michigan and SPF inflation forecasts are available. All standard errors are corrected for heteroskedasticity and serial correlation using a Newey-West procedure (a Bartlett kernel) with four lags. Results are not sensitive to the choice of lags.

to the object required by the theory. (For details of index construction, see Curtin [10].)

Measuring the forecasts that people are assumed to encounter in the news media is a thornier problem. But typical newspaper articles on inflation tend to quote professional forecasters, and so it seems reasonable to use the mean forecast from the Survey of Professional Forecasters (SPF) as a proxy for what the news media are reporting.

Carroll [9] estimates eq. (10) using the Michigan survey index for M_t and the SPF for N_t. Results are reproduced in the upper panel of table 2 (where N_t changes to S_t to indicate the use of the SPF).

The first line of the table ("Memo:") presents results for the simplest possible model: that the value of the Michigan index of inflation expectations $M_t[\pi_{t,t+4}]$ is equal to a constant, α_0. By definition the $\bar{R}^2$ is equal to zero; the standard error of the estimate is 0.88. The last column is reserved for reporting the results of various tests; for example, the test performed in the "Memo:" equation is for whether the average value of the expectations index is zero, $\alpha_0 = 0$, which is rejected at a very high level of statistical significance, as indicated by a p-value of zero.

Equation 1 in the table reflects the estimation of an equation of the form

$$M_t[\pi_{t,t+4}] = \alpha_1 S_t[\pi_{t,t+4}] + \alpha_2 M_t[\pi_{t-1,t+3}] + \nu_t. \tag{11}$$

Comparing this to eq. (10) provides the testable restriction that $\alpha_2 = 1 - \alpha_1$ or, equivalently,

$$\alpha_1 + \alpha_2 = 1. \tag{12}$$

The point estimates in eq. (1) of $\alpha_1 = 0.36$ and $\alpha_2 = 0.66$ suggest that the restriction (12) is very close to holding true, and the last column confirms that the proposition is easily accepted by the data (the p-value is far above the usual critical level of 0.05 which would signal a rejection).

Estimation results when the restriction (12) is imposed in estimation are presented in the next row of the table, yielding our central estimate of the model's main parameter: $\lambda = 0.27$. This point estimate is remarkably close to the value of 0.25 assumed by Mankiw and Reis [16, 17] in their simulation experiments; unsurprisingly, the test reported in the last column for eq. (2) indicates that the proposition $\alpha_1 = \lambda = 0.25$ is easily accepted by the data. Thus, the model implies that in each quarter, only about one fourth of households have a completely up-to-date forecast of the inflation rate over the coming year. On the other hand, this estimate also indicates that only about 32 percent ($= (1 - 0.25)^4$) of households have inflation expectations that are more than a year out of date.

Intuitively it might seem that if almost 70 percent of agents have inflation expectations that are of a vintage of a year or less, the behavior of the macroeconomy could not be all that different from what would be expected if all expectations were completely up-to-date. The surprising message of Roberts [20, 21] and Mankiw and Reis [16, 17] is that this intuition is wrong. Mankiw and Reis show that an economy with $\lambda = 0.25$ behaves in ways that are sharply different from an economy with fully rational expectations ($\lambda = 1$), and argue that in each case where behavior is different the behavior of the $\lambda = 0.25$ economy corresponds better with empirical evidence.

Equation 3 in the table reports some bad news for the model: When a constant term is permitted in the regression equation, it turns out to be highly statistically significant. The model (10) did not imply the presence of a constant term, so this is somewhat disappointing. On the other hand, despite being statistically significant, the constant term does not improve the fit of the equation much: the standard error of the estimate only declines from 0.43 to 0.35. Furthermore, a version of the model with a constant term cannot be plausibly interpreted as a true "structural" model of the expectations process, since it implies that even if the inflation rate were to go to zero forever, and all forecasters were to begin forecasting zero inflation forever, households would never catch on. A more plausible interpretation of the positive constant term is that it may reflect some form of misspecification of the model. Below, I will present simulation results showing that if expectations are transmitted from person to person in addition to through the news media, and an equation of the form of (10) is estimated on the data generated by the modified model, the regression equation returns a positive and statistically significant constant term; thus, the presence of the constant term can be interpreted as evidence that the simple "common source" epidemiological model postulated here may be a bit too simple.

The bottom panel of the table presents results for estimating an equation for unemployment expectations that is parallel to the estimate for inflation expectations.[6] Equation 2 of this panel presents the version of the model that restricts the coefficients to sum to 1; the point estimate of the fraction of updaters is $\lambda = 0.31$, but this estimate is not significantly different from the estimate of $\lambda = 0.27$ obtained for inflation expectations or from the $\lambda = 0.25$ postulated by Mankiw and Reis [16, 17]. The last equation shows that the unemployment expectations equation does not particularly want an intercept term, so the model actually fits better for unemployment expectations than for inflation expectations.

In sum, it seems fair to say that the simple "common-source" epidemiological eq. (10) does a remarkably good job of capturing much of the predictable behavior of both the inflation and the unemployment expectations indexes.

3   AGENT-BASED MODELS OF INFLATION EXPECTATIONS

One of the most fruitful trends in empirical macroeconomics over the last fifteen years has been the effort to construct rigorous microfoundations for macroeconomic models. Broadly speaking, the goal is to find empirically sensible models for the behavior of individual agents (people, firms, banks), which can then be aggregated to derive implications about macroeconomic dynamics. Separately, but in a similar spirit, researchers at the Santa Fe Institute, the CSED, and elsewhere have been exploring "agent-based" models that examine the complex behavior that can sometimes emerge from the interactions between collections of simple agents.

One of the primary attractions of an agent-based or microfounded approach to modeling macroeconomic behavior is the prospect of being able to test a model using large microeconomic datasets. This is an opportunity that has largely been neglected so far in the area of expectations formation; I have found only three existing research papers that have examined the raw household-level expecta-

---

[6]Some data construction was necessary to do this, because the Michigan survey does not ask people directly what their expectations are for the level of the unemployment rate, but instead asks whether they think the unemployment rate will rise or fall over the next year. See Carroll [9] for details about how the unemployment expectations data are constructed.

tions data from the Michigan survey. Two are by Nicholas Souleles [23, 24]. For present purposes, the more interesting of these is Souleles [23], which demonstrates (among other things) that there are highly statistically significant differences across demographic groups in forecasts of several macroeconomic variables. Clearly, in a world where everyone's expectations are purely rational, there should be no demographic differences in such expectations.

An agent-based version of the epidemiological model above could, in principle, account for such demographic differences. The simplest approach would be to assume that there are differences across demographic groups in the propensity to pay attention to economic news (different λ's); it is even conceivable that one could calibrate these differences using existing facts about the demographics of newspaper readership (or CNBC viewership).

Without access to the underlying microdata it is difficult to tell whether demographic heterogeneity in λ would be enough to explain Souleles' findings about systematic demographic differences in macro expectations. Even without the raw microdata, however, an agent-based model has considerable utility. In particular, an agent-based approach permits us to examine the consequences of relaxing some of the model's assumptions to see how robust its predictions are. Given our hypothesis that Souleles' results on demographic differences in expectations might be due to differences in λ across groups, the most important application of the agent-based approach is to determine the consequences of heterogeneity in λ.[7]

3.1   HETEROGENEITY IN λ

Consider a model in which there are two categories of people, each of which makes up half the population, but with different newspaper-reading propensities, λ_1 and λ_2.

For each group it will be possible to derive an equation like (10),

$$M_{i,t}[\pi_{t,t+4}] = \lambda_i N_t[\pi_{t,t+4}] + (1 - \lambda_i) M_{i,t-1}[\pi_{t-1,t+3}] . \qquad (13)$$

But note that (dropping the π arguments for simplicity) aggregate expectations will just be the population-weighted sum of expectations for each group,

$$M_t = (M_{1,t} + M_{2,t})/2 \qquad (14)$$

$$= \left(\frac{\lambda_1 + \lambda_2}{2}\right) N_t + \frac{(1 - \lambda_1) M_{1,t-1} + (1 - \lambda_2) M_{2,t-1}}{2} . \qquad (15)$$

---

[7]The final paper I know of that examines the microdata underlying the Michigan inflation expectations index is by Branch [7], who proposes an interesting model in which individual consumers dynamically choose between competing models for predicting inflation, but are subject to idiosyncratic errors. He finds evidence that people tend to switch toward whichever model has recently produced the lowest mean squared error in its forecasts. This interesting approach deserves further study.

Replace $M_{1,t-1}$ by $M_{t-1}+(M_{1,t-1}-M_{t-1})$ and similarly for $M_{2,t-1}$ to obtain

$$
M_t = \left(\frac{\lambda_1 + \lambda_2}{2}\right) N_t + \left(1 - \left(\frac{\lambda_1 + \lambda_2}{2}\right)\right) M_{t-1} + \overbrace{\left(\frac{M_{1,t-1} + M_{2,t-1}}{2}\right) - M_{t-1}}^{=0}
$$
$$
- \left(\frac{\lambda_1(M_{1,t-1} - M_{t-1}) + \lambda_2(M_{2,t-1} - M_{t-1})}{2}\right) \tag{16}
$$

$$
M_t = \hat{\lambda} N_t + (1 - \hat{\lambda}) M_{t-1} - \left(\frac{\lambda_1(M_{1,t-1} - M_{t-1}) + \lambda_2(M_{2,t-1} - M_{t-1})}{2}\right) \tag{17}
$$

where $\hat{\lambda} = (\lambda_1 + \lambda_2)/2$.

Thus, the dynamics of aggregate inflation expectations with heterogeneity in λ have a component $\hat{\lambda} N_t + (1 - \hat{\lambda}) M_{t-1}$ that behaves just like a version of the model when everybody has the same λ equal to the average value in the population, plus a term (in big parentheses in eq. (17)) that depends on the joint distribution of λ's and the deviation by group of the difference between the previous period's rational forecast and the group's forecast.

Now consider estimating the baseline equation

$$
M_t = \lambda N_t + (1 - \lambda) M_{t-1} \tag{18}
$$

on a population with heterogeneous λ's. The coefficient estimates will be biased in a way that depends on the correlations of N_t, M_{t-1} and M_t with the last term in eq. (17), $((\lambda_1(M_{1,t-1} - M_{t-1}) + \lambda_2(M_{2,t-1} - M_{t-1}))/2)$. There is no analytical way to determine the magnitude or nature of the bias without making a specific assumption about the time series process for N_t, and even with such an assumption all that could be obtained is an expected asymptotic bias. The bias in any particular small sample would depend on the specific history of N_t in that sample.

The only sensible way to evaluate whether the bias problem is likely to be large, given the actual history of inflation and inflation forecasts in the U.S., is to simulate a model with households of people who have heterogeneous λ's and to estimate the baseline equation on aggregate statistics generated by that sample.

Specifically, the experiment is as follows. A population of P agents is created, indexed by i; each of them begins by drawing a value of λ_i from a uniform distribution on the interval $(\underline{\lambda}, \overline{\lambda})$. In an initial period 0, each agent is endowed with an initial value of $M_{i,0} = 2$ percent. Thus the population mean value $M_0 = (1/P)\sum_{i=1}^{P} M_{i,0} = 2$. For period 1, each agent draws a random variable distributed on the interval $[0, 1]$. If that draw is less than or equal to the agent's λ_i, the agent updates $M_{i,1} = N_1$ where N_1 is taken to be the "newspaper" forecast of the next year's inflation rate in period t; if the random draw is less than λ_i the agent's $M_{i,1} = M_{i,0}$. The population-average value of M_1 is calculated, and the simulation then proceeds to the next period.

TABLE 3 Estimating the baseline model on simulated data with heterogeneous λs.

Estimating $M_t[\pi_{t,t+4}] = \alpha_1 S_t[\pi_{t,t+4}] + \alpha_2 M_{t-1}[\pi_{t-1,t+3}] + \epsilon_t$					
λ				Durbin-	
Range	α_1	α_2	$\bar{R}^2$	Watson	StdErr
$[0.25, 0.25]$	0.250	0.750	1.000	1.94	0.006
	$(0.001)^{***}$	$(0.001)^{***}$			
$[0.00, 0.50]$	0.265	0.743	0.999	0.11	0.039
	$(0.010)^{***}$	$(0.009)^{***}$			
$[0.20, 0.30]$	0.249	0.751	1.000	2.03	0.005
	$(0.001)^{***}$	$(0.001)^{***}$			
$[0.15, 0.35]$	0.244	0.756	1.000	0.64	0.009
	$(0.002)^{***}$	$(0.002)^{***}$			

$M_t[\pi_{t,t+4}]$ is mean inflation expectations in quarter t, $N_t[\pi_{t,t+4}]$ is the news signal corresponding to the SPF mean inflation forecast after 1981q3 and the previous year inflation rate before 1981q3. All equations are estimated over the period 1981q3 to 2001q2.

For the simulations, the "news" series N_t is chosen as the concatenation of (1) the actual inflation rate from 1960q1 to 1981q2 and (2) the SPF forecast of inflation from 1981q3 to 2001q2. Then regression equations corresponding to eq. (18) are estimated on the subsample corresponding to the empirical subsample, 1981q3 to 2001q2. Thus, the simulation results should indicate the dynamics of M_t that would have been observed if actual newspaper forecasts of inflation had been a random walk until 1981q2 and then had tracked the SPF once the SPF data began to be published.

The results of estimating eq. (10) on the data generated by this simulation when the population is $P = 250,000$ are presented in table 3. For comparison, and to verify that the simulation programs are working properly, eq. (1) presents results when all agents' λ's are exogenously set to 0.25. As expected, the simulation returns an estimate of $\lambda = 0.25$, and the equation fits so precisely that there are essentially no residuals.

The remaining rows of the table present the results in the case where λ values are heterogeneous in the population. The second row presents the most extreme example, $[\underline{\lambda}, \bar{\lambda}] = [0.00, 0.50]$. Fortunately, even in this case the regression yields an estimate of the speed-of-adjustment parameter λ that, at around 0.26, is still quite close to the true average value 0.25 in the population. Interestingly, however, one consequence of the heterogeneity in λ is that there is now a very large amount of serial correlation in the residuals of the equation; the Durbin-Watson statistic indicates that this serial correlation is positive and a Q test shows it to be highly statistically significant.

Heterogeneous λ's induce serial correlation primarily because the views of people with λ's below $\bar{\lambda}$ are slow to change. For example, if the "rational" forecast is highly serially correlated, an agent with a λ close to zero will be expected to make errors of the same size and direction for many periods in a row after a shock to the fundamental inflation rate, until finally updating.

The comparison of the high serial correlation that emerges from this simulation to the low serial correlation that emerged in the empirical estimation in table 2 suggests that heterogeneity in λ is probably not as great as the assumed uniform distribution between 0.0 and 0.5. Results are, therefore, presented for a third experiment, in which λ's are uniformly distributed between 0.2 and 0.3. Estimation on the simulated data from this experiment yields an estimate of λ very close to 0.25 and a Durbin-Watson statistic that indicates much less serial correlation than emerged with the broad $[0, 0.5]$ range of possible λ's. Finally, the last row presents results when λ is uniformly distributed over the interval $[0.15, 0.35]$. This case is intermediate: the estimate of λ is still close to 0.25, but the Durbin-Watson statistic now begins to indicate substantial serial correlation.

On the whole, the simulation results suggest that the serial correlation properties of the empirical data are consistent with a moderate degree of heterogeneity in λ, but not with extreme heterogeneity. It is important to point out, however, that empirical data contain a degree of measurement and sampling error that is absent in the simulated data. To the extent that these sources can be thought of as white noise, they should bias the Durbin-Watson statistic up in comparison to the "true" Durbin-Watson, so the scope for heterogeneity in λ is probably considerably larger than would be indicated by a simple comparison of the measured and simulated Durbin-Watson statistics. Furthermore, since the error term is very tiny (the standard errors are less than 4/100 of one percentage point), any serial correlation properties it has cannot be of much econometric consequence. Thus, the serial correlation results should not be taken as very serious evidence against substantial heterogeneity in λ.

A few last words on serial correlation. The important point in Mankiw and Reis [16, 17], as well as in work by Ball [3] and others, is that the presence of some people whose expectations are not fully and instantaneously forward-looking profoundly changes the behavior of macro models. Thus, the possibility of heterogeneity in λ, and the resulting serial correlation in errors, has an importance here beyond its usual econometric ramifications for standard errors and inference. If there are some consumers whose expectations are very slow to update, they may be primarily responsible for important deviations between the rational expectations model and macroeconomic reality.

3.2 MATCHING THE STANDARD DEVIATION OF INFLATION EXPECTATIONS

Thus far, all our tests of the model have been based on its predictions for behavior of mean inflation expectations. Of course, the model also generates predictions for other statistics like the standard deviation of expectations across households at a point in time. Some households will have expectations that correspond to the most recent inflation forecast, while others will have expectations that are out

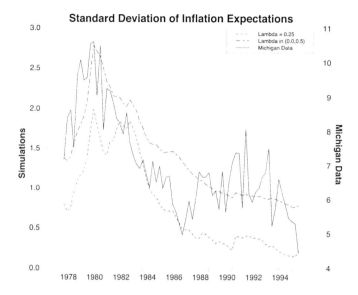

FIGURE 1   Standard deviation of inflation expectations from data and simulations.

of date by varying amounts. One prediction of the model is that (for a constant λ) if SPF inflation forecasts have remained stable for a long time, the standard deviation of expectations across households should be low, while if there have been substantial recent changes in the rational forecast of inflation we should expect to see more cross-section variability in households' expectations.

This is testable. Curtin [10] reports average values for the standard deviation for the Michigan survey's inflation expectations over the period from 1978 to 1995; results are plotted as the solid line in figure 1. It is true that the empirical standard deviation was higher in the early 1980s, a time when inflation rates and SPF inflation expectations changed rapidly over the course of a few years, than later, when the inflation rate was lower and more stable.

The short- and long-dashed loci in the figure depict the predictions of the homogeneous $\lambda = 0.25$ and heterogeneous $\lambda \in [0.0, 0.5]$ versions of the agent-based model. There is considerable similarity between the time paths of the actual and simulated standard deviations: the standard deviation is greatest for both simulated and actual data in the late 1970s and early 1980s, because that is the period when the levels of both actual and expected inflation changed the most. In both simulated and real data the standard deviation falls gradually over time, but shows an uptick around the 1990 recession and recovery before returning to its downward path.

However, the *levels* of the standard deviations are very different between the simulations and the data; the scale for the Michigan data on the right axis ranges from 4 to 11, while the scale for the simulated standard deviations on the left axis ranges from 0 to 3. Over the entire sample period, the standard deviation of household inflation expectations is about 6.5 in the real data, compared to only about 0.5 in the simulated data.

Curtin [10] analyzes the sources of the large standard deviation in inflation expectations across households. He finds that part of the high variability is attributable to small numbers of households with very extreme views of inflation. Curtin's interpretation is that these households are probably just ill-informed, and he proposes a variety of other ways to extract the data's central tendency that are intended to be robust to the presence of these outlying households. However, even Curtin's preferred measure of dispersion in inflation expectations, the size of the range from the 25th to the 75th percentile in expectations, has an average span of almost five percentage points over the 81q3-95q4 period, much greater than would be produced by any of the simulation models considered above.[8]

The first observation to make about the excessive cross-section variability of household inflation expectations is that such variability calls into question almost all standard models of wage setting in which well-informed workers demand nominal wage increases in line with a rational expectation about the future inflation rate.[9] If a large fraction of workers have views about the future inflation rate that are a long way from rational, it is hard to believe that those views have much impact on the wage-setting process. Perhaps it is possible to construct a model in which equilibrium is determined by average inflation expectations, with individual variations making little or no difference to individual wages. Constructing such a model is beyond the scope of this chapter; but whether or not such a model is proposed, it seems likely that any thorough understanding of the relation between inflation expectations in the aggregate and actual inflation will need a model of how individuals' inflation expectations are determined.

The simplest method of generating extra individual variability in expectations is to assume that when people encounter a news report on inflation, the process of committing the associated inflation forecast to memory is error-prone.[10]

---

[8]Curtin advocates use of the median rather than the mean as the summary statistic for "typical" inflation expectations. However, the epidemiological model has simple analytical predictions for the mean but not the median of household expectations, so the empirical work in this chapter uses the mean.

[9]The only prominent exception I am aware of is the two papers by Akerlof, Dickens, and Perry [1, 2] mentioned briefly above. In these models workers do not bother to learn about the inflation rate unless it is high enough to make the research worthwhile. However, such a model would presumably imply a modest upper bound to inflation expectation errors, since people who suspected the inflation rate was very high would have the incentive to learn the truth. In fact, Curtin [10] finds that the most problematic feature of the empirical data is the small number of households with wildly, implausibly high forecasts.

[10]Alternatively, one could assume that retrieval from memory is error-prone. The implications are very similar but not identical.

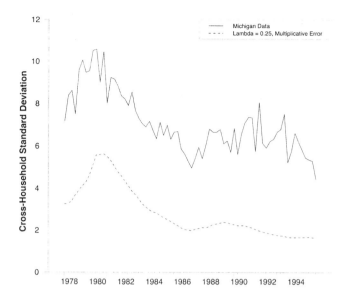

FIGURE 2   Standard deviation of inflation expectations from simulation with memory errors.

To be specific, suppose that whenever an agent encounters a news report and updates his expectations, the actual expectation stored in memory is given by the expectation printed in the news report times a mean-one lognormally distributed storage error. Since the errors average out in the population as a whole, this assumption generates dynamics of aggregate inflation expectations that are identical to those of the baseline model. Figure 2 plots the predictions for the standard deviation of inflation expectations across households of the baseline $\lambda = 0.25$ model with a lognormally distributed error with a standard error of 0.5. The figure shows that the change in the standard deviation of inflation residuals over time is very similar in the model and in the data, but the level of the standard deviation is still considerably smaller in the model. This could, of course, be rectified by including an additive error in addition to the multiplicative error. Such a proposed solution could be tested by examining more detailed information on the structure of expectations at the household level, like that examined by Souleles [23].

3.3   SOCIAL TRANSMISSION OF INFLATION EXPECTATIONS

As noted above, the standard model of disease transmission is one in which illness is transmitted by person-to-person contact. Analogously, it is likely that some people's views about inflation are formed by conversations with others

TABLE 4   Estimating baseline model on random mixing simulations.

Prob. of Social Exchange	α_0	α_1	α_2	$\bar{R}^2$	Durbin-Watson	StdErr	Test p-value
			Estimating $M_t = \alpha_0 + \alpha_1 S_t + \alpha_2 M_{t-1} + \epsilon_t$				
$p = 0.25$		0.311	0.689	1.000	2.26	0.020	$\alpha_1 + \alpha_2 = 1$
		$(0.003)^{***}$	$(0.003)^{***}$				0.1357
	0.009	0.303	0.694	1.000	2.15	0.020	$\alpha_0 = 0$
	(0.009)	$(0.006)^{***}$	$(0.006)^{***}$				0.2939
$p = 0.10$		0.276	0.724	1.000	1.69	0.009	$\alpha_1 + \alpha_2 = 1$
		$(0.001)^{***}$	$(0.001)^{***}$				0.2172
	0.000	0.274	0.725	1.000	1.66	0.009	$\alpha_0 = 0$
	(0.004)	$(0.0030)^{***}$	$(0.003)^{***}$				0.9006

M_t is the mean value of inflation expectations across all agents in the simulated population; S_t is the actual annual inflation rate from 1960q1 to 1981q2, and the SPF inflation forecast from 1981q3 to 2000q2. Estimation is restricted to the simulation periods corresponding to 1981q3 to 2000q2 for which actual SPF data are available. All standard errors are corrected for heteroskedasticity and serial correlation using a Newey-West procedure (a Bartlett kernel) with four lags. Results are not sensitive to the choice of lags.

rather than by direct contact with news reports. For the purposes of this chapter the most important question is whether the simple formula (10) would do a reasonably good job of capturing the dynamics of inflation expectations even when social transmission occurs.

Simulation of an agent-based model with both modes of transmission is straightforward. The extended model works as follows. In each period, every person has a probability λ of obtaining the latest forecast by reading a news story. Among the $(1 - \lambda)$ who do not encounter the news source, the algorithm is as follows. For each person i, there is some probability p that he will have a conversation about inflation with a randomly-selected other person j in the population. If j has an inflation forecast that is of more recent vintage than i's forecast, then i adopts j's forecast, and vice-versa.[11]

Table 4 presents results of estimating eq. (10) on the aggregate inflation expectations data that result from this agent-based simulation under a uniform fixed $\lambda = 0.25$ probability of news-reading. The first two rows present results when the probability of a social transmission event is $p = 0.25$. The primary effect of social transmission is to bias upward the estimated speed of adjustment term. The point estimate is about 0.31, or about 6 percentage points too high. However, the $\bar{R}^2$ of the equation is virtually 100 percent, indicating that even when there is social transmission of information, the common-source model does an excellent

---

[11]This rules out the possibility that the less recent forecast would be adopted by the person with more recent information. The reason to rule this out is that if there were no directional bias (more recent forecasts push out older ones), the swapping of information would not change the distribution of forecasts in the population and, therefore, would not result in aggregate dynamics any different from those that occur when no social communication is allowed.

TABLE 5   Estimating baseline model on local interactions simulations.

Up-to-date Agents	α_0	α_1	α_2	$\bar{R}^2$	Durbin-Watson	StdErr	Test p-value
		Estimating $M_t = \alpha_0 + \alpha_1 S_t + \alpha_2 M_{t-1} + \epsilon_t$					
$\eta = 0.25$		0.234	0.696	0.992	0.10	0.135	$\alpha_1 + \alpha_2 = 1$
		$(0.025)^{***}$	$(0.034)^{***}$				0.0000
	0.386	0.315	0.499	1.000	1.03	0.007	$\alpha_0 = 0$
	$(0.003)^{***}$	$(0.001)^{***}$	$(0.001)^{***}$				0.0000
$\eta = 0.15$		0.098	0.853	0.988	0.13	0.117	$\alpha_1 + \alpha_2 = 1$
		$(0.017)^{***}$	$(0.027)^{***}$				0.0000
	0.475	0.185	0.587	1.000	1.15	0.008	$\alpha_0 = 0$
	$(0.004)^{***}$	$(0.001)^{***}$	$(0.001)^{***}$				0.0000

M_t is the mean value of inflation expectations across all agents in the simulated population; S_t is the actual annual inflation rate from 1960q1 to 1981q2, and the SPF inflation forecast from 1981q3 to 2000q2. Estimation is restricted to the simulation periods corresponding to 1981q3 to 2000q2 for which actual SPF data are available. All standard errors are corrected for heteroskedasticity and serial correlation using a Newey-West procedure (a Bartlett kernel) with four lags. Results are not sensitive to the choice of lags.

job of explaining the dynamics of aggregate expectations. The next row shows the results when the rate of social transmission is $p = 0.10$. Unsurprisingly, the size of the bias in the estimate of λ is substantially smaller in this case, and the model continues to perform well in an $\bar{R}^2$ sense.

A potential objection to these simulations is that they assume "random mixing." That is, every member of the population is equally likely to encounter any other member. Much of the literature on agent-based models has examined the behavior of populations that are distributed over a landscape in which most interactions occur between adjacent locations on the landscape. Often models with local but no global interaction yield quite different outcomes from "random mixing" models.

To explore a model in which social communication occurs locally but not globally, I constructed a population distributed over a two-dimensional lattice, of size 500×500, with one agent at each lattice point. I assumed that a fraction η of agents are "well informed"—that is, as soon as a new inflation forecast is released, these agents learn the new forecast with zero lag. Other agents in the population obtain their views of inflation solely through interaction with neighbors.[12] Thus, in this model, news travels out in concentric patterns (one step on the landscape per period) from its geographical origination points (the news agents, who are scattered randomly across the landscape). As in the random mixing model, I assume that new news drives out old news.

---

[12] For the purposes of the simulation, an agent's neighbors are the agents in the eight cells surrounding him. For agents at the borders of the grid, neighborhoods are assumed to wrap around to the opposite side of the grid; implicitly this assumes the agents live on a torus.

Results from estimating the baseline model on data produced by the "local interactions" simulations are presented in table 5. For comparability with the baseline estimate of $\lambda = 0.25$ in the common-source model, I have assumed that proportion $\eta = 0.25$ of the agents in the new model are the well-informed types whose inflationary expectations are always up to date. Interestingly, estimating the baseline model yields a coefficient of about $\alpha_1 = 0.22$ on the SPF forecast, even though 25 percent of agents always have expectations exactly equal to the SPF forecast. The coefficient on lagged expectations gets a value of about 0.71, and the last column indicates that a test of the proposition that $\alpha_1 + \alpha_2 = 1$ now rejects strongly. However, the regression still has an $\bar{R}^2$ of around 0.99, so the basic common-source model still does an excellent job of capturing the dynamics of aggregate inflation expectations.

The most interesting result, however, is shown in the next row: the estimation now finds a highly statistically significant role for a nonnegligible constant term. Recall that the only real empirical problem with the common-source model was that the estimation found a statistically significant role for a constant term.

Results in the next rows show what happens when the proportion of news agents is reduced to $\eta = 0.15$. As expected, the estimate of α_1 falls; indeed, the downward bias is now even more pronounced than with 25 percent well informed. However, when a constant is allowed into the equation, the constant term itself is highly significant and the estimate of α_1 jumps to about 0.18, not far from the fraction of always-up-to-date agents in the population.

What these simulation results suggest is that the empirical constant term may somehow be reflecting the fact that some transmission of inflation expectations is through social exchange rather than directly through the news media. Furthermore, and happily, it is clear from the structure of the local interactions model that this population would eventually learn the true correct expectation of inflation if the SPF forecasts permanently settled down to a nonstochastic steady state. Thus it is considerably more appealing to argue that the constant term reflects misspecification of the model (by leaving out social interactions) than to accept the presence of a true constant term (and its associated implication of permanent bias).

A final caveat is in order. The central lesson of Mankiw and Reis [16, 17] and others is that the extent to which inflation can be reduced without increasing unemployment depends upon the speed with which a new view of inflation can be communicated to the *entire* population. It is not at all clear that the predictions about the medium-term inflation/unemployment tradeoff of a model with social transmission of expectations, or even of the common-source model with heterogeneous λ's, are similar to the predictions of the homogeneous λ model examined by Mankiw and Reis [16, 17]. Investigating this question should be an interesting project for future research.

4 CONCLUSIONS

This chapter was written to provide a specific example of a more general proposition: that many of the puzzles confronting standard macroeconomic models today could be resolved by abandoning the mathematically elegant but patently false assumptions of rational expectations models and replacing them with more realistic and explicit models of how people obtain their ideas about economic topics, which involve some form of learning or social transmission of knowledge and information. While the chapter confines itself to presenting results from agent-based simulations of such a model of inflation expectations, the closely related work by Mankiw and Reis [16, 17] shows that macroeconomic dynamics are much more plausible when expectations are governed by a model like the ones explored here.

Other puzzles that might yield to such an approach are legion. For example, excess smoothness in aggregate consumption (releative to the rational expectations benchmark) may reflect precisely the same kind of inattention posited for inflation expectations here (I am actively pursuing this possibility in ongoing work). A plausible explanation for the equity premium puzzle might be to suppose that it has taken a long time for news of the favorable risk/return tradeoff of stocks to spread from experts like Mehra and Prescott [18] to the general population. The strong systematic relationship of productivity growth and the natural rate of unemployment documented, for example, by Staiger, Stock, and Watson [25] and Ball and Moffitt [5] may reflect workers' imperfect knowledge about productivity growth (and the slow social transmission of such information). The detailed dynamics of productivity itself can surely be captured better by models in which new technologies spread gradually in a population than by models in which new technologies instantaneously boost productivity upon the date of invention (which is the conventional "technology shock" approach in rational expectations models). And a substantial literature now exists arguing that social transmission of information in a population of investing agents may be able to explain the excess volatility of asset prices compared to the rational expectations benchmark (see LeBaron [14] for a summary).

REFERENCES

[1] Akerlof, George, William Dickens, and George Perry. "The Macroeconomics of Low Inflation." *Brookings Papers in Economic Activity* **1** (1996): 1–76.

[2] Akerlof, George, William Dickens, and George Perry. "Near-Rational Wage and Price Setting and the Long-Run Phillips Curve." *Brookings Papers in Economic Activity* **1** (2000): 1–60.

[3] Ball, Laurence. "Near-Rationality and Inflation in Two Monetary Regimes." Working Paper No. W7988, National Bureau of Economic Research, Cambridge, MA, 2000.

[4] Ball, Laurence. "What Determines the Sacrifice Ratio?" In *Monetary Policy*, edited by N. Gregory Mankiw, ch. 5. Chicago, IL: University of Chicago Press, 1994.

[5] Ball, Laurence, and Robert Moffitt. "Productivity Growth and the Phillips Curve." Working Paper Number 450, Department of Economics, Johns Hopkins University, Baltimore, MD, 2001.

[6] Barsky, Robert B. "The Fisher Hypothesis and the Forecastability and Persistence of Inflation." *J. Monetary Econ.* **19** (1987): 3–24.

[7] Branch, William A. "The Theory of Rationally Heterogeneous Expectations: Evidence from Survey Data on Inflation Expectations." Manuscript, Department of Economics, College of William and Mary, Washington, DC, 2001.

[8] Calvo, Guillermo A. "Staggered Contracts in a Utility-Maximizing Framework." *J. Monetary Econ.* **12** (1983): 383–398.

[9] Carroll, Christopher D. "Macroeconomic Expectations of Households and Professional Forecasters." *Quart. J. Econ.* **118(1)** (2003): 269–298.

[10] Curtin, Richard T. "Procedure to Estimate Price Expectations." Manuscript, University of Michigan Survey Research Center, Ann Arbor, MI, 1996.

[11] Evans, George W., and Seppo Honkapohja. *Learning and Expectations in Macroeconomics.* Princeton, NJ: Princeton University Press, 2001.

[12] Fraser, D. W., T. R. Tsai, W. Orenstein, W. E. Parkin, H. J. Beecham, R. G. Sharrar, J. Harris, G. F. Mallison, S. M. Martin, J. E. McDade, C. C. Shepard, and P. S. Brachman. "Legionnaires' Disease: Description of an Epidemic of Pneumonia." *New England J. Med.* **297(22)** (1977): 1189–1197.

[13] Keynes, John Maynard. *The General Theory of Employment, Interest, and Money.* New York: Harcourt, Brace, 1936.

[14] LeBaron, Blake. "Agent Based Computational Finance: Suggested Readings and Early Research." *J. Econ. Dynamics & Control* **24** (2000): 679–702.

[15] Mankiw, N. Gregory. "The Inexorable and Mysterious Tradeoff Between Inflation and Unemployment." *Econ. J.* **111(471)** (2001): C45–C61.

[16] Mankiw, N. Gregory, and Ricardo Reis. "Sticky Information: A Model of Monetary Nonneutrality and Structural Slumps." Working Paper Number 8614, National Bureau of Economic Research, Cambridge, MA, 2001.

[17] Mankiw, N. Gregory, and Ricardo Reis. "Sticky Information Versus Sticky Prices: A Proposal to Replace the New Keynesian Phillips Curve." *Quart. J. Econ.* **117(4)** (2002): 1295–1328.

[18] Mehra, Rajnish, and Edward C. Prescott. "The Equity Premium: A Puzzle." *J. Monetary Econ.* **15** (1985): 145–161.

[19] Roberts, John M. "Inflation Expectations and the Transmission of Monetary Policy." Working Paper Number 1998-43, Federal Reserve Board FEDS, 1998.

[20] Roberts, John M. "Is Inflation Sticky?" *J. Monetary Econ.* (1997): 173–196.

[21] Roberts, John M. "New Keynesian Economics and the Phillips Curve." *J. Money, Credit, and Banking* **27(4)** (1995): 975–984.

[22] Sargent, Thomas J. *Bounded Rationality in Macroeconomics*. Oxford: Oxford University Press, 1993.

[23] Souleles, Nicholas. "Consumer Sentiment: Its Rationality and Usefulness in Forecasting Expenditure; Evidence from the Michigan Micro Data." *J. Money, Credit, and Banking* (2004): forthcoming.

[24] Souleles, Nicholas S. "Household Securities Purchases, Transactions Costs, and Hedging Motives." Manuscript, University of Pennsylvania, Philadelphia, PA, 2000.

[25] Staiger, Douglas, James H. Stock, and Mark W. Watson. "Prices, Wages, and the U.S. NAIRU in the 1990s." Working Paper Number 8320, National Bureau of Economic Research, Cambridge, MA, 2001.

Social Learning and the Adoption of Innovations

Charles F. Manski

1 INTRODUCTION

Social scientists have long wanted to understand the manner in which decision-makers learn about and choose innovations. A common scenario envisions an initial condition in which decisionmakers choose among a set of actions with known attributes. At some point, a new alternative yielding unknown outcomes becomes available. From then on, successive cohorts of decisionmakers choose among the expanded choice set, with later cohorts observing the experiences of earlier ones and possibly learning from them.

It has often been conjectured, and sometimes observed, that the fraction of decisionmakers choosing the new alternative increases with time in the manner of an S-shaped curve—first rising slowly, then rapidly, and finally converging to some limit value (e.g., Griliches [2]). However, this certainly is not the only possible dynamic for adoption of an innovation. The fraction of decisionmakers choosing the new alternative could begin high and then decrease with time, or the time path could be non-monotone.

The Economy as an Evolving Complex System III,
edited by Lawrence E. Blume and Steven N. Durlauf, Oxford University Press

The shape of the time path of adoption should depend on the beliefs that decisionmakers hold when the innovation is introduced and on how those beliefs evolve as experience accumulates. Manski [6] showed that processes of social learning can generate potentially complex time paths for the adoption of innovations. The present chapter carries this work further. Section 2 reviews the general analysis of social learning in Manski [6] and the specific findings on adoption of innovations. Section 3 reports a set of computational experiments that enrich understanding of the dynamics of information accumulation and decisionmaking after introduction of an innovation. Section 4 examines the implications for the welfare of the population of decisionmakers. Section 5 concludes.

2 SOCIAL LEARNING FROM PRIVATE EXPERIENCES

Manski [6] analyzes social interaction processes that stem from the successive endeavors of new cohorts of heterogeneous decisionmakers to learn from the experiences of past cohorts. The members of each new cohort observe the actions chosen and outcomes realized by past cohorts, and then make decisions that produce new experiences observable by future cohorts. I emphasize that decisionmakers face a basic identification problem, the *selection problem*, as they seek to learn from the experiences of others. The problem is that only the outcomes of chosen actions are observable; one cannot observe the outcomes that earlier decisionmakers would have experienced if they had selected other actions. The logical impossibility of observing counterfactual outcomes has long been recognized to pose a fundamental difficulty for empirical research in the social sciences. It is no less an impediment to social learning.

I study the dynamics of information accumulation and decision making when new cohorts have no prior knowledge of the outcomes associated with alternative actions, nor of the decision processes of past cohorts. I assume that new decisionmakers must choose their actions at a specified time and cannot revise their choices once made. Thus, they cannot undertake *learning-by-doing* and cannot otherwise wait for empirical evidence to accumulate before making decisions. These simplifying assumptions imply that each decisionmaker faces a single choice problem with predetermined information. Thus, dynamics emerge purely out of the process of social learning across successive cohorts. Individuals do not themselves face dynamic choice problems.

The analysis assumes only one regularity condition and one form of prior information. The regularity condition is that, for each feasible action, successive cohorts of decisionmakers share the same distribution of outcomes. The informational assumption is that decisionmakers know about this stationarity. The stationarity assumption implies that empirical evidence accumulates over time, each successive cohort being able to draw inferences from a longer history of experiences.

A medical illustration may help to envision the process of adoption of innovations under study here. Suppose that each year persons who are newly diagnosed with an illness must choose a treatment. Originally, only one treatment was available. This treatment was the universal choice and so its properties could readily be learned by observation of its success rate in curing the illness. At some point, a new treatment with *a priori* unknown properties is introduced. From then on, persons diagnosed with the illness choose between the old treatment and the new one. Initially, there is no empirical evidence about the success rate of the new treatment, so the persons who first choose the innovation tend to be those who are either most "optimistic" (in a sense to be made precise) about its success rate or who have the lowest cost of treatment, relative to the alternative. As empirical evidence accumulates, persons who are less "optimistic" or who have higher cost of treatment may adopt the innovation. These processes tend to make the rate of adoption grow over time, but a countervailing force may exist to the degree that empirical evidence shows optimism about the new treatment to be unwarranted. Hence the rate of adoption of the new treatment may increase, decrease, or be non-monotone over time.

Section 2.1 summarizes the basic analysis of information accumulation. Section 2.2 considers how decisionmakers may use the available empirical evidence to choose actions. Section 2.3 applies the findings to the adoption of innovations. The propositions and corollaries stated below are taken directly from Manski [6] and are proved there.

2.1 INFORMATION ACCUMULATION

To begin, I formalize the idea of a succession of cohorts who learn from past experiences. Suppose that at each integer date $T \geq 1$, each member of a cohort J_T of decisionmakers must choose an action from a finite time-invariant choice set C. Each person $j \in J_T$ has a response function $y_j(\cdot) : C \to Y$ that maps actions into outcomes, which take values in space Y. Let $z_j \in C$ denote the action chosen by person j. Then person j realizes outcome $y_j \equiv y_j(z_j)$. The counterfactual outcomes $y_j(c), c \neq z_j$ are unobservable.

To formalize needed distributional concepts, let each cohort J_T be a probability space, say (J_T, Ω_T, P_T), with Ω_T the σ-algebra and P_T the probability measure. For each $c \in C$, let $P_T[y(c)]$ be the outcome distribution for action c in this cohort. $P_T[y(c)]$ is the outcome distribution that would be realized if a randomly drawn member of J_T were to choose c. It is not the distribution among members of J_T who actually choose c. That is $P_T[y(c)|z = c]$.

The analysis of information accumulation rests on two maintained assumptions:

Assumption 1 (Observability of Past Actions and Outcomes): *Let $T \geq 1$. Before choosing actions, the members of cohort J_T observe the distributions $\{P_t(y, z), 1 \leq t \leq T - 1\}$ of actions chosen and outcomes realized by earlier cohorts.* ∎

Assumption 2 (Stationarity of Outcome Distributions): *For each $c \in C$, there exists a time-invariant probability distribution $P[y(c)]$ on the outcome space Y such that $P_T[y(c)] = P[y(c)], \forall T \geq 1$. This stationarity of outcome distributions is common knowledge.* ∎

Assumption 1 asserts that members of each cohort can observe the experiences of past cohorts. Assumption 2 asserts the stationarity of outcome distributions that enables decisionmakers of each cohort to learn about their own outcome distributions by observing past experiences.

The main findings are

Proposition 1: *Let Assumptions 1 and 2 hold. Let Γ denote the set of all probability distributions on Y. Let $T \geq 2$ and $c \in C$. The members of cohort J_T learn that*

$$P[y(c)] \in H(T, c) \equiv \cap_{1 \leq t \leq T-1} \{P_t(y|z = c)P_t(z = c) + \gamma_t \cdot P_t(z \neq c), \gamma_t \in \Gamma\}. \tag{1}$$

The identification region for $\{P[y(c)], c \in C\}$ is $[H(t, c), c \in C]$. ∎

Corollary 1: *Let Assumptions 1 and 2 hold. Let $T \geq 2$ and $c \in C$. Let $\eta \in \Gamma$ be a specified probability distribution on Y. Given any measurable set $A \subset Y$, define*

$$\pi_{Tc}(A) \equiv \max_{1 \leq t \leq T-1} P_t(y \in A|z = c)P_t(z = c). \tag{2}$$

(a) Then $\eta \in H(T, c)$ if and only if $\eta(A) \geq \pi_{Tc}(A), \forall A \subset Y$.
(b) Let Y be countable. Then $\eta \in H(T, c)$ if and only if $\eta(y) \geq \pi_{Tc}(y), \forall y \in Y$.
(c) Let Y be countable. Let $S(T, c) \equiv \sum_{y \in Y} \pi_{Tc}(y)$. Then $H(T, c)$ contains a unique distribution if and only if $S(T, c) = 1$. When $S(T, c) = 1$, the unique feasible distribution is $\eta_{Tc}(y), y \in Y$.[1] ∎

Proposition 1 shows that learning is a process of sequential reduction in ambiguity.[2] At date $T = 1$, decisionmakers have no knowledge at all of their outcome distributions. From $T = 2$ on, decisionmakers can use observations of

---

[1] The event $S(T, c) > 1$ cannot occur under Assumptions 1 and 2; this event implies that $H(T, c)$ is empty. The distribution η_{Tc} is distinct from π_{Tc}, which is sub-additive and hence not a probability distribution; that is, $\eta_{Tc}(y) = \pi_{Tc}(y)$ for $y \in Y$ but $\eta_{Tc}(A) \geq \pi_{Tc}(A)$ for $A \subset Y$.

[2] A decisionmaker with a known choice set who wishes to maximize an unknown objective function is said to face a problem of choice under ambiguity. A common source of ambiguity is incomplete knowledge of a probability distribution describing a relevant population—the decisionmaker may know only that the distribution of interest is a member of some set of distributions. This is the generic situation of a decisionmaker who seeks to learn a population distribution empirically, but whose data and prior information do not suffice to identify the distribution. Thus, identification problems in empirical analysis induce ambiguity in decision making.

past cohorts to learn about their outcome distributions. For each $c \in C$, the set $H(T+1, c)$ of distributions that are feasible at date $T+1$ is a subset of the corresponding set $H(T, c)$ at T. Because the process of information accumulation is monotone, it must converge to a *terminal information state*. That is, there necessarily exists a $[H(c), c \in C]$ such that

$$\lim_{T \to \infty} [H(T, c), c \in C] = [H(c), c \in C]. \tag{3}$$

The characterization of the set of feasible distributions given in Proposition 1 is simple but abstract. Corollary 1 gives a useful alternative characterization of $H(T, c)$. The basic finding is that a distribution is feasible if and only if the probability it places on each measurable subset of Y is no less than an easily computed lower bound. This characterization is particularly useful when the outcome space Y is countable. Then one need only consider the probability placed on each atom of Y. The Corollary shows that when Y is countable, the vector $[\pi_{Tc}(y), y \in Y]$ is a sufficient statistic for $H(T, c)$. Observe that $H(T, c)$ shrinks as $[\pi_{Tc}(y), y \in Y]$ increases.

2.2 DECISION MAKING

Now consider how decisionmakers may behave in the setting described in section 2.1. For $T \geq 2$ and $j \in J_T$, let $U_j(\cdot, \cdot) : C \times Y \to R^1$ denote the utility function that person j uses to evaluate actions. The utility $U_j[c, y(c)]$ that person j associates with action c may depend on the outcome $y(c)$, which the person does not know when facing the choice problem, as well as on attributes of c that the person does know.

Economists often assume that decisionmakers have rational expectations and choose actions that maximize expected utility. However, decisionmakers do not have rational expectations under Assumptions 1 and 2. Person j knows only that $\{P_T[y(c)], c \in C\}$, the vector of objective distributions of outcomes within his cohort, is an element of the set $[H(T, c), c \in C]$ specified in Proposition 1.

How might a person behave in this setting? A pervasive idea in research on social learning has been that a person views himself as a member of some observable *reference group* and predicts that, if he were to choose a given action, he would experience an outcome drawn at random from the distribution of outcomes in this group. We can formalize this idea by assuming that person j views himself as a member of cohort J_T, predicts that his outcome under each action $c \in C$ is drawn from $P_T[y(c)]$, and aims to solve the problem

$$\max_{c \in C} \int U_j[c, y(c)] dP_T[y(c)]. \tag{4}$$

The study of choice under ambiguity dates back at least to Keynes [4] and Knight [5], who used the term *uncertainty*. Ellsberg [1] introduced the term *ambiguity* and posed the problem in a particularly evocative way through a thought experiment requiring subjects to draw a ball from either of two urns, one with a known distribution of colors and the other with an unknown distribution of colors.

Problem (4) expresses a limited-information version of the usual rational expectations model, one in which person j conditions his expectations only on the information that he belongs to cohort J_T rather than on his full information set.

ELIMINATION OF DOMINATED ACTIONS

Problem (4) may not be solvable if $H[(T, c), c \in C]$ contains multiple distributions. However, decisionmakers can eliminate actions that are dominated. Assumption 3 asserts that decisionmakers do not choose dominated actions:

Assumption 3 (Elimination of Dominated Actions): *Let Assumptions 1 and 2 hold. Let $T \geq 2$ and $j \in J_T$. For $c \in C$ and $\gamma \in \Gamma$, let $\int U_j(c, y) d\gamma$ be the expected utility of action c if outcome y were distributed γ. Action $c' \in C$ is dominated if there exists another action $c'' \in C$ such that $\int U_j(c', y) d\eta' \leq \int U_j(c'', y) d\eta''$ for all $(\eta', \eta'') \in [H(T, c'), H(T, c'')]$ and $\int U_j(c', y) d\eta' < \int U_j(c'', y) d\eta''$ for some $(\eta', \eta'') \in [H(T, c'), H(T, c'')]$. Person j does not choose a dominated action.* ∎

The abstract characterization of dominated actions given in Assumption 3 becomes more transparent when the outcome space Y is countable and utility is bounded. In this case, Proposition 2 yields a simple description of the dominated actions.

Proposition 2: Let Y be countable. Let $T \geq 2$ and $j \in J_T$. Let $K_{0jc} \equiv \min_{y \in Y} U_j(c, y)$ and $K_{1jc} \equiv \max_{y \in Y} U_j(c, y)$ exist for all $c \in C$. Let

$$d \in \arg \max_{c \in C} \sum_{y \in Y} \pi_{Tc}(y) \cdot U_j(c, y) + [1 - S(T, c)] \cdot K_{0jc}. \tag{5}$$

Action $c' \in C$ is dominated if

$$\begin{aligned}\sum_{y \in Y} \pi_{Tc'}(y) \cdot U_j(c', y) + [1 - S(T, c')] \cdot K_{1jc'} \\ < \sum_{y \in Y} \pi_{Td}(y) \cdot U_j(d, y) + [1 - S(T, d)] \cdot K_{0jd}\end{aligned} \tag{6a}$$

or if

$$\begin{aligned}\sum_{y \in Y} \pi_{Tc'}(y) \cdot U_j(c', y) + [1 - S(T, c')] \cdot K_{1jc'} = \\ \sum_{y \in Y} \pi_{Td}(y) \cdot U_j(d, y) + [1 - S(T, d)] \cdot K_{0jd}\end{aligned} \tag{6b}$$

and

$$\min[S(T, c'), S(T, d)] < 1. \tag{6c}$$

Action c' is undominated if neither (6a) nor (6b)–(6c) holds. ∎

Proposition 2 shows that if utility is bounded, the accumulation of empirical evidence over time can enlarge the set of actions that decisionmakers may eliminate as dominated. Consider a sequence of decisionmakers who share the same bounded utility function but who make decisions at successive dates. Let $c' \in C$. The upper bound on the expected utility of this action, given on the left side of (6a), decreases with T. The greatest lower bound of the expected utility of all actions, on the right side of (6a), increases with T. Hence action c' may be undominated at early dates but dominated later on. It is not possible for c' to be dominated early but undominated later.

CHOICE AMONG UNDOMINATED ACTIONS

Assumption 3 leaves open how decisionmakers choose among undominated actions. There is no "optimal" way to make this choice, but many "reasonable" decision rules have been suggested over the years. In particular, Wald [7] proposed the maximin rule, which solves the problem

$$\max_{c \in C} \inf_{\eta \in H(T,c)} \int U_j[c, y(c)]d\eta. \tag{7}$$

Hurwicz [3] suggested maximization of a weighted average of the minimum and maximum values of the objective function that are feasible for each action. Thus person j would solve the problem

$$\max_{c \in C} \lambda_j \left\{ \inf_{\eta \in H(T,c)} \int U_j[c, y(c)]d\eta \right\} + (1 - \lambda_j)\left\{ \sup_{\eta \in H(T,c)} \int U_j[c, y(c)]d\eta \right\} \tag{8}$$

for some $\lambda_j \in [0, 1]$. Rule (8) provides a simple way of expressing degrees of pessimism and optimism; $\lambda_j = 1$ means that person j uses the maximin rule and $\lambda_j = 0$ that he uses the maximax rule.

Bayesian decision theorists suggest that the decisionmaker assert a subjective distribution on the space of feasible outcome distributions and maximize subjective expected utility with respect to this distribution. Thus person j would solve the problem

$$\max_{c \in C} \int \left\{ \int U_j[c, y(c)]d\eta \right\} dQ_{jc}(\eta), \tag{9}$$

where Q_{jc} is the subjective distribution that person j places on $H(T, c)$. Despite their widespread application in economic theory, Bayes decision rules have no particular normative force in the absence of credible prior information.

2.3   LEARNING ABOUT AND CHOOSING INNOVATIONS

I now specialize the foregoing analysis to adoption of innovations. Assumption 4 specifies a model whose structure is very simple, yet which can generate a rich variety of dynamics.

Assumption 4:   Assumption 3 holds. Moreover,

(a) The choice set is $C = (e, n)$. At date $T = 1$, all persons choose action e. The outcome space is $Y = \{0, 1\}$. The utilities that person j associates with actions e and n are $U_j[e, y(e)] = y(e)$ and $U_j[n, y(n)] = y(n) + u_j$, where $u_j \in R^1$. Person j knows u_j before choosing an action.

(b) Person j uses the Hurwicz criterion (8) with parameter λ_j to choose among undominated actions.

(c) There exists a time-invariant probability distribution $P[y(e), y(n), u, \lambda]$ such that $P_T[y(e), y(n), u, \lambda] = P[y(e), y(n), u, \lambda], \forall T \geq 1$. The distribution of u is continuous. ∎

Part (a) specializes Assumption 3 in various respects. Action e is the only pre-existing alternative, which all persons choose at $T = 1$. Action n is the innovation. The outcome y is binary, taking the value zero or one. Utility functions are separable in y. Parts (b) and (c) go beyond Assumption 3. Part (b) asserts that, to choose among undominated actions, each decisionmaker maximizes some weighted average of the lower and upper bounds on expected utility. Part (c) strengthens the stationarity condition asserted in Assumption 2. Successive cohorts of decisionmakers not only have the same outcome distributions, but have the same joint distributions of decision rules and outcomes.[3] Requiring that $P(u)$ be continuous ensures that indifference between actions e and n occurs with probability zero, so the model yields well-defined choice probabilities.

THE DYNAMICS OF CHOICE

Proposition 3 describes the time path of adoption of the innovation.

Proposition 3:   *Let Assumption 4 hold. At each date $T \geq 2$,*

$$P_t(z = n) = P\{\lambda \cdot \pi_{Tn}(1) + (1 - \lambda) \cdot [1 - \pi_{Tn}(0)] + u > P[y(e) = 1]\}. \quad (10)$$

∎

Proposition 3 shows how adoption of the innovation depends on $[\pi_{Tn}(1), \pi_{Tn}(0)]$, which weakly increase with time as empirical evidence accumulates. Consider date $T = 2$. No one chose action n at $T = 1$, so $\pi_{2n}(0) = \pi_{2n}(1) = 0$. Hence $P_2(z = n) = P\{1 - \lambda + u > P[y(e) = 1]\}$. From then on, $\pi_{(T+1)n}(1)$ and $\pi_{(T+1)n}(0)$ are given by the updating rule

$$\pi_{(T+1)n}(1) = \max[\pi_{Tn}(1), P_T(y = 1|z = n)P_T(z = n)] \quad (11a)$$
$$\pi_{(T+1)n}(0) = \max[\pi_{Tn}(0), P_T(y = 0|z = n)P_T(z = n)]. \quad (11b)$$

---

[3]Part (c) does not strengthen the information condition asserted in Assumption 2. Here, as before, decisionmakers only know that outcome distributions are stationary.

Moreover,

$$
\begin{aligned}
P_T(y = 1 | z = n) &= P\{y(n) = 1 | \lambda \cdot \pi_{Tn}(1) + (1 - \lambda)[1 - \pi_{Tn}(0)] \\
&\quad + u > P[y(e) = 1]\} \tag{12a} \\
P_T(y = 1 | z = e) &= P\{y(e) = 1 | \lambda \cdot \pi_{Tn}(1) + (1 - \lambda)[1 - \pi_{Tn}(0)] \\
&\quad + u < P[y(e) = 1]\} . \tag{12b}
\end{aligned}
$$

Taken together, eqs. (10)–(12) show how $P[y(e), y(n), u, \lambda]$, the stationary distribution of outcomes and decision rules, determines the dynamics of learning and choice.

Under Assumption 3, the decision rule that persons would use if $P[y(n) = 1]$ were known is to choose n if $P[y(n) = 1] + u > P[y(e) = 1]$ and choose e otherwise. The rate of adoption of the innovation would be $p^* \equiv P\{P[y(n) = 1] + u > P[y(e) = 1]\}$. Observe that $\pi_{Tn}(1) \leq P[y(n) = 1] \leq 1 - \pi_{Tn}(0)$. Hence the actual fraction of a cohort who choose action n can be below or above p^*, depending on the population distribution of (u, λ).

It is revealing to consider two extreme cases, one in which all decisionmakers use the maximin rule ($\lambda = 1$) and the other in which all use the maximax rule ($\lambda = 0$). If everyone uses the maximin rule, then $P_T(z = n) = P\{\pi_{Tn}(1) + u > P[y(e) = 1]\}$. Hence the fraction of a cohort who choose the innovation weakly increases with time, but always remains less than or equal to p^*. If all use the maximax rule, $P_T(z = n) = P\{1 - \pi_{Tn}(0) + u > P[y(e) = 1]\}$. In this case, the fraction who choose the innovation weakly decreases with time, but always remains greater than or equal to p^*.

THE TERMINAL INFORMATION STATE

The terminal information state is determined by the stationary distribution of outcomes and decision rules. Some sense of the possibilities is given by considering the special case in which all persons have the same value of $\lambda, y(n)$ is statistically independent of u, and u has support R^1.

Let $P(\lambda = L) = 1$, where $L \in [0, 1]$. Let $b \equiv P[y(n) = 1]$. Let $p_t \equiv P_t(z = n), t \geq 1$. By (11), statistical independence of $y(n)$ and u implies that for each $T \geq 2$,

$$
\begin{aligned}
\pi_{Tn}(1) &= P[y(n) = 1] \cdot \{\max_{1 \leq t \leq T-1} P_t(z = n)\} \\
&= b \cdot (\max_{1 \leq t \leq T-1} p_t) \tag{13a} \\
\pi_{Tn}(0) &= P[y(n) = 0] \cdot \{\max_{1 \leq t \leq T-1} P_t(z = n)\} \\
&= (1 - b) \cdot (\max_{1 \leq t \leq T-1} p_t) . \tag{13b}
\end{aligned}
$$

This and Proposition 3 yield

$$
\begin{aligned}
p_T &= P\{L \cdot b \cdot (\max_{1 \leq t \leq T-1} p_t) + (1 - L) \cdot [1 - (1 - b) \cdot (\max_{1 \leq t \leq T-1} p_t)] \\
&\quad + u > P[y(e) = 1]\} \\
&= P\{(L + b - 1) \cdot (\max_{1 \leq t \leq T-1} p_t) + 1 - L + u > P[y(e) = 1]\} . \tag{14}
\end{aligned}
$$

Inspection of eq. (14) shows that the sign of $(L + b - 1)$ determines the qualitative dynamics of decision making and information accumulation. If $(L + b - 1)$ is positive, the probability of choosing the innovation increases with time. Thus $\max_{1 \leq t \leq T-1} p_t = p_{(T-1)}$ and eq. (14) reduces to

$$p_T = p\{(L + b - 1) \cdot p_{(T-1)} + 1 - L + u > P[y(e) = 1]\}. \qquad (15)$$

Recall that, by assumption, $p_1 = 0$. Hence eq. (15) generates a monotone increasing rate of adoption whose limit as $T \to \infty$ is the value p' yielding the smallest solution to the equation

$$p' = P\{(L + b - 1) \cdot p' + 1 - L + u > P[y(e) = 1]\}. \qquad (16)$$

The terminal information state is $[\pi_n(1) = b \cdot p', \pi_n(0) = (1 - b) \cdot p']$. The value p' lies in the open interval $(0, 1)$. Hence the terminal information state is informative about b but does not completely identify it.

If $(L + b - 1)$ is non-positive, the situation is entirely different. Consider dates $T = 2, 3$, and 4. The following hold:

$$
\begin{aligned}
p_2 &= P\{1 - L + u > P[y(e) = 1]\} & (17a) \\
p_3 &= P\{(L + b - 1) \cdot p_2 + 1 - L + u > P[y(e) = 1]\} & (17b) \\
p_4 &= P\{(L + b - 1) \cdot p_2 + 1 - L + u > P[y(e) = 1]\}. & (17c)
\end{aligned}
$$

Equation (17a) holds because $p_1 = 0$, eq. (17b) because $p_2 \geq 0$, and eq. (17c) because $p_3 \leq p_2$. Hence information accumulation ceases at $T = 3$ and the terminal information state is $[\pi_n(1) = b \cdot p_2, \pi_n(0) = (1 - b) \cdot p_2]$.

Thus the qualitative dynamics of decision making and information accumulation depend critically on how decisionmakers choose among undominated actions. If they act pessimistically (i.e., $L > 1 - b$), the adoption rate of the innovation increases with time. If they act optimistically (i.e., $L \leq 1 - b$), the adoption rate begins high and then immediately falls to a steady state value. However decisionmakers behave, social learning takes place but remains incomplete.

3   COMPUTATIONAL EXPERIMENTS

Computational experiments with particular specifications of the time-invariant probability distribution $P[y(e), y(n), u, \lambda]$ can enhance understanding of the model of adoption of innovations studied in section 2.3. The experiments reported here aim to illuminate how behavior under ambiguity affects information accumulation and decision making.

3.1   EXPERIMENTAL DESIGN

The experiments fix many features of $P[y(e), y(n), u, \lambda]$ but consider a broad set of nine specifications for the distribution of the parameter λ, which governs behavior under ambiguity. The maintained assumptions are

- $P[y(e), y(n), u, \lambda] = P[y(e)] \cdot P[y(n)] \cdot P(u) \cdot P[\lambda|y(n)]$
- $P[y(e) = 1] = P[y(n) = 1] = 0.5$
- $P(u) \sim N(0, 1)$
- λ can take the values $\{0, 0.5, 1\}$.

Thus, the random variables $[y(e), y(n), u]$ are statistically independent and have specified marginal distributions. The distribution of λ may vary with the outcome $y(n)$, but all decisionmakers use one of three decision rules: the maximin rule ($\lambda = 1$), the maximax rule ($\lambda = 0$), or the intermediate rule giving equal weight to the lower and upper bounds on expected utility ($\lambda = 0.5$).

The nine specifications for the distributions $P[\lambda|y(n)]$ are

Case 1: $P[\lambda = 0|y(n) = 0] = 1$ $\qquad$ $P[\lambda = 0|y(n) = 1] = 1$
Case 2: $P[\lambda = 0|y(n) = 0] = 1$ $\qquad$ $P[\lambda = k|y(n) = 1] = 1/3, k \in \{0, 0.5, 1\}$
Case 3: $P[\lambda = 0|y(n) = 0] = 1$ $\qquad$ $P[\lambda = 1|y(n) = 1] = 1$
Case 4: $P[\lambda = k|y(n) = 0] = 1/3, k \in \{0, 0.5, 1\}$ $\qquad$ $P[\lambda = 0|y(n) = 1] = 1$
Case 5: $P[\lambda = k|y(n) = 0] = 1/3, k \in \{0, 0.5, 1\}$ $\qquad$ $P[\lambda = k|y(n) = 1] = 1/3, k \in \{0, 0.5, 1\}$
Case 6: $P[\lambda = k|y(n) = 0] = 1/3, k \in \{0, 0.5, 1\}$ $\qquad$ $P[\lambda = 1|y(n) = 1] = 1$
Case 7: $P[\lambda = 1|y(n) = 0] = 1$ $\qquad$ $P[\lambda = 0|y(n) = 1] = 1$
Case 8: $P[\lambda = 1|y(n) = 0] = 1$ $\qquad$ $P[\lambda = k|y(n) = 1] = 1/3, k \in \{0, 0.5, 1\}$
Case 9: $P[\lambda = 1|y(n) = 0] = 1$ $\qquad$ $P[\lambda = 1|y(n) = 1] = 1$.

Cases 1 and 9 express the extreme possibilities that all persons use the maximax rule (Case 1) or all use the maximin rule (Case 9). Cases 2 through 7 specify various forms of heterogeneity in behavior under ambiguity; some persons use the maximin rule, others use the maximax rule, and still others use the intermediate rule with $\lambda = 0.5$. The nine cases also express varied forms of dependence between λ and the outcome $y(n)$ that a person would experience if he were to choose the innovation; λ and $y(n)$ are statistically independent in cases (1, 5, 9), but are dependent in the other cases.

3.2 FINDINGS

Figure 1 plots the time path for dates $T = 2, \ldots, 10$ of adoption of the innovation in each of the nine cases specified above. Table 1 presents the same findings in numerical form. Figure 2 and table 2 present the identification regions for $P[y(n) = 1]$; that is, $[\pi_{Tn}(1), 1 - \pi_{Tn}(0)]$, $T = 2, \ldots, 10$.

The figures and tables show that the time path of adoption is monotone increasing in cases (6, 9), monotone decreasing in cases (1, 2, 4), slightly non-monotone in cases (3, 7, 8), and flat in case 5. The terminal information state is always reached by $T = 7$, but as soon as $T = 3$ in some cases.

The steady state rate of adoption of the innovation varies considerably across the nine cases, from a low of 0.3779 if all persons use the maximin rule to a high

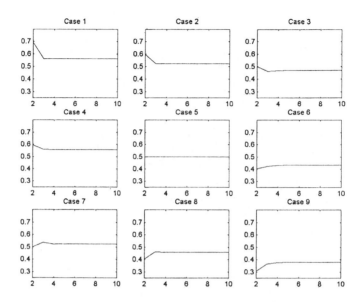

FIGURE 1 $P[z = n]$ as a function of T.

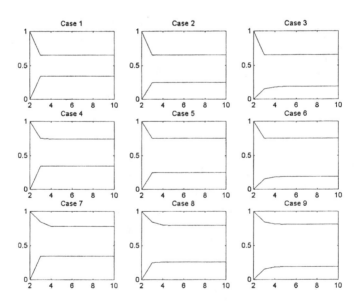

FIGURE 2   Identification region for $P[y(n) = 1]$ as a function of T.

TABLE 1   Rate $P_T(z = n)$ of Adoption of the Innovation

T	Case 1	Case 2	Case 3	Case 4	Case 5
1	0	0	0	0	0
2	0.6915	0.5957	0.5000	0.5957	0.5000
3	0.5613	0.5212	0.4630	0.5588	0.5000
4	0.5613	0.5212	0.4683	0.5560	0.5000
5	0.5613	0.5212	0.4694	0.5560	0.5000
6	0.5613	0.5212	0.4695	0.5560	0.5000
7	0.5613	0.5212	0.4696	0.5560	0.5000
8	0.5613	0.5212	0.4696	0.5560	0.5000
9	0.5613	0.5212	0.4696	0.5560	0.5000
10	0.5613	0.5212	0.4696	0.5560	0.5000

TABLE 1   continued

T	Case 6	Case 7	Case 8	Case 9
1	0	0	0	0
2	0.4043	0.5000	0.4043	0.3085
3	0.4231	0.5370	0.4599	0.3648
4	0.4311	0.5246	0.4581	0.3754
5	0.4326	0.5246	0.4580	0.3774
6	0.4329	0.5246	0.4580	0.3778
7	0.4330	0.5246	0.4580	0.3779
8	0.4330	0.5246	0.4580	0.3779
9	0.4330	0.5246	0.4580	0.3779
10	0.4330	0.5246	0.4580	0.3779

TABLE 2   Identification region for $P[y(n) = 1]$

	Case 1		Case 2		Case 3		Case 4		Case 5	
T	LB	UB	LB	UB	LB	UB	LB	UB	LB	UB
2	0	1	0	1	0	1	0	1	0	1
3	0.3457	0.6543	0.25	0.6543	0.1543	0.6543	0.3457	0.75	0.25	0.75
4	0.3457	0.6543	0.25	0.6543	0.1824	0.6543	0.3457	0.7406	0.25	0.75
5	0.3457	0.6543	0.25	0.6543	0.1877	0.6543	0.3457	0.7406	0.25	0.75
6	0.3457	0.6543	0.25	0.6543	0.1887	0.6543	0.3457	0.7406	0.25	0.75
7	0.3457	0.6543	0.25	0.6543	0.1889	0.6543	0.3457	0.7406	0.25	0.75
8	0.3457	0.6543	0.25	0.6543	0.1889	0.6543	0.3457	0.7406	0.25	0.75
9	0.3457	0.6543	0.25	0.6543	0.1889	0.6543	0.3457	0.7406	0.25	0.75
10	0.3457	0.6543	0.25	0.6543	0.1889	0.6543	0.3457	0.7406	0.25	0.75

TABLE 2   continued

	Case 6		Case 7		Case 8		Case 9	
T	LB	UB	LB	UB	LB	UB	LB	UB
2	0	1	0	1	0	1	0	1
3	0.1543	0.75	0.3457	0.8457	0.25	0.8457	0.1543	0.8457
4	0.1824	0.75	0.3457	0.7807	0.2593	0.7994	0.1824	0.8176
5	0.1877	0.75	0.3457	0.7807	0.2593	0.7976	0.1877	0.8123
6	0.1887	0.75	0.3457	0.7807	0.2593	0.7976	0.1887	0.8113
7	0.1889	0.75	0.3457	0.7807	0.2593	0.7976	0.1889	0.8111
8	0.1889	0.75	0.3457	0.7807	0.2593	0.7976	0.1889	0.8111
9	0.1889	0.75	0.3457	0.7807	0.2593	0.7976	0.1889	0.8111
10	0.1889	0.75	0.3457	0.7807	0.2593	0.7976	0.1889	0.8111

of 0.5613 if all persons use the maximax rule. If $P[y(n) = 1]$ were known, the rate of adoption would be

$$P\{P[y(n) = 1] + u > P[y(e) = 1]\} = P(u > 0) = 0.5.$$

Coincidentally, this also is the rate of adoption in Case 5. I say "coincidentally" because decisionmakers have only partial knowledge of $P[y(n) = 1]$ in Case 5; the adoption rate turns out to be 0.5 only because of the specific assumptions made about the distribution of λ.

The terminal information state also varies considerably across the nine cases. Cases 1 and 9 give the extreme outcomes of the learning process. If all decision-makers use the maximax rule, they learn as soon as $T = 3$ that $P[y(n) = 1]$ lies in the interval $[0.3457, 0.6543]$. If all decisionmakers use the maximin rule, the terminal state is reached at $T = 7$ and they learn that $P[y(n) = 1]$ lies in the interval $[0.1889, 0.8111]$. The former and latter intervals for $P[y(n) = 1]$ have widths 0.3086 and 0.6222, respectively.

Thus, in these computational experiments, the way that decisionmakers be-have under ambiguity very substantially affects both the steady state rate of adoption of the innovation and the amount of learning that takes place.

4   WELFARE ANALYSIS

How does incomplete knowledge of the outcomes associated with alternative actions affect the welfare of each cohort of decisionmakers? To address this ques-tion, I adopt the conventional perspective of public economics, in which the objective is to maximize a utilitarian social welfare function. Then we can com-pare the welfare realized when decisionmakers make choices under ambiguity with the welfare they would realize in other scenarios.

4.1   WELFARE IN VARIOUS SCENARIOS

Fix T and let J_T be the cohort of interest. In terms of the general discussion of decision making in section 2.2, the utilitarian social welfare realized by this cohort is

$$W_T \equiv \int \left\{ \sum_{c \in C} U_j[c, y_j(c)] 1[z_j = c] dP_T(j) \right\}, \tag{18}$$

where $1[\cdot]$ is the indicator function taking the value one if the condition in the brackets holds and zero otherwise. In the simple setting of Assumption 4, (18) reduces to

$$W_T \equiv \int \{ [y_j(n) + u_j] 1[z_j = n] + y_j(e) 1[z_j = e] \} dP_T(j)$$
$$= P_T[y(n) = 1, z = n] + E_T\{ u \cdot 1[z = n] \} + P_T[y(e) = 1, z = e]. \tag{19}$$

There are several welfare expressions with which W_T may be usefully compared. One is the ideal welfare that could be realized if decisionmakers had perfect foresight (PF); that is, if each person j were to know his outcomes $[y_j(e), y_j(n)]$. Then person j would choose action n if $y_j(n) + u_j > y_j(e)$, and choose action e otherwise. Realized welfare would be

$$W_{PF} \equiv \max[y(n) + u, y(e)] dP[y(e), y(n), u]. \tag{20}$$

Another is the welfare that would be realized if decisionmakers were able to identify the reference-group (RG) outcome distributions $\{ P[y(e)], P[y(n)] \}$ and solve problem (4). Then person j would choose action n if $P[y(n) = 1] + u_j > P[y(e) = 1]$. Realized welfare would be

$$W_{RG} \equiv P\{ y(n) = 1, u > P[y(e) = 1] - P[y(n) = 1] \}$$
$$+ E\{ u \cdot 1[u > P[y(e) = 1] - P[y(n) = 1]] \}$$
$$+ P\{ y(e) = 1, u < P[y(e) = 1] - P[y(n) = 1] \}. \tag{21}$$

One more welfare expression with which W_T may usefully be compared is W_1, the welfare realized at date $T = 1$, when all persons must choose the existing alternative. This is

$$W_1 = P[y(e) = 1]. \tag{22}$$

The welfare W_{PF} achievable with perfect foresight must be at least as large as each of the welfare expressions (W_T, W_{RG}, W_1), whatever the distribution $P[y(e), y(n), u, \lambda]$ may be. The ranking of (W_T, W_{RG}, W_1) relative to one another depends on the form of this distribution. Inspection of (21) shows that $W_{RG} \geq W_1$ if u is statistically independent of $[y(e), y(n)]$, but this inequality does not necessarily hold under some forms of dependence between u and $[y(e), y(n)]$. It appears difficult to say much of anything a priori about the ranking of W_T relative to W_{RG} and W_1. However, we can usefully calculate the various welfare expressions for the particular specifications of $P[y(e), y(n), u, \lambda]$ considered in the computational experiments of section 3. Section 4.2 gives the findings.

4.2   WELFARE IN THE COMPUTATIONAL EXPERIMENTS

The distributional assumptions of the computational experiments imply these values for the welfare expressions (W_{PF}, W_{RG}, W_1):

$$W_{PF} = 1.0114 \qquad W_{RG} = 0.8989 \qquad W_1 = 0.5 \,.$$

The welfare W_T depends on the date T and on the specification for $P[\lambda | y(n)]$. I focus here on $T = 10$, which always yields the terminal information state. The results for the nine cases are:

	Case 1	Case 2	Case 3	Case 4	Case 5	Case 6	Case 7	Case 8	Case 9
W_{10}	0.8942	0.8797	0.8552	0.9156	0.9012	0.8684	0.9434	0.9255	0.8801

Perhaps the most striking finding is that in each of the nine cases, W_{10} is reasonably close to the value of W_{RG}; whereas $W_{RG} = 0.8989$, W_{10} takes values in the interval $[0.8552, 0.9434]$. In Section 3.2, we found that the way decisionmakers behave under ambiguity has strong quantitative effects on the rate of adoption of the innovation and on the terminal state of the learning process. Here, in contrast, we find only moderate quantitative effects on welfare. Moreover, realized welfare is relatively high in all cases, much closer to the ideal WPF than to the welfare that would be experienced in the absence of the innovation.

It is easy to see why Cases 3 and 7 yield the lowest and highest values for W_{10}. The ambiguity parameter λ and the outcome $y(n)$ are strongly dependent in these cases. In Case 3, the persons who behave optimistically, and so tend to choose the innovation, tend to have bad draws of $y(n)$; those who behave pessimistically, and so tend to choose action e, tend to have good draws of $y(n)$. Hence the members of each new cohort J_T observe small values for the probabilities $[P_t(y = 1 | z = n), t < T]$ that earlier decisionmakers who chose the innovation had good outcomes. In Case 7, the nature of the dependency between λ and $y(n)$ is reversed.

One perhaps unintuitive finding is that W_{10} slightly exceeds W_{RG} in Case 5, where λ and $y(n)$ are statistically independent. This ranking is possible, albeit hard to explain, because decisionmakers who behave according to Assumption 4 make choices using knowledge of $[P_t(y | z = n), t < T]$. This information is not used in solving problem (4).

5   CONCLUSION

This chapter has used computational experiments to shed further light on the theoretical analysis of the dynamics of social learning in Manski [6]. These experiments illustrate quantitatively the qualitative theme, advanced in my earlier paper, that social learning from private experiences is a process of *complexity within regularity*. The process is complex because the dynamics of learning and the properties of the terminal information state flow from the subtle interaction of information accumulation and decision making. Yet a basic regularity constrains how the process evolves, as accumulation of empirical evidence over time (weakly) reduces the ambiguity that successive cohorts face.

Theoretical analysis and computational experiments are valuable in understanding complex economic processes, but I see a pressing need for new empirical research as well. In the present context, the critical empirical question is how decisionmakers actually cope with ambiguity. It is clear that the way decisionmakers choose among undominated actions can critically affect the dynamics of learning and choice. An improved empirical understanding of decision making under ambiguity is necessary to guide theoretical and computational research in productive directions.

6 ACKNOWLEDGMENTS

This research was supported in part by National Science Foundation grants SES-0001436 and SES-0314312. I am grateful to Francesca Molinari for research assistance and comments.

REFERENCES

[1] Ellsberg, D. "Risk, Ambiguity, and the Savage Axioms." *Quart. J. Econ.* **75** (1961): 643–669.

[2] Griliches, Z. "Hybrid Corn: An Exploration in the Economics of Technological Change." *Econometrica* **25** (1957): 501–522.

[3] Hurwicz, L. "Some Specification Problems and Applications to Econometric Models." *Econometrica* **19** (1951): 343–344.

[4] Keynes, J. *A Treatise on Probability.* London: MacMillan, 1921.

[5] Knight, F. *Risk, Uncertainity, and Profit.* Boston, MA: Houghton-Mifflin, 1921.

[6] Manski, C. "Social Learning from Private Experiences: The Dynamics of the Selection Problem." *Rev. Econ. Stud.* **71** (2004): 443–458.

[7] Wald, A. *Statistical Decision Functions.* New York: Wiley, 1950.

Rationality and Selection in Asset Markets

Lawrence E. Blume
David Easley

1 INTRODUCTION

In this chapter we ask a simple question: What does rational behavior on the part of asset market participants imply about equilibrium asset prices? "Rationality" has a variety of meanings in economic thought, so to answer this question we must first be clear about what we intend by "rational behavior." Here we take "rationality" to mean that investor preferences satisfy the Savage [14] axioms or some modern refinement of them. Thus, the investor is a subjective expected utility (SEU) maximizer. The existence of an SEU representation implies that the investor is a Bayesian, but it does not otherwise restrict the investor's beliefs about future prices. In particular, without ancillary assumptions on prior beliefs, it does not imply that the investor has correct beliefs, or even that he will eventually learn the truth.

The hypothesis of rationality can be strengthened by ancillary assumptions on the nature of beliefs. One such belief restriction is the requirement that investors' beliefs are conditional forecast distributions from prior beliefs over a

The Economy as an Evolving Complex System III,
edited by Lawrence E. Blume and Steven N. Durlauf, Oxford University Press

class of models which includes the "true" model. A sharper belief restriction is the rational expectations hypothesis, that investors *are certain of* the true model. In other words, investors' beliefs are correct. In terms of prior beliefs, the first assumption has the support of the prior belief distribution containing the true model. The second assumption has the support of the prior belief distribution containing only the true model. In other words, the true model receives prior probability 1.

Here we examine the implications of this hierarchy of rationality hypotheses for equilibrium asset prices. The economy we analyze has investors who live forever, have stochastic endowments of a single consumption good, and trade in each period a dynamically complete set of Arrow securities. We do not explicitly consider richer sets of securities, but even with the weakest of our rationality hypotheses security prices are arbitrage proof, so more complex assets can be priced by arbitrage from the prices of the Arrow securities.

A belief-based learning rule is a map from partial histories of states into a forecast distribution on the next state. We show that any belief-based learning rule is consistent with Bayesian updating, and thus is consistent with subjective expected utility maximization. Consequently, any map from partial histories into prices of the Arrow securities is consistent with rational behavior of the first type. In this market model, restrictions on asset prices cannot come from the hypothesis of SEU maximization.

Belief restrictions, on the other hand, do have power. For example, if investors beliefs are generated by a prior on a set of models for the economy that includes the true model, then investors will learn the true model (if it is identified) and, under some assumptions, prices will converge to their rational expectations equilibrium values. If we further strengthen the rationality hypothesis to require correct beliefs from the outset, then prices will always be at their rational expectations equilibrium values.

It is important for these rational expectations equilibrium conclusions that belief restrictions as well as SEU rationality are required of all investors. This is surely problematic. How is it that all investors know the truth or even place positive probability on it? Where does this knowledge or prior restriction come from? It cannot be derived from learning, as the rationality model with a prior restriction is itself supposed to be a model of the learning process. What happens if, more realistically, we assume that some, but not all, investors know the truth or are able to learn it? This requires an analysis of an economy with heterogeneous investors.

In an economy in which investors have heterogeneous beliefs or heterogeneous learning rules, structure on long-run prices arises from the forces of market selection. It has long been assumed that those with better beliefs will make better decisions, driving out those with worse beliefs, and thus determining long run asset prices correctly. This argument is usually attributed to Alchian [1] and Friedman [11], and to Cootner [7] and Fama [10] for its application to financial markets. More generally the idea is that rational (in a strong sense) decisionmakers will drive out irrational decisionmakers. Thus, according to this argument, long-run asset prices will be correct. But until recently there was little formal investigation of this conjecture.

Delong, Shleifer, Summers, and Waldman [8, 9] provide one of the first formal analyses of wealth flows between rational and irrational traders. They argue that irrationally overconfident noise traders can come to dominate an asset market in which prices are set exogenously; a claim that contradicts Alchian's and Friedman's intuition. In Blume and Easley [5] we addressed the same issue in a general equilibrium model. We showed that if savings rates are equal across investors, general equilibrium wealth dynamics need not lead to investors making portfolio choices as if they were subjective expected utility maximizers with correct beliefs. We did not study the emergence of fully intertemporal expected utility maximization, nor did we say much about the emergence of beliefs. Sandroni [13] addressed the latter question. He built economies with intertemporal expected utility maximizers and studied the emergence of rational expectations. He showed in a Lucas trees economy that, controlling for discount factors, only investors with rational expectations, or those whose forecasts merge with rational expectations forecasts, survive. He also showed that even if no such investors are present, no investor whose forecasts are persistently wrong survives in the presence of a learner. In Blume and Easley [4] we showed that whenever markets are complete, and investors have a common discount factor, investors with correct beliefs drive out those with incorrect beliefs and thus drive prices to their rational expectations equilibrium values. Here we apply the analysis of Sandroni [13] and Blume and Easley [4] to show how selection works in the Arrow securities economy.

In the following sections we describe a simple model of an economy with Arrow securities (section 2), show that subjective expected utility maximizers are Bayesians (section 3), consider other non-SEU behavior (section 4), show the implications of various definitions of rationality for asset prices (section 5), and show how wealth dynamics work (section 6).

2   A SIMPLE MODEL

We consider the implications of SEU rationality and various belief restrictions for asset pricing in a simple infinite-horizon general equilibrium model. Time is discrete and is indexed by $t \in \{0, 1, \ldots, T\}$ with $T \leq \infty$. At each date $t \geq 1$, a state from the finite set of states $\{1, \ldots, S\}$ is realized. A *path* of states is denoted $\sigma = (\sigma_1, \sigma_2 \ldots)$, where each $\sigma_t \in S$. The set of paths is denoted Σ and its product sigma-field is denoted $\mathcal{F}$. States evolve according to a **"true" probability** p on $(\Sigma, \mathcal{F})$.

All random variables dated t are assumed to be date-t measurable; that is, their value depends only on the realization of states through date t. Formally, $\mathcal{F}_t$ is the σ-field of events measurable at date t, and each such random variable is assumed to be $\mathcal{F}_t$-measurable. For a given path σ, σ_t is the state at date t and $\sigma^t = (\sigma_1, \ldots, \sigma_t)$ is the *partial history* through date t. Let $\mathcal{H}$ denote the set of all partial histories. Let 0 denote the empty partial history.

There is a single, non-storable consumption good available at each date. Also at each date, S Arrow [3] securities are available. One unit of security s available at date t pays one unit of the consumption good at date $t + 1$ if and only if state s occurs at date $t + 1$.[1] The price of the consumption good is one at each date. The prices of Arrow securities are random variables denoted as $q_t = (q_t^1, \ldots, q_t^S)$.

There are I investors, indexed by i. Investors have stochastic endowments of the good. The endowment stream for investor i is given by the random variable $e^i = (e_0^i, e_1^i \ldots)$, where $e_t^i \in \mathbf{R}_{++}$ is investor i's endowment of the good at date t. A consumption plan for investor i is a random variable denoted $c^i = (c_0^i, c_1^i \ldots)$, where $c_t^i \in \mathbf{R}_{++}$ is i's consumption of the good at date t. The set of consumption plans is denoted C.

Investors have preferences over entire consumption plans. Investor i's preference order over plans is denoted by $\succeq^i$. Under standard assumptions (see Savage [14] or Anscombe and Aumann [2]), these preferences have a subjective expected utility (SEU) representation.

Definition 1. *Preferences $\succeq$ have a **subjective expected utility** representation if there exists a **payoff function** $U : C \to \mathbf{R}$ and **subjective beliefs**, a probability p on Σ, such that $c \succeq c'$ if and only if*

$$E_p U(c) \geq E_p U(c').$$

We assume that investors' utility functions are *time separable* and permit *geometric discounting*, that is, there is a discount factor β and a function $u : c \mapsto \mathbf{R}$ such that

$$E_p U(c) = E_p \left\{ \sum_t \beta^t u(c_t) \right\}. \tag{1}$$

This representation provides a utility function for consumption u, a discount factor β and, most importantly for our purposes, beliefs p over paths. The representation places no restrictions on beliefs other than the obvious requirement that they are a probability on $(\Sigma, \mathcal{F})$. One important special case is that of beliefs generated by iid forecasts. If trader i believes that all the σ_t are iid draws from a common distribution ρ, then p^i is the corresponding distribution on infinite sequences. In this case, the marginal probability on σ^t is $p_t^i(\sigma) = \prod_{\tau=1}^t \rho(\sigma_\tau)$.

---

[1] We index both states and Arrow securities by s because each Arrow security can be identified with the state in which it pays off. Our assumption that markets are dynamically complete is not important for our analysis of individual behavior, but we do use it in two places. First, it is important for the interpretation of pricing all possible securities by arbitrage. Second, it is important for the results about selection for rationality in section 6. If markets are incomplete, then irrational investors can drive out rational investors. See Blume and Easley [4].

The subjective expected utility representation also allows for investors who are uncertain about the process on states and who learn about it as Bayesians. In fact, it allows for no other learning rules. To formalize this claim we first need to define conditional preferences and Bayes' rule.

3 BAYESIAN LEARNING

If a preference order $\succeq$ satisfies the Savage axioms, then there is a well-defined notion of conditional preference order. We say that one consumption plan c is at least as good as another consumption plan c' given some set of paths A, $c \succeq_A c'$, if the ranking between these two plans depends only on how they behave on A.

For c and c' in C, and $A \in \mathcal{F}$, define

$$c_A c'_t(\sigma^t) = \begin{cases} c_t(\sigma^t) & \text{if } \sigma^t \in A, \\ c'_t(\sigma^t) & \text{if } \sigma^t \notin A. \end{cases} \tag{2}$$

Definition 2. *Consumption plan c is **at least as good as** c' **given** A, $c \succeq_A c'$, if for all plans $c'' \in C$, $c_A c'' \succeq c'_A c''$.*

Given that the path will be in A, only how plans compare on A matters to a subjective expected utility maximizer. If the individual's beliefs over paths are p^i, then only beliefs conditional on A matter when A is known to occur. These conditional beliefs are given by the Bayes rule.

Definition 3. *For $A \in \mathcal{F}$ with $p(A) > 0$ and any $B \in \mathcal{F}$ define p_A by*

$$p_A(B) = \frac{p(B \cap A)}{p(A)}.$$

First we recall the elementary fact that SEU maximization implies Bayesian updating.[2] If a decisionmaker ranks consumption plans with beliefs p then, given knowledge of A, he ranks consumption plans using conditional beliefs p_A.

Theorem 1. *Suppose $\succeq$ has an SEU representation (U, p). Then for any $A \in \mathcal{F}$ with $p(A) > 0$ and $c, c' \in C$, $c \succeq_A c'$ if and only if $E_{p_A} U(c) \geq E_{p_A} U(c')$, where p_A is p conditioned on A.*

Proof Choose any $c'' \in C$. The following are all equivalent:

$$c \succeq_A c'$$
$$c_A c'' \succeq c'_A c''$$
$$E_p U(c_A c'') \geq E_p U(c'_A c'')$$

---

[2] A set of axioms that characterize Bayesian updating is explored more fully in Ghirardato [12]

$$p(A)E_p\{U(c)|A\} + p(A^c)E_p\{U(c'')|A^c\} \geq p(A^c)E_p\{U(c')|A\}$$
$$+p(A^c)E_p\{U(c'')|A^c\}$$
$$p(A)E_p\{U(c)|A\} \geq p(A)E_p\{U(c')|A\}$$
$$E_{p_A}U(c) \geq E_{p_A}U(c').$$

∎

4   CONTINGENT DECISION PROBLEMS

In asset markets investors make a sequence of decisions: a choice at the outset, a choice after observing the state at date 1, a choice after observing the states at dates 1 and 2, and so forth. We call these contingent decision problems. Each contingency has its own preference order with respect to which choice, given that contingency is maximal.

Formally, let Σ_{σ^t} denote the set of all paths with initial partial history σ^t, and let $\mathcal{F}_{\sigma^t}$ denote the restriction of $\mathcal{F}$ to subsets of Σ_{σ^t}.

The elements of the decision problem D_{σ^t} for contingency σ^t are the set of all consumption plans $C_{\sigma^t} = \{(c_{t+1}, \ldots) : c \in C\}$ and on this set a preference order $\succeq^{\sigma^t}$.

Definition 4.   *A contingent preference structure is a collection* $D = \{(D_{\sigma^t}, \succeq^{\sigma^t}) : \sigma^t \in \mathcal{H}\}$. Combining the framework with appropriate budget constraints defines contingent decision problems from which asset demand can be derived.

One source of contingent preference structures is conditional SEU preferences. We know from Theorem 1 that SEU preferences imply Bayesian learning, so we call the decision framework they induce *Bayes*.

Definition 5.   *A contingent preference structure D is **Bayes** if there is a payoff function U and a belief p on Σ such that $\succeq^{\sigma^t}$ is represented by (U, p_{σ^t}) where each p_{σ^t} is defined from p by Bayes' rule.*

The SEU framework imposes a coherency over preferences in these different decision problems. If σ^t is a partial history, and σ^{t+k} is an extension of that partial history, then preferences in the decision problem after having observed partial histories σ^t and σ^{t+k} each have an SEU representation. The payoff functions are the same in both representations, and the beliefs at σ^{t+k} are the conditional probability of future events from the probability distribution representing beliefs at σ^t given the additional observations $\sigma_{t+1}, \ldots, \sigma_{t+k}$. This, of course, is a consequence of Theorem 1. This works both ways. The coherency condition just described is necessary as well as sufficient for a contingent preference structure to be Bayes. The following claim is trivially true but it makes an important point, that when conditional preferences are SEU, Bayesian behavior is nothing more nor less than the path-consistency of preferences.

Theorem 2. *Let D be a contingent preference structure such that each $\succeq^{\sigma^t}$ has an SEU representation. Then D is Bayes if and only if for each partial history σ^t and extension σ^{t+k}, the conditional preference order defined from $\succeq^{\sigma^t}$ given σ^{t+k}, denoted $\succeq^{\sigma^t}_{-\sigma^{t+k}}$, is identical to the preference order $\succeq^{\sigma^{t+k}}$.*

Proof That every collection of conditional preference orders derived from SEU preferences has this property is obvious. Going the other way, let (U, p) represent the preference order $\succeq^0$, and consider any expected utility representation (U', p') for $\succeq^{\sigma^t}$. Since $\succeq^0_{\sigma^t}$ and $\succeq^{\sigma^t}$ are identical, the uniqueness of the SEU representation implies that $p' = p_{\sigma^t}$ and that there exist numbers α and $\beta > 0$ such that $U' = \alpha + \beta U$. So (U, p_{σ^t}) represents $\succeq^{\sigma^t}$. Thus D is Bayes. ∎

It is often argued that this Bayesian coherence imposes a significant restriction on beliefs, and therefore on behavior. A common "remedy" is to suppose that preferences after different partial histories have SEU representations with identical payoff functions, but to allow arbitrary belief evolution. Specifically, consider a decisionmaker who has initial beliefs p_1 on states at time 1. Suppose that the individual's beliefs on states at time 2, conditional on the realization of the time 1 state σ_1, are given by a learning rule $p_2(\sigma_1, \cdot)$. Similarly, for each partial history σ^t, the individual's beliefs on states at time $t + 1$ are given by a learning rule $p_{t+1}(\sigma^t, \cdot)$. An individual who follows this procedure uses a *belief-based learning rule*.

Definition 6. *A **belief-based learning rule** is a probability p_1 on S and a sequence of $\mathcal{F}_t$-measurable functions $\{p_{t+1}(\sigma^t, \cdot)\}$, for $t \geq 1$, from partial histories into probabilities on S. A contingent preference structure D has a **belief-based expected utility (BBEU) representation** if there exists a $U : C \to \mathbf{R}$ and a belief-based learning rule $\{p_t\}_{t=1}^{\infty}$ such that $\succeq^{\sigma^t}$ is represented by $(U, p_{t+1}(\sigma^t, \cdot))$.*

So many papers on bounded rationality employ this remedy that we resist the opportunity to single out one or two to pick on. But our point is that this is no remedy at all. If a contingent preference structure has a BBEU representation, then it is Bayes.

Theorem 3. *If $\{p_t\}_{t=1}^{\infty}$ is a belief-based learning rule, then there is a subjective belief p on Σ such that*

1. *For all $A \subset S$, $p_1(A) = p(\sigma_1 \in A)$, and*
2. *For all partial histories σ^t and $A \subset S$, $p_{t+1}(\sigma^t, A) = p(\sigma_{t+1} \in A | \sigma^t)$.*

In other words, any belief-based learning rule is realizable as a collection of conditional expectations from a subjective belief distribution p.

Proof The functions p_t, are conditional probabilities, and p_1 is a probability distribution. The initial beliefs p_1 and the conditional distributions $p_2, \ldots p_{T-1}$ can be integrated to generate a marginal distribution q_T on partial histories σ^T such that the marginal distribution of σ^T with respect to any q_{T+k} is just q_T. The Kolmogorov extension theorem then states there is a distribution p on Σ with the given marginals q_T. ∎

Any BBEU representation is Bayes. Thus, requiring an individual to be a Bayesian places no restrictions on his sequence of one-period forecasts. Restrictions on these forecasts are typically obtained by placing restrictions on the set of models for the stochastic process that the individual considers and by restricting his prior on the model set. It is worth emphasizing that even if we can observe an individual's entire sequence of one period ahead forecasts, observations that contradict Bayesian behavior, and thus a subjective expected utility representation, are not possible unless the observer has some prior knowledge about the individual's beliefs.

The usual method of employing this false remedy is to pose a problem with a space of models and a prior distribution (or class of prior distributions) on that space. Then one rejects Bayesian updating in favor of some other updating rule. Of course such learning rules can lead to conclusions different from Bayesian updating, but what is being rejected is not Bayesian behavior but the choice of the model space. This is a belief restriction, not a rationality hypothesis. The only implication of SEU rationality is coherence. We explore coherence violations in the next section.

5   NON-SUBJECTIVE EXPECTED UTILITY MOTIVATED BEHAVIOR PREFERENCES

Beliefs, and the maximization of expected utility using those beliefs, are obviously important for asset pricing. These beliefs could come from preferences over random consumption streams as in the subjective expected utility setting. Alternatively, they could be arbitrary beliefs of investors who are not operationally subjective expected utility maximizers. In this section we consider more general, or seeming more general, forms of behavior and ask if these behaviors are different from those generated by subjective expected utility maximizers. We show that any investor who correctly anticipates his future beliefs acts as if he is a Bayesian, although perhaps one with rather odd beliefs. Such investors are indistinguishable from subjective expected utility maximizers. Equilibria in economies populated with these investors thus cannot be differentiated from those arising in economies populated by subjective expected utility maximizers.

As we have already shown that the hypothesis that investors are subjective expected utility maximizers places no restrictions on learning rules, this claim is perhaps not surprising. However, the hypothesis that investors are subjective expected utility maximizers does impose consistency restrictions on plans. These restrictions arise from the hypothesis that the investor knows his preferences. This, in turn, implies that he acts as if he knows his belief-based learning rule and thus correctly anticipates how his beliefs will evolve along any path. Alternatively, a investor who does not correctly anticipate his future beliefs may not act according to his plans and thus may not behave as a subjective expected utility maximizer. This is the reason for the qualification that the behavior of any investor who correctly anticipates his future beliefs is not distinguishable from that of a subjective expected utility maximizer.

To see these claims most clearly we consider a simple three-period, two-state model, $S = (s_1, s_2)$. Let w_0 be the present discounted value at $t = 0$ of the investor's endowment stream. At date 0 the investor has to allocate this wealth between consumption and purchases of date 0 Arrow securities. At date 1 she receives the proceeds from the Arrow securities that pay off in the realized state and she re-allocates between consumption and new Arrow security purchases. Finally, at date 2, she consumes the proceeds of the Arrow securities that pay off at date 2.

At date 0 the investor has beliefs p^i on sample paths (σ_1, σ_2). These beliefs induce a probability p_1^i on states at date 1 and two conditional probabilities at date 1 on states at date 2. Denote these conditional probabilities by $p_2^i(s_1, \cdot)$ if state s_1 occurs at date 1, and $p_2^i(s_2, \cdot)$ if state s_2 occurs at date 1.

Because markets are complete, the investor's sequential decision problem can be collapsed into a static problem in which she chooses consumption plans subject to a single budget constraint. Let $q_t^{\sigma_{t+1}}(\sigma_t)$ be the price of consumption in state σ_{t+1} given σ_t.

$$P_0: \quad \max u(c_0) + \beta E_p u\big(c_1(\sigma_1)\big) + \beta^2 E_p u\big(c_2(\sigma_1, \sigma_2)\big)$$
$$\text{s.t.} \quad c_0 + \sum_{\sigma_1} q_0^{\sigma_1} c_1(\sigma_1) + \sum_{\sigma_1, \sigma_2} q_0^{\sigma_1} q_1^{\sigma_2}(\sigma_1) c_2(\sigma_1, \sigma_2)$$
$$= w_0.$$

Let the plans that solve this decision problem be denoted $\{c_0, c_1(\sigma_1), c_2(\sigma_1, \sigma_2)\}$.

When period 1 arrives, this investor will carry out her plans as long as her beliefs at that point are as predicted. A subjective expected utility maximizer always correctly predicts the evolution of her beliefs along each path and thus always carries out her plans. We also want to allow for the possibility that the investor's beliefs are not as predicted. The investor's actual beliefs about states at date $t = 2$, given σ_1, are denoted by $r_{\sigma_1}(\sigma_2)$. We say that an investor is naïve if she does not always correctly anticipate how her beliefs will evolve; otherwise she is sophisticated.

Definition 7. *A investor is* naïve *if for some* $\{\sigma_1, \sigma_2\}$, $p_1(\sigma_1, \sigma_2) \neq r_{\sigma_1}(\sigma_2)$. *Otherwise she is* sophisticated.

Investors who are subjective expected utility maximizers are sophisticated. They are Bayesians who act as if they understand how their beliefs will evolve. But an investor does not need to be a Bayesian to be sophisticated. For example, an investor who uses maximum likelihood to estimate a parameter for an iid distribution on states and who correctly anticipates how the maximum likelihood estimate will change, given any partial history is sophisticated. However, a maximum likelihood estimator who does not anticipate how her estimate will change over time is naïve.

The decision problem for an investor at time 1 if state σ_1 has occurred is

$$P_{\sigma_1}: \quad \max u\big(d_1(\sigma_1)\big) + \beta E_{r_{\sigma_1}} u\big(d_2(\sigma_1, \sigma_2)\big)$$

$$\text{s.t.} \quad d_1(\sigma_1) + \sum_{\sigma_2} q_1^{\sigma_2}(\sigma_1) d_2(\sigma_1, \sigma_2) = w(\sigma_1)$$

$$w(\sigma_1) = c_1(\sigma_1) + \sum_{\sigma_2} q_1^{\sigma_2}(\sigma_1) c_2(\sigma_1, \sigma_2).$$

Let the decisions that solve this problem be denoted $\{d_1(\sigma_1), d_2(\sigma_1, \sigma_2)\}$.

Definition 8. *The investor is* plan consistent *if for each* (σ_1, σ_2)

$$c_1(\sigma_1) = d_1(\sigma_1)$$
$$c_2(\sigma_1, \sigma_2) = d_2(\sigma_1, \sigma_2).$$

Subjective expected utility maximizers are obviously sophisticated investors and are plan consistent. In fact, any sophisticated investor solves a decision problem that can be recast as if the investor was a Bayesian who solves problem P_0. These investors are operationally Bayesian and are indistinguishable from subjective expected utility maximizers. They are thus plan consistent.

Definition 9. *An investor is* observationally equivalent *to a subjective expected utility maximizer if there are beliefs* p^i *on paths, a discount factor* β_i *and a utility function* u^i *which generate her plans as a solution to problem* P_0.

Theorem 4. *In the framework of this section:*

1. *All subjective expected utility maximizers are sophisticated investors.*
2. *All sophisticated investors are plan consistent.*
3. *All sophisticated investors are observationally equivalent to subjective expected utility maximizers.*
4. *Naïve investors need not be plan consistent.*

Proof

1. Obvious.
2. Rewrite the investor's objective function in P_0 as

$$\max u(c_0) + \beta \sum_{\sigma_1} p_0(\sigma_1) u\big(c_1(\sigma_1)\big)$$
$$+ \sum_{\sigma_1} p_0(\sigma_1)\beta^2 \sum_{\sigma_2} p_1(\sigma_1, \sigma_2) u\big(c_2(\sigma_1, \sigma_2)\big).$$

3. Let $p_0(\sigma_1) = r(\sigma_1)$. Let $p_1(\sigma_1, \sigma_2) = r_{\sigma_1}(\sigma_2)$. The sophisticated investor has the same plan as would a Bayesian with beliefs $p(\sigma_1, \sigma_2) = p_0(\sigma_1)p_1(\sigma_1, \sigma_2)$.
4. To prove this we provide an example of a naïve, plan inconsistent investor. Suppose that all asset prices are 1 and that $u(c) = \gamma^{-1}c^\gamma$. Let $g = 1/(1 - \gamma)$.

The investor is naïve and a maximum likelihood learner. At date 0 her forecast for period 1 is $(r, 1 - r)$. At date 1 her conditional forecasts are $r_{s_1}(\cdot) = (r, 1 - r)$ and $r_{s_2}(\cdot) = (p, 1 - p) \neq (r, 1 - r)$.

At date 0 she plans in each state to allocate

$$\alpha(r) = \frac{r^g}{r^g + (1 - r)^g}$$

to the state s_1 security. At date 1 she in fact chooses

$$s_1: \quad \alpha(r) = \frac{r^g}{r^g + (1-r)^g}$$
$$s_2: \quad \alpha(p) = \frac{p^g}{p^g + (1-p)^g}.$$

Since her planned and actual date 1-state s_2 investment allocations differ, her planned and actual date 2 consumptions must differ on the event $\sigma_1 = s_1$ ∎

6 EQUILIBRIUM PRICES

Because subjective expected utility maximization places no restrictions on beliefs, it places few restrictions on equilibrium prices. To see this in the simplest setting suppose that there is only one investor, i.e., $(I = 1)$, whose endowment is constant over time and states, $e_t(\sigma^t) = e \in \mathbf{R}_+$ for all σ^t and t. Let $p_{t+1}^1(\sigma^t, \cdot)$ be the investor's date t forecast of the conditional probability on states at date $t + 1$. If the investor's discount factor is β_1 then it is easy to see that the following prices support the investor's endowment and so form an equilibrium. An equilibrium price of Arrow security s given partial history σ^t is

$$q_t^s(\sigma^t) = \beta_1 p_{t+1}^1(\sigma^t, s). \tag{3}$$

The prices do not depend on the investor's utility function or on the amount of the endowment.[3] This is true in a multiple investor economy also as long as the investors have common beliefs and a common discount factor.

Theorem 5. *Consider an economy with I investors with common beliefs p^1 and a common discount factor β. Suppose that each investor's endowment is constant over time and states, i.e., for each i there is a $e^i \in \mathbf{R}_+$ such that $e^i_t(\sigma^t) = e^i$ for all σ^t and t. Then, for each $s \in S$ and partial history σ^t the equilibrium price of Arrow security s given partial history σ^t is*

$$q^s_t(\sigma^t) = \beta p^1_{t+1}(\sigma^t, s). \tag{4}$$

Proof Because markets are dynamically complete, it is sufficient to consider the present value of investors' endowments and their complete market demands. At prices $q^s_t(\sigma^t) = \beta p^1_{t+1}(\sigma^t, s)$ the present value of investor i's endowment is $e^i/(1 - \beta)$. Calculation shows that, regardless of the investor's utility function, at a date 0 optimum he saves fraction β of this value and invests a fraction of this savings in each Arrow security equal to the probability of its associated state. Thus, at date 0 he consumes e^i units of the good. This is clearly an equilibrium at date 0. The date 1 present value of his wealth will be $e^i/(1 - \beta)$ no matter what state occurs at date 1. So he again consumes e^i units of the good and we have an equilibrium at date 1. Repeating this argument shows that we have an equilibrium at each date. ∎

We know from Theorem 3 that the beliefs are arbitrary. So equilibrium Arrow security prices are arbitrary. Of course there are restrictions on prices of securities that can be represented as bundles, over time or over states, of Arrow securities. Although these redundant securities are not present in our model, we could easily include them and price them by arbitrage. Inclusion of such securities would lead to falsifiable restrictions on security prices. But note that rejecting these restrictions would do far more than reject Bayesian learning—it would reject any decision theory in which individuals recognize and take advantage of arbitrage opportunities.

To obtain restrictions on asset prices in the simple economy of Theorem 5 we would need to have restrictions on investors' beliefs. For example, if we assume that these beliefs are correct, $p^i = p$ for all i, then prices will also be "correct." Or we could assume that all investors are learning about the true model. If the true model p is in the set of models they consider and if it is identified, they will learn it and prices will converge to "correct" prices.[4] But how is it that all investors come to know the truth or to have it in their model set? What happens if some

---

[3]The assumption that the endowment is constant does matter.
[4]See Blume and Easley [6]

investors know the truth, have rational expectations, and others do not? Will the rational investors drive out the incorrect ones and force prices to converge to their "correct" values? These questions are addressed in the next section.

7 WEALTH DYNAMICS

If investors have differing beliefs and or differing discount factors then they may make differing investment choices. Both the level of savings and the portfolio rule that investors choose may be affected by these individual factors. This will cause wealth to flow between the investors over time. In this section we analyze these wealth flows and their implications for asset prices. The analysis in this section is an application of the results in Sandroni [13] and Blume and Easley [4].

In order to do this analysis we make the following assumptions. First we assume that investors are strictly risk averse and that marginal utility converges to infinity as consumption converges to 0.

A.1. *The payoff functions u_i are C^1 functions from $\mathbf{R}_+$ to $\mathbf{R}_+$ which are strictly concave, strictly monotonic, and satisfy an Inada condition at 0.*

We next assume that the aggregate endowment is uniformly bounded from above and away from 0:

A.2. $\infty > F = \sup_{t,\sigma} \sum_i e_t^i(\sigma) \geq \inf_{t,\sigma} \sum_i e_t^i(\sigma) = f > 0.$

Finally, we assume that investors believe to be possible anything which is possible.

A.3. *For all investors i, all dates t and all paths σ, $p_t(\sigma) > 0$ and $p_t^i(\sigma) > 0$.*

The economy has a full set of Arrow securities so by the First Welfare Theorem any competitive equilibrium allocation is a Pareto optimal allocation. Further, because each investor has a strictly positive endowment, she must receive a strictly positive utility in any competitive equilibrium. So the relevant Pareto optimal allocations are those in which every investor has strictly positive utility. Our approach is to characterize this set of Pareto optimal allocations. Any property that holds for all of them must hold for any competitive equilibrium.[5]

Theses Pareto optimal allocations maximize a weighted sum of utilities with strictly positive welfare weights for each investor. If $c^* = (c^{1*}, \ldots, c^{i*})$ is such a Pareto optimal allocation, then there is a vector of welfare weights $(\lambda^1, \ldots, \lambda^i) \gg \mathbf{0}$ such that c^* solves the problem

$$\max_{(c^1,\ldots,c^i)} \quad \sum_i \lambda^i U^i(c) \tag{5}$$

---

[5]We do not ask whether competitive equilibrium exists. However, we have computed examples in which it does exist so the following results are not empty.

$$\text{such that} \quad \sum_i c^i - e \leq 0 \tag{6}$$

$$\forall t, \sigma \; c_t^i(\sigma) \geq 0 \tag{7}$$

where $e_t = \sum_i e_t^i$.

From the first-order conditions for problem (5) it can be shown that for any investors i and j there is a constant K_{ij} such that for any path σ and for all t,

$$\frac{u^{i'}(c_t^i(\sigma))}{u^{j'}(c_t^j(\sigma))} = K_{ij} \frac{\beta_j^{t-1}}{\beta_i^{t-1}} \frac{p_t^j(\sigma)}{p_t^i(\sigma)}. \tag{8}$$

The left side of eq. (8) is not a marginal rate of substitution. It is the ratio of marginal utilities for two investors along the path σ. This ratio conveys information about the investors' consumption and wealth. To see this, note that because the aggregate endowment, and thus consumption, is bounded away from 0 and from above, our conditions on utility functions imply that:

$$\text{If} \quad \frac{u^{i'}(c_t^i(\sigma))}{u^{j'}(c_t^j(\sigma))} \to \infty \quad \text{then} \quad c_t^i(\sigma) \to 0. \tag{9}$$

$$\text{If} \quad c_t^i(\sigma)) \to 0 \quad \text{then for some } j, \quad \limsup \frac{u^{i'}(c_t^i(\sigma))}{u^{j'}(c_t^j(\sigma))} \to \infty. \tag{10}$$

So we can study the limit behavior of i's consumption, and thus his wealth and affect on prices, by studying the right side of eq. (8). The right side does not involve utility functions so we immediately have the result that, within the class of preferences that we consider, attitudes toward risk are irrelevant for long survival. All that matters are discount factors and beliefs.

7.1 AN IID ECONOMY

When the truth is iid and all investors have iid beliefs, the right side of (8) can be analyzed with a straightforward application of the strong law of large numbers. Suppose that the distribution of states is given by independent draws from a probability distribution q on S, and forecasts p^i and p^j are distributions on paths induced by iid draws from strictly positive distributions q^i and q^j on S, respectively. Then $p_t^i(\sigma)$ is

$$p_t^i(\sigma) = \prod_{s=1}^{S} (q_s^i)^{n_t^s(\sigma)}, \tag{11}$$

where $n_t^s(\sigma)$ is the number of occurrences of state s by date t in partial history σ^t. Taking logs of Eq. (8) and dividing by t gives

$$\frac{1}{t} \log \frac{u^{i'}(c_t^i(\sigma))}{u^{j'}(c_t^j(\sigma))} = \frac{1}{t} K_{ij} + \log \frac{\beta_j}{\beta_i} + \frac{1}{t} \sum_s n_t^s(\sigma)(\log q_s^j - \log q_s^i). \tag{12}$$

By the strong law of large numbers, the left side converges p-a.s. to

$$\left(\log \beta_j - I_p(p^j)\right) - \left(\log \beta_i - I_p(p^i)\right), \tag{13}$$

where $I_r(\pi)$ is the relative entropy of r with respect to π,

$$I_r(\pi) = \sum_{s \in S} r(s) \log \frac{r(s)}{\pi(s)}. \tag{14}$$

Relative entropy is a measure of distance. $I_r(\pi) \geq 0$ and $I_r(\pi) = 0$ if and only if $\pi = r$.

If the limit in eq. (13) is positive, the ratio of marginal utilities diverges, and so $\lim_t c_t^i(\sigma) \to 0$ almost surely. The expression $\log \beta_i - I_p(p^i)$ measures the potential for trader i to survive. This analysis shows that in the iid case a necessary condition for investor i's survival is that this value be maximal in the population.

When investors have identical discount factors, those who survive are those whose forecasts are closest in relative entropy to the truth. An investor with rational expectations survives, and any investor who does not have rational expectations vanishes. If there is at least one investor who has rational expectations, then Arrow securities prices must converge to their rational expectations values.

When discount factors differ, higher discount factors can offset bad forecasts. An investor with incorrect forecasts may care enough about the future that she puts more weight on future consumption even in states which she considers unlikely, than does an investor with correct forecasts, who considers those same states likely, but cares little about tomorrow. In this case, prices need not converge to their rational expectations values

Next, we ask what happens for more general stochastic processes. Allowing the process on states to be arbitrary is important, but far more important is allowing an investor's beliefs on paths to be general. Even if the world is iid, and an investor knows this, beliefs will not be iid unless the investor knows the true process. In the natural case in which the investor is uncertain about the true process, forecasts will depend on history through the dependence of posteriors on history.

7.2   RATIONAL EXPECTATIONS

We consider economies in which all investors have the same discount factor, $\beta_i = \beta_j$ for all i and j. We say that investor i *survives* if $\limsup c_t^i > 0$ p-almost surely and that she *vanishes* if $\lim c_t^i = 0$ p-almost surely.

Blume and Easley [4] show, in a more general analysis, that any investor with rational expectations survives almost surely. So no matter what other investors believe about the economy, a trader with rational expectations cannot be driven out of the market and his beliefs determine Arrow security prices asymptotically.

Theorem 6. *Suppose that $\beta_i = \beta_j$ for all i and j. If investor i is a subjective expected utility maximizer with correct beliefs, $p^i = p$, then investor i survives p-almost surely.*

This result does not imply that traders whose beliefs are not correct vanish. The fate of these traders depends on whether their conditional forecasts converge to correct conditional forecasts and on how fast this convergence occurs. In Blume and Easley [4] we provide a rate analysis that shows how various learning rules perform.

8 CONCLUSION

The hypothesis of rational investor behavior has few implications for asset prices. The power of rationality lies in the ancillary assumptions of various restrictions on beliefs. Rational expectations impose strong conditions on asset prices. Belief restrictions guaranteeing that rational expectations are learnable imply strong conditions on asset prices in the long run. We believe that these assumptions on traders' beliefs are unreasonable, but that most mispricings of assets with reference to the rational expectations asset pricing formula are consistent with Bayesian rationality. We agree that behavioral models can provide convenient representations of preferences which highlight particular properties of asset price behavior that differ from conventional asset pricing predictions. But it is wrong to assert that the source of these differences must lie in the rejection of SEU preferences.

Assuming that some investors may have more accurate beliefs than others is more plausible than rational expectations assumptions. We have reported on some restrictions on asset prices that can be derived from economic models with heterogeneous beliefs. In the short run, investors with incorrect expectations can influence asset prices. But in the long run they may lose out to those with better expectations who choose better portfolio rules. Expectations also affect savings rates, and investors with incorrect expectations can be induced to oversave, so the conjecture that they are driven out is far from obvious. We show that if markets are dynamically complete and investors have a common discount factor, then in fact the market is dominated in the long run by those with correct expectations. In the long run, asset prices converge to their rational expectations values.

The assumptions that markets are complete and that investors have a common discount factor are both important for this selection result. In Blume and Easley [4] we provide an analysis of the tradeoff between the size of discount factors and the distance of beliefs from the truth. Investors with high discount factors and incorrect beliefs can drive out those with correct beliefs and lower discount factors, and this will cause even longrun asset prices to be incorrect. More importantly, we also show that if markets are not dynamically complete then, even when discount factors are common, investors with incorrect beliefs can drive out those with correct beliefs.

REFERENCES

[1] Alchian, Armen. "Uncertainty, Evolution, and Economic Theory." *J. Pol. Econ.* **58** (1950): 211–221.

[2] Anscombe, F., and Robert Aumann. "A Definition of Subjective Probability." *Annl. Math. Stat.* **34** (1963): 199–205.

[3] Arrow, K. "The Role of Securities in the Optimal Allocation of Risk-Bearing." *Rev. Econ. Stud.* **31** (1964): 91–96.

[4] Blume, Lawrence, and David Easley. "If You're so Smart, Why Aren't You Rich? Belief Selection in Complete and Incomplete Markets." Unpublished, Cornell University, Ithaca, NY, 2000.

[5] Blume, Lawrence, and David Easley. "Evolution and Market Behavior." *J. Econ. Theor.* **58(1)** (1992): 9–40.

[6] Blume, Lawrence, and David Easley. "Rational Expectations and Rational Learning." In *Organizations with Incomplete Information: Essays in Economic Analysis*, edited by Mukul Majumdar, 61–109. Cambridge, UK: Cambridge University Press, 1998.

[7] Cootner, Paul. *The Random Character of Stock Market Prices.* Cambridge, MA: MIT Press, 1964.

[8] DeLong, J. Bradford, Andrei Shleifer, Lawrence Summers, and Robert Waldman. "The Survival of Noise Traders in Financial Markets." *J. Bus.* **64(1)** (1991): 1–19.

[9] DeLong, J. Bradford, Andrei Shleifer, Lawrence Summers, and Robert Waldman. "Noise Trader Risk in Financial Markets." *J. Pol. Econ.* **98(4)** (1990): 703–738.

[10] Fama, Eugene. "The Behavior of Stock Market Prices." *J. Bus.* **38(1)** (1965): 34–105.

[11] Friedman, Milton. *Essays in Positive Economics.* Chicago, IL: University of Chicago Press, 1953.

[12] Ghirardato, Paolo. "Revisiting Savage in a Conditional World." *Econ. Theor.* **20** (2002): 83–92.

[13] Sandroni, Alvaro. "Do Markets Favor Agents Able to Make Accurate Predictions." *Econometrica* **68(6)** (2000): 1303–1342.

[14] Savage, Leonard. *On the Foundations of Statistics.* New York: Wiley, 1954.

Statistical Physics and Economic Fluctuations

H. Eugene Stanley
Xavier Gabaix
Parameswaran Gopikrishnan
Vasiliki Plerou

We present an overview of recent research—much of it carried out in collaborations between economists and physicists—which is focused on applying ideas of statistical physics to try to better understand puzzles regarding economic fluctuations. One of our questions is how to describe outliers, phenomena that lie outside of patterns of statistical regularity. We review evidence consistent with the possibility that such outliers may not exist. This possibility is supported by the extensive numerical analysis of a huge database, containing every trade, which results in power-law descriptions of a number of quantities whose fluctuations are of interest. It is also supported by recent analysis by Plerou et al. of a database containing the bid, the ask, and the sale price of each trade of every stock. Further, the Plerou et al. analysis is consistent with a possible theoretical framework for understanding economic fluctuations in which a financial market alternates between being in an *equilibrium phase* where market behavior is split roughly equally between buying and selling, and an *out-of-equilibrium phase* where the market is mainly either buying or selling.

1   INTRODUCTION

Collaborative work joining economists and physicists has begun to lead to modest progress in answering questions of interest to both economists and physicists. In particular, these collaborations have the potential to change the paradigm for understanding economic fluctuations. Until relatively recently, theories of economic fluctuations invoked the label of *outlier* (bubbles and crashes) to describe fluctuations that do not agree with existing theory. These outliers are of interest, as they correspond to extremely large and unpredictable changes of magnitude sufficient to wreak havoc.

The paradigm of *statistical regularity plus outliers* which does not exist in the traditional economic theory is not always sufficient to predict all the outliers. Recent analysis of gargantuan databases suggests that classic theories fail not only for a few outliers, but that there occur similar outliers of every possible size. In fact, if one analyzes only a small data set (say, 10^4 data points), then outliers appear to occur as rare events. However, when orders of magnitude more data (10^8 data points) are analyzed, one finds orders of magnitude more outliers—thus ignoring them is not a responsible option, and studying their properties becomes a realistic goal. One finds that the statistical properties of these outliers are identical to the statistical properties of everyday fluctuations. For example, a histogram giving the number of fluctuations of a given magnitude x for fluctuations ranging in magnitude from everyday fluctuations to extremely rare fluctuations (*financial earthquakes*) that occur with a probability of only 10^{-8} is a perfect straight line in a double-log plot.

An analogy with earthquake research is perhaps not entirely inappropriate. If one studies limited data sets that correspond to everyday experience, an entirely natural paradigm arises in which there are everyday (unnoticeable except by sensitive seismometer) *tremors*, punctuated from time to time by *earthquakes* (rare events). Thanks to the empirical work, we now know that the partition of shocks into tremors and earthquakes is not valid. Rather, if one examines enough data, one sees that the shocks occur for all possible magnitudes. The empirical law named after Gutenberg and Richter, refers to a statistical formula that gives all the data from the smallest tremors all the way up to the *big one*. This empirical law states that the histogram giving the number of shocks of a given size is a straight line in a log-log plot [54, 131]. Since this straight line fits all the data, there are no outliers in earthquake research. The utility of this empirical law is at least twofold: (1) it motivates understanding the big ones (that matter!) by extensive analysis of small ones (that do not matter), and (2) it enables *quantitative* estimates of the risk of large earthquakes, thereby making possible safer design of buildings by guiding engineers to have just enough vibration protection to reduce the risk to an acceptable level.

Our experience with thinking about earthquakes teaches us that an inappropriate paradigm can arise when a limited quantity of data is considered, since if one has only a handful of rare events, it is natural to partition data into everyday events (often describable by one statistical law) and rare events (which, since they are not described by the law, are termed outliers). Has an inappropriate paradigm arisen in economic research? In economic research, there are fluctuations in stock prices, in number of shares trading hands, and in total number of fluctuations, and so forth. Recent empirical studies calculating histograms for all recordable quantities are linear on log-log plots (albeit with different slopes). In mathematical language, the occurrence probability of such a quantity's fluctuations appears to be described by a power law.

In economics, neither the existence of power laws nor the exact exponents measured (the slopes of the above-mentioned log-log plots) has an accepted theoretical basis. Professionally, empirical laws such as power laws are called *stylized facts*, a term in physics that would be regarded as dismissive, since physics is a discipline grounded on empirical facts, and facts that are observed and confirmed by independent observation are called *laws*. Accordingly, some theoretical understanding is urgently needed or else these empirical laws will continue to be regarded as largely uninteresting, if not irrelevant. Of course facts, even facts without any interpretation, may have practical value. If the Gütenberg-Richter law enables one to accurately calculate the risk of a shock (tremor or earthquake) of a given magnitude, and hence informs the building codes of Los Angeles and Tokyo, could the empirical laws governing economic fluctuations perhaps enable one to accurately calculate the risk of an economic shock of a given magnitude?

The lack of a coherent theory is unfortunate—especially in economics, where to be faced with facts bereft of any theoretical foundation is considered deplorable. Accordingly, my collaborators and I have been seeking to develop a theoretical framework within which to interpret these new empirical facts, and recently some progress is beginning to occur [41, 42]. This work is potentially significant, since it provides a theoretical framework within which to interpret the new empirical laws. Specifically, the model fulfills these requirements for such a basic *microscopic* model of the stock market. It is founded on realistic features of the stock market, and reflects the view that market participants have of the functioning of the market, as well as the main determinants of their trading behavior.

2   FIRST DISCOVERY OF SCALING AND UNIVERSALITY

That at least *some* economic phenomena are described by power-law tails has been recognized for over 100 years, ever since Pareto investigated the statistical character of the wealth of individuals by modeling them using the *scale-invariant* distribution

$$f(x) \sim x^{-\alpha}, \tag{1}$$

where $f(x)$ denotes the number of people having income x or greater than x, and α is an exponent that Pareto estimated to be 1.5 [96, 117]. Pareto noticed that his result was *universal* in the sense that it applied to nations "as different as those of England, of Ireland, of Germany, of the Italian cities, and even of Peru" [96]. A physicist would say that the universality class of the scaling law, eq. (1), includes all the aforementioned countries as well as Italian cities since, by definition, two systems belong to the same universality class if they are characterized by the same exponents.

In the century following Pareto's discovery, the twin concepts of scaling and universality have proved to be important in a number of scientific fields [17, 79, 85, 119, 123, 124, 129]. A striking example was the elucidation of the puzzling behavior of systems near their critical points. Over the past few decades it has come to be appreciated that the scale-free nature of fluctuations near critical points also characterizes a huge number of diverse systems that in turn are characterized by strong fluctuations. This set of systems includes examples that at first sight are as far removed from physics as is economics. For example, consider the percolation problem, which in its simplest form consists of placing pixels on a fraction p of randomly chosen plaquettes of a computer screen. A remarkable fact is that the largest connected component of pixels magically spans the screen at a threshold value p_c. This purely geometrical problem has nothing to do, at first sight, with critical point phenomena. Nonetheless, the fluctuations that occur near $p = p_c$ are scale-free and functions describing various aspects of the incipient spanning cluster that appears at $p = p_c$ are described by power laws characterized by exponent values that are universal in the sense that they are independent of the details of the computer screen's lattice (square, triangle, honeycomb). Nowadays, the concepts of scaling and universality provide the conceptual framework for understanding the geometric problem of percolation.

It is becoming clear that almost any system comprised of a large number of interacting units has the potential of displaying power-law behavior. Since economic systems are comprised of a large number of interacting units, it is perhaps not unreasonable to examine economic phenomena within the conceptual framework of scaling and universality [17, 79, 85, 119, 123, 124, 129]. We will discuss this topic in detail below.

3   SCALING AND UNIVERSALITY: TWO CONCEPTS OF MODERN STATISTICAL PHYSICS

Statistical physics deals with systems comprising a very large number of interacting subunits, for which predicting the exact behavior of the individual subunit would be impossible. Hence, one is limited to making statistical predictions regarding the collective behavior of the subunits. Recently, it has come to be appreciated that many such systems consisting of a large number of interacting subunits obey universal laws that are independent of the microscopic details. The finding, in physical systems, of universal properties that do not depend on the specific form of the interactions gives rise to the intriguing hypothesis that universal laws or results may also be present in economic and social systems [79, 85].[1]

3.1 BACKGROUND

Suppose we have a small bar magnet made up of 10^{12} strongly interacting subunits called *spins*. We know it is a magnet because it is capable of picking up thumbtacks, the number of which is called the order parameter M. As we heat this system, M decreases and eventually, at a certain critical temperature T_c, it reaches zero. Since M approaches zero at T_c with infinite slope, the transition is remarkably sharp, hence M is not an analytic function. Such singular behavior is an example of a *critical phenomenon*. Recently, the field of critical phenomena has been characterized by several important conceptual advances, two of which are scaling and universality.

3.1.1 Scaling.
The scaling hypothesis has two categories of predictions, both of which have been remarkably well verified by a wealth of experimental data on diverse systems. The first category is a set of relations, called *scaling laws*, that serve to relate the various critical-point exponents characterizing the singular behavior of functions such as M.

The second category is a sort of *data collapse*, which is perhaps best explained in terms of our simple example of a uniaxial magnet. We may write the equation of state as a functional relationship of the form $M = M(H, \tau)$, where M is the order parameter, H is the magnetic field, and $\tau \equiv (T - T_c)/T_c$ is a dimensionless measure of the deviation of the temperature T from the critical temperature T_c. Since $M(H, \tau)$ is a function of two variables, it can be represented graphically and M vs. τ for a sequence of different values of H. The scaling hypothesis predicts that all the curves of this family can be *collapsed* onto a single curve provided one plots not M vs. τ but rather a *scaled M* (M divided by H to some power) vs. a *scaled τ* (τ divided by H to some different power).

The predictions of the scaling hypothesis are supported by a wide range of experimental work, and also by numerous calculations on model systems. Moreover, the general principles of scale invariance used here have proved useful

---

[1] An often-expressed concern regarding the application of physics methods to the social sciences is that physical laws are said to apply to systems with a very large number of subunits (of the order of $\approx 10^{20}$), while social systems comprise a much smaller number of elements. However, the *thermodynamic limit* is reached in practice for rather small systems. For example, in early computer simulations of gases or liquids, reasonable results are already obtained for systems with 20–30 atoms.

in interpreting a number of other phenomena, ranging from elementary particle physics and galaxy structure to finance [79, 81, 82].

3.1.2 Universality. The second theme goes by the name *universality*. It was found empirically that two systems with the same values of critical point exponents and scaling functions are said to belong to the same universality class. Thus the fact that the exponents and scaling functions are the same for all five materials implies they all belong to the same universality class. Hence we can pick a tractable system to study and the results we obtain will hold for all other systems in the same universality class.

3.2 SCALING AND UNIVERSALITY IN SYSTEMS OUTSIDE OF PHYSICS

At one time, many imagined that the *scale-free* phenomena are relevant to only a fairly narrow slice of physical phenomena [11, 119, 124]. However, the range of systems that apparently display power law and hence scale-invariant correlations has increased dramatically in recent years, ranging from base pair correlations in noncoding DNA [88, 98], lung inflation [126], and interbeat intervals of the human heart to complex systems involving large numbers of interacting subunits that display *free will*, such as city growth, and even populations of birds [64].

4 TOWARDS A THEORY OF THE FIRM

Having embarked on a path guided by these two theoretical concepts, what does one do? Initially, critical phenomena research—guided by the Pareto principles of scaling and universality—was focused on finding which systems display scaling phenomena, and on discovering the actual values of the relevant exponents. This initial empirical phase of critical phenomena research proved vital, for only by carefully obtaining empirical values of exponents such as α could scientists learn which systems have the same exponents (and thus belong to the same *universality class*). The fashion in which physical systems partition into disjoint universality classes proved essential to such later theoretical developments as the renormalization group [119]—which offered some insight into why scaling and universality seem to hold; ultimately, it led to a better understanding of the critical point.

Similarly, our group's initial research in economics—guided by the Pareto principles—has largely been concerned with establishing which systems display scaling phenomena, and with measuring the numerical values of the exponents with sufficient accuracy that one can begin to identify universality classes if they exist. Economic systems differ from often-studied physical systems in that the number of interacting subunits is much smaller. The macroscopic samples in physical systems contain a huge number of interacting subunits (as many as Avogadro's number 6×10^{23}). In contrast, in an economic system, one initial work was limited to analyzing time series comprising of the order of magnitude 10^3 terms, and nowadays, with high frequency data being the standard, one may have 10^8 terms. Scaling laws of the form of eq. (1) are found that hold over a range of a factor of $\approx 10^6$ on the x-axis [3, 9, 20, 121, 122]. Moreover, these scaling laws appear to be universal in that they, like the Pareto scaling law, hold for different countries [128], for countries themselves [21, 69], for other social organizations [71], and even for bird populations [63, 64].

One aspect of this work has come to the attention of a particular group of social scientists: the research community that studies S&T (science and technology) systems. Earlier findings for the growth of economic organizations [22, 31, 34, 36, 45, 55, 57, 76, 78, 96, 115, 123] prompted investigations to ask if similar laws may hold for the time evolution of S&T systems. To this end, Plerou et al. [1, 91, 107] analyzed the fluctuations in the growth rates of university research activities, using five different measures of research activity. Plerou et al. studied the production of research both from the point of view of inputs (R&D funding) and outputs (publications and patents).

Recent attempts to make models that reproduce the empirical scaling relationships suggest that significant progress on understanding firm growth may be well underway [2, 16, 19, 23, 27, 127, 133], leading to the hope of ultimately developing a clear and coherent "theory of the firm." One utility of the recent empirical work is that now any acceptable theory must respect the fact that power laws hold over typically six orders of magnitude. As Axtell put the matter rather graphically: "the power-law distribution is an unambiguous target that any empirically accurate theory of the firm must hit" [9].

5   INVERSE CUBIC LAW OF STOCK AND COMMODITY PRICE FLUCTUATIONS

With this background on power laws and scale invariance in geometry and in economics, we now turn to the well-studied problem of finance fluctuations, where a consistent set of empirical facts is beginning to emerge. One fact that has been confirmed by numerous, mostly independent, studies is that stock price fluctuations are characterized by a scale-invariant cumulative distribution function of the power-law form (1) with $\alpha \approx 3$ [49, 77, 105]. This result is also universal, in the sense that this inverse cubic law exponent is within the error bars of results for different segments of the economy, different time periods, and different countries—and is the same for stock averages as different as the S&P and the Hang Seng [48].

This *inverse cubic law* disagrees with the classic work of Mandelbrot [79] on price fluctuations of cotton, which appear to have displayed scale-free behavior (*no outliers*) but with much fatter tails characterized by $\alpha \approx 1.7$; this work is of interest because if $\alpha < 2$, then the distribution is of the Lévy form. To understand this discrepancy, Matia and collaborators have suggested that perhaps cotton has fatter tails because it is a commodity; commodities exist in limited supply, and one must sometimes pay exorbitant prices (e.g., electricity in California). Accordingly, they analyzed a large number of commodities, but found that these commodities have tails described not by $\alpha < 2$ but rather by $\alpha \approx 3$ [89, 90]. Another possible reason is that Mandelbrot analyzed three data sets, each containing only about 2000 points, while the results on stocks typically contain about 40,000 points per stock (and 1000 stocks, or 40,000,000 total data points). This possibility was tested by randomly choosing 2000 points to analyze, but again $\alpha < 2$ could not be obtained. A third possible explanation of this discrepancy is that the cotton market was out of equilibrium, and that such out-of-equilibrium markets have fatter tails—a possibility consistent with a recent analysis of stock price fluctuations [99, 100]. A fourth possible explanation is that, at the time Mandelbrot collected his data, commodities were intrinsically different from what commodities are today. The modern commodities market, the source of the Matia data, is much more similar to the stock market than it was in 1963. Still another possibility is that the cotton distribution has $\alpha < 2$ in the central region analyzed in 1963, but ultimately crosses over to a power law in the distant tails (which were not analyzed in 1963). This disagreement led to the development of a class of mathematical processes called *truncated* Lévy distributions [58, 80, 82, 83, 108, 109, 116]—which has attracted the attention of a number of mathematicians and is actually taught in Columbia University's Graduate School of Finance. In any case, one of the challenges of econophysics is to resolve current results with the classic 1963 analysis of Mandelbrot [79].

6   DATABASES ANALYZED

Our results are based on the analysis of different databases covering securities traded in the three major US stock exchanges, namely, (1) the New York Stock Exchange (NYSE), (2) the American Stock Exchange (AMEX), and (3) the National Association of Securities Dealers Automated Quotation (NASDAQ).

For studying short time-scale dynamics, we analyze the Trades and Quotes (TAQ) database, from which we select the four-year period January 1994 to December 1997. Nasdaq and AMEX merged on October 1998, after the end of the period studied in this work. The TAQ database, which is published by NYSE since 1993, covers *all* trades at the three major US stock markets. This huge database is available in the form of CD-ROMs. The rate of publication was one CD-ROM per month for the period studied, but has recently increased to two to four CD-ROMs per month. The total number of transactions for the largest 1000 stocks is of the order of 10^9 in the four-year period studied. They analyze the largest 1000 stocks, by capitalization on January 3, 1994, which survived through December 31, 1995. From the set of these 1000 stocks, they select a subset consisting of 880 stocks which survive through the further two years 1996–1997.

The data are adjusted for stock splits and dividends. The data are also filtered to remove spurious events that occur due to inevitable recording errors. The most common error is missing digits which appears as a large spike in the time series of returns. These are much larger than usual fluctuations and can be removed by choosing an appropriate threshold. We tested a range of thresholds and found no effect on the results.

To study the dynamics at longer time horizons, they also analyze the Center for Research and Security Prices (CRSP) database. The CRSP Stock Files cover common stocks listed on the NYSE beginning in 1925, the AMEX beginning in 1962, and the NASDAQ Stock Market beginning in 1972. The files provide complete historical descriptive information and market data including comprehensive distribution information, high, low, and closing prices, trading volumes, shares outstanding, and total returns. In addition to adjusting for stock splits and dividends, they have also detrended the data for inflation.

The CRSP Stock Files provide monthly data for NYSE beginning in December 1925 and daily data beginning July 1962. For the AMEX, both monthly and daily data begin in July 1962. For the NASDAQ Stock Market, both monthly and daily data begin in July 1972.

They also analyze the S&P 500 index, which comprises 500 stocks chosen for market size, liquidity, and industry group representation in the U.S. In our study, we first analyze high-frequency data that covers the 13-year period 1984–1996, with a recording frequency of less than 1 minute. The total number of records in this database exceeds 4.5×10^6. To investigate longer time scales, we also study daily records of the S&P 500 index for the 35-year period 1962–1996, and monthly records for the 71-year period 1926–1996.

7   THE DISTRIBUTION OF STOCK PRICE FLUCTUATIONS

The nature of the distribution of price fluctuations in financial time series has been a topic of interest for over 100 years [10]. A reasonable *a priori* assumption, motivated by the central limit theorem, is that the returns are independent, identically Gaussian distributed (iid) random variables, which results in a Gaussian random walk in the logarithm of price.

Empirical studies [39, 40, 49, 77, 79, 82, 86, 87, 93, 95, 105] show that the distribution of returns has pronounced tails, in striking contrast to that of a Gaussian. In addition to being non-Gaussian, the process of returns shows another interesting property: *time scaling*—that is, the distributions of returns for various choices of Δt, ranging from one day up to one month have similar functional forms [79]. These results together would suggest that the distribution of returns is consistent with a Lévy stable distribution [40, 70, 79, 96], the rationale for which arises from the generalization of the central limit theorem to random variables which do not have a finite second moment. Empirical studies suggest, however, that the tails of the return distribution are inconsistent with the stable Paretian hypothesis [12, 25, 48, 49, 75, 77, 82, 93, 94, 105, 111]. In particular, alternative hypotheses for modeling the return distribution were proposed, which include a log-normal mixture of Gaussians [25], Student t-distributions [12, 94, 111], and exponentially truncated Lévy distributions [82, 83, 108].

7.1   UNIVERSALITY OF THE DISTRIBUTION OF RETURNS

Conclusive results on the distribution of returns are difficult to obtain and require a large amount of data to study the rare events that give rise to the tails. We analyze approximately 40 million records of stock prices sampled at 5-minute intervals for the 1,000 leading US stocks for the two-year period 1994–1995 and 30 million records of daily returns for 6,000 US stocks for the 35-year period 1962–1996.

The basic quantity studied for individual companies is the price $S_i(t)$. The time t runs over the working hours of the stock exchange—removing nights, weekends and holidays. For each company, we calculate the return

$$G_i \equiv G_i(t, \Delta t) \equiv \ln S_i(t + \Delta t) - \ln S_i(t). \tag{2}$$

For small changes in $S_i(t)$, the return $G_i(t, \Delta t)$ is approximately the forward relative change, $G_i(t, \Delta t) \approx [S_i(t + \Delta t) - S_i(t)]/S_i(t)$. For time scales shorter than one day, we analyze the data from the TAQ database.

We then calculate the cumulative distributions—the probability of a return larger than or equal to a threshold—of returns G_i for $\Delta t = 5$ min. For each stock $i = 1, \ldots, 1000$, the asymptotic behavior of the functional form of the cumulative distribution is consistent with a power law,

$$P\{G_i > x\} \sim \frac{1}{x^{\alpha_i}}, \tag{3}$$

where α_i is the exponent characterizing the power-law decay. In order to compare the returns of different stocks with different volatilities, we define the normalized return $g_i \equiv (G_i - \langle G_i \rangle_T)/v_i$, where $\langle \ldots \rangle_T$ denotes a time average over the 40,000 data points of each time series for the two-year period studied, and the time-averaged volatility v_i of company i is the standard deviation of the returns over the two-year period $v_i^2 \equiv \langle G_i^2 \rangle_T - \langle G_i \rangle_T^2$. Values of the exponent α_i can be estimated by a power-law regression on each of these distributions $P\{g > x\} \sim x^{-\alpha}$, whereby we obtain the average value for the 1000 stocks,

$$\alpha = \begin{cases} 3.10 \pm 0.03 & \text{(positive tail)} \\ 2.84 \pm 0.12 & \text{(negative tail)} \end{cases}, \tag{4}$$

where the fits are performed in the region $2 \leq g \leq 80$. These estimates of the exponent α are well outside the stable Lévy range, which requires $0 < \alpha < 2$, and is, therefore, consistent with a finite variance for returns. However, moments larger than three, in particular the kurtosis, seem to be divergent [75, 95]. Our results are consistent with the results of the analysis of the daily returns of 30 German stocks comprising the DAX index [77], daily CRSP returns [95], and foreign exchange rates [93].

In order to obtain an alternative estimate for α, we use the methods of Hill [49, 77, 95, 105]. We calculate the inverse local slope of the cumulative distribution function $P(g)$, $\gamma \equiv -(d\log P(g)/d\log g)^{-1}$ for the negative and the positive tails. We obtain an estimator for γ by sorting the normalized increments by their size, $g^{(1)} > g^{(2)} > ... > g^{(N)}$. The cumulative distribution can then be written as $P(g^{(k)}) = k/N$, and we obtain for the local slope

$$\gamma = \left[(N-1)\sum_{i=1}^{N-1}\log g^{(i)}\right] - \log g^{(N)}, \tag{5}$$

where N is the number of tail events used. We use the criterion that N does not exceed 10% of the sample size, simultaneously ensuring that the sample is restricted to the tail events [95]. We thereby obtain the average estimates for 1000 stocks,

$$\alpha = \begin{cases} 2.84 \pm 0.12 & \text{(positive tail)} \\ 2.73 \pm 0.13 & \text{(negative tail)} \end{cases}. \tag{6}$$

Removing overnight events yields the average values of $\alpha = 3.11 \pm 0.15$ for the positive tail and $\alpha = 3.03 \pm 0.21$ for the negative tail. Currently, we are also investigating the dependence of the exponent α on the time of day by splitting a trading day into three equal parts of 130 min each. A parallel analysis on the S&P 500 index shows consistent asymptotic behavior [48], although the central part of the distribution seems to display Lévy behavior for short time scales (< 30 min) [82]. One reason for a different behavior at the central part of the distribution of S&P 500 returns is the discreteness of the prices of individual stocks (which causes a cut-off for low values of returns) that comprise the S&P 500 index.

7.2   SCALING OF THE DISTRIBUTIONS OF RETURNS AND CORRELATIONS IN THE VOLATILITY

Since the values of α we find are inconsistent with a statistically stable law, we expect the distribution of returns $P(G)$ on larger time scales to converge to Gaussian. In contrast, our analysis of daily returns from the CRSP database suggests that the distributions of returns retain the same functional form for a wide range of time scales Δt, varying over three orders of magnitude, 5 min$\leq$ $\Delta t \leq 6240$ min $= 16$ days. The *onset* of convergence to a Gaussian starts to occur only for $\Delta t > 16$ days [48, 105]. In contrast, n-partial sums of computer-simulated time series of the same length and probability distribution display Gaussian behavior for $n \geq 256$ [17, 48]. Thus, the rate of convergence of $P(G)$ to a Gaussian is remarkably slow, indicative of time dependencies that violate the conditions necessary for the central limit theorem to apply.

To test for time dependencies, we analyzed the autocorrelation function of returns, which we denote as $\langle G(t)G(t+\tau)\rangle$, using 5-minute returns of 1000 stocks. Our results show pronounced short-time (< 30 min) anti-correlations, consistent with the bid-ask bounce [113]. For larger time scales, the correlation function is at the level of noise (for some portfolios of common stocks Lo [74] has reported long memory), consistent with the efficient market hypothesis [37, 38, 39]. Lack of linear correlation does not imply independent returns, since higher-order correlations may exist. Our recent studies [72] show that the amplitude of the returns measured by the absolute value or the square has long-range correlations with persistence [51, 52] up to several months,

$$\langle |G(t)|\, |G(t+\tau)|\rangle \sim \tau^{-a}, \tag{7}$$

where a has the average value $a = 0.34 \pm 0.09$ for the 1000 stocks studied.

7.3   STATISTICS OF TRADING ACTIVITY

In order to understand the reasons for slow decaying tails in the return distribution and long-range correlations in volatility, we follow an approach in the spirit of models of time deformation proposed by Clark [25], Tauchen and Pitts [130], Stock [125], Lamoureux and Lastrapes [67], Ghysels and Jasiak [44], and Engle and Russell [35].

Returns G over a time interval Δt can be expressed as the sum of several changes δp_i due to the $i = 1, \ldots, N_{\Delta t}$ trades in the interval $[t, t + \Delta t]$,

$$G_{\Delta t} = \sum_{i=1}^{N_{\Delta t}} \delta p_i. \tag{8}$$

If Δt is such that $N_{\Delta t} \gg 1$, and δp_i have finite variance, then one can apply the classic version of the central limit theorem, whereby one would obtain the result that the unconditional distribution $P(G)$ is Gaussian [25]. It is implicitly assumed in this description that $N_{\Delta t}$ has only *narrow* Gaussian fluctuations, in other words, it has a standard deviation much smaller than the mean $\langle N_{\Delta t}\rangle$.

Our investigation of $N_{\Delta t}$ suggests it is in stark contrast to a Gaussian time series with the same mean and variance—there are several events of the magnitude of tens of standard deviations which are inconsistent with Gaussian statistics [7, 25, 35, 47, 53, 84, 104, 125, 130]. For each stock analyzed, we chose sampling time intervals Δt such that it contains sufficient $N_{\Delta t}$; for actively traded stocks $\Delta t = 15$ min, and for stocks with the least frequency of trading, $\Delta t = 390$ min (one day) [104]. We find that the distribution of $N_{\Delta t}$ appears to display an asymptotic power-law decay

$$P\{N_{\Delta t} > x\} \sim x^{-\beta} \quad (x \gg 1). \tag{9}$$

For the 1000 stocks that we analyze, we estimate β using Hill's method and obtain a mean value $\beta = 3.40 \pm 0.05$. Note that $\beta > 2$ is outside the Lévy stable domain $0 < \beta < 2$ and is inconsistent with a stable distribution for $N_{\Delta t}$, and with the log-normal hypothesis of Clark [25].

7.4 PRICE FLUCTUATIONS AND TRADING ACTIVITY

Since we find that $P\{G_{\Delta t} > x\} \sim x^{-\alpha}$, we can ask whether the value of β we find for $P\{N_{\Delta t} > x\}$ is sufficient to account for the fat tails of returns. To test this possibility, we implement, for each stock, the ordinary least squares regression

$$\ln|G_{\Delta t}(t)| = a + b\ln N_{\Delta t}(t) + \psi(t), \tag{10}$$

where $\psi(t)$ has mean zero and the equal time covariance $\langle N_{\Delta t}\psi(t)\rangle = 0$. Our results on 30 actively traded stocks yield the average value of $b = 0.57 \pm 0.09$.

Values of $b \approx 0.5$ are consistent with what we would expect from eq. (8), if δp_i are iids with finite variance. In other words, suppose δp_i are chosen *only from the interval* $[t, t + \Delta t]$, and let us hypothesize that *these* δp_i are mutually independent, with a common distribution $P(\delta p_i | t \in [t, t + \Delta t])$ having a finite variance $W_{\Delta t}^2$. Under this hypothesis, the central limit theorem, applied to the sum of δp_i in eq. (8), implies that the ratio

$$\epsilon \equiv \frac{G_{\Delta t}}{W_{\Delta t}\sqrt{N_{\Delta t}}} \tag{11}$$

must be a Gaussian-distributed random variable with zero mean and unit variance. We can test this hypothesis by analyzing the distribution $P(\epsilon)$ and the correlations in ϵ.

Our results on 30 actively traded stocks seem to indicate that the distribution $P(\epsilon)$ is consistent with a Gaussian, with mean values of excess kurtosis ≈ 0.1. This is noteworthy since, for the unconditional distribution $P(G_{\Delta t})$, the kurtosis is divergent (empirical estimates yield mean values ≈ 80 for 1000 stocks).

If our hypothesis that $P(\epsilon)$ is consistent with a Gaussian is borne out by the data, this would imply that the fat tails of $P\{G_{\Delta t} > x\} \sim x^{-\alpha}$ cannot be caused solely by $P\{N_{\Delta t} > x\} \sim x^{-\beta}$ because, by conservation of probabilities, $P\{\sqrt{N_{\Delta t}} > x\} \sim x^{-2\beta}$ with $2\beta \approx 6.8$. Equation (11) then implies that $N_{\Delta t}$ alone cannot explain the value $\alpha \approx 3$.

Since $N_{\Delta t}$ is not sufficient to account for the fat tails in $G_{\Delta t}$, one other possibility is that it arises from $W_{\Delta t}$. By definition, $W_{\Delta t}$ is the variance of all δp_i in Δt, which is difficult to estimate when one does not have sufficient $N_{\Delta t}$. We can investigate the statistics of $W_{\Delta t}$ and examine if the distribution of $W_{\Delta t}$ is sufficient to explain the value of α found for $P\{G_{\Delta t} > x\}$. Our results on 30 actively traded stocks suggest that

$$P\{W_{\Delta t} > x\} \sim x^{-\gamma}, \tag{12}$$

where we obtain rough estimates $\gamma = 2.85 \pm 0.20$, consistent with the estimates of α for the same 30 stocks. Estimates of γ are obtained by choosing $\Delta t = 15$ min for these stocks, at the same time ensuring that $N_{\Delta t} > 20$.

7.5   VOLATILITY CORRELATIONS AND TRADING ACTIVITY

Thus far we have discussed eq. (11) from the point of view of distributions. Next, we analyze time correlations in $N_{\Delta t}$ and relate them to the time correlations of $|G_{\Delta t}|$. Our studies on the same 30 actively traded stocks indicate that the autocorrelation function $\langle N_{\Delta t}(t)N_{\Delta t}(t+\tau)\rangle \sim \tau^{-\nu}$, with a mean value of the estimates of $\nu = 0.32 \pm 0.09$ using the detrended fluctuation analysis method [97]. To detect genuine long-range correlations, the marked U-shaped intra-daily pattern [132] in $N_{\Delta t}$ is removed [72]. We substantiate this analysis using semi-parametric estimators such as those due to Robinson [112]. We can then test the dependence of the exponent ν on (1) the type of industry sector and (2) the market capitalization.

   Our long-term goal is to relate the exponent ν of the autocorrelation function of $N_{\Delta t}$ to that of $|G_{\Delta t}|$. To this end, we also estimate, in parallel, the time correlations in $W_{\Delta t}$ and $|\epsilon|$. Since our investigations on the 30 stocks seem to indicate the absence of long-range correlations in $W_{\Delta t}$, the above investigation of correlations could yield the interesting statement that the long-range correlations in volatility are due to those of $N_{\Delta t}$. Together with the above discussion on distribution functions, these results suggest an interesting result—that the fat tails of returns $G_{\Delta t}$ arise from $W_{\Delta t}$ and the long-range volatility correlations arise from trading activity $N_{\Delta t}$.

7.6   STATISTICS OF SHARE VOLUME TRADED

Understanding the equal-time correlations between volume and volatility and, more importantly, understanding how the number of shares traded impacts the price has long been a topic of great interest [7, 25, 43, 47, 59, 62, 104, 130]. The number of shares traded in Δt is the sum

$$Q_{\Delta t} \equiv \sum_{i=1}^{N_{\Delta t}} q_i, \qquad (13)$$

where q_i traded for all $i = 1, \ldots, N_{\Delta t}$ transactions in Δt. So it is clear that $Q_{\Delta t}$ must be positively correlated with $N_{\Delta t}$.

   The results of Plerou et al. on 30 actively traded stocks suggest that the probability distributions $P\{Q_{\Delta t} > x\}$ are consistent with a power-law asymptotic behavior

$$P\{Q_{\Delta t} > x\} \sim x^{-\lambda}. \qquad (14)$$

Using Hill's estimator, they obtain an average value $\lambda = 1.7 \pm 0.2$, which, as a further test for Lévy stability of $Q_{\Delta t}$, we can investigate the scaling behavior of the sum

$$Q_n \equiv \sum_{i=1}^{n} q_i. \qquad (15)$$

where n is a fixed number of trades. We first analyze the asymptotic behavior of $P(Q_n)$ for increasing n. For a Lévy stable distribution, $n^{1/\lambda} P([Q_n - \langle Q_n \rangle]/n^{1/\lambda})$ should have the same functional form as $P(q)$, where $\langle Q_n \rangle = n \langle q \rangle$ and $\langle \ldots \rangle$ denotes average values. We can also perform an independent test and estimate λ by analyzing the scaling behavior of the moments

$$\mu_r(n) \equiv \langle |Q_n - \langle Q_n \rangle|^r \rangle, \tag{16}$$

where $r < \lambda$. For a Lévy stable distribution

$$[\mu_r(n)]^{1/r} \sim n^{1/\lambda}. \tag{17}$$

Hence, by regressing $[\mu_r(n)]^{1/r}$ as a function of n, we obtain an inverse slope which would yield an estimate of λ.

7.7 SHARE VOLUME TRADED AND NUMBER OF TRADES

If our hypothesis is true that $Q_{\Delta t}$ and q_i are consistent with a one-sided Lévy stable process, then $N_{\Delta t}^{1/\lambda} P([Q_{\Delta t} - \langle q \rangle N_{\Delta t}]/N_{\Delta t}^{1/\lambda})$ from eq. (13) should have the same distribution as any of the q_i. Thus, we hypothesize that the dependence of $Q_{\Delta t}$ on $N_{\Delta t}$ can be separated by defining

$$\chi \equiv \frac{Q_{\Delta t} - \langle q \rangle N_{\Delta t}}{N_{\Delta t}^{1/\lambda}}, \tag{18}$$

where χ is a one-sided Lévy-distributed variable with zero mean and exponent λ. To test this hypothesis, we first analyze $P(\chi)$ for consistent asymptotic behavior to $P(Q_{\Delta t})$.

7.8 TIME CORRELATIONS IN SHARE VOLUME TRADED

We also study extensively the time correlations in $Q_{\Delta t}(t)$. A difficulty arises due to the divergent second moment of the distribution $P(Q_{\Delta t})$. To circumvent this problem, we consider the family of correlation functions $\langle [Q_{\Delta t}(t)]^a [Q_{\Delta t}(t+\tau)]^a \rangle$, where the parameter a $(< \lambda/2)$ is required to ensure that the correlation function is well defined. Instead of analyzing the correlation function directly, we apply detrended fluctuation analysis [97], which has been successfully used to study long-range correlations in a wide range of complex systems. Our results suggest that $Q_{\Delta t}(t)$ has strong long-range correlations, while the number of shares traded in each transaction q_i eq. (13) displays only short-range correlations, suggesting that long-range correlations in $Q_{\Delta t}$ can in turn be related to those of $N_{\Delta t}$, if eq. (18) is found to be valid.

7.9 RETURNS AND SHARE VOLUME TRADED

An interesting implication is an explanation for the previously observed [43, 59, 62] equal-time correlations between $Q_{\Delta t}$ and volatility $V_{\Delta t}$, which is the local standard deviation of price changes $G_{\Delta t}$. Now, $V_{\Delta t} = W_{\Delta t} \sqrt{N_{\Delta t}}$ from eq. (11). Consider the equal-time correlation $\langle Q_{\Delta t} V_{\Delta t} \rangle$, where the means are subtracted from $Q_{\Delta t}$ and $V_{\Delta t}$. Since $Q_{\Delta t}$ depends on $N_{\Delta t}$ through $Q_{\Delta t} = \langle q \rangle N_{\Delta t} + N_{\Delta t}^{1/\zeta} \chi$, and if the equal-time correlations $\langle N_{\Delta t} W_{\Delta t} \rangle$, $\langle N_{\Delta t} \chi \rangle$, and $\langle W_{\Delta t} \chi \rangle$ are small (correlation coefficients ≈ 0.1), it follows that the equal-time correlation $\langle Q_{\Delta t} V_{\Delta t} \rangle \propto \langle N_{\Delta t}^{3/2} \rangle - \langle N_{\Delta t} \rangle \langle N_{\Delta t}^{1/2} \rangle$, which is positive due to the Cauchy-Schwartz inequality.

8   ARE POWER LAWS REALLY THERE?

Newcomers to the field of scale invariance often ask why a power law does not extend forever as it would for a mathematical power law of the form $f(x) = x^{-\alpha}$. This legitimate concern is put to rest by reflecting on the fact that power laws for natural phenomena are not equalities, but rather asymptotic relations of the form $f(x) \sim x^{-\alpha}$. Here the tilde denotes *asymptotic equality*. Thus $f(x)$ is not approximately equal to a power law, making the notation $f(x) \approx x^{-\alpha}$ inappropriate. Similarly, $f(x)$ is not proportional to a power law, so the notation $f(x) \propto x^{-\alpha}$ is also inappropriate. Rather, asymptotic equality means that $f(x)$ becomes increasingly like a power law as $x \to \infty$. Moreover, crossovers abound in financial data, such as the crossover from power-law behavior to simple Gaussian behavior as the time horizon Δt over which fluctuations are calculated increases beyond about a year (i.e., the power-law behavior holds for time horizons up to a month or even a year, but for horizons exceeding a year there is a distinct crossover to Gaussian behavior). Such crossovers are also characteristic of other scale-free phenomena in the physical sciences [119, 124], where the Yule distribution often proves quite useful.

For reasons of this sort, standard statistical fits to data are inappropriate, and often give distinctly erroneous values of the exponent α. Rather, one reliable way of estimating the exponent α is to form successive slopes of pairs of points on a log-log plot, since these successive slopes will be monotonic and converge to the true asymptotic exponent α. One finds that successive slopes for the empirical data converge rapidly to a value $\alpha \approx 3$, while successive slopes for the model diverge. While it is clear that a simple three-factor model [68] cannot generate power-law behavior, it is less clear why the empirical data analyzed appear at first glance to be well approximated by the model. The first fact is that the region of linearity of the data is not as large as in typical modern studies because the total quantity of data analyzed is not that large, since only a low-frequency time series comprising daily data is used. Only 28,094 records are analyzed [68] (not 4×10^7 as in recent studies [48, 105]) and the model simulations are presented for a limited sample size. The second fact is that when one superposes a curved line (the model) on a straight line (the data), the untrained eye is easily tempted to find agreement where none exists—and closer inspection of figs. 2–5 of LeBaron [68] reveals actually a rather poor agreement between model and data due to the pronounced downward curvature of the model's predictions [118].

9　OTHER SCALE-INVARIANT QUANTITIES DESCRIBING ECONOMIC FLUCTUATIONS

Other quantities characterizing stock movements (such as the volatility), share volume decays that are different for different quantities; it is tempting to conjecture that in finance there may exist a set of relations among the power-law exponents found, just as relations exist among the exponents characterizing different quantities near the critical point. Finally, it is well known that while the autocorrelation function of price returns decays rapidly, the autocorrelation function of the absolute values of price returns is power-law correlated in time (see Liu et al. [72] and extensive earlier work cited therein).

Consider, for example, the volatility. There are several possible definitions of this quantity, all of which seem to give the same scale invariant properties. But why care about volatility at all? On the cover of the May 15, 2000, issue of *Forbes* magazine is a large photograph of Henk Paulson, CEO of Goldman Sachs, and the headline quotation "Volatility is Our Friend." This is the case because it is known that volatility *clusters*; in other words, there are time correlations in this quantity. Our group has attempted to quantify these correlations, and has found evidence of power-law behavior [24, 72, 73, 110]. If we plot an economic earthquake such as Black Monday (October 19, 1987), a date on which most worldwide stock indices dropped 25–50 percent, and then plot and compare the volatility (the absolute value of the fluctuations), we see a big peak in the volatility curve on Black Monday. But even prior to Black Monday the value of the volatility on our graph seems to be particularly unstable; there is some precursor to Black Monday evident in its behavior. One can imagine a computer program that would monitor volatility, not necessarily for the entire market but certainly for an individual stock, and the volatility calculation would need to be updated in real time.

There are correlations in the stock price change, but those correlations have a very short range—on the order of a few minutes—and they decay exponentially in time. Our group calculated the autocorrelation function of stock-price changes and plotted the logarithm of the function linearly in time; since the logarithm of e^{-x} is $-x$, we get a straight line. In contrast, for the volatility we find that the autocorrelation function is linear on log-log paper, meaning that the correlations in the volatility are power law in nature. That, in turn, translates to mean they are much, much longer-range in time.

In order to quantify long-range power-law volatility correlations, we developed a method of analyzing a non-stationary time series. The volatility of a financial market is non-stationary: there are days when the volatility is quiet and days when it is active. The statistical properties of a volatility time series are changing in time. The standard deviation of that time series is fluctuating wildly on every scale, which is the reason conventional methods are not effective. The method our group has been developing—detrended fluctuation analysis (DFA)—gets rid of trends in the raw data [60, 61, 97]. We take a graph of the volatility expressed in absolute values (i.e., it is always positive) in which we see the peaks that indicate it is a very *noisy* or non-stationary time series, we integrate this time series, and we subtract the mean. This produces an up-and-down *landscape*. We then look for correlations in this landscape. We do this by partitioning the landscape into *windowboxes* of a fixed size (e.g., 200) and asking whether the regression fits the fluctuations in that windowbox. We then calculate for each box the RMS fluctuation around the regression line. Finally, we average the RMS fluctuation for all 40,000 windowboxes of the entire series. With that many windowboxes, we get a very accurate measurement. We call the quantity *f*. We repeat the entire calculation for windowboxes one-half as big (size 100). Obviously, the smaller the windowbox, the less the fluctuation. This gives us the circle for size 100. We repeat this a number of times. When that fluctuation is plotted as a function of windowbox size we find, contrary to what we might expect—that in almost all correlated signals the fluctuations increase as the square root of the windowbox size—the fluctuations instead increase more rapidly than that. That means there is some positive correlation in the signal. This analysis method produces results with very little noise. The data fall very close to the straight line, and the exponent can be obtained with a high degree of accuracy. All this allows us to analyze quantitatively the behavior of the volatility as a function of time and elucidate its correlations. This could be very useful information for people actually working in financial markets.

The distribution of volatility fluctuations has also been the object of extensive study. It was at one time believed by many that the volatility follows a log-normal distribution—that is, the number of times the volatility has a certain value follows not a Gaussian but a log-normal distribution (one has $e^{-(\log x)^2}$ not e^{-x^2}). But until our group's work, no one had studied *all* the data, in other words, *every* trade [72]. Our doing it meant we could study relatively rare events, those occurring much less frequently than everyday events. What we find is that the log-normal part of the curve—the middle—though true for the middle, does not describe the tails. The huge volatilities in the tails are described by a different exponent μ. We also see that volatility clusters—that is, volatility is correlated in time.

10   CROSS-CORRELATIONS AMONG FLUCTUATIONS OF DIFFERENT STOCKS

Another possible application of an appropriately designed software package could be the ability to determine how the fluctuations of one stock price correlate with those of another. This question of cross-correlation is one we have been studying

[46, 66, 101, 106]. For example, to quantify cross-correlations, we draw a circle corresponding to the stock price x and draw a second circle corresponding to the stock price x five minutes later. If we make the difference in the radii proportional to G, the stock price change, then we can think of the market as thousands of circles, each growing and shrinking—a kind of pulsation that is a function of time. The key is that these correlations change in time. Car sales by Ford and GM may be anti-correlated during some time periods and positively correlated during others.

The standard approach to this problem is to calculate, by brute force, a huge square matrix that has as many rows as there are companies in the database. Each element of the matrix is the correlation between the price change of company i and the price change of company j, but to find a genuine correlation we have to be able to distinguish correlations from coincidences. In order to do that we draw on something developed by Wigner in his work in nuclear physics—random matrix theory. Random matrix theory compares the matrix calculated by brute force from stock market data with a random matrix that also has 1000 rows and 1000 columns—but with every number generated randomly. Somewhere hidden in the huge matrix calculated by brute force from stock market data are the true correlations. To uncover them, we first diagonalize the matrix in order to determine its eigenvalues, and then make a histogram that gives the number of times each given eigenvalue is found. The histogram curve of a random matrix, unlike this one from real data, can be predicted exactly. For a random matrix there is never an eigenvalue larger than 2.0. The histogram of the empirical stock price data, on the other hand, contains a significant number of eigenvalues larger than 2.0. Some are as big as 5.0. These eigenvalues of necessity must correspond to genuine correlations.

The eigenvalue of a matrix has a corresponding eigenvector—a column matrix of 1000 elements—each element of which is a different weight from each of the 1000 stocks. Thus we can look at the column vectors that correspond to these deviating, genuinely correlated eigenvalues and ask: what kinds of stocks entered into each of these eigenvectors? What we found, fortunately, has implications for portfolios. If we restart the graph at 2.0—removing the distortions of the random values—and look at the 20 eigenvalues larger than 2.0, we see that the stocks that make up most of the weights in the corresponding eigenvectors are almost entirely transportation stocks in the first case, almost entirely paper in the second, almost entirely pharmaceuticals in the third, and so on. In other words, the market *automatically* partitions itself into separate business sectors [46, 101, 114]. Thus a physicist who knows nothing about the stock market can mathematically partition the economy into separate business sectors!

The sectors and the quantitative degree to which each constituent firm conforms to the sector can be monitored and updated as a function of time, that is, every 15 minutes. Firms that belong to the same business sector can be monitored in a kind of rainbow spectrum. The *good* firms sticking to the business sector are assigned to the *violet* end of the spectrum, and the *bad* firms deviating from the sector are assigned to the *red*. When a firm first starts to move to the red end of the spectrum (i.e., starts to deviate), the trader is alerted to consider action.

11 EQUILIBRIUM VS. OUT-OF-EQUILIBRIUM MARKET PHASES

Before concluding, we ask what sort of understanding could eventually develop if one takes seriously the power laws that appear to characterize finance fluctuations. It is tempting to imagine that there might be analogies between finance and known physical processes displaying similar scale-invariant fluctuations. One initially promising analogy was with turbulence: In turbulence, one adds energy at a large scale and this energy is dissipated at smaller and smaller scales in a scale-invariant fashion. Similarly, if external news is added at a large scale, then this news is dissipated by traders at smaller and smaller scales in a scale-invariant fashion. Despite some initial claims, these similarities are not borne out by quantitative analysis—although one finds non-Gaussian statistics, and intermittency, for both turbulence fluctuations and stock price fluctuations, the time evolution of the second moment and the shape of the probability density functions are different for turbulence and for stock market dynamics [86, 87].

More recent work pursues a rather different analogy: phase transitions in spin systems. One might be tempted to say that the set of all firm fluctuations is like a set of subunit fluctuations in a physics system such as a spin glass (the simplest spin glass is a set of Ising spins, each interacting with other spins by means of an interaction whose sign and range are chosen from a probability distribution). Similarly, in economic fluctuations, the sign of the fluctuation can be up or down, and can be of any magnitude; fluctuations interact with one another via interactions that are certainly long-range and of both signs. Further, the interactions change with time. A given subunit fluctuation is influenced (1) by other fluctuations (so the exchange interactions among spins is somewhat like the *herd effect*), and (2) by forces external to the system (so the external field is somewhat like *news*, which plays a role in determining the sign and magnitude of fluctuations). Economists all appreciate these (and all other!) facts—but for physicists they are truly reminiscent of a cooperative system for which emergent behavior can result from the collective behavior of subunits, each obeying relatively simple and *local* rules.

If this crude analogy were to hold even approximately, then a first step should perhaps be to seek to identify the analogs for the price fluctuation problem of field and temperature in the magnetic problem. Stock prices respond to demand, just as the magnetization of an interacting spin system responds to the magnetic field. Periods with a large number of market participants buying the stock imply mainly positive changes in price, analogous to a magnetic field causing spins in a magnet to align. Recent work [102] quantifies the relations between price change and demand fluctuations, and finds results reminiscent of phase transitions in spin systems (fig. 1), where the divergent behavior of the response function at the critical point (zero magnetic field) leads to large fluctuations [124]. More precisely, buying and selling behavior in complex financial markets are driven by demand, which can be quantified by the imbalance in the number of shares transacted by buyers and sellers over a time interval Δt.

If demand is the analog of the magnetic field, what is the analog of temperature? To answer this question, Plerou et al. [99, 100] analyze the probability distribution of demand, conditioned on its local noise intensity Σ, and find the surprising existence of a critical threshold Σ_c separating two market phases (fig. 2). Their findings for the financial market problem are identical to what is known to occur in all phase transition phenomena, wherein the behavior of a system undergoes a qualitative change at a critical threshold K_c of some control parameter K. Plerou et al. interpret these two market phases as corresponding to two distinct conditions of the financial market: (1) The "$\Sigma < \Sigma_c$ market phase," where the distribution of demand is single-peaked with the most probable value being zero, they interpret to be the market equilibrium phase, since the price of the stock is such that the probability of a transaction being buyer initiated is equal to the probability of a transaction being seller initiated, and (2) the "$\Sigma > \Sigma_c$ market phase," where the distribution of demand is bimodal, they interpret to be the out-of-equilibrium phase, since the price of the stock is such that there is an excess of either buyers or of sellers and there is a non-zero net demand for the stock.

It should be possible to design a software package that could be on every trader's desk allowing instant access to data regarding any firm in which time is partitioned into two different phases: equilibrium and out-of-equilibrium. Qualitatively and informally many people use those terms in reference to the stock market, but in this case we would be actually *quantifying* the extent to which the market is in or out of equilibrium. If we graph the price-change of a particular stock as a function of time for a sequence of 15-minute intervals and use two different symbols for data points when the market is in equilibrium and for those for when it is out of equilibrium, we notice that, in general, a stock price is not changing when the market is in equilibrium and is changing when the market is out of equilibrium. This could be useful in that it could be an indicator of the relative stability of an individual stock. When the market is out of equilibrium, the probability that a stock price is going to change is higher than when the market is in equilibrium.

12 DISCUSSION

Since the evidence for an analogy between stock price fluctuations and magnetization fluctuations near a critical point is backed up by quantitative analysis of finance data, it is legitimate to demand a theoretical reason for this analogy. To

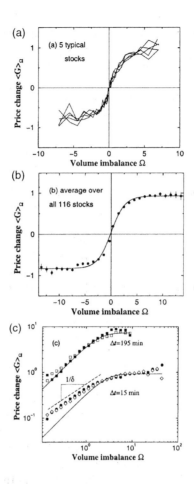

FIGURE 1 (a) Conditional expectation $\langle G \rangle_\Omega$ for 5 typical stocks over a time interval $\Delta t = 15$ min, where Ω is defined as the difference in number of shares traded in buyer and seller initiated trades. We normalize G to have zero mean and unit variance. Since Ω has a tail exponent $\zeta = 3/2$ which implies divergent variance, we normalize Ω by the first moment $\langle |\Omega - \langle \Omega \rangle| \rangle$. (b) Conditional expectation $\langle G \rangle_\Omega$ averaged over all 116 stocks studied. We calculate G and Ω for $\Delta t = 15$ min. The solid line shows a fit to the function $B_0 \tanh(B_1 \Omega)$. (c) $\langle G \rangle_\Omega$ on a log-log plot for different Δt. For small Ω, $\langle G \rangle_\Omega \simeq \Omega^{1/\delta}$. For $\Delta t = 15$ min find a mean value $1/\delta = 0.66 \pm 0.02$ by fitting $\langle G \rangle_\Omega$ for all 116 stocks individually. The same procedure yields $1/\delta = 0.34 \pm 0.03$ at $\Delta t = 5$ min (interestingly close to the value of the analogous critical exponent in mean field theory). The solid curve shows a fit to the function $B_0 \tanh(B_1 \Omega)$. For small Ω, $B_0 \tanh(B_1 \Omega) \sim \Omega$, and therefore disagrees with $\langle G \rangle_\Omega$, whereas for large Ω the fit shows good agreement. For $\Delta t = 195$ min ($\frac{1}{2}$ day) (squares), the hyperbolic tangent function shows good agreement.

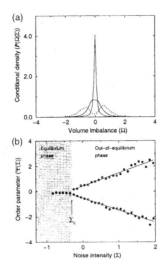

FIGURE 2   Empirical evidence supporting the existence of two distinct phases in a complex financial market. (a) Conditional density $P(\Omega|\Sigma)$ for varying local noise intensity Σ computed using data for all stocks. For each stock, Ω and Σ are normalized to zero mean and unit first centered moment. The distribution displays a single peak for $\Sigma < \Sigma_c$ (solid line). For $\Sigma \approx \Sigma_c$ (dotted line), the distribution flattens near the origin, and for $\Sigma > \Sigma_c$, $P(\Omega|\Sigma)$ displays two peaks (dashed line). (b) Order parameter, Ψ (positions of the maxima of the distribution $P(\Omega|\Sigma)$), as a function of Σ. For small Σ, $P(\Omega|\Sigma)$ displays a single maximum whereas for large Σ two maxima appear. To locate the extrema as accurately as possible, we compute all probability densities using the density estimator of Holy [56]. Also shown, via shading, is a schematic phase diagram representing the two distinct market phases. Here $\Delta t = 15$ min; we have tested that our results hold for Δt ranging from 15 min up to approximately 1/2 day, beyond which we have insufficient data.

this end, we discuss briefly one possible theoretical understanding for the origin of scaling and universality in economic systems. As mentioned above, economic systems consist of interacting units just as critical point systems consist of inter-acting units. Two units are correlated in what might seem a hopelessly complex fashion—consider, for example, two spins on a lattice, which are correlated re-gardless of how far apart they are. The correlation between two given spins on a finite lattice can be partitioned into the set of all possible topologically linear paths connecting these two spins—indeed this is the starting point of one of the solutions of the two-dimensional Ising model (see Appendix B of Stanley [124]). Since correlations decay exponentially along a one-dimensional path, the correla-tion between two spins would at first glance seem to decay exponentially. Now it is a mathematical fact that the total number of such paths grows exponentially with the distance between the two spins—to be very precise, the number of paths is given by a function which is a product of an exponential and a power law. The constant of the exponential *decay* depends on temperature while the constant for the exponential *growth* depends only on the geometric properties of the system [124]. Hence, by tuning the temperature it is possible to achieve a threshold temperature where these two *warring exponentials* balance each other, allowing a previously negligible power-law factor that enters into the expression for the number of paths to dominate. Thus power-law scale invariance emerges as a result of canceling exponentials, and universality emerges from the fact that the interaction paths depend not on the interactions but rather on the connectivity. Similarly, in economics, two units are correlated through a myriad of different correlation paths; "everything depends on everything else" is the adage expressing the intuitive fact that when one firm changes, it influences other firms. A more careful discussion of this argument is presented, not for the economy but for the critical phenomena problem, in Stanley [119].

Consider the following thought experiment. Measure the temperature in an extremely tiny region of a glass of water—say in a cube measuring only 10 Å on a side. Set the macroscopic water temperature to be exactly at water's critical temperature (about 647° K). The measured *local* temperature will fluctuate in time from being above or below the actual crtical temperature. Hence, the tiny cube will fluctuate from being in the liquid or the gas phase as a function of time. Similarly, it appears that the market fluctuates from being in one phase to another as a function of time [99, 100].

13   CONCLUDING REMARKS

In summary, physicists are finding this emerging field fascinating. For a long time, physicists and economists had noticed the potential for useful collaborations but, notwithstanding some stellar insights [5, 4, 8, 13, 14, 15, 18, 29, 30, 32, 33, 65, 92], not too many new results were discovered by physicists. A major reason for this is that, until recently, the amount of data routinely recorded concerning financial transactions was insufficient to be useful to physicists. That fact is no longer true. Now every trade is recorded, along with bid-ask quotes for every trade, and these data are available.

Part of the reason for the invention [120] of the neologism *econophysics* (in the tradition of the neologisms biophysics, astrophysics, and geophysics, etc.) was to enable our physics students to persuade the departmental administrators that their dissertation research topics actually belonged in the physics department. The neologism seems to have caught on, and there are now several conferences each year with the word *econophysics* in their titles.

Finally, a word of humility with respect to our esteemed economics colleagues is perhaps not inappropriate. Physicists may care passionately if there are analogies between physics systems they understand (like critical point phenomena) and economics systems they do not understand. But why should anyone else care? One reason is that the scientific understanding of earthquakes moved ahead after it was recognized [54, 131] that extremely rare events—previously regarded as statistical outliers requiring for their interpretation a theory quite distinct from the theories that explain everyday shocks—in fact possess the identical statistical properties as everyday events; that is, all earthquakes fall on the same straight line on an appropriate log-log plot. Since economic phenomena possess the analogous property, the challenge is to develop a coherent understanding of financial fluctuations that incorporates not only everyday fluctuations but also those extremely rare financial earthquakes.

According to the economist Neil A. Chriss—who is affiliated with ICor Brokerage Incorporated in New York:

> The aim of modern financial theory (or at least that part of modern finance having to do with financial markets) might be described as an attempt to produce theoretical models describing the behavior of financial markets, with an eye toward causal mechanisms, statistical laws, and even predictive power. Starting with assumptions about the behavior of rational economic agents, one makes restrictions on the set of possible laws describing financial markets. Adding simplifying assumptions such as frictionless markets, an absence of transaction costs, and unlimited short selling, the analysis is brought into the realm of the tractable. By observing the behavior of actual financial markets, through the collection and analysis of time series of financial data, one ultimately eliminates many models that are *a priori* possible but contrary to observed behavior [26].

Thus, one prevalent paradigm in economics is to marry finance with mathematics, with the fruit of this marriage being the development of clever models, some of which are used in everyday trading. In physics, we also develop and make use of models (or *artificial worlds*). However, a large number of physicists are fundamentally empirical in our approach to science—indeed, some physicists never make reference to models at all (other than in classroom teaching situations). This empirical approach has led to advances when theory has grown out of experiment; one such example is the understanding of phase transitions and critical phenomena. Such a basic and deep grounding in empirical facts could have an influence on the way physicists approach economics. Our approach has been to follow the paradigm of experimental physics, that is, to first examine the empirical facts as thoroughly as possible before we begin to construct models.

ACKNOWLEDGMENTS

We thank the NSF economics program (SES-0215823 and SRS-0140554) for financial support and we thank our collaborators: S. V. Buldyrev, D. Canning, P. Cizeau, S. Havlin, Y. Lee, Y. Liu, P. Maass, R. N. Mantegna, K. Matia, M. Meyer, B. Rosenow, M. A. Salinger, and M. H. R. Stanley, and most especially L. A. N. Amaral. We also thank L. Blume and S. Durlauf for organizing the May 2001 Santa Fe Institute conference in which these ideas were first discussed, and P. W. Anderson, J. K. Arrow, and D. Pines for organizing the first of this series of conferences 15 years ago [5].

REFERENCES

[1] Amaral, L. A. N., P. Gopikrishnan, K. Matia, V. Plerou, and H. E. Stanley. "Application of Statistical Physics Methods and Concepts to the Study of Science and Technology Systems." [Proceedings of the 2000 International Conference on Science and Technology Indicators, Leiden.] *Sociometrics* **51** (2001): 9–36.

[2] Amaral, L. A. N., S. V. Buldyrev, S. Havlin, M. A. Salinger, and H. E. Stanley. "Power Law Scaling for a System of Interacting Units with Complex Internal Structure." *Phys. Rev. Lett.* **80** (1998): 1385–1388.

[3] Amaral, L. A. N., S. V. Buldyrev, S. Havlin, H. Leschhorn, P. Maass, M. A. Salinger, H. E. Stanley, and M. H. R. Stanley. "Scaling Behavior in Economics: I. Empirical Results for Company Growth." *J. Phys. I France* **7** (1997): 621–633.

[4] Anderson, P. W. "More is Different." *Science* **177** (1972): 393–396.

[5] Anderson, P. W., J. K. Arrow and D. Pines, eds. *The Economy as a Complex Evolving System II*. Santa Fe Institute Studies in the Sciences of Complexity, Proc. Vol. V. Redwood City, CA: Addison-Wesley, 1988.

[6] Anderson, T., T. Bollerslev, F. X. Diebold, and P. Labys. "The Distribution of Exchange Rate Volatility." Working Paper WP6961, National Bureau of Economic Research, Cambridge, MA, 1999.

[7] Ane, T., and H. Geman. "Order Flow, Transaction Clock, and Normality of Asset Returns." *J. Fin.* (October 2000).

[8] Arthur, W. B., S. Durlauf, and D. Lane, eds. *The Economy as a Complex Evolving System II*. Santa Fe Institute Studies in the Sciences of Complexity, Proc. Vol. XXVII. Redwood City, CA: Addison-Wesley, 1997.

[9] Axtell, R. L. "Zipf Distribution of US Firm Sizes." *Science* **293** (2001): 1818–1821.

[10] Bachelier, L. "Théorie de la spéculation." [Ph.D. thesis in mathematics]. *Annales Scientifiques de l'Ecole Normale Supérieure* **III-17** (1900): 21–86.

[11] Barabasi, A.-L., and H. E. Stanley. *Fractal Concepts in Surface Growth*. Cambridge, MA: Cambridge University Press, 1995.

[12] Blattberg, R. C., and N. Gonedes. "A Comparison of the Stable Paretian and Student Distributions as Statistical Models for Prices." *J. Bus.* **47** (1974): 244–280.

[13] Blume, L. "The Statistical Mechanics of Strategic Interaction." *Games and Econ. Behav.* **5** (1993): 387–424.

[14] Blume, L., and S. Durlauf. "Equilibrium Concepts for Social Interaction Models." Mimeo, Department of Economics, Cornell University, Ithaca, NY, 1998.

[15] Blume, L., and S. Durlauf. "The Interactions-Based Approach to Socioeconomic Behavior." Mimeo, Department of Economics, University of Wisconsin, Madison, WI, 1998.

[16] Bottazzi, G., and A. Secchi. "A Stochastic Model of Firm Growth." *Physica A* **324** (2003): 213–219.

[17] Bouchaud, J. P., and M. Potters. *Theory of Financial Risk.* Cambridge, MA: Cambridge University Press, 2000.

[18] Brock, W., and C. Hommes. "Rational Routes to Randomness." *Econometrica* **65** (1998): 1059–1096.

[19] Buldyrev, S. V., M. A. Salinger, and H. E. Stanley. "A Statistical Physics Implementation of Coase's Theory of the Firm." Paper presented at the Haas School, Berkeley, CA, April 29, 2004.

[20] Buldyrev, S. V., L. A. N. Amaral, S. Havlin, H. Leschhorn, P. Maass, M. A. Salinger, H. E. Stanley, and M. H. R. Stanley. "Scaling Behavior in Economics: II. Modeling of Company Growth." *J. Phys. I France* **7** (1997): 635–650.

[21] Canning, D., L. A. N. Amaral, Y. Lee, M. Meyer, and H. E. Stanley. "A Power Law for Scaling the Volatility of GDP Growth Rates with Country Size." *Econ. Lett.* **60** (1998): 335–341.

[22] Carroll, G. R. "National City-Size Distribution: What do We Know After 67 Years of Research?" *Progress in Human Geography* **VI** (1982): 1–43.

[23] Cecconi, F., M. Marsili, J. R. Banavar, and A. Maritan. "Diffusion, Peer Pressure, and Tailed Distributions." *Phys. Rev. Lett.* **89** (2002): 088102.

[24] Cizeau, P., Y. Liu, M. Meyer, C.-K. Peng, and H. E. Stanley. "Volatility Distribution in the S&P 500 Stock Index." *Physica A* **245** (1997): 441–445.

[25] Clark, P. K. "A Subordinated Stochastic Process Model with Finite Variance for Speculative Prices." *Econometrica* **41** (1973): 135–155.

[26] Criss, N. A. "Review of Mantegna and Stanley: An Introduction to Econophysics." *Physics Today* **53(12)** (2000): 70.

[27] De Fabritiis, G., F. Pammolli, and M. Riccaboni. "On Size and Growth of Business Firms." *Physica A* **324** (2003): 38–44.

[28] Ding, Z., C. W. J. Granger, and R. F. Engle. "A Long Memory Property of Stock Market Returns and a New Model." *J. Emp. Fin.* **1** (1993): 83–105.

[29] Durlauf, S. N. "Nonergodic Economic Growth." *Rev. Econ. Stud.* **60** (1993): 349–366.

[30] Durlauf, S. N. "A Theory of Persistent Income Inequality." *J. Econ. Growth* **1** (1996): 75–93.

[31] Durlauf, S. N. "On the Convergence and Divergence of Growth Rates." *Econ. J.* **106** (1996): 1016–1018.

[32] Durlauf, S. N. "Statistical Mechanics Approaches to Socioeconomic Behavior." In *The Economy as a Complex Evolving System II*, edited by W. B. Arthur, S. Durlauf, and D. Lane, 81–104. Santa Fe Institute Studies in the Sciences of Complexity, Proc. Vol. XXVII. Redwood City, CA: Addison-Wesley, 1997.

[33] Durlauf, S. N. "How Can Statistical Mechanics Contribute to Social Science?" *Proc. Natl. Acad. Sci. USA* **96** (1999): 10582–10584.

[34] Durlauf, S. N., and P. Johnson. "Multiple Regimes and Cross-Country Growth Behavior." *J. Appl. Econ.* **10** (1995): 365–384.

[35] Engle, R. F., and J. R. Russell. "Autoregressive Conditional Duration: A New Model for Irregularly Spaced Transaction Data." *Econometrica* **66** (1998): 1127–1162.

[36] Evans, D. S. "Tests of Alternative Theories of Firm Growth." *J. Pol. Econ.* **95** (1987): 657–674.

[37] Fama, E. F. "Efficient Capital Markets: II." *J. Fin.* **46** (1991): 1575–1617.

[38] Fama, E. F. "Efficient Capital Markets: A Review of Theory and Empirical Work." *J. Fin.* **25(2)** (1970): 383–417.

[39] Fama, E. F. "The Behavior of Stock Market Prices." *J. Bus.* **38** (1965): 34–105.

[40] Fama, E. F. "Mandelbrot and the Stable Paretian Distribution." *J. Bus.* **36** (1963): 420–429.

[41] Gabaix, X., P. Gopikrishnan, V. Plerou, and H. E. Stanley. "A Theory of Power-Law Distributions in Financial Market Fluctuations." *Nature* **423** (2003): 267–270.

[42] Gabaix, X., P. Gopikrishnan, V. Plerou, and H. E. Stanley. "A Simple Theory of Asset Market Fluctuations, Motivated by the Cubic and Half Cubic Laws of Trading Activity in the Stock Market." *Quart. J. Econ.* (submitted).

[43] Gallant, A. R., P. E. Rossi, and G. Tauchen. "Stock-Prices and Volume." *Rev. Fin. Stud.* **5** (1992): 199–242.

[44] Ghysels, E., and J. Jasiak. "Stochastic Volatility and Time Deformation: An Application to Trading Volume and Leverage Effects." Preprint, CRDE, Université de Montreal.

[45] Gibrat, R. *Les Inégalités Economiques.* Paris: Sirey, 1931.

[46] Gopikrishnan, P., B. Rosenow, V. Plerou, and H. E. Stanley. "Quantifying and Interpreting Collective Behavior in Financial Markets." *Phys. Rev. E: Rapid Communications* **64** (2001): 035106.

[47] Gopikrishnan, P., V. Plerou, X. Gabaix, and H. E. Stanley. "Statistical Properties of Share Volume Traded in Financial Markets." *Phys. Rev. E (Rapid Communications)* **62** (2000): 4493–4496.

[48] Gopikrishnan, P., V. Plerou, L. A. N. Amaral, M. Meyer, and H. E. Stanley. "Scaling of the Distributions of Fluctuations of Financial Market Indices." *Phys. Rev. E* **60** (1999): 5305–5316.

[49] Gopikrishnan, P., M. Meyer, L. A. N. Amaral, and H. E. Stanley. "Inverse Cubic Law for the Distribution of Stock Price Variations." *Eur. Phys. J. B* **3** (1998): 139–140.

[50] Granger, C. W. J., and Z. Ding. "Varieties of Long Memory Models." *J. Econometrics* **73** (1996): 61–77.

[51] Granger, C. W. J. "Long Memory Relationships and the Aggregation of Dynamic Models." *J. Econometrics* **14** (1980): 227–238.

[52] Granger, C. W. J. "The Typical Spectral Shape of an Economic Variable." *Econometrica* **34** (1966): 150–161.

[53] Guillaume, D. M., O. V. Pictet, U. A. Muller, and M. M. Dacorogna. "Unveiling Non-Linearities through Time Scale Transformations." Olsen group preprint OVP.1994-06-26 (1995), available at ⟨http://www.olsen.ch/research/working-papers.html⟩.

[54] Gutenberg, B., and C. F. Richter. *Seismicity of the Earth and Associated Phenomena.* 2d ed. Princeton, NJ: Princeton University Press, 1954.

[55] Hall, B. H. "The Relationship between Firm Size and Firm Growth in the U.S. Manufacturing Sector." *The J. Indust. Econ.* **35** (1987): 583–606.

[56] Holy, T. E. "Analysis of Data from Continuous Probability Distributions." *Phys. Rev. Lett.* **79** (1997): 3545–3548.

[57] Ijiri, Y., and H. A. Simon. *Skew Distributions and the Sizes of Business Firms.* Amsterdam: North Holland, 1977.

[58] Ivanov, P. Ch., B. Podobnik, Y. Lee, and H. E. Stanley. "Truncated Lévy Process with Scale-Invariant Behavior." [Proc. NATO Advanced Research Workshop on Application of Physics in Economic Modeling, Prague.s] *Physica A* **299** (2001): 154–160.

[59] Jones, C., K. Gautam, and M. Lipson. "Transactions, Volumes and Volatility." *Rev. Fin. Stud.* **7** (1994): 631–651.

[60] Kantelhardt, J. W., Y. Ashkenazy, P. Ch. Ivanov, A. Bunde, A. L. Goldberger, S. Havlin, T. Penzel, J.-H. Peter, and H. E. Stanley. "Characterization of Sleep Stages by Correlations in the Magnitude and Sign of Heartbeat Increments." *Phys. Rev. E* **65** (2002): 051908-1 to 051908-6.

[61] Kantelhardt, J. W., S. Zschiegner, E. Koscielny-Bunde, S. Havlin, A. Bunde, and H. E. Stanley. "Multifractal Detrended Fluctuation Analysis of Nonstationary Time Series." *Physica A* **316** (2002): 87.

[62] Karpoff, J. "Price Variability and Volume: A Review." *J. Fin. & Quant. Anal.* **22** (1987): 109.

[63] Keitt, T. H., L. A. N. Amaral, S. V. Buldyrev, and H. E. Stanley. "Scaling in the Growth of Geographically Subdivided Populations: Scale-Invariant Patterns from a Continent-Wide Biological Survey." [Focus issue: The Biosphere as a Complex Adaptive System.] *Phil. Trans. Roy. Soc. B: Biol. Sci.* **357** (2002): 627–633.

[64] Keitt, T., and H. E. Stanley. "Scaling in the Dynamics of North American Breeding-Bird Populations." *Nature* **393** (1998): 257.

[65] Krugman, P. *The Self-Organizing Economy.* Oxford: Basil Blackwell, 1996.

[66] Laloux, L., P. Cizeau, J.-P. Bouchaud and M. Potters. "Noise Dressing of Financial Correlation Matrices." *Phys. Rev. Lett.* **83** (1999): 1469–1482.

[67] Lamoureux, C. G., and W. D. Lastrapes. "Heteroskedasticity in Stock Return Data: Volume Versus GARCH Effects." *J. Fin.* **45** (1990): 221–229.

[68] LeBaron, B. "Stochastic Volatility as a Simple Generator of Financial Power Laws and Long Memory." *Quant. Fin.* **2** (2001): 621–631.

[69] Lee, Y., L. A. N. Amaral, D. Canning, M. Meyer, and H. E. Stanley. "Universal Features in the Growth Dynamics of Complex Organizations." *Phys. Rev. Lett.* **81** (1998): 3275–3278.

[70] Lévy, P. *Théorie de l'Addition des Variables Aléatoires.* Paris: Gauthier-Villars, 1937.

[71] Liljeros, F., C. R. Edling, L. A. N. Amaral, H. E. Stanley, and Y. Åberg. "The Web of Human Sexual Contacts." *Nature* **411** (2001): 907–908.

[72] Liu, Y., P. Gopikrishnan, P. Cizeau, M. Meyer, C.-K. Peng and H. E. Stanley. "The Statistical Properties of the Volatility of Price Fluctuations." *Phys. Rev. E* **60** (1999): 1390–1400.

[73] Liu, Y., P. Cizeau, M. Meyer, C.-K. Peng, and H. E. Stanley. 'Quantification of Correlations in Economic Time Series." *Physica A* **245** (1997): 437–440.

[74] Lo, A. "Long Term Memory in Stock Market Prices." *Econometrica* **59** (1991): 1279–1313.

[75] Loretan, M., and P. C. B. Phillips. "Testing the Covariance Stationarity of Heavy-Tailed Time Series: An Overview of Applications to Several Financial Data Sets." *J. Emp. Fin.* **1** (1994): 211–248.

[76] Lotka, A. J. "The Frequency Distribution of Scientific Productivity." *J. Washington Acad. Sci.* **12** (1926): 317–323.

[77] Lux, T. "The Stable Paretian Hypothesis and the Frequency of Large Returns: An Examination of Major German Stocks." *Appl. Fin. Econ.* **6** (1996): 463–475.

[78] Mabe, M., and M. Amin. "Growth Dynamics of Scholarly and Scientific Journals." *Scientometrics* **51** (2001): 147–162.

[79] Mandelbrot, B. B. "The Variation of Certain Speculative Prices." *J. Bus.* **36** (1963): 394–419.

[80] Mantegna, R. N., and H. E. Stanley. "Modeling of Financial Data: Comparison of the Truncated Lévy Flight and the ARCH(1) and GARCH(1,1) Processes." [Proceedings of the International IUPAP Conference on Statistical Physics, held in Taipei.] *Physica A* **254** (1998): 77–84.

[81] Mantegna, R. N., and H. E. Stanley. "Physics Investigation of Financial Markets." In *Proceedings of the International School of Physics "Enrico*

Fermi," *Course CXXXIV*, edited by F. Mallamace and H. E. Stanley. Amsterdam: IOS Press, 1997.

[82] Mantegna, R. N., and H. E. Stanley. "Scaling Behavior in the Dynamics of an Economic Index." *Nature* **376** (1995): 46–49.

[83] Mantegna, R. N., and H. E. Stanley. "Stochastic Process with Ultraslow Convergence to a Gaussian: the Truncated Lévy Flight." *Phys. Rev. Lett.* **73** (1994): 2946–2949.

[84] Mandelbrot, B. B., and H. Taylor. "On the Distribution of Stock Price Differences." *Oper. Resh.* **15** (1962): 1057–1062.

[85] Mantegna, R. N., and H. E. Stanley. *An Introduction to Econophysics: Correlations and Complexity in Finance.* Cambridge, MA: Cambridge University Press, 2000.

[86] Mantegna, R. N., and H. E. Stanley. "Stock Market Dynamics and Turbulence: Parallel Analysis of Fluctuation Phenomena." [Proceedings of the International Conference on Pattern Formation in Fluids and Materials.] *Physica A* **239** (1997): 255–266.

[87] Mantegna, R. N., and H. E. Stanley. "Turbulence and Exchange Markets." *Nature* **383** (1996): 587–588.

[88] Mantegna, R. N., S. V. Buldyrev, A. L. Goldberger, S. Havlin, C.-K. Peng, M. Simons, and H. E. Stanley. "Systematic Analysis of Coding and Noncoding DNA Sequences Using Methods of Statistical Linguistics." *Phys. Rev. E* **52** (1995): 2939–2950.

[89] Matia, K., Y. Ashkenazy, and H. E. Stanley. "Multifractal Properties of Price Fluctuations of Stocks and Commodities." *Europhys. Lett.* **6** (2003): 422.

[90] Matia, K., L. A. N. Amaral, S. Goodwin, and H. E. Stanley. "Non-Lévy Distribution of Commodity Price Fluctuations." *Phys. Rev. E: Rapid Communications* **66** (2002): 045103. Also available at ⟨http://arxiv.org/abs/cond-matt/0202028⟩.

[91] Moed, H. F., and M. Luwel. "Science Policy: the Business of Research." *Nature* **400** (1999): 411–412.

[92] Montroll, E. W., and W. W. Badger. *Introduction to Quantitative Aspects of Social Phenomena.* New York: Gordon & Breach, 1974.

[93] Muller, U. A., M. M. Dacorogna, and O. V. Pictet. "Heavy Tails in High-Frequency Financial Data." In *A Practical Guide to Heavy Tails*, edited by R. J. Adler, R. E. Feldman, and M. S. Taqqu, 83–311. Boston: Birkhäuser Publishers, 1998.

[94] Officer, R. R. "The Distribution of Stock Returns." *J. Amer. Stat. Assoc.* **67** (1972): 807–812.

[95] Pagan, A. "The Econometrics of Financial Markets." *J. Emp. Fin.* **3** (1996): 15–102.

[96] Pareto, V. *Cours d'Economie Politique.* Lausanne and Paris, 1897.

[97] Peng, C. K., S. V. Buldyrev, S. Havlin, M. Simons, H. E. Stanley, and A. L. Goldberger. "Mosaic Organization of DNA Nucleotides." *Phys. Rev. E* **49** (1994): 1685–1689.

[98] Peng, C. K., S. Buldyrev, A. Goldberger, S. Havlin, F. Sciortino, M. Simons, and H. E. Stanley. "Long-Range Correlations in Nucleotide Sequences." *Nature* **356** (1992): 168–171.

[99] Plerou, V., P. Gopikrishnan, and H. E. Stanley. "Two-Phase Behaviour of Financial Markets." *Nature* **421** (2003): 130.

[100] Plerou, V., P. Gopikrishnan, and H. E. Stanley. "Symmetry Breaking in Stock Demand." *Phys. Rev. E* (2001): submitted. cond-mat/0111349. Also available at ⟨http://arxiv.org/abs/cond-mat/0111349⟩.

[101] Plerou, V., P. Gopikrishnan, B. Rosenow, L. A. N. Amaral, T. Guhr, and H. E. Stanley, "A Random Matrix Approach in Financial Data." *Phys. Rev. E* **65** (2002): 066126.

[102] Plerou, V., P. Gopikrishnan, X. Gabaix, and H. E. Stanley. "Quantifying Stock Price Response to Demand Fluctuations." *Phys. Rev. E* **66** (2002): 027104.

[103] Plerou, V., P. Gopikrishnan, X. Gabaix, L. A. N. Amaral, and H. E. Stanley. "Price Fluctuations, Market Activity, and Trading Volume." *Quant. Fin.* **1** (2001): 262–269.

[104] Plerou, V., P. Gopikrishnan, L. A. N. Amaral, X. Gabaix, and H. E. Stanley. "Diffusion and Economic Fluctuations." *Phys. Rev. E (Rapid Communications)* **62** (2000): 3023–3026.

[105] Plerou, V., P. Gopikrishnan, L. A. N. Amaral, M. Meyer, and H. E. Stanley. "Scaling of the Distribution of Price Fluctuations of Individual Companies." *Phys. Rev. E* **60** (1999): 6519–6529.

[106] Plerou, V., P. Gopikrishnan, B. Rosenow, L. A. N. Amaral, and H. E. Stanley. "Universal and Nonuniversal Properties of Financial Cross-Correlation Matrices." *Phys. Rev. Lett.* **83** (1999): 1471–1475.

[107] Plerou, V., L. A. N. Amaral, P. Gopikrishnan, M. Meyer, and H. E. Stanley. "Similarities between the Growth Dynamics of University Research and of Competitive Economic Activities." *Nature* **400** (1999): 433–437.

[108] Podobnik, B., P. Ch. Ivanov, Y. Lee, A. Chessa, and H. E. Stanley. "Systems with Correlations in the Variance: Generating Power Law Tails in Probability Distributions." *Europhys. Lett.* **50** (2000): 711–717.

[109] Podobnik, B., P. Ch. Ivanov, Y. Lee, and H. E. Stanley. "Scale-Itnvariant Truncated Lévy Process." *Europhys. Lett.* **52** (2000): 491–497.

[110] Podobnik, B., K. Matia, A. Chessa, P. Ch. Ivanov, Y. Lee, and H. E. Stanley. "Time Evolution of Stochastic Processes with Correlations in the Variance: Stability in Power-Law Tails of Distributions." *Physica A* **300** (2001): 300–309.

[111] Praetz, P. D. "The Distribution of Share Price Changes." *J. Bus.* **45** (1972): 49–55.

[112] Robinson, P. M. "Gaussian Semiparametric Estimation of Long Range Dependence." *Ann. Stat.* **23** (1995): 1630–1661.

[113] Roll, R. "A Simple Implicit Measure of the Effective Bid-Ask Spread in an Efficient Market." *J. Fin.* **39** (1984): 1127–1140.

[114] Rosenow, B., V. Plerou, P. Gopikrishnan, and H. E. Stanley. "Portfolio Optimization and the Random Magnet Problem." *Europhys. Lett.* **59** (2002): 500–506.

[115] Singh, A., and G. Whittington. "The Size and Growth of Firms." *Rev. Econ. Stud.* **42** (1975): 15–26.

[116] Skjeltorp, J. A. "Scaling in the Norwegian Stock Market." *Physica* **283** (2001): 486–528.

[117] Solomon, S., and P. Richmond. "Stable Power Laws in Variable Economies; Lotka-Volterra Implies Pareto-Zipf." *Eur. Phys. J. B* **27** (2002): 257–261.

[118] Stanley, H. E., and V. Plerou. "Scaling and Universality in Economics: Empirical Results and Theoretical Interpretation." *Quant. Fin.* **1** (2001): 563–567.

[119] Stanley, H. E. "Scaling, Universality, and Renormalization: Three Pillars of Modern Critical Phenomena." *Rev. Mod. Phys.* **71** (1999): S358–S366.

[120] Stanley, H. E., V. Afanasyev, L. A. N. Amaral, S. V. Buldyrev, A. L. Goldberger, S. Havlin, H. Leschhorn, P. Maass, R. N. Mantegna, C.-K. Peng, P. A. Prince, M. A. Salinger, M. H. R. Stanley, and G. M. Viswanathan. "Anomalous Fluctuations in the Dynamics of Complex Systems: From DNA and Physiology to Econophysics." *Physica A* **224** (1996): 302–321.

[121] Stanley, M. H. R., L. A. N. Amaral, S. V. Buldyrev, S. Havlin, H. Leschhorn, P. Maass, M. A. Salinger, and H. E. Stanley. "Scaling Behavior in the Growth of Companies." *Nature* **379** (1996): 804–806.

[122] Stanley, M. H. R., S. V. Buldyrev, S. Havlin, R. Mantegna, M. A. Salinger, and H. E. Stanley. "Zipf Plots and the Size Distribution of Firms." *Econ. Lett.* **49** (1996): 453–457.

[123] Stanley, H. E. "Power Laws and Universality." *Nature* **378** (1995): 554–555.

[124] Stanley, H. E. *Introduction to Phase Transitions and Critical Phenomena.* Oxford: Oxford University Press, 1971.

[125] Stock, J. "Estimating Continuous Time Processes Subject to Time Deformation." *J. Amer. Stat. Assoc.* **83** (1988): 77–85.

[126] Suki, B., A.-L. Barabási, Z. Hantos, F. Peták, and H. E. Stanley. "Avalanches and Power Law Behaviour in Lung Inflation." *Nature* **368** (1994): 615–618.

[127] Sutton, J. "The Variance of Firm Growth Rates: The 'Scaling' Puzzle." *Physica A* **312** (2002): 577–590.

[128] Takayasu, H., and K. Okuyama. "Country Dependence on Company Size Distributions and a Numerical Model Based on Competition and Cooperation." *Fractals* **6** (1998): 67–79.

[129] Takayasu, H. ed. *Empirical Science of Financial Fluctuations: The Advent of Econophysics.* Berlin: Springer, 2002.

[130] Tauchen, G., and M. Pitts. "The Price Variability-Volume Relationship on Speculative Markets." *Econometrica* **57** (1983): 485–505.

[131] Turcotte, D. L. *Fractals and Chaos in Geology and Geophysics.* Cambridge, MA: Cambridge University Press, 1992.

[132] Wood, R. A., T. H. McInish, and J. K. Ord. "An Investigation of Transactions Data for NYSE Stocks." *J. Fin.* **40** (1985): 723–739.

[133] Wyart, M., and J.-P. Bouchaud. "Statistical Models for Company Growth." E-print archive, Condensed Matter Physics, Cornell University. October 2002. ⟨http:/xxx.lanl.gov/abs/cond-mat/0210479⟩.

Market Efficiency, the Pareto Wealth Distribution, and the Lévy Distribution of Stock Returns

The Pareto (power-law) wealth distribution, which is empirically observed in many countries, implies rather extreme wealth inequality. For instance, in the U.S. the top 1% of the population holds about 40% of the total wealth. What is the source of this inequality? The answer to this question has profound political, social, and philosophical implications. We show that the Pareto wealth distribution is a robust consequence of a fundamental property of the capital investment process: it is a stochastic multiplicative process. Moreover, the Pareto distribution implies that inequality is driven primarily by chance, rather than by differential investment ability. This result is closely related to the concept of market efficiency, and may have direct implications regarding the economic role and social desirability of wealth inequality. We also show that the Pareto wealth distribution may explain the Lévy distribution of stock returns, which has puzzled researchers for many years. Thus, the Pareto wealth distribution, market efficiency, and the Lévy distribution of stock returns are all closely linked.

The Economy as an Evolving Complex System III,
edited by Lawrence E. Blume and Steven N. Durlauf, Oxford University Press

1 INTRODUCTION

In this study we focus on three seemingly unrelated issues: (a) the distribution of wealth and wealth inequality, (b) market efficiency (do some investors have stock selection or market "timing" ability, or are success and failure in capital investments primarily due to chance?), and (c) the distribution of stock returns (in particular, the "fat tailed" Lévy distribution observed by Mandelbrot [52, 53], and recently precisely measured by Mantegna and Stanley [57] and others). We show in this chapter that although it seems that these are three unrelated research topics (the first in economics and the other two in finance), they are, in fact, very closely related.

The Pareto wealth distribution is shown to be a robust consequence of the stochastic multiplicative nature of the investment process. However, we find that the Pareto distribution can occur only if the market is efficient—which implies that success and failure in investments is primarily due to chance, rather than to differential investment ability. Thus, it is chance which drives the Pareto wealth distribution and the rather extreme inequality which it implies. Furthermore, the Pareto wealth distribution can explain the (truncated) Lévy distribution of stock returns. The mechanism we suggest implies a surprising and empirically testable prediction: the exponent of the Lévy return distribution should be equal to the Pareto constant. Cross-country empirical investigation reveals striking agreement between these two *a priori* unrelated parameters:

	α_L	α_W
U.S.	1.37	1.25
U.K.	1.08	1.06
France	1.82	1.83

where α_L is the Lévy characteristic exponent and α_W is the Pareto constant. Thus, the Pareto wealth distribution, market efficiency, and the Lévy distribution of stock returns, are all tightly linked.

When examining the wealth distribution in society, one typically finds two distinct regions. At the lower-wealth range the distribution of wealth can be approximated by the log-normal distribution. At the high-wealth range the distribution is described by the Pareto distribution (see, for example, Stiendl [75]). In this chapter we focus on the Pareto distribution, which characterizes the high-wealth range. This range is extremely important because, although it accounts for a relatively small part of the population (typically about 5%), it accounts for most of the wealth.[1] In addition, when considering wealth accumulation through capital investments, it is the high-wealth range which is relevant to the analysis.[2]

A century ago, Pareto [60] discovered that at the high-wealth range, wealth (and also income) are distributed according to a power-law distribution. The parameters of this distribution may change across societies, but regardless of the social or political conditions, taxation, and so on, Pareto claimed that the wealth distribution obeys this general distribution law, which became known as the Pareto distribution or Pareto law. The Pareto distribution is given by the following probability density function:

$$P(W) = CW^{-(1+\alpha)} \qquad \text{for } W \geq W_0 \tag{1}$$

where W stands for wealth, $P(W)$ is the density function, W_0 is the lower end of the high-wealth range, C is a normalization constant, and α is known as the Pareto constant.

Pareto's finding has been shown in numerous studies to provide an excellent fit to the empirical wealth distribution in various countries (see, for example, Steindl [75], Atkinson and Harrison [4], Persky [63], and Levy and Solomon [46]). Several researchers claim that the Pareto law is very universal. Davis [15] argues that:

> No one however, has yet exhibited a stable social order, ancient or modern, which has not followed the Pareto pattern at least approximately. (p. 395)

Snyder [73] writes:

> Pareto's curve is destined to take its place as one of the great generalizations of human knowledge. (p. 417)

---

[1] According to Wolff [80] the top 1% of the population in the U.S. holds more than 40% of the total wealth. Díaz-Giménez, Quadrini, and Ríos-Rull [16] report that the top 5% of the population hold 55% of the wealth.

[2] Several researchers employ neoclassical growth models with uninsurable idiosyncratic earning shocks in order to explain the entire empirically observed wealth and income distributions (see Auerbach and Kotlikoff [5], Aiyagari [2], Ríos-Rull [66], Huggett [34], Krusell and Smith [40], and Castaneda, Díaz-Giménez, and Rios-Rull [10]. This is a formidable task as it aims to explain the distribution both at the high-wealth range and the low-wealth range with a single model. This is difficult because the main factors influencing the wealth of a person at the lower range are usually labor income and consumption, while the wealth of individuals in the high-wealth range typically changes mainly due to capital investments. Indeed, as Quadrini and Ríos-Rull [65] report, these models typically produce distributions of wealth which differ significantly from the empirical U.S. wealth distribution. Regarding the fit of income distributions to the Pareto distribution Blinder [7] asserts:

> It may well be no accident that the upper tails of almost all income distributions, where **returns to capital dominate** and earnings play a minor role, exhibit a striking resemblance to the Pareto distribution (pp. 7–8).

Here we focus only on capital investments and on the high-wealth range.

Several examples of the fit of the Pareto law to the empirical wealth distribution are provided by figures 8–10, which depict the wealth distribution in France, the U.K., and the U.S. These figures are discussed in detail in section 5.

The first to suggest an explanation for the Pareto distribution of wealth was Pareto himself (Pareto [60]). Pareto suggested that the distribution of wealth corresponds to an underlying distribution of human abilities. However, Pareto has not offered a mathematical model that would explain the distribution of abilities and its relation to the Pareto law. Pareto's explanation was advanced by Davis, who introduced the "law of the distribution of special abilities" which asserts that the probability of an additional unit of ability was independent of the level of ability (Davis [15]). This model, however, leads to a normal distribution of ability and, therefore, presumably to a normal, rather than Pareto, distribution of wealth. A different model for the distribution of ability was formulated by Boissevain [8] who considered the distribution of abilities that could be represented as a product of several factors, each of which follows a binomial distribution. Boissevain's model explains the positive skewness in the distributions of wealth and income, but leads to a log-normal distribution, not the empirically observed Pareto distribution.

The main models that offer an explanation for the precise form of the Pareto wealth distribution are the Markov chain model of Champernowne [11], the stream model of Simon [71], and the birth-and-death model of Wold and Whittle [79].[3] Although these models are quite different from each other and make various different assumptions, in all of these models the wealth accumulation process is a stochastic *multiplicative* process. A stochastic multiplicative process is a process in which the value of each element is *multiplied* by a random variable with each time step. Many economic processes, and in particular the accumulation of wealth via investment of capital, are stochastic and multiplicative by nature. For example, if a person invests her money in a portfolio which yields 10% with probability 1/2 and −5% with probability 1/2 each year, her wealth will follow a stochastic multiplicative process. The main difference between multiplicative and additive processes is that in additive processes (such as random walks) the changes in value are independent of the value, whereas in multiplicative processes the changes are proportional to the value.

In this chapter we argue that the multiplicative nature of the capital investment process is the reason for the empirically observed Pareto wealth distribution. Indeed, starting with an arbitrary non-degenerate initial wealth distribution, any process which is stochastically multiplicative and homogeneous leads to the Pareto law. The homogeneity of the process in essence means that individuals do not possess differential investment abilities and cannot "beat the market." This idea is closely related to the concept of market efficiency: in an efficient market one would not expect to find investors who consistently outper-

---

[3]For a review of models generating Pareto distributions see Steindl [75], Arnold [3], and Slottje [72].

form their peers. We show that non-homogeneous multiplicative processes lead to a wealth distribution which is different from the Pareto distribution. Thus, the Pareto distribution implies market efficiency. Our analysis leads us to conclude that the extreme inequality in modern western society is a very fundamental and robust outcome of the nature of the capital investment process. Furthermore, this inequality is driven primarily by chance, rather than by differential ability.

The structure of this chapter is as follows. In section 2 we present the framework of stochastically multiplicative investment processes. We prove that homogeneous processes lead to the Pareto wealth distribution, and to the extreme inequality which it implies. In section 3 we discuss non-homogeneous processes and show that they lead to wealth distributions different than the Pareto distribution. This section reveals that the Pareto distribution is closely related to market efficiency, and puts an upper bound on the degree of market inefficiency. In section 4 we show that the Lévy distribution of stock returns can be explained by the Pareto wealth distribution. The theoretical prediction resulting from this analysis is empirically tested in section 5. In section 6, we present our conclusions.

2   STOCHASTIC MULTIPLICATIVE PROCESSES

A stochastic multiplicative wealth accumulation process is given by:

$$W_i^{t+1} = W_i^t \tilde{\lambda}_i^t \tag{2}$$

where W_i^t is the wealth of investor i at time t and $\tilde{\lambda}_i^t$ represents the stochastic return, which is a random variable drawn from some distribution $g_i(\tilde{\lambda})$. Generally, each investor may have a different distribution of returns on his investment, hence the sub-index i in $g_i(\tilde{\lambda})$.

For people at the high-wealth range, changes in wealth are mainly due to financial investment, and are, therefore, typically multiplicative. For people at the lower-wealth range, changes in wealth are mainly due to labor income and consumption, which are basically additive rather than multiplicative. Here we are only interested in modeling wealth dynamics in the high-wealth range. There are many ways one could model the boundary between these two regions. We start by considering the most simple model in which there is a sharp boundary between the two regions. The specific modeling of the boundary does not change our general results. As the stochastic multiplicative process (eq. (2)) describes the dynamics only at the higher-wealth range, we introduce a threshold wealth level, W_0, above which the dynamics are multiplicative. We assume that only those people with wealth exceeding W_0 participate in the stochastic multiplicative investment process. Formally, we require that:

$$W_i^t \geq W_0 \qquad \text{for all } i, \text{ and for all } t. \tag{3}$$

In the case that there is an overall drift towards lower-wealth values (as in Champernowne [11]) one can define the lower bound W_0 in absolute terms. In general, however, we would expect the drift to be towards higher-wealth values (as when there is inflation or a growing economy, for example). In this case, an absolute lower-bound value becomes meaningless, and one has to define the lower bound in real terms. A natural way to define the lower bound is in terms of the average wealth. We define the lower bound, W_0, as $W_0 = \omega(1/N) \sum_{i=1}^{N} W_i^t$ where N is the number of investors and ω is a threshold given in absolute terms ($\omega < 1$).

As people's wealth changes, they may cross the boundary between the upper and lower-wealth regions. We do not model the dynamics at the lower-wealth range, and for the sake of simplicity, we assume that the market has reached an equilibrium in which the flow of people across the boundary is equal in both directions, that is, the number of people participating in the stochastic multiplicative investment process remains constant. The above assumption simplifies the analysis, but the results presented here are robust to the relaxation of this assumption.

In a homogeneous process all investors face the same return distribution. The homogeneous process is thus described by:

$$W_i^{t+1} = W_i^t \tilde{\lambda}_i^t, \, W_i^t \geq W_0, \text{ and } g_i(\tilde{\lambda}) = g(\tilde{\lambda}) \text{ for all investors } i. \quad (4)$$

Note that although all investors face the same return distribution $g(\tilde{\lambda})$, $\tilde{\lambda}$ is drawn separately for each investor. One way to think of this is to think of investors who have the same objective but different expectations, and, therefore, hold different portfolios. At each period every investor will have a different realized return, but if all investors have the same stock-picking and market-timing abilities, none of them achieves a return distribution better than the others', and they draw their returns from the same distribution (see also footnote 8). A "lucky" investor is one for whom many high values of λ are drawn. Such a lucky investor will become richer than the others. Note that in the homogeneous case investors face the same distribution of returns, and thus the differentiation in wealth is entirely due to chance.

The next theorem shows that the Pareto wealth distribution is a very robust result of homogeneous multiplicative processes.

Theorem 1 *For any initial wealth distribution and non-trivial return distribution* (var $(\lambda) > 0$), *the wealth accumulation process given by eq. (4) leads to a convergence of the wealth distribution to the Pareto distribution.*

Proof: Denote the cumulative wealth distribution at time t and at time $t + 1$ by $F(W, t)$ and $F(W, t + 1)$, respectively. Then, because the wealth of the ith investor changes from W_i^t at time t to $W_i^t \tilde{\lambda}_i^t$ at time $t + 1$, that is, $W_i^{t+1} = W_i^t \tilde{\lambda}_i^t$ (see eq. (1)), the cumulative wealth distribution at $t + 1$ is given by:

$$F(W, t + 1) = \int_0^{+\infty} F\left(\frac{W}{\lambda}, t\right) g(\lambda) d\lambda \quad (5)$$

where all values of λ such that the wealth at $t+1$ is equal to $(W/\lambda)\lambda = W$ are accounted for.[4]

Equation (5) describes a process in which the probability $F(W)$ at time $t+1$ is a weighted average of the probability at points surrounding W (points W/λ) at time t. Thus, starting from an arbitrary probability density, $F(W,0)$, the distribution $F(W)$ undergoes a continuous "smoothing" process. In the presence of an effective lower bound on wealth ($W_i^t \geq W_0$), this smoothing process is analogous to diffusion towards a barrier (see Levy and Solomon [47]). Such a process is well known to lead to the convergence of $F(W)$ to a stationary distribution (Boltzmann [9] and Feynman, Leighton, and Sands [24]). For the limiting stationary wealth distribution we have $F(W, t+1) = F(W,t) = F(W)$ and eq. (5) becomes:

$$F(W) = \int_0^{+\infty} F\left(\frac{W}{\lambda}\right) g(\lambda)d\lambda. \tag{6}$$

Differentiating with respect to W we obtain the density function:

$$f(W) = \int_0^{+\infty} f\left(\frac{W}{\lambda}\right) \frac{1}{\lambda} g(\lambda)d\lambda. \tag{7}$$

In order to show that the Pareto distribution is a solution to eq. (7), substitute the Pareto probability density function (eq. (1)) for $f(W)$ in eq. (7) to obtain:

$$\frac{\alpha k^\alpha}{W^{\alpha+1}} = \int_0^{+\infty} \frac{\alpha k^\alpha}{(W/\lambda)^{\alpha+1}} \frac{1}{\lambda} g(\lambda)d\lambda = \frac{\alpha k^\alpha}{W^{\alpha+1}} \int_0^{+\infty} \lambda^\alpha g(\lambda)d\lambda. \tag{8}$$

Thus, it is evident that the Pareto distribution with α satisfying $\int_0^{+\infty} \lambda^\alpha g(\lambda)d\lambda = 1$ is a solution to eq. (6). The Pareto distribution is also the unique positive solution to (6) because the only positive g-harmonic functions on $\Re$ are exponentials (see Choquet [12], Loomis [50], Furstenberg [27, Theorem B, p. 291], and Levy [44].).[5] ∎

Theorem 1 shows that the Pareto distribution is a limit distribution of homogeneous stochastic multiplicative wealth accumulation processes, as given by eq. (4). We would like to emphasize that the analysis is quite general and does not rely on any specific form of the return distribution $g(\lambda)$, as long as this distribution is non-trivial.

Monte Carlo simulations of the homogeneous multiplicative wealth accumulation process illustrate the result of Theorem 1, and provide an estimate of the

---

[4]As $\tilde\lambda$ represents the total return on capital investment, it can not be less than 0 (which corresponds to a rate of return of -100%).

[5]Notice that the results of Champernowne [11] and Wold and Whittle [79] can be viewed as special cases of Theorem 1. The theorem is also closely related to Kesten [39] who investigates processes of the type $x_i^{t+1} = x_i^t \tilde\lambda_i^t + \tilde\varepsilon_i^t$, which are similar to eq. (1), with the additive random variable $\tilde\varepsilon_i^t$ replacing the role of the lower bound. Recently, Gabaix [28] employs similar arguments to explain Zipf's [83] Law for the distribution of city sizes.

time it takes the wealth distribution to converge to the Pareto distribution. We have conducted simulations in which all investors start out with an identical initial wealth level of \$100,000. The return distribution $g(\tilde{\lambda})$ is taken as:

λ	probability
1.10	1/2
0.95	1/2

thus, at every time period each investor has an equal probability of gaining 10% or losing 5%. The lower-wealth bound (W_0) is set to 20% of the average wealth. We have recorded the distribution of wealth at different times. The results are shown in Figure 1, which is a two-way logarithmic plot of the probability density as a function of wealth (in units of the average wealth). The dashed vertical line at 0.2 represents the minimal wealth threshold W_0. Note that the theoretical Pareto distribution (eq. (1)) is a power-law distribution, and it is, therefore, linear when plotted on a double-logarithmic scale.[6] The distribution after 10 investment periods (fig. 1(a)) is still rather symmetric, and centered around the average wealth (1.0 on the horizontal axis). However, after 100 time periods, the wealth distribution is very close to the Pareto distribution (fig. 1(b)). The distribution remains Paretian from then on.[7] Figure 1(c) shows the wealth distribution after 10,000 time periods.

The homogeneity of the process ($g_i(\lambda) = g(\lambda)$ for all i) implies an efficient market: no investor is able to achieve a superior distribution of returns which dominates $g(\lambda)$. In the next section we show that this is indeed a necessary condition for the emergence of a Pareto distribution.[8] If the market is inefficient and $g_i(\lambda) \neq g_j(\lambda)$, a wealth distribution which is different than the Pareto distribution emerges.

3　NON-HOMOGENEOUS MULTIPLICATIVE PROCESSES AND MARKET EFFICIENCY

As a first step toward the analysis of the general heterogeneous model ($g_i(\lambda) \neq g_j(\lambda)$), we analyze the case of two subpopulations. Consider a market in which

---

[6]Take the logarithm of both sides of eq. (1) to obtain: $\log[P(W)] = \log[C] - (1 - \alpha)\log[W]$.

[7]The slope of the line in figures 2(b) and 2(c) is -2.25, which implies $1 + \alpha = 2.25$ or $\alpha = 1.25$. This value is typical of western countries, and it is between the value of α in the U.K. (1.06) and the value of α in the U.S. (1.35) (see section 5).

[8]Market efficiency is necessary, but not sufficient. Even if all investors have similar investment talent, they may still have different distributions of returns, due to different attitudes towards risk. However, if investors have long horizons (which seems reasonable for the high-wealth range), then under mild assumptions regarding preferences, they should all seek to find the investment which maximizes the geometric mean (see Latané [41], Markowitz [58], and Leshno and Levy [42]). If this is the case, they have the same goal, and in an efficient market they are likely to draw returns from similar distributions.

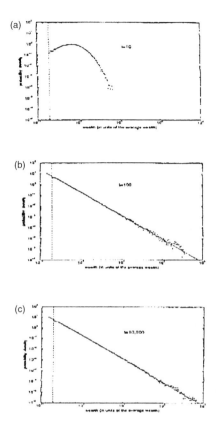

FIGURE 1 the evolution of the wealth distribution in a simulation of a stochastic multiplicative process. Initially, all investors have the same wealth. (a) After $t = 10$ time steps the distribution is still centered around the average wealth. (b) After $t = 100$ time steps the Pareto distribution (straight line on the double-logarithmic scale) is obtained. (c) From that time onwards, the Pareto distribution remains as the steady state.

some of the population has *normal* investment skills and faces the return distribution $g_{normal}(\tilde{\lambda})$, while a minority of *smart* investors are able to take advantage of market inefficiencies and to obtain the superior distribution $g_{smart}(\tilde{\lambda})$, such that $\sigma(g_{smart}) = \sigma(g_{normal})$ and $E(g_{smart}) > E(g_{normal})$. The resulting wealth distribution will be different from the Pareto distribution, as the theorem below shows.

Theorem 2: *In the case of two different subpopulations, as described above, the wealth distribution converges to a distribution which does not conform with the Pareto Law.*

Proof: Over time the "smart" investors become, on average, richer than the "normal" investors. As the "normal" investors become relatively poorer, more and more of them will cross the lower wealth threshold, W_0, and will exit the market. One might suspect that in the long run the "normal" population will be completely wiped out. However, recall that there is an inflow of investors into the market. This is an inflow of investors from below the threshold who have acquired enough wealth in order to participate in the investment process. (We do not model the process of wealth accumulation below the threshold, but assume that the market is in a steady state in which the inflow of new investors balances the outflow of investors leaving the market. This assumption simplifies the analysis but is not essential to our results.) Some of the new investors entering the market are of the "normal" type.[9] As the number of "normal" investors declines, so does their proportion in the outflow from the market. Eventually, a balance is reached when the outflow of investors of each type matches the inflow of that type, and the size of each subgroup converges to a certain (mean) value.

As the population of each subgroup is homogeneous, the wealth distribution of each subgroup is subject to the dynamics described by eq. (4).[10] From the result of Theorem 1, it follows that the wealth of each subgroup will be divided between the members of that subgroup according to the Pareto distribution. Thus, the wealth distribution among "normal" investors is:

$$P_{\text{normal}}(W) = C_{\text{normal}} W^{-(1+\alpha_{\text{normal}})} \tag{9}$$

and the wealth distribution among "smart" investors is:

$$P_{\text{smart}}(W) = C_{\text{smart}} W^{-(1+\alpha_{\text{smart}})}. \tag{10}$$

Both distributions are Paretian, but with different parameters C and α. As the average wealth of the smart population is greater than the average wealth of the normal population, we will have $\alpha_{\text{smart}} < \alpha_{\text{normal}}$.[11] The aggregate distribution of wealth is given by:

$$P(W) = C_1 W^{-(1+\alpha_{\text{normal}})} + C_2 W^{-(1+\alpha_{\text{smart}})} \tag{11}$$

---

[9]One can think of different ways in which to compose the population of new investors: (a) for each investor exiting the market an investor of the same type enters; (b) each new investor has a certain probability p for being "smart" and probability $(1-p)$ of being "normal." The choice between the above two alternatives, and the value of the probability p, may change the specific parameters of the steady state wealth distribution, but not its essential features, as described below.

[10]The interaction between the different subgroups is only through the lower bound W_0, which depends on the average wealth of all investors in the market.

[11]The lower the value of the exponent α of the Pareto distribution, the higher the average wealth. $-(1 + \alpha)$ is the slope of the distribution function on the double-logarithmic scale. It is, therefore, intuitively clear that the more moderate the slope (smaller α) the more weight is

which is *not* a Pareto distribution.[12,13] ∎

The result of Theorem 2 can be directly generalized to the case of many subpopulations: in this case the wealth distribution *within* each subpopulation follows the Pareto law, but as each subpopulation is characterized by a different parameter α, the aggregate distribution is not Paretian.

Monte Carlo simulations can help illustrate the result of Theorem 2, and confirm that this result holds for the general case of many subpopulations. Figure 2 shows the wealth distribution in the two-population case, where the "normal" population faces the return process:

$$g_{\text{normal}}(\tilde{\lambda}): \quad \begin{array}{cc} \underline{\lambda} & \underline{\text{probability}} \\ 1.10 & 1/2 \\ 0.95 & 1/2 \end{array}$$

while the "smart" investors face the following superior return process:

$$g_{\text{smart}}(\tilde{\lambda}): \quad \begin{array}{cc} \underline{\lambda} & \underline{\text{probability}} \\ 1.11 & \frac{1}{2} \\ 0.96 & \frac{1}{2} \end{array}$$

Figure 2 shows that although the distribution of wealth within each subpopulation follows the Pareto law ($\alpha_{\text{normal}} = 1.67, \alpha_{\text{smart}} = 0.63$), the aggregate distribution (solid line) does not. This is evident from the convexity of the aggregate distribution, while a Pareto distribution should be linear on a double-logarithmic scale (see footnote 6). The same convex pattern that contradicts the

---

given to higher-wealth states. Formally:

$$E(W) = \int_{W_0}^{+\infty} P(W)W \, dW = C \int_{W_0}^{+\infty} W^{-(1+\alpha)}W \, dW = \frac{C}{(\alpha - 1)} W_0^{1-\alpha}.$$

(We assume $\alpha > 1$, otherwise $E(W)$ is infinite. Empirical values of α are typically in the range 1.2–1.6.) From the normalization condition $\int_{W_0}^{+\infty} P(W)dW = 1$ we obtain $C = \alpha W_0^\alpha$. Substituting in the above equation we obtain:

$$E(W) = W_0 \frac{\alpha}{(\alpha - 1)},$$

which is a monotonically decreasing function of α.

   [12]C_1 and C_2 replace C_{normal} and C_{smart} because the normalization constraints have changed, and depend on the relative proportions of the two subgroups, i.e.: $C_1 = \frac{N_{\text{normal}}}{N} C_{\text{normal}}; C_2 = \frac{N_{\text{smart}}}{N} C_{\text{smart}}$.

   [13]The wealth distribution given in eq. (11) is asymptotically Paretian, i.e., as $W \to \infty, P(W) \approx C_2 W^{-(1+\alpha_{\text{smart}})}$. Thus, it is approximately Paretian in the wealth range where the investor population is homogeneous (in the range where all the investors are "smart"). Hence, if we empirically observe that the wealth distribution is closely approximated by the Pareto distribution for the top 5% of the population, we may conclude that among these top 5% investment ability is homogeneous.

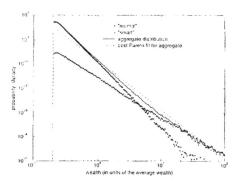

FIGURE 2 The wealth distribution with two different subpopulations. While the wealth distribution within each subpopulation is Paretian (circles and triangles). The aggregate distribution (solid line) is not. The straight dashed line is the best Pareto fit to the aggregate distribution.

Pareto distribution is also obtained in the general case with many investor subpopulations. Figure 3 depicts the steady-state wealth distribution in a market in which each investor faces a different return distribution. For all investors the return distribution $g_i(\tilde{\lambda})$ is taken as a normal distribution with a standard deviation of 20%. However, the mean of the distribution $g_i(\tilde{\lambda})$, μ_i, is different for each investor. We assume that μ is distributed normally in the population with a mean value of 10% and a standard deviation of 2%. Even though the distribution of talent is rather narrow (for 68% of the investors μ_i is in the range 8%–12%), the resulting distribution of wealth is clearly different than the Pareto distribution (see fig. 3). The Kolmogorov-Smirnov goodness-of-fit test confirms that one can safely reject the hypothesis that the generated distribution is Paretian. Comparing the cumulative distributions of the sample distribution with the best fit Pareto distribution (with 1000 investors) we obtain a D value of 0.310, which is much larger than the critical D value of 0.052 ($= 1.63/\sqrt{1000}$) needed in order to reject the hypothesis that the distribution is Paretian at a 99% confidence level.

While the Pareto wealth distribution cannot precisely hold in an inefficient market with differential investment ability, it can be consistent with some degree of market inefficiency (and differential investment ability) in the sense that the Pareto distribution cannot be statistically rejected. Levy and Levy [45] employ numerical analysis to show that the Pareto distribution cannot be statistically rejected if the annual average return across different investor subgroups is within approximately 1%. Thus, the empirically observed wealth distribution, which is very close to a Pareto distribution, does not imply a perfectly efficient market, but it does impose a rather tight upper bound on market inefficiency.

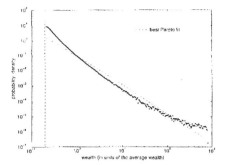

FIGURE 3   The wealth distribution in a non-homogeneous market with a continuum of investor types.

4   THE PARETO WEALTH DISTRIBUTION AND THE LÉVY DISTRIBUTION OF STOCK RETURNS

In this section we suggest that the Pareto wealth distribution can explain the Lévy distribution of short-term stock returns. We proceed with a brief review of the distribution of short-term stock returns. Our theoretical result regarding the distribution of stock returns and its relation to the wealth distribution is given in Theorem 3. This result has a surprising and testable prediction, which we empirically investigate in section 5.

4.1   THE LÉVY DISTRIBUTION OF STOCK RETURNS—REVIEW

It has long been known that the distributions of returns on stocks, especially when calculated for short time intervals, are not fitted well by the normal distribution. Rather, the distributions of stock returns are leptokurtic, or "fat tailed." Mandelbrot [52, 53] proposed an *exact functional form* for return distributions. To be specific, he has suggested that log-returns are distributed according to the symmetrical Lévy probability distribution defined by:

$$L_{\alpha_L}^\gamma(x) \equiv \frac{1}{\pi} \int_0^\infty \exp(-\gamma \Delta t q^{\alpha_L}) \cos(qx) dq \qquad (12)$$

where $L_{\alpha_L}^\gamma(x)$ is the Lévy probability density function at x, α_L is the characteristic exponent of the distribution, $\gamma \Delta t$ is a general scale factor, γ is the scale factor for $\Delta t = 1$, and q is an integration variable (for this formulation of the Lévy distribution see, for example, Mantegna and Stanley [57]).[14]

---

[14]This distribution is also known as the "stable-Paretian" distribution. In order to avoid confusion, we will use only the term "Lévy distribution" throughout this chapter.

Mandelbrot's pioneering work gained enthusiastic support in the first few years after its publication.[15] Subsequent works, however, have questioned the Lévy distribution hypothesis (Hsu, Miller and Wichern [33] and Joyce, Brorsen, and Irwin [38]), and this hypothesis has temporarily lost favor. In the 1990s the Lévy distribution hypothesis made a dramatic comeback. Recent extensive analysis of short-term returns has shown that price differences, log-returns, and rates of return[16] are described extremely well by a *truncated* Lévy distribution. This is not a sharp truncation in the usual mathematical sense, but rather, it describes a smooth fall-off of the empirical distribution from the Lévy distribution at some value (for a general picture of the empirical short-term rate of return distribution, see fig. 5). Mantegna and Stanley [57] analyze tick-by-tick data on the S&P 500 index and find excellent agreement with a Lévy distribution up to six standard deviations away from the mean (in both directions). For more extreme observations, the distribution they find falls off faster than the Lévy distribution.[17] Similar results have been found in the examination of the Milan Stock Exchange (Mantegna [55]), the CAC40 index (Zajdenweber [82]), individual French stocks (Belkacem [6]), and foreign exchange markets (Pictet and Muller [64], Guillaume et al. [31], and Cont, Potters, and Bouchaud [14]).

The revival of the (truncated) Lévy distribution awakens an old question: *Why are returns distributed in this very specific way?* Below we suggest that the answer may lie with the Pareto distribution of wealth.

4.2   THE PARETO WEALTH DISTRIBUTION AND THE LÉVY RETURN DISTRIBUTION

The Lévy distribution describes the distribution of returns in the short term. We therefore formulate the framework of our analysis in terms of the most "atomistic" return—a single trade return. Theorem 3 below shows that if investors' wealth is distributed according to the Pareto distribution, and if the effect of an investor's trade on the stock price is proportional (in a stochastic sense) to the investor's wealth, the short-term returns will be distributed according to the Lévy distribution. The assumption of proportionality between the investor's wealth and the price impact of the investor's trade seems natural: it is intuitive that the actions of an investor with $100 million will, on average, affect prices roughly ten times as much as the actions of a similar investor with only $10 mil-

---

[15]See Fama [17, 18, 19], Teichmoeller [78], and Officer [59]. Roll [67] extended the analysis from stocks to Treasury Bills. Fama and Roll [21, 22] developed methodologies in order to estimate the parameters of the Lévy distribution. Efficient portfolio selection in a market with Lévy distributions was analyzed by Fama [20] and Samuelson [68].

[16]Some studies examine the distribution of price differences, some of log-returns, and some of rates of return. As the focus is on short time intervals (a few seconds to a few days), all of the above are very closely related. See also the discussion in Appendix A.

[17]Several authors investigate this fall-off, and find it to be approximated by a power law with an exponent in the range 2-5 (see Jansen and de Vries [36], Longin [49], Gopikrishnan, Meyer, Amaral, and Stanley [30], Stanley et al. [74], and Cont [13]).

lion. This is also consistent with models of constant relative risk aversion, which imply that investors make decisions regarding *proportions* of their wealth (see, for example, Levy and Markowitz [43] and Samuelson [69]), and with the finding that the price impact of a trade is roughly proportional to the volume of the trade, especially for high-volume trades (see fig. 4 in Hausman, Lo, and MacKinlay [32]). To be more specific, if investors make decisions regarding proportions of their wealth, then the volume of a trade is (stochastically) proportional to the investor's wealth. If the effect of the trade on the price is proportional to the volume of the trade (as implied by market clearance in most models, and as documented by Lo and MacKinlay), then the effect that an investor's trade has on the price is (stochastically) proportional to the investor's wealth. We should stress we do not make any assumptions regarding the investors' reason for trading: it can be due to the arrival of new information, liquidity constraints, portfolio rebalancing, etc.

Theorem 3: *If the wealth of investors is distributed according to the Pareto law with exponent α_W, and the effect of each investor's trade on the price is stochastically proportional to the investor's wealth, then the resulting return distribution (and the price-change distribution) is given by the Lévy distribution with an exponent $\alpha_L = \alpha_W$.*

Proof: See Appendix A.

Theorem 3 not only suggests an explanation for the Lévy distribution of returns, but it also makes a surprising prediction: the exponent of the Lévy return distribution, α_L, should be equal to the Pareto wealth distribution constant, α_W. This prediction is surprising, because these two parameters are associated with different research arenas, and seem to be *a priori* unrelated. In the next section we test this prediction empirically.

5 EMPIRICAL EVIDENCE

In this section we empirically estimate and compare α_L and α_W for three countries: the U.S., the U.K., and France.

5.1 ESTIMATION OF α_L

For the estimation of α_L we follow the methodology used by Mantegna and Stanley [57]. They denote the density of the symmetric Lévy distribution eq. (12) at 0 by p_0, and employ the relation below in order to estimate α_L:

$$p_0 \equiv L_{\alpha_L}^{\gamma}(0) = \frac{\Gamma(1/\alpha_L)}{\pi\alpha_L(\gamma\Delta t)^{1/\alpha_L}} \tag{13}$$

where Γ is the Gamma function, Δt is the horizon for which rates of return are being calculated, and γ is the scale factor for $\Delta t = 1$ (for proof of the relationship (13) see Appendix B). Thus, the probability density at 0 decays as $\Delta t^{-1/\alpha_L}$. Mantegna and Stanley estimate the density at $0, p_0$, for various time intervals, Δt. In order to estimate α_L they run the regression:

$$\log[p_0(\Delta t)]_i = A + B \log[\Delta t]_i \varepsilon_i \qquad (14)$$

and estimate α_L as $-1/\hat{B}$. We employ the same technique here. Our data set consists of:

S&P 500: all 1,780,752 records of the index between 1990-1995, obtained from the Chicago Mercantile Exchange;

FTSE 100: all 75,606 records of the index between January 1997 and August 1997, obtained from the Futures Industry Institute; and

CAC 40: all 234,501 records of the index in 1996, obtained from the Bourse de Paris.

Following Mantegna and Stanley, for each of these series we estimate the density $p_0(\Delta t)$ by going over the entire data set and calculating the rates of return for all intervals of Δt. We count the number of rates of return within the range $[-0.0001, 0.0001]$ and divide this number by the total number of observations in order to get the probability of rate of return in this range.[18] Then we divide the result by the size of the range, 0.0002, in order to get the probability density at $0, p_0$. We repeat this procedure for different sampling time intervals Δt. The values of p_0 as a function of Δt are reported in figures 4, 6, and 7. In order to obtain an estimate of α_L, we employ the regression in eq. (14). For the S&P 500 we obtain $\alpha_L = 1.37$ (fig. 4). The standard error of this estimation is 0.04, and the correlation coefficient is -0.987. This estimated value that we find for α_L is very close to the value of 1.40 reported by Mantegna and Stanley [57] for the S&P 500, during the sample period 1984-89.

In order to verify that the empirical rate of return distribution is indeed well fitted by the symmetric Lévy distribution with the estimated α_L of 1.37, we compare these two distributions in figure 5. The empirical distribution is calculated for 1-minute rates of return, and the plot is semi-logarithmic.[19] Figure 5 shows an excellent agreement between the empirical and theoretical distributions up to rates of return on the order of 0.001 (or 0.1%), which are about six standard deviations away from the mean.[20] For more extreme returns, the empirical distribution falls off from the Lévy distribution. This is the so-called truncation, which will be discussed below.[21]

---

[18]Similar estimations of α_L are obtained for different choices of small ranges around 0.

[19]The empirical distribution is estimated by a non-parametric density estimate with a Gaussian kernel and the "normal reference rule" (see Scott [70, p. 131]).

[20]The standard deviation of the 1-minute rate of return distribution for the period 1990-1995 is approximately 0.00016 or 0.016%.

[21]It is interesting to note the secondary peak of the empirical distribution at a rate of return of about -0.001. A similar bimodal distribution was observed by Jackwerth and

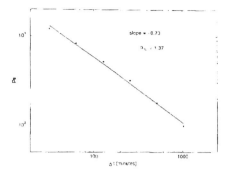

FIGURE 4   The density of the S&P 500 return distribution at 0 as a function of return interval Δt.

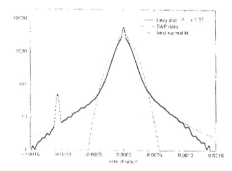

FIGURE 5   The S&P 500 1-minute rate of return distribution. Notice that the vertical axis is logarithmic. The parabola is the best normal fit to the empirical data. The solid line is the Lévy distribution with $\alpha_L = 1.37$, as estimated in figure 4.

For the FTSE 100 we find $\alpha_L = 1.08$ (fig. 6). The standard error of this estimation is 0.03, the correlation coefficient is -0.996, and the t-value is -59.7. This number is close to the α_L value of 1.10 which is calculated from the 1993 FTSE 100 data reported by Abhyankar, Copeland, and Wong [1].

For the CAC 40 we find $\alpha_L = 1.82$ (fig. 7). The standard error of this estimation is 0.05, the correlation coefficient is -0.978, and the t-value is -35.9.

Rubinstein [35]. We do not have an explanation for this phenomenon in the framework of the present model.

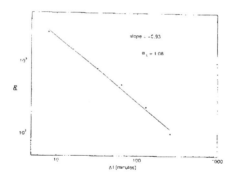

FIGURE 6   The density of the FTSE 100 return distribution at 0 as a function of return interval Δt.

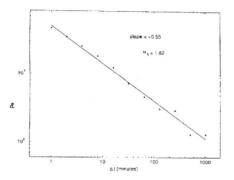

FIGURE 7   The density of the CAC 40 return distribution at 0 as a function of return interval Δt.

5.2   ESTIMATION OF α_W

Estimating the Pareto wealth distribution exponent α_W requires data regarding the "right-tail" of the distribution, that is, data about the wealth of the wealthiest individuals. The French almanac *Quid* provides wealth data on the top 162,370 individuals in France. This data is in aggregate form, in other words, the numbers of individuals with wealth exceeding certain wealth levels are reported. According to the Pareto law (eq. (1)), the number of individuals with wealth exceeding a certain level W_x should be proportional to $W_x^{-\alpha_W}$:

$$N(W > W_x) = N \int_{W_x}^{\infty} f(W)dW = NC \int_{W_x}^{\infty} W^{-(1+\alpha_W)}dW = \frac{NC}{\alpha_W}W_x^{-\alpha_W} \quad (15)$$

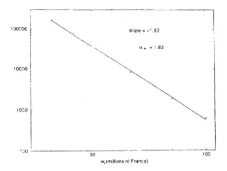

FIGURE 8   Wealth distribution in France. Regression (16) yields correlation of -0.999, and implies $\alpha_W = 1.83$.

where $N(W > W_x)$ is the number of individuals with wealth exceeding W_x, and N is the total number of individuals. If the Pareto distribution is valid, one expects that when plotting $N(W > W_x)$ as a function of W_x on a double-logarithmic graph, the data points should fall on a straight line with slope $-\alpha_W$. Figure 8 is a double logarithmic plot of $N(W > W_x)$ as a function of W_x for the French data provided by *Quid*. This figure shows an excellent agreement between the empirical wealth distribution and the Pareto law. In order to estimate α_W for France, we run the regression:

$$\log[N(W > W_x)] = A + B \log[W_x]_i + \varepsilon_i . \tag{16}$$

The absolute value of the slope of the regression line, which is the estimate for α_W, is 1.83 (standard error = 0.03, correlation coefficient = -0.999 t-value = -59.5).

For the U.S. and the U.K. the available data regarding the wealthiest people is more detailed but also more limited in scope. For these countries, lists with the ranking and wealth of several hundred of the wealthiest individuals are published. We use the methods suggested by Levy and Solomon [46] in order to estimate α_W from these data. A Pareto law distribution of wealth with exponent α_W implies the following relation between the rank of an individual in the wealth hierarchy and her wealth:

$$W(n) = An^{-1/\alpha_W} , \tag{17}$$

where n is the rank (by wealth), and W is the wealth. The constant A is given by $A = (\alpha_W/NC)^{-1/\alpha_W}$, where N is the total number of individuals in the population, and C is the normalization constant from eq. (1) (for a mathematical derivation of this relationship see Johnson and Kotz [37]).

For the U.S. we obtain data from the 1997 Forbes 400 list. Wealth as a function of rank is plotted in double logarithmic form in figure 9. Running the

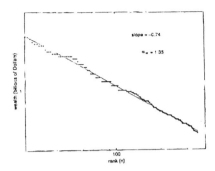

FIGURE 9   Wealth distribution in the U.S.—wealth vs. rank. Regression (18) yields $1/\alpha_W = 0.74$, or $\alpha_W = 1.35$.

TABLE 1   Summary of the empirical results. The table provides the values of the Lévy rate of return distribution exponent, α_L, and the Pareto wealth distribution exponent, α_W, as empirically estimated for the U.S. and U.K. and France (and the standard errors for these figures).

	α_L	α_W
U.S.	1.37 ± 0.04	1.35 ± 0.005
U.K.	1.08 ± 0.03	1.06 ± 0.004
France	1.82 ± 0.05	1.83 ± 0.030

regression:

$$\log[W(n)]_i = A + B \log[n]_i + \varepsilon_i \tag{18}$$

we estimate the slope of the regression as -0.74. This is the estimation of $-1/\alpha_W$, and it corresponds to an estimation of $\alpha_W = 1.35$ for the U.S. The standard error of this estimation is 0.005. We would like to clarify that we do not assume that only the wealthiest 400 individuals determine the S&P rate of return distribution. Rather, we use the data that we are able to obtain in order to estimate the Pareto constant for the entire upper wealth range. Our estimation of $\alpha_W = 1.35$ for the U.S., is close to the estimate of $1.35 \leq \alpha_W \leq 1.42$ which is obtained by the data provided by Wolff [81] regarding the percentage of wealth held by the top 1%, 5%, and 10% of the population (see appendix C).v

For the U.K. we obtain data from the *Sunday Times* "Rich List" [76]. The data are plotted in Figure 10. We obtain a slope of -0.94 which corresponds to a value of $1/0.94 = 1.06$ for α_W (standard error 0.004).

The summary of our empirical results appears in table 1. This evidence shows a striking agreement between the values of (the *a priori* unrelated) α_W and α_L for the three countries investigated.

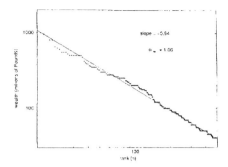

FIGURE 10   Wealth distribution in the U.K.—wealth vs. rank. Regression (18) yields $1/\alpha_W = 0.94$, or $\alpha_W = 1.06$.

6   CONCLUDING REMARKS

The process of wealth accumulation by capital investment is stochastic and multiplicative by nature. This chapter shows that homogeneous stochastic processes lead to a Pareto wealth distribution. Thus, the Pareto wealth distribution, and the rather extreme inequality which it implies, is a fundamental and robust outcome of the nature of the capital investment process. Non-homogeneous processes, in which investors have differential investment abilities, lead to a wealth distribution which is different than the Pareto distribution. Thus, the Pareto distribution implies that chance, rather than differential investment ability, is the main source of inequality at the high-wealth range.

The Pareto distribution is closely related to market efficiency. A precise Pareto distribution implies market efficiency. In practice, some degree of market inefficiency can be consistent with the Pareto distribution, in the sense that the resulting distribution cannot be statistically rejected. However, the Pareto distribution does impose a rather tight upper bound on market inefficiency. The closer the wealth distribution to the Pareto distribution, the smaller the tolerable level of market inefficiency.

The Pareto wealth distribution can also explain the (truncated) Lévy distribution of short-term returns, a phenomenon which has puzzled researchers for many years. Our theoretical analysis links between two different research arenas: the distribution of wealth, which is a central issue in economics, and the distribution of stock returns, which plays an important role in finance. The analysis leads to a surprising prediction: the Pareto exponent α_W should be equal to α_L, the exponent of the Lévy return distribution. Empirical evidence from the U.S., the U.K., and France reveals a striking agreement between these *a priori* unrelated parameters (U.S.: $\alpha_L = 1.37$, $\alpha_W = 1.35$; U.K.: $\alpha_L = 1.08$, $\alpha_W = 1.06$; France: $\alpha_L = 1.82$, $\alpha_W = 1.83$).

7 ACKNOWLEDGMENTS

I am grateful to Tony Bernardo, Michael Brennan, Doyne Farmer, Haim Levy, Victor Ríos-Rull, Richard Roll, Eduardo Schwartz, Joel Slemrod, Sorin Solomon, Gene Stanley, Ed Wolff, and participants of the third conference on The Economy as an Evolving Complex System for their helpful comments and suggestions. This study has been financially supported by the Zagagi Fund.

APPENDIX A: PROOF OF THEOREM 3

Theorem 3: *If the wealth of investors is distributed according to the Pareto law with exponent α_W, and the effect of each investor's trade on the price is stochastically proportional to the investor's wealth, then the resulting price-change (and return) distribution is given by the Lévy distribution with an exponent $\alpha_L = \alpha_W$.*

Proof: Suppose a single investor is drawn at random to trade with a market maker, and that the effect of the investor on the price is (stochastically) proportional to the investor's wealth. We first prove that in this case a Pareto wealth distribution leads to a Lévy price-change distribution. Then this result is extended to the return distribution, and to the case of a stochastic number of investors trading at each period.

Let us denote the single-trade price change at period t as z_t. z_t is given by:

$$\tilde{z}_t = \tilde{q}_t \tilde{W}_t\,, \tag{19}$$

where $\tilde{W}_t$ is the wealth of the investor randomly chosen to trade at time t, and $\tilde{q}_t$ is a stochastic proportionality factor which is uncorrelated with $\tilde{W}_t$, and which is distributed according to some probability density function $h(\tilde{q})$. In what follows, we derive the distribution for single-trade price changes, and the price change distribution which results from a larger number of trades.

When analyzing the probability of single-trade price changes it is convenient to separate the discussion to the case of positive price changes ($z > 0$), and negative price changes ($z < 0$). The probability of obtaining a positive single-trade price change which is smaller or equal to a certain value $z(z > 0)$ is given by:

$$G(z) = \int_{-\infty}^{\infty} h(q) F\left(\frac{z}{q}\right) dq\,, \qquad \text{for } z > 0\,, \tag{20}$$

where $G(z)$ and $F(z/q)$ are the cumulative distributions of $\tilde{z}$ and $\tilde{W}$, respectively. Thus, the density function of z is given by:

$$g(z) = \int_{-\infty}^{\infty} h(q) f\left(\frac{z}{q}\right) \frac{1}{q} dq\,, \qquad \text{for } z > 0\,. \tag{21}$$

Since we are dealing with the case $z > 0$, and since the Pareto density function $f(W)$ is non-zero only for $W > W_0$, the contribution to the integral in eq. (21) is only for values of q such that $z/q > W_0$. Thus, the contribution is non-zero only for $0 < q < z/W_0$ (if $q < 0$ then $z/q < 0$ and $f(z/q) = 0$; if $q > z/W_0$ then $z/q < W_0$ and again $f(z/q) = 0$). Hence, eq. (21) can be written as:

$$g(z) = \int_0^{\frac{z}{W_0}} h(q) f\left(\frac{z}{q}\right) \frac{1}{q} dq, \qquad \text{for } z > 0. \tag{22}$$

Similarly, for negative price changes ($z < 0$) we obtain[22]:

$$g(z) = \int_{z/W_0}^0 h(q) f\left(\frac{z}{q}\right) \frac{-1}{q} dq, \qquad \text{for } z < 0. \tag{23}$$

Combining eqs. (22) and (23), and employing the Pareto wealth distribution (eq. (1)) for f, we obtain:

$$g(z) = \begin{cases} z > 0 & z^{-(1+\alpha_W)} C \int_0^{z/W_0} h(q) \left(\frac{1}{q}\right)^{-\alpha_W} dq \\ z < 0 & |z|^{-(1+\alpha_W)} C \int_{z/W_0}^0 h(q) \left(-\frac{1}{q}\right)^{-\alpha_W} dq \end{cases}. \tag{24}$$

The important property of $g(z)$ is that it is asymptotically Paretian. Namely, as $z \to \infty$ $g(z) \to D_1 z^{-(1+\alpha_W)}$, and as $z \to -\infty$ $g(z) \to D_2 |z|^{-(1+\alpha_W)}$, where D_1 and D_2 are given by:

$$D_1 = C \int_0^\infty h(q) \left(\frac{1}{q}\right)^{-\alpha_W} dq, \, D_2 = C \int_{-\infty}^0 h(q) \left(-\frac{1}{q}\right)^{-\alpha_W} dq. \tag{25}$$

(Asymptotically Paretian distributions are distributions that have power-law "tails," see, for example, Fama [19, p. 423].)

Thus, the single-trade price-change distribution generated by a market in which investors' wealth is distributed according to the Pareto law with exponent α_W is asymptotically Paretian with the same exponent α_W. The price change after n single trades is simply the sum of these single-trade price changes. The Doblin-Gnedenko result states that the sum of many iid random variables which are asymptotically Paretian with some exponent α converges to a Lévy distribution with characteristic exponent α (Gnedenko and Kolmogorov [29], Fama [18, 19], Feller [23]). Thus, the distribution of the total price change, which is the sum of many single-trade price changes, converges to the Lévy distribution. Moreover, since the single-trade price changes are asymptotically Paretian with the same exponent as the Pareto-law wealth exponent α_W, by the Doblin-Gnedenko result the price-change Lévy distribution will be characterized by the same exponent, that is, $\alpha_L = \alpha_W$. ∎

---

[22]For $z < 0$ we have $G(z) = \int_{-\infty}^\infty h(q)(1 - F(z/q)) dq$ and therefore $g(z) = \int_{-\infty}^\infty h(q) f(z/q)(-1/q) dq$, and the only non-zero contribution to the integral is for values of q in the range $z/W_0 < q < 0$.

Similar considerations to those discussed in Theorem 3 lead to a Lévy distribution with $\alpha_L = \alpha_W$ for rates of return and for log-returns as well for price changes. If the price remains at a fairly constant level during the sample period, it is straightforward that a Lévy price-change distribution implies a Lévy rate of return distribution: since the rate of return is just the price change divided by the price, if the price level is fairly constant, the rate of return is just the price change divided by an (almost) constant number, and, therefore, if price changes are distributed according to the Lévy distribution, so are rates of return. This result can also be extended to the case where the price does change considerably over the sample period, if one also takes into account the effect of the price level on the average wealth.

Extension: Variable Trading Frequency. In the preceding Theorem 3 we have assumed that at time period t only one investor is chosen to trade with the market-maker. This assumption can be relaxed to allow for a stochastic number of investors to trade at each time period. The stochastic price change due to the effect of a single trade is given by:

$$\tilde{z} = \tilde{q}W \, .$$

In Theorem 3 it was shown that $g(z)$, the probability density function of z, is asymptotically Paretian with exponent α_W. Let us denote the sum of m iid random variables z by S_m: $S_m \equiv z^1 + z^2 + \ldots + z^m$. Notice that because the z's are asymptotically Paretian with exponent α_W, so is their sum S_m (Gnedenko and Kolmogorov [29]). Let us denote the density function of S_m by k_m. The number of trades taking place at a given time period is a discrete random variable which we denote by $\tilde{m}$:

$$\tilde{m} = \begin{cases} & \text{probability} \\ 1, & \pi_1 \\ 2, & \pi_2 \\ \vdots & \vdots \\ m, & \pi_\infty \\ \vdots & \vdots \end{cases} \tag{26}$$

The probability density function of an aggregate price change z_t at time period t is given by:

$$g(z_t) = \sum_{m=1}^{\infty} \pi_m k_m(z_t) \tag{27}$$

where m is the number of trades, $k_m(z_t)$ is the density function of S_m at z_t, and the summation is over all possible numbers of trades in a single time period. As the k_m's are asymptotically Paretian distributions with an exponent α_W, so is $g(z_t)$, their weighted average. (To see this, note that if $k_i(z_t) \to d_i z_t^{-(1+\alpha_w)}$ as $z_t \to \infty$, and $k_j(z_t) \to d_j z_t^{-(1+\alpha_w)}$ as $z_t \to \infty$ then $\pi_i k_i(z_t) + \pi_j k_j(z_t) \longrightarrow$

$(\pi_i d_i + \pi_j d_j)z_t^{-(1+\alpha_w)}$ as $z_t \to \infty$, which implies that the weighted average is also asymptotically Paretian.)

As the z_t's have been shown to be asymptotically Paretian with exponent α_W even if the number of trades per period is stochastic, according to the Doblin-Gnedenko result, for a large number of trades, the price-change distribution converges to the Lévy distribution with the same exponent α_W, which is the Pareto constant of the wealth distribution. Thus, the result of the model is robust to a stochastic number of trades at each time period.

APPENDIX B: DERIVATION OF THE LÉVY PROBABILITY DENSITY FUNCTION AT 0

Denote the value of the Lévy p.d.f at 0 by p_0.

Lemma:

$$p_0 \equiv L_{\alpha_L}^{\gamma}(0) = \frac{\Gamma(1/\alpha_L)}{\pi \alpha_L (\gamma \Delta t)^{1/\alpha_L}} \tag{28}$$

Proof: From the definition of $L_{\alpha_L}^{\gamma}(x)$ in eq. (12):

$$L_{\alpha_L}^{\gamma}(0) = \frac{1}{\pi} \int_0^{\infty} \exp(-\gamma \Delta t q^{\alpha_L}) \cos(q \times 0) dq = \frac{1}{\pi} \int_0^{\infty} \exp(-\gamma \Delta t q^{\alpha_L}) dq. \tag{29}$$

Define a new variable $u = \gamma \Delta t q^{\alpha_L}$, and note that $dq = \alpha_L^{-1}(\gamma \Delta t)^{-\frac{1}{\alpha_L}} u^{\left(\frac{1}{\alpha_L}-1\right)} du$. Substituting in eq. (29) we obtain:

$$L_{\alpha_L}^{\gamma}(0) = \frac{1}{\pi \alpha_L (\gamma \Delta t)^{\frac{1}{\alpha_L}}} \int_0^{\infty} \exp(-u) u^{\left(\frac{1}{\alpha_L}-1\right)} du. \tag{30}$$

Recalling that the integral is the definition of $\Gamma(1/\alpha_L)$ we have:

$$L_{\alpha_L}^{\gamma}(0) = \frac{\Gamma(1/\alpha_L)}{\pi \alpha_L (\gamma \Delta t)^{1/\alpha_L}}. \tag{31}$$

APPENDIX C: ALTERNATIVE ESTIMATE OF THE PARETO CONSTANT α_W FOR THE U.S.

Wolff's [81] findings regarding the holdings of the top 1%, top 5%, and top 10% of the U.S. population in 1992 are reported in table 2 below:

In this table, P_k denotes the percentage of total wealth held by the top k percent of the population. A Pareto-law wealth distribution with exponent α_W implies the following relationship for any two k's:

$$\frac{P_{k_1}}{P_{k_2}} = \left(\frac{k_1}{k_2}\right)^{1-\frac{1}{\alpha_W}}. \tag{32}$$

TABLE 2   The percent of total wealth held by the top 1%, 5%, and 10% of the population in the U.S. (Adapted from Wolff [81].)

k	P_k
1%	37.2%
5%	60.0%
10%	71.8%

(See proof below.) Employing this relationship we can estimate α_W for the U.S. by using the data in table 2. By comparing the holdings of the top 1% with the holdings of the top 5% we obtain:

$$\frac{0.372}{0.600} = \left(\frac{0.01}{0.05}\right)^{1-\frac{1}{\alpha_W}} \tag{33}$$

which yields $\alpha_W = 1.42$. A similar comparison of the holdings of the top 1% with the holdings of the top 10% yields $\alpha_W = 1.42$. Comparing the holdings of the top 5% with the holdings of the top 10% yields $\alpha_W = 1.35$.

Lemma: *A Pareto-law wealth distribution with exponent α_W implies the following relationship for any two k's:*

$$\frac{P_{k_1}}{P_{k_2}} = \left(\frac{k_1}{k_2}\right)^{1-\frac{1}{\alpha_W}} . \tag{34}$$

Proof: Assuming the Pareto law (eq. (1)), the number of individuals with wealth exceeding W is given by:

$$n(W) = N \int_W^\infty f(x)dx = NC \int_W^\infty x^{-(1+\alpha_W)} = \frac{NC}{\alpha_W} W^{-\alpha_W} , \tag{35}$$

where N is the total number of individuals. This number of individuals corresponds to a proportion $k = (n(W)/N) = (C/\alpha_W)W_k^{-\alpha_w}$ of the population. The above result can be restated in the following way. The wealth of the poorest individual in the top k% of the population is given by:

$$W_k = \left(\frac{k\alpha_W}{C}\right)^{-\frac{1}{\alpha_W}} \tag{36}$$

(where k is expressed as a proportion, i.e., $0 \leq k \leq 1$). The aggregate wealth held by the top k% of the population is given by:

$$N \int_{W_k}^\infty f(W)WdW = NC \int_{W_k}^\infty W^{-(1+\alpha_W)}WdW = \frac{NC}{\alpha_W - 1} W_k^{1-\alpha_W} \tag{37}$$

$$= \left(\frac{NC^{1/\alpha_W}}{\alpha_W - 1} \right) \alpha_W^{(1 - \frac{1}{\alpha_W})} k^{(1 - \frac{1}{\alpha_W})}, \tag{38}$$

where the last equality is obtained by substituting W_k from eq. (33). The *percentage* of wealth held by the top $k\%$ of the population is:

$$P_k = \frac{1}{W_{\text{total}}} \left(\frac{NC^{1/\alpha_W}}{\alpha_W - 1} \right) \alpha_W^{(1 - \frac{1}{\alpha_W})} k^{(1 - \frac{1}{\alpha_W})}, \tag{39}$$

where W_{total} is the total wealth of all the population. Comparing the percentage of wealth held by the top $k_1\%$ of the population, with the percentage of wealth held by the top $k_2\%$ of the population, we obtain:

$$\frac{P_{k_1}}{P_{k_2}} = \left(\frac{k_1}{k_2} \right)^{1 - \frac{1}{\alpha_W}}. \tag{40}$$

Note: In the above proof we have assumed that the Pareto wealth distribution holds for all wealth levels. However, it is straightforward to show that the above result is also valid if one assumes a Pareto distribution in the high-wealth range but a different wealth distribution in the low-wealth range (as long as the k's are in the high-wealth range, in which the Pareto wealth distribution holds).

REFERENCES

[1] Abhyankar, A., L. S. Copeland, and W. Wong. "Nonlinear Dynamics in Real-Time Equity Market Indices: Evidence From the United Kingdom." *Econ. J.* **105** (1995): 864–880.

[2] Aiyagari, S. R. "Uninsured Idiosyncratic Risk and Aggregate Saving." *Quart. J. Econ.* **109** (1994): 659–684.

[3] Arnold, B. C. *Pareto Distributions.* Maryland: International Co-operative Publishing House, 1983.

[4] Atkinson, A. B., and A. J. Harrison. *Distribution of Total Wealth in Britain.* Cambridge, MA: Cambridge University Press, 1978.

[5] Auerbach, A. J., and L. J. Kotlikoff. *Dynamic Fiscal Policy.* New York: Cambridge University Press, 1987.

[6] Belkacem, L. *Processus Stables et Applications en Finance.* Thése de Doctorat, Université Paris IX, 1996.

[7] Blinder, A. S. *Towards an Economic Theory of Income Distribution.* Cambridge, MA: The MIT Press, 1974.

[8] Boissevain, C. H. "Distribution of Abilities Depending on Two or More Independent Factors." *Metron* **13** (1939) 49–58.

[9] Boltzmann, L. *Lectures on Gas Theory.* Berkeley, CA: University of California Press, 1964.

[10] Castaneda, A., J. Díaz-Giménez, and J. V. Ríos-Rull. "Unemployment Spells, Cyclically Moving Factor Shares and Income Distribution Dynamics." Manuscript, Federal Reserve Bank of Minneapolis, 1997.

[11] Champernowne, D. G. "A Model of Income Distribution." *Econ. J.* **63** (1953): 318–351.

[12] Choquet, G. "Le théoreme de representation integrale dans les ensembles convees compacts." *Ann. Inst. Fourier* **10** (1960): 333.

[13] Cont, R. "Empirical Properties of Asset Returns: Stylized Facts and Statistical Issues." *Quant. Fin.* **1** (2001): 223–236.

[14] Cont, R., M. Potters, and J. P. Bouchaud. "Scaling in Stock Market Prices: Stable Laws and Beyond." Working Paper 97-02, Science and Finance Research Group, 1997.

[15] Davis, H. "The Analysis of Economic Time Series." San Antonio: The Principia Press of Trinity University, 1963. Originally as monograph No. 6 of the Cowles Commission for Research in Economics, 1941.

[16] Díaz-Giménez, J., V. Quadrini, and J. V. Ríos-Rull. "Dimensions of Inequality: Facts on the U.S. Distributions of Earnings, Income, and Wealth." *Quart. Rev. Fed. Res. Bank of Minneapolis* **21(2)** (1997): 3–21.

[17] Fama, E. F. "The Behavior of Stock Prices." *J. Bus.* **38(1)** (1965): 34–105.

[18] Fama, E. F. "The Distribution of the Daily First Differences of Stock Prices: A Test of Mandelbrot's Stable Paretian Hypothesis." Unpublished Ph.D. diss., University of Chicago, 1963.

[19] Fama, E. F. "Mandelbrot and the Stable Paretian Hypothesis." *J. Bus.* **36** (1963): 4.

[20] Fama, E. F. "Portfolio Analysis in a Stable Paretian Market." *Mgmt. Sci.* **2** (1965): 3.

[21] Fama, E. F., and R. Roll. "Parameter Estimates for Symmetric Stable Distributions." *J. Am. Stat. Assoc.* **66** (1971): 331–338.

[22] Fama, E. F., and R. Roll. "Some Properties of Symmetric Stable Distributions." *J. Am. Stat. Assoc.* **63** (1968): 817–836.

[23] Feller, W. *An Introduction to Probability Theory and Its Applications*, vol. 2, 2d ed. New York: Wiley, 1971.

[24] Feynman, R. P., R. B. Leighton, and M. Sands. *The Feynman Lectures on Physics*, vol. 1. Reading MA: Addison Wesley, 1964.

[25] *Forbes*. Special 400 List Issue, October 13, 1997.

[26] Fremy, D., ed. *QUID*. Paris: RTL, 1998.

[27] Furstenberg, H. *Bull. Am. Math. Soc.* **71** (1965): 271–326.

[28] Gabaix, X. "Zipf's Law for Cities: An Explanation." *Quart. J. Econ.* (1999): 739–767.

[29] Gnedenko, B. V., and A. N. Kolmogorov. *Limit Distributions for Sums of Independent Variables*, ch. 7. Translated by K. L. Chung. Cambridge, MA: Addison-Wesley, 1954.

[30] Gopikrishnan, P., M. Meyer, L. A. N. Amaral, and H. E. Stanley. "Inverse Cubic Law for the Probability Distribution of Stock Price Variations." *Europ. J. Phys. B* **3** (1998): 139–140.

[31] Guillaume, D. M., M. M. Dacorogna, R. D. Davé, U. A. Müller, R. .B. Olsen, and O. V. Pictet. "From the Bird's Eye to the Microscope: A Survey of New Stylized Facts of the Intra-daily Foreign Exchange Markets." *Fin. & Stoc.* **1** (1997): 95–129.

[32] Hausman, J. A., A. W. Lo, and A. C. MacKinlay. "An Ordered Probit Analysis of Transaction Stock Prices." *J. Fin. Econ.* **31(3)** (1992): 319–379.

[33] Hsu, D. A., R. B. Miller, and D. W. Wichern. "On the Stable Paretian Behavior of Stock-Market Prices." *J. Am. Stat. Assoc.* **68** (1974): 34.

[34] Huggett, M. "Wealth Distribution in Life-Cycle Economies." *J. Monetary Econ.* **38** (1996): 953–969.

[35] Jackwerth, J. C., and M. Rubinstein. "Recovering Probability Distributions from Option Prices." *J. Fin.* **51(5)** (1996): 1611–1632.

[36] Jansen, D. W., and C. G. de Vries. "On the Frequency of Large Stock Returns: Putting Booms and Busts into Perspective." *Rev. Econ. & Stat.* **73** (1991): 18–24.

[37] Johnson, N. L., and S. Kotz. *Continuous Univariate Distributions - 1*. New York: John Wiley and Sons, 1970.

[38] Joyce, H. A., W. Brorsen, and S. H. Irwin. "The Distribution of Futures Prices: A Test of the Stable Paretian and Mixture of Normals Hypotheses." *J. Fin. & Quant. Analysis* **24** (1989): 1.

[39] Kesten, H. "Random Difference Equations and Renewal Theory for Products of Random Matrices." *Acta Mathematica* **81** (1973): 207–248.

[40] Krusell, P., and A. A. Smith. "Income and Wealth Heterogeneity in the Macroeconomy." *J. Pol. Econ.* **106(5)** (1998): 867–896.

[41] Latané, H. E. "Criteria for Choice Among Risky Ventures." *J. Pol. Econ.* **LVII** (1959): 144–155.

[42] Leshno, M., and H. Levy. "Almost Stochastic Dominance." *Mgmt. Sci.* **48(8)** (2002): 1074–1085.

[43] Levy, H., and H. M. Markowitz. "Approximating Expected Utility by a Function of Mean and Variance." *Am. Econ. Rev.* **69(3)** (1979): 308–317.

[44] Levy, M. "Are Rich People Smarter?" *J. Econ. Theor.* **110** (2003): 42–64.

[45] Levy, M., and H. Levy. "Investment Talent and the Pareto Wealth Distribution: Theoretical and Experimental Analysis." *Rev. Econ. Stat.* **85(3)** (2003): 709–725.

[46] Levy, M., and S. Solomon. "New Evidence for the Power-Law Distribution of Wealth." *Physica A* **242** (1997): 90–94.

[47] Levy, M., and S. Solomon. "Power Laws are Logarithmic Boltzmann Laws." *Int'l. J. Mod. Phys. C* **7** (1996): 65–72.

[48] Lévy, P. *Calcul des Probabilitiés*, part II, ch. 6. Paris: Gauthier Villars, 1925.

[49] Longin, F. "The Asymptotic Distribution of Extreme Stock Market Returns." *J. Bus.* **63** (1996): 383–408.

[50] Loomis, L., "Unique Direct Integral Decompositions on Convex Sets." *Am. J. Math.* **84** (1962): 509–526.

[51] Mandelbrot, B. *Fractals and Scaling in Finance: Discontinuity, Concentration, and Risk.* New York: Springer-Verlag, 1997.

[52] Mandelbrot, B. "New Methods in Statistical Economics." *J. Pol. Econ.* **61** (1963): 421–440.

[53] Mandelbrot, B. "The Variation of Certain Speculative Prices." *J. Bus.* **36** (1963): 4.

[54] Mankiw, N. G., and S. P. Zeldes. "The Consumption of Stockholders and Nonstockholders." *J. Fin. Econ.* **29** (1991): 131–135.

[55] Mantegna, R. N. "Lévy Walks and Enhanced Diffusion in the Milan Stock Exchange." *Physica A* **179** (1991).

[56] Mantegna, R. N., and H. E. Stanley. "Stochastic Process with Ultraslow Convergence to a Gaussiaan: The Truncated Lévy Flight." *Phys. Rev. Lett.* **73** (1994): 2946–2949.

[57] Mantegna, R. N., and H. E. Stanley. "Scaling Behavior in the Dynamics of an Economic Index." *Nature* **376** (1995): 46–49.

[58] Markowitz, H. "Investment for the Long Run: New Evidence for an Old Rule." *J. Fin.* **31** (1976): 1273–1286.

[59] Officer, R. R. "The Distribution of Stock Returns." *J. Am. Stat. Assoc.* **67** (1972): 340.

[60] Pareto, V. *Cours d'Economique Politique*, vol 2, 1897. Also see: *Manual of Political Economy.* New York: Augustus M. Kelley, 1971. Translated from the original 1906 *Manuale d'Economia Politica.*

[61] Pareto, V. *Manual of Political Economy.* New York: Augustus M. Kelley, 1971. Translated from the original 1906 *Manuale d'Economia Politica.*

[62] Pedrosa, M., and R. Roll. "Systematic Risk in Corporate Bond Credit Spreads." *J. Fixed Income* **8** (1998): 7–26.

[63] Persky, J. "Retrospectives: Pareto's Law." *J. Econ. Perspectives* **6** (1992): 181–192.

[64] Pictet, O. V., and U. A. Muller. "Statistical Study of Foreign Exchange Rates, Empirical Evidence of a Price Change Scaling Law and Intra-day Analysis." *J. Bank. & Fin.* **14** (1995): 1189–1208.

[65] Quadrini, V., and J. V. Ríos-Rull. "Understanding the U.S. Distribution of Wealth." *Quart. Rev. Fed. Reserve Bank of Minneapolis* **21(2)** (1997): 22–36.

[66] Ríos-Rull, J. V. "Models with Heterogeneous Agents." In *Frontiers of Business Cycle Research*, edited by T. F. Cooley, 98–125. Princeton, NJ: Princeton University Press, 1995.

[67] Roll, R. "The Efficient Market Model Applied to U.S. Treasury Bill Rates." Unpublished Ph.D. diss., University of Chicago, Chicago, IL, 1968.

[68] Samuelson, P. A. "Efficient Portfolio Selection for Pareto-Lévy Investments." *J. Fin. & Quant. Analysis* **2(2)** (1967): 107–122.

[69] Samuelson, P. A. "The Judgment of Economic Science on Rational Portfolio Management: Indexing, Timing, and Long-Horizon Effects." *J. Portfolio Mgmt.* (1989): 4–12.

[70] Scott, D. W. *Multivariate Density Estimation.* New York: Wiley, 1992.

[71] Simon, H. "On a Class of Skew Distributions." *Biometrica* **45** (1955): 425–440. (Reprinted in Simon, H., Models of Man, 1957.)

[72] Slottje, D. J. *The Structure of Earnings and the Measurement of Income Inequality in the U.S.* New York: Elsevier Science Publishers, 1989.

[73] Snyder, C. *Capitalism the Creator.* Macmillan, 1940.

[74] Stanley, H. E., L. A. N. Amaral, D. Canning, P. Gopikrishnan, Y. Lee, and Y. Liu. "Econophysics: Can Physicists Contribute to the Science of Economics?" *Physica A* **269** (1999): 156–169.

[75] Steindl, J. *Random Processes and the Growth of Firms—A Study of the Pareto Law.* London: Charles Griffin & Company, 1965.

[76] *The Sunday Times.* "Rich List." 1997. ⟨http://www.sunday-times.co.uk/news/pages/resources/library1.n.html?2286097⟩

[77] Takayasu, H. *Fractals in the Physical Sciences.* Wiley, 1990.

[78] Teichmoeller, J. "A Note on the Distribution of Stock Price Changes." *J. Amer. Stat. Assoc.* **66** (1971).

[79] Wold, H., and P. Whittle. "A Model Explaining the Pareto Distribution of Wealth." *Econometrica* **25** (1957): 591–95.

[80] Wolff, E. N. "How the Pie is Sliced." *The American Prospect* **6(22)** (1995): 58–64.

[81] Wolff, E. "Trends in Household Wealth During 1989-1992." Submitted to the Department of Labor. New York University, New York, 1996.

[82] Zajdenweber, D. "Propriétés Autosimilaires du CAC40." *Rev. d'Econ. Polit.* **104** (1994): 408–434.

[83] Zipf, G. *Human Behavior and the Principle of Least Effort.* Cambridge, MA: Addison-Wesley, 1949.

A Random Order Placement Model of Price Formation in the Continuous Double Auction

J. Doyne Farmer
László Gillemot
Giulia Iori
Supriya Krishnamurthy
D. Eric Smith
Marcus G. Daniels

Most modern financial markets use a continuous double auction mechanism to store and match orders and facilitate trading. In this chapter we use a microscopic dynamical statistical model for the continuous double auction under the assumption of IID random order flow. The analysis is based on simulation, dimensional analysis, and theoretical tools based on mean-field approximations. The model makes testable predictions for all the basic properties of markets, including price volatility, the depth of stored supply and demand, the bid-ask spread, the price impact function, and the time and probability of filling orders. These predictions are based on properties of order flow such as share volume of market and limit orders, cancellations, typical order size, and tick size. Because these quantities can all be measured directly in real data sets there are no free parameters. We show that the order size, which can be cast as a nondimensional granularity parameter, is in most cases a more significant determinant of market behavior than tick size. We also provide an explanation for the observed highly concave nature of the price impact function. On a broader level, this work demonstrates how stochastic models based on zero-intelligence agents may be useful in probing the structure of market institutions. Like the model of perfect rationality, a stochastic zero-intelligence model can be used to make strong predictions based on a compact set of assumptions. Preliminary evidence suggests that this model explains many aspects of real markets.

1 INTRODUCTION

1.1 MOTIVATION

In this chapter we analyze the continuous double auction trading mechanism under the assumption of random order flow, giving an overview of the work described in Daniels et al. [12] and Smith et al. [26]. This analysis produces quantitative predictions about the most basic properties of markets, such as volatility, depth of stored supply and demand, the bid-ask spread, the price impact, and probability and time to fill. These predictions are based on the rate at which orders flow into the market, and other parameters of the market, such as order size and tick size. The predictions are falsifiable with no free parameters. This extends the original random walk model of Bachelier [1] by providing a basis for the diffusion rate of prices. The model also provides a possible explanation for the highly concave nature of the price impact function. Even though some of the assumptions of the model are too simple to be literally true, preliminary results suggest that it explains several aspects of price formation and transaction costs in the London Stock Exchange [11] and the New York Stock Exchange [20]. Furthermore, the model provides a framework onto which more realistic assumptions may easily be added.

The model demonstrates the importance of financial institutions in setting prices, and how solving a necessary economic function such as providing liquidity can have unanticipated side effects. In a world of imperfect rationality and imperfect information, the task of demand storage necessarily causes persistence. Under perfect rationality, all traders would instantly update their orders with the arrival of each piece of new information, but this is clearly not true for real markets. The limit order book, which is the queue used for storing unexecuted orders, has long memory when there are persistent orders. It can be regarded as a device for storing supply and demand, somewhat like a capacitor is a device for storing charge. We show that even under completely random IID order flow and cancellations, the price process displays anomalous diffusion and interesting temporal structure. The converse is also interesting: For prices to be effectively random, incoming order flow must be non-random, in just the right way to compensate for the persistence. (See the remarks in section 4.3.)

This work is also of interest from a fundamental point of view because it suggests an alternative approach to doing economics. The assumption of perfect rationality has been popular in economics because it provides a parsimonious model that makes strong predictions. In the spirit of Gode and Sunder [17], we show that the opposite extreme of zero-intelligence random behavior provides another reference model that also makes very strong predictions. Like perfect rationality, zero-intelligence is an extreme simplification that is obviously not literally true. But as we show here, it provides a useful tool for probing the behavior of financial institutions. The resulting model may easily be extended by introducing simple boundedly rational behaviors. We also differ from standard treatments in that we do not attempt to understand the properties of prices from fundamental assumptions about utility. Rather, we split the problem in two. We attempt to understand how prices depend on order flow rates, leaving the problem of what determines these order flow rates for the future.

One of our main results concerns the average price impact function. The liquidity for executing a market order can be characterized by a price impact function $\Delta p = \phi(\omega, \tau, t)$. Δp is the shift in the logarithm of the price at time $t + \tau$ caused by a market order of size ω placed at time t. Understanding price impact is important for practical reasons such as minimizing transaction costs, and also because it is closely related to an excess demand function,[1] providing a natural starting point for theories of statistical or dynamical properties of markets [4, 15]. A naive argument predicts that the price impact $\phi(\omega)$ should increase at least linearly. This argument goes as follows: Fractional price changes should not depend on the scale of price. Suppose buying a single share raises the price by a factor $k > 1$. If k is constant, buying ω shares in succession should raise it by k^ω. Thus, if buying ω shares all at once affects the price at least as much as buying them one at a time, the ratio of prices before and after impact should increase at least exponentially. Taking logarithms implies that the price impact as we have defined it above should increase at least linearly.[2]

In contrast, from empirical studies $\phi(\omega)$ for buy orders appears to be concave [16, 18, 19, 20, 24, 28]. Lillo et al. have shown for that for stocks in the NYSE the concave behavior of the price impact is quite consistent across different stocks [20]. Our model produces concave price impact functions that are in qualitative agreement with these results. Furthermore, members of our group have recently begun to analyze data from the London Stock Exchange, which provides every action taken by each trader, and allows us to measure order flows in the way they are defined here. Preliminary results suggest that the model has a remarkable ability to predict the bid-ask spread, and that when plotted in the nondimensional coordinates defined here, the price impact collapses onto a universal function that is consistent through time and across stocks [11].

---

[1]In financial models it is common to define an excess demand function as demand minus supply; when the context is clear the modifier "excess" is dropped, so that demand refers to both supply and demand.

[2]This has practical implications. It is common practice to break up orders in order to reduce losses due to market impact. With a sufficiently concave market impact function, in contrast, it is cheaper to execute an order all at once.

Our work also demonstrates the value of physics techniques for economic problems. Our analysis makes extensive use of dimensional analysis, the solution of a master equation through a generating functional, and a mean-field approach that is commonly used to analyze non-equilibrium reaction-diffusion systems and evaporation-deposition problems.

1.2   BACKGROUND: THE CONTINUOUS DOUBLE AUCTION

Most modern financial markets operate continuously. The mismatch between buyers and sellers that typically exists at any given instant is solved via an order-based market with two basic kinds of orders. Impatient traders submit *market orders*, which are requests to buy or sell a given number of shares immediately at the best available price. More patient traders submit *limit orders*, or *quotes* which also state a limit price, corresponding to the worst allowable price for the transaction. (Note that the word "quote" can be used either to refer to the limit price or to the limit order itself.) Limit orders often fail to result in an immediate transaction, and are stored in a queue called the *limit order book*. Buy limit orders are called *bids*, and sell limit orders are called *offers* or *asks*. We use the logarithmic price $a(t)$ to denote the position of the best (lowest) offer and $b(t)$ for the position of the best (highest) bid. These are also called the *inside quotes*. There is typically a non-zero price gap between them, called the *spread* $s(t) = a(t) - b(t)$. Prices are not continuous, but rather have discrete quanta called *ticks*. Throughout this chapter, all prices will be expressed as logarithms, and, to avoid endless repetition, the word *price* will mean the logarithm of the price. The minimum interval that prices change on is the *tick size dp* (also defined on a logarithmic scale; note this is not true for real markets). Note that dp is *not* necessarily infinitesimal.

As market orders arrive they are matched against limit orders of the opposite sign in order of first price and then arrival time, as shown in figure 1.

Because orders are placed for varying numbers of shares, matching is not necessarily one-to-one. For example, suppose the best offer is for 200 shares at \$60 and the next best is for 300 shares at \$60.25; a buy market order for 250 shares buys 200 shares at \$60 and 50 shares at \$60.25, moving the best offer $a(t)$ from \$60 to \$60.25. A high density of limit orders per price results in high *liquidity* for market orders, in other words, it decreases the price movement when a market order is placed. Let $n(p, t)$ be the stored density of limit order volume at price p, which we will call the *depth profile* of the limit order book at any given time t. The total stored limit order volume at price level p is $n(p, t)dp$. For unit order size the shift in the best ask $a(t)$ produced by a buy market order is given by solving the equation

$$\omega = \sum_{p=a(t)}^{p'} n(p, t)dp \tag{1}$$

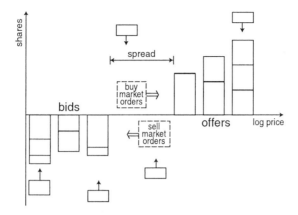

FIGURE 1   A schematic illustration of the continuous double auction mechanism and our model of it. Limit orders are stored in the limit order book. We adopt the arbitrary convention that buy orders are negative and sell orders are positive. As a market order arrives, it has transactions with limit orders of the opposite sign, in order of price (first) and time of arrival (second). The best quotes at prices $a(t)$ or $b(t)$ move whenever an incoming market order has sufficient size to fully deplete the stored volume at $a(t)$ or $b(t)$. Our model assumes that market order arrival, limit order arrival, and limit order cancellation follow a Poisson process. New offers (sell limit orders) can be placed at any price greater than the best bid, and are shown here as "raining down" on the price axis. Similarly, new bids (buy limit orders) can be placed at any price less than the best offer. Bids and offers that fall inside the spread become the new best bids and offers. All prices in this model are logarithmic.

for $p\prime$. The shift in the best ask is $p\prime - a(t)$, where eq. (1) is the instantaneous price impact for buy market orders. A similar statement applies for sell market orders, where the price impact can be defined in terms of the shift in the best bid. (Alternatively, it is also possible to define the price impact in terms of the change in the midpoint price.)

We will refer to a buy limit order whose limit price is greater than the best ask, or a sell limit order whose limit price is less than the best bid, as a *crossing limit order* or *marketable limit order*. Such limit orders result in immediate transactions, with at least part of the order immediately executed.

1.3   THE MODEL

This model, introduced in Daniels et al. [12], is designed to be as analytically tractable as possible while capturing key features of the continuous double auction. All the order flows are modeled as Poisson processes. We assume that market orders arrive in chunks of σ shares, at a rate of μ shares per unit time. The market order may be a "buy" order or a "sell" order with equal probability.

(Thus the rate at which buy orders or sell orders arrive individually is $\mu/2$.) Limit orders arrive in chunks of σ shares as well, at a rate of α shares per unit price and per unit time for buy orders and also for sell orders. Offers are placed with uniform probability at integer multiples of a tick size dp in the range of price $b(t) < p < \infty$, and similarly for bids on $-\infty < p < a(t)$. When a market order arrives it causes a transaction; under the assumption of constant order size, a buy market order removes an offer at price $a(t)$, and if it was the last offer at that price, moves the best ask up to the next occupied price tick. Similarly, a sell market order removes a bid at price $b(t)$, and if it is the last bid at that price, moves the best bid down to the next occupied price tick. In addition, limit orders may also be removed spontaneously by being canceled or by expiring, even without a transaction having taken place. We model this by letting them be removed randomly with constant probability δ per unit time.

While the assumption of limit order placement over an infinite interval is clearly unrealistic, it provides a tractable boundary condition for modeling the behavior of the limit order book near the midpoint price $m(t) = (a(t) + b(t))/2$, which is the region of interest since it is where transactions occur. Limit orders far from the midpoint are usually canceled before they are executed (we demonstrate this later in figure 5), and so far from the midpoint, limit order arrival and cancellation have a steady state behavior characterized by a simple Poisson distribution. Although under the limit order placement process the total number of orders placed per unit time is infinite, the order placement per unit price interval is bounded and thus the assumption of an infinite interval creates no problems. Indeed, it guarantees that there is always an infinite number of limit orders of both signs stored in the book, so that the bid and ask are always well-defined and the book never empties. (Under other assumptions about limit order placement this is not necessarily true, as demonstrated in Smith et al.) We are also considering versions of the model involving more realistic order placement functions (see the discussion in section 4.2).

In this model, to keep things simple, we are using the conceptual simplification of *effective market orders* and *effective limit orders*. When a crossing limit order is placed, part of it may be executed immediately. The effect of this part on the price is indistinguishable from that of a market order of the same size. Similarly, given that this market order has been placed, the remaining part is equivalent to a non-crossing limit order of the same size. Thus a crossing limit order can be modeled as an effective market order followed by an effective (non-crossing) limit order.[3] Working in terms of effective market and limit orders affects data analysis: The effective market order arrival rate μ combines both pure market orders and the immediately executed components of crossing limit orders, and similarly the limit order arrival rate α corresponds only to the components of limit orders that are not executed immediately. This is consistent

---

[3] In assigning independently random distributions for the two events, our model neglects the correlation between market and limit order arrival induced by crossing limit orders.

with the boundary conditions for the order placement process, since an offer with $p \leq b(t)$ or a bid with $p \geq a(t)$ would result in an immediate transaction, and thus would be effectively the same as a market order. Defining the order placement process with these boundary conditions realistically allows limit orders to be placed anywhere inside the spread.

Another simplification of this model is the use of logarithmic prices, both for the order placement process and for the tick size dp. This has the important advantage that it ensures that prices are always positive. In real markets price ticks are linear, and the use of logarithmic price ticks is an approximation that makes both the calculations and the simulation more convenient. We find that the limit $dp \to 0$, where tick size is irrelevant, is a good approximation for many purposes. We find that tick size is less important than other parameters of the problem, which provides some justification for the approximation of logarithmic price ticks.

Assuming a constant probability for cancellation is clearly *ad hoc*, but in simulations we find that other assumptions with well-defined timescales, such as constant duration time, give similar results. For our analytic model we use a constant order size σ. In simulations we also use variable order size, for example, half-normal distributions with standard deviation $\sqrt{\pi/2}\sigma$, which ensures that the mean value remains σ. As long as these distributions have thin tails, the differences do not qualitatively affect most of the results reported here, except in a trivial way. As discussed in section 4.2, decay processes without well-defined characteristic times and size distributions with power-law tails give qualitatively different results and will be treated elsewhere.

Even though this model is simply defined, the time evolution is not trivial. One can think of the dynamics as being composed of three parts: (1) the buy market order/sell limit order interaction, which determines the best ask; (2) the sell market order/buy limit order interaction, which determines the best bid; and (3) the random cancellation process. Processes (1) and (2) determine each other's boundary conditions. That is, process (1) determines the best ask, which sets the boundary condition for limit order placement in process (2), and process (2) determines the best bid, which determines the boundary conditions for limit order placement in process (1). Thus processes (1) and (2) are strongly coupled. It is this coupling that causes the bid and ask to remain close to each other, and guarantees that the spread $s(t) = a(t) - b(t)$ is a stationary random variable, even though the bid and ask are not. It is the coupling of these processes through their boundary conditions that provides the nonlinear feedback that makes the price process complex.

1.4 SUMMARY OF PRIOR WORK

There are two independent lines of prior work, one in the financial economics literature, and the other in the physics literature. The models in the economics literature are directed toward empirical analysis, and treat the order process as static. In contrast, the prior models in the physics literature are conceptual toy models, but they allow the order process to react to changes in prices, and are thus fully dynamic. Our model bridges this gap. This is explained in more detail below.

The first model of this type that we are aware of was due to Mendelson [23], who modeled random order placement with periodic clearing. This was developed along different directions by Cohen et al. [10], who used techniques from queuing theory, but assumed only one price level and addressed the issue of time priority with that price level (motivated by the hypothesized existence of a specialist who pins prices to make them stationary). Domowitz and Wang [13] and Bollerslev et al. [3] further developed this to allow more general order placement processes that depend on prices, but without solving the full dynamical problem. This allows them to get a stationary solution for prices. In contrast, in the physics models reviewed below, the prices that emerge make a random walk, and so are much more realistic. In our case, to get a solution for the depth of the order book we have to go into price coordinates that comove with the random walk. Dealing with the feedback between order placement and prices makes the problem much more difficult, but it is key for getting reasonable results.

The models in the physics literature incorporate price dynamics, but have tended to be conceptual toy models designed to understand the anomalous diffusion properties of prices. This line of work begins with a paper by Bak et al. [2] which was developed by Eliezer and Kogan [14] and by Tang [27]. They assume that limit orders are placed at a fixed distance from the midpoint, and that the limit prices of these orders are then randomly shuffled until they result in transactions. It is the random shuffling that causes price diffusion. This assumption, which we feel is unrealistic, was made to take advantage of the analogy to a standard reaction-diffusion model in the physics literature. Maslov [22] introduced an alternative model that was solved analytically in the mean-field limit by Slanina [25]. Each order is randomly chosen to be either a buy or a sell, and either a limit order or a market order. If a limit order, it is randomly placed within a fixed distance of the current price. This again gives rise to anomalous price diffusion. A model adding Poisson order cancellation was proposed by Challet and Stinchcombe [7]. Iori and Chiarella [9] have numerically studied a model including fundamentalists and technical traders.

The model studied in this chapter was introduced by Daniels et al. [12]. This adds to the literature by introducing a model that (like the other physics models above) treats the feedback between order placement and price movement, but unlike them is defined so that the parameters of the model can be measured and its predictions tested against real data. The prior models in the physics literature have tended to focus primarily on the anomalous diffusion of prices. While interesting and important for refining risk calculations, this is a second order effect. In contrast, we focus on the first order effects of primary interest to market participants, such as the bid-ask spread, volatility, depth profile, price impact, and the probability and time to fill an order. We demonstrate how dimensional analysis becomes a useful tool in an economic setting, and develop mean-field theories in a context that is more challenging than that of the toy models of previous work.

Subsequent to Daniels et al. [12], Bouchaud et al. [5] demonstrated that, under the assumption that prices execute a random walk, by introducing an additional free parameter they can derive a simple equation for the depth profile. In this chapter we show how to do this from first principles without introducing a free parameter.

2 OVERVIEW OF PREDICTIONS OF THE MODEL

In this section we give an overview of the phenomenology of the model. Because this model has five parameters, understanding all their effects would generally be a complicated problem in and of itself. This task is greatly simplified by the use of dimensional analysis, which reduces the number of independent parameters from five to two. Thus, before we can even review the results, we need to first explain how dimensional analysis applies in this setting. One of the surprising aspects of this model is that one can derive several powerful results using the simple technique of dimensional analysis alone.

Unless otherwise mentioned, the results presented in this section are based on simulations. A brief overview of the theoretical methods used and their agreement to the simulations is given in section 3.

2.1 DIMENSIONAL ANALYSIS

Because dimensional analysis is not commonly used in economics, we first present a brief review. For more details see Bridgman [6].

Dimensional analysis is a technique that is commonly used in physics and engineering to reduce the number of independent degrees of freedom by taking advantage of the constraints imposed by dimensionality. For sufficiently constrained problems it can be used to guess the answer to a problem without doing a full analysis. The idea is to write down all the factors that a given phenomenon can depend on, and then find the combination that has the correct dimensions. For example, consider the problem of deriving the correct formula for the period of a pendulum: The period T has dimensions of *time*. Obvious candidates that it might depend on are the mass of the bob m (which has units of *mass*), the length l (which has units of *distance*), and the acceleration of gravity g (which has units of $distance/time^2$). There is only one way to combine these to produce something with dimensions of *time*, i.e., $T \sim \sqrt{l/g}$. This determines the correct formula for the period of a pendulum up to a constant. Note that it makes it clear that the period does not depend on the mass, a result that is not obvious *a priori*. We were fortunate because in this problem there were three parameters and three dimensions, with a unique combination of the parameters having the

TABLE 1   The five parameters that characterize this model. α, μ, and δ are order flow rates, and dp and σ are discreteness parameters.

Parameter	Description	Dimensions
α	limit order rate	$shares/(price\ time)$
μ	market order rate	$shares/time$
δ	order cancellation rate	$1/time$
dp	tick size	$price$
σ	characteristic order size	$shares$

right dimensions. In general, dimensional analysis can only be used to reduce the number of free parameters through the constraints imposed by their dimensions.

For this problem the three fundamental dimensions in the model are *shares*, *price*, and *time*. Note that by *price*, we mean the logarithm of price; as long as we are consistent, this does not create problems with the dimensional analysis. There are five parameters: three rate constants and two discreteness parameters. The *order flow rates* are μ, the market order arrival rate, with dimensions of *shares per time*; α, the limit order arrival rate per unit price, with dimensions of *shares per price per time*; and δ, the rate of limit order decays, with dimensions of *1/time*. These play a role similar to rate constants in physical problems. The two *discreteness parameters* are the price tick size dp, with dimensions of *price*, and the order size σ, with dimensions of *shares*. This is summarized in table 1.

Dimensional analysis can be used to reduce the number of relevant parameters. Because there are five parameters and three dimensions (*price, shares, time*), and because in this case the dimensionality of the parameters is sufficiently rich, the dimensional relationships reduce the degrees of freedom, so that all the properties of the limit order book can be described by functions of two parameters. It is useful to construct these two parameters so that they are nondimensional.

We perform the dimensional reduction of the model by guessing that the effect of the order flow rates is primary to that of the discreteness parameters. This leads us to construct nondimensional units based on the order flow parameters alone, and take nondimensionalized versions of the discreteness parameters as the independent parameters whose effects remain to be understood. As we will see, this is justified by the fact that many of the properties of the model depend only weakly on the discreteness parameters. We can thus understand much of the richness of the phenomenology of the model through dimensional analysis alone.

There are three order flow rates and three fundamental dimensions. If we temporarily ignore the discreteness parameters, there are unique combinations of the order flow rates with units of shares, price, and time. These define a characteristic number of shares $N_c = \mu/2\delta$, a characteristic price interval $p_c = \mu/2\alpha$, and a characteristic timescale $t_c = 1/\delta$. This is summarized in table 2. The

TABLE 2   Important characteristic scales and nondimensional quantities. We summarize the characteristic share size, price, and times defined by the order flow rates, as well as the two nondimensional scale parameters dp/p_c and ϵ that characterize the effect of finite tick size and order size. Dimensional analysis makes it clear that all the properties of the limit order book can be characterized in terms of functions of these two parameters.

Parameter	Description	Expression
N_c	characteristic number of shares	$\mu/2\delta$
p_c	characteristic price interval	$\mu/2\alpha$
t_c	characteristic time	$1/\delta$
dp/p_c	nondimensional tick size	$2\alpha dp/\mu$
ϵ	nondimensional order size	$2\delta\sigma/\mu$

factors of two occur because we have defined the market order rate for either a buy or a sell order to be $\mu/2$. We can thus express everything in the model in nondimensional terms by dividing by N_c, p_c, or t_c as appropriate, for example, to measure shares in nondimensional units $\hat{N} = N/N_c$, or to measure price in nondimensional units $\hat{p} = p/p_c$.

The value of using nondimensional units is illustrated in figure 2.

Figure 2(a) shows the average depth profile for three different values of μ and δ with the other parameters held fixed. When we plot these results in dimensional units the results look quite different. However, when we plot them in terms of nondimensional units, as shown in figure 2(b), the results are indistinguishable. As explained below, because we have kept the nondimensional order size fixed, the collapse is perfect. Thus, the problem of understanding the behavior of this model is reduced to studying the effects of tick size and order size.

To understand the effects of tick size and order size it is useful to do so in nondimensional terms. The nondimensional scale parameter based on tick size is constructed by dividing by the characteristic price, that is, $dp/p_c = 2\alpha dp/\mu$. The theoretical analysis and the simulations show that there is a sensible continuum limit as the tick size $dp \to 0$, in the sense that there is non-zero price diffusion and a finite spread. Furthermore, the dependence on tick size is weak, and for many purposes the limit $dp \to 0$ approximates the case of finite tick size fairly well. As we will see, working in this limit is essential for getting tractable analytic results.

A nondimensional scale parameter based on order size is constructed by dividing the typical order size (which is measured in shares) by the characteristic number of shares N_c, i.e., $\epsilon \equiv \sigma/N_c = 2\delta\sigma/\mu$. ϵ characterizes the "chunkiness" of the orders stored in the limit order book. As we will see, ϵ is an important determinant of liquidity, and it is a particularly important determinant of volatility. In the continuum limit $\epsilon \to 0$ there is no price diffusion. This is because price

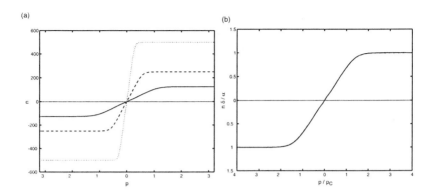

FIGURE 2 The usefulness of nondimensional units. (a) We show the average depth profile for three different parameter sets. The parameters $\alpha = 0.5$, $\sigma = 1$, and $dp = 0$ are held constant, while δ and μ are varied. The line types are: (dotted) $\delta = 0.001$, $\mu = 0.2$; (dashed) $\delta = 0.002$, $\mu = 0.4$ and (solid) $\delta = 0.004$, $\mu = 0.8$. (b) is the same, but plotted in nondimensional units. The horizontal axis has units of *price*, and so has nondimensional units $\hat{p} = p/pc = 2\alpha p/\mu$. The vertical axis has units of n *shares/price*, and so has nondimensional units $\hat{n} = np_c/N_c = n\delta/\alpha$. Because we have chosen the parameters to keep the nondimensional order size ϵ constant, the collapse is perfect. Varying the tick size has little effect on the results other than making them discrete.

diffusion can occur only if there is a finite probability for price levels outside the spread to be empty, thus allowing the best bid or ask to make a persistent shift. If we let $\epsilon \to 0$ while the average depth is held fixed, the number of individual orders becomes infinite, and the probability that spontaneous decays or market orders can create gaps outside the spread becomes zero. This is verified in simulations. Thus the limit $\epsilon \to 0$ is always a poor approximation of a real market. ϵ is a more important parameter than the tick size dp/p_c. In the mean-field analysis in section 3, we let $dp/p_c \to 0$, reducing the number of independent parameters from two to one, and in many cases find that this is a good approximation.

The order size σ can be thought of as the order *granularity*. Just as the properties of a beach with fine sand are quite different from those of one populated by fist-sized boulders, a market with many small orders behaves quite differently from one with a few large orders. N_c provides the scale against which the order size is measured, and ϵ characterizes the granularity in relative terms. Alternatively, $1/\epsilon$ can be thought of as the annihilation rate from market orders expressed in units of the size of spontaneous decays. Note that in nondimensional units the number of shares can also be written $\hat{N} = N/N_c = N\epsilon/\sigma$.

The construction of the nondimensional granularity parameter illustrates the importance of including a spontaneous decay process in this model. If $\delta = 0$ (which implies $\epsilon = 0$) there is no spontaneous decay of orders, and depending

TABLE 3   Estimates from dimensional analysis for the scaling of a few market properties based on order flow rates alone. α is the limit order density rate, μ is the market
order rate, and δ is the spontaneous limit order removal rate. These estimates are constructed by taking the combinations of these three rates that have the proper units.
They neglect the dependence on the order granularity ϵ and the nondimensional tick
size dp/p_c. More accurate relations from simulation and theory are given in table 4.

Quantity	Dimensions	Scaling relation
Asymptotic depth	$shares/price$	$d \sim \alpha/\delta$
Spread	$price$	$s \sim \mu/\alpha$
Slope of depth profile	$shares/price^2$	$\lambda \sim \alpha^2/\mu\delta = d/s$
Price diffusion rate	$price^2/time$	$D_0 \sim \mu^2\delta/\alpha^2$

on the relative values of μ and α, generically either the depth of orders will
accumulate without bound or the spread will become infinite. As long as $\delta > 0$,
in contrast, this is not a problem.

For some purposes the effects of varying tick size and order size are fairly
small, and we can derive approximate formulas using dimensional analysis based
only on the order flow rates. For example, in table 3 we give dimensional scaling
formulas for the average spread, the market order liquidity (as measured by the
average slope of the depth profile near the midpoint), the volatility, and the
asymptotic depth (defined below). Because these estimates neglect the effects of
discreteness, they are only approximations of the true behavior of the model,
which do a better job of explaining some properties than others. Our numerical
and analytical results show that some quantities also depend on the granularity
parameter ϵ and to a weaker extent on the tick size dp/p_c. Nonetheless, the
dimensional estimates based on order flow alone provide a good starting point
for understanding market behavior.

A comparison to more precise formulas derived from theory and simulations
is given in table 4.

An approximate formula for the mean spread can be derived by noting that
it has dimensions of $price$, and the unique combination of order flow rates with
these dimensions is μ/α. While the dimensions indicate the scaling of the spread,
they cannot determine multiplicative factors of order unity. A more intuitive argument can be made by noting that inside the spread, removal due to cancellation is dominated by removal due to market orders. Thus, the total limit order
placement rate inside the spread, for either buy or sell limit orders αs, must
equal the order removal rate $\mu/2$, which implies that spread is $s = \mu/2\alpha$. As we
will see later, this argument can be generalized and made more precise within
our mean-field analysis, which then also predicts the observed dependence on
the granularity parameter ϵ. However, this dependence is rather weak and only
causes a variation of roughly a factor of two for $\epsilon < 1$ (see fig. 10), and the factor

TABLE 4   The dependence of market properties on model parameters based on simulation and theory, with the relevant figure numbers. These formulas include corrections
for order granularity ϵ and finite tick size dp/p_c. The formula for asymptotic depth
from dimensional analysis in table 3 is exact with zero tick size. The expression for the
mean spread is modified by a function of ϵ and dp/p_c, though the dependence on them
is fairly weak. For the liquidity λ, corresponding to the slope of the depth profile near
the origin, the dimensional estimate must be modified because the depth profile is no
longer linear (mainly depending on ϵ) and so the slope depends on price. The formulas
for the volatility are empirical estimates from simulations. The dimensional estimate
for the volatility from Table 3 is modified by a factor of $\epsilon^{-0.5}$ for the early time price
diffusion rate and a factor of $\epsilon^{0.5}$ for the late time price diffusion rate.

Quantity	Scaling relation	Figure
Asymptotic depth	$d = \alpha/\delta$	3
Spread	$s = (\mu/\alpha)f(\epsilon, dp/p_c)$	10
Slope of depth profile	$\lambda = (\alpha^2/\mu\delta)g(\epsilon, dp/p_c)$	3
Price diffusion ($\tau \to 0$)	$D_0 = (\mu^2\delta/\alpha^2)\epsilon^{-0.5}$	11, 14(c)
Price diffusion ($\tau \to \infty$)	$D_\infty = (\mu^2\delta/\alpha^2)\epsilon^{0.5}$	11, 14(c)

of $1/2$ derived above is a good first approximation. Note that this prediction of
the mean spread is just the characteristic price p_c.

It is also easy to derive the mean *asymptotic depth*, which is the density
of shares far away from the midpoint. The asymptotic depth is an artificial
construct of our assumption of order placement over an infinite interval; it should
be regarded as providing a simple boundary condition so that we can study the
behavior near the midpoint price. The mean-asymptotic depth has dimensions
of *shares/price*, and is, therefore, given by α/δ. Furthermore, because removal
by market orders is insignificant in this regime, it is determined by the balance
between order placement and decay, and far from the midpoint the depth at any
given price is Poisson distributed. This result is exact.

The average slope of the depth profile near the midpoint is an important
determinant of liquidity, since it affects the expected price response when a
market order arrives. The slope has dimensions of *shares/price*^{2}, which implies
that in terms of the order flow rates it scales roughly as $\alpha^2/\mu\delta$. This is also the
ratio of the asymptotic depth to the spread. As we will see later, this is a good
approximation when $\epsilon \sim 0.01$, but for smaller values of ϵ the depth profile is not
linear near the midpoint, and this approximation fails.

The last two entries in table 4 are empirical estimates for the price diffusion
rate D, which is proportional to the square of the volatility. That is, for normal
diffusion, starting from a point at $t = 0$, the variance v after time t is $v = Dt$. The
volatility at any given timescale t is the square root of the variance at timescale
t. The estimate for the diffusion rate based on dimensional analysis in terms of
the order flow rates alone is $\mu^2\delta/\alpha^2$. However, simulations show that short time

diffusion is much faster than long time diffusion, due to negative autocorrelations in the price process, as shown in figure 11. The initial and the asymptotic diffusion rates appear to obey the scaling relationships given in table 4. Though our mean-field theory is not able to predict this functional form, the fact that early and late time diffusion rates are different can be understood within the framework of our analysis, as discussed in section 3. Anomalous diffusion of this type implies negative autocorrelations in midpoint prices. Note that we use the term "anomalous diffusion" to imply that the diffusion rate is different on short and long timescales. We do not use this term in the sense that it is normally used in the physics literature, in other words, that the long-time diffusion is proportional to t^γ with $\gamma \neq 1$ (for long times $\gamma = 1$ in our case).

2.2   VARYING THE GRANULARITY PARAMETER ϵ

We first investigate the effect of varying the order granularity ϵ in the limit $dp \to 0$. As we will see, the granularity has an important effect on most of the properties of the model, and particularly on depth, price impact, and price diffusion. The behavior can be divided into three regimes, roughly as follows:

- **Large ϵ, i.e.,** $\epsilon \gtrsim 0.1$. This corresponds to a large accumulation of orders at the best bid and ask, nearly linear market impact, and roughly equal short and long time price diffusion rates. This is the regime in which the mean-field approximation used in the theoretical analysis works best.
- **Medium ϵ, i.e.,** $\epsilon \sim 0.01$. In this range the accumulation of orders at the best bid and ask is small, and near the midpoint price the depth profile increases nearly linearly with price. As a result, as a crude approximation the price impact increases as roughly the square root of order size.
- **Small ϵ, i.e.,** $\epsilon \lesssim 0.001$. The accumulation of orders at the best bid and ask is very small, and near the midpoint the depth profile is a convex function of price. The price impact is very concave. The short time price diffusion rate is much greater than the long time price diffusion rate.

Since the results for bids are symmetric with those for offers about $p = 0$, for convenience we only show the results for offers, that is, buy market orders and sell limit orders. In this subsection prices are measured relative to the midpoint, and simulations are in the continuum limit where the tick size $dp \to 0$. The results in this section are from numerical simulations. Also, bear in mind that far from the midpoint the predictions of this model are not valid due to the unrealistic assumption of an order placement process with an infinite domain. Thus the results are potentially relevant to real markets only when the price p is at most a few times as large as the characteristic price p_c.

2.2.1   Depth Profile.   The *mean-depth profile*, in other words, the average number of shares per price interval, and the mean-cumulative depth profile are shown in

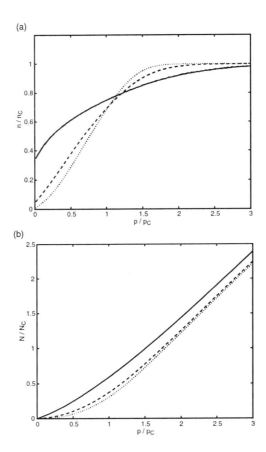

FIGURE 3 The mean-depth profile and cumulative depth versus $\hat{p} = p/p_c = 2\alpha p/\mu$. The origin $p/p_c = 0$ corresponds to the midpoint. (a) is the average depth profile n in nondimensional coordinates $\hat{n} = np_c/N_c = n\delta/\alpha$. (b) is nondimensional cumulative depth $N(p)/N_c$. We show three different values of the nondimensional granularity parameter: $\epsilon = 0.2$ (solid), $\epsilon = 0.02$ (dash), $\epsilon = 0.002$ (dot), all with tick size $dp = 0$.

figure 3, and the standard deviation of the cumulative profile is shown in figure 4. Since the depth profile has units of *shares/price*, nondimensional units of depth profile are $\hat{n} = np_c/N_c = n\delta/\alpha$.

The cumulative depth profile at any given time t is defined as

$$N(p,t) = \sum_{\tilde{p}=0}^{p} n(\tilde{p},t)dp.$$ (2)

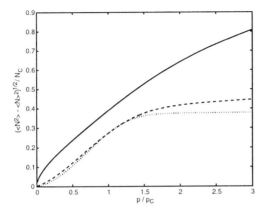

FIGURE 4   Standard deviation of the nondimensionalized cumulative depth versus nondimensional price, corresponding to figure 3.

This has units of shares and so in nondimensional terms is $\hat{N}(p) = N(p)/N_c = 2\delta N(p)/\mu = N(p)\epsilon/\sigma$.

In the high ϵ regime the annihilation rate due to market orders is low (relative to $\delta\sigma$), and there is a significant accumulation of orders at the best ask, so that the average depth is much greater than zero at the midpoint. The mean-depth profile is a concave function of price. In the medium ϵ regime the market order removal rate increases, depleting the average depth near the best ask, and the profile is nearly linear over the range $p/p_c \leq 1$. In the small ϵ regime the market order removal rate increases even further, making the average depth near the ask very close to zero, and the profile is a convex function over the range $p/p_c \leq 1$.

The standard deviation of the depth profile is shown in figure 4. We see that the standard deviation of the cumulative depth is comparable to the mean depth, and that as ϵ increases, near the midpoint there is a similar transition from convex to concave behavior.

The uniform order placement process seems at first glance one of the most unrealistic assumptions of our model, leading to depth profiles with a finite asymptotic depth (which also implies that there is an infinite number of orders in the book). However, orders far away from the spread in the asymptotic region almost never get executed and thus do not affect the market dynamics. To demonstrate this in figure 5 we show the comparison between the limit order depth profile and the depth n_e of only those orders which eventually get executed.[4]

---

[4]Note that the ratio n_e/n is not the same as the probability of filling orders (fig. 12) because in that case the price p/p_c refers to the distance of the order from the midpoint at the time when it was placed.

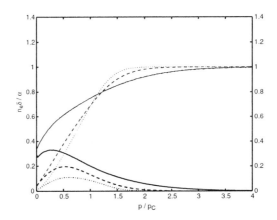

FIGURE 5 A comparison between the depth profiles and the effective depth profiles as defined in the text, for different values of ϵ. Heavy lines refer to the effective depth profiles n_e and the light lines correspond to the depth profiles.

The density n_e of executed orders decreases rapidly as a function of the distance from the mid-price. Therefore, we expect that near the midpoint our results should be similar to alternative order placement processes, as long as they also lead to an exponentially decaying profile of executed orders (which is what we observe above). However, to understand the behavior further away from the midpoint we are also working on enhancements that include more realistic order placement processes grounded on empirical measurements of market data, as summarized in section 4.2.

2.2.2 Liquidity for Market Orders: The Price Impact Function.

In this subsection we study the *instantaneous price impact* function $\phi(t, \omega, \tau \to 0)$. This is defined as the (logarithm of the) midpoint price shift immediately after the arrival of a market order in the absence of any other events. This should be distinguished from the asymptotic price impact $\phi(t, \omega, \tau \to \infty)$, which describes the permanent price shift. While the permanent price shift is clearly very important, we do not study it here. The reader should bear in mind that all prices—p, $a(t)$, etc.—are logarithmic.

The price impact function provides a measure of the liquidity for executing market orders. (The liquidity for limit orders, in contrast, is given by the probability of execution, studied in section 2.2.5.) At any given time t, the instantaneous ($\tau = 0$) price impact function is the inverse of the cumulative depth profile. This follows immediately from eqs. (1) and (2), which in the limit $dp \to 0$

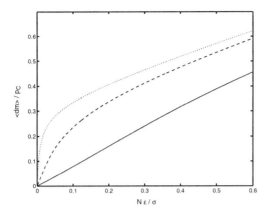

FIGURE 6 The average price impact corresponding to the results in figure 3. The average instantaneous movement of the nondimensional mid-price, $\langle dm \rangle/p_c$ caused by an order of size $N/N_c = N\epsilon/\sigma$. $\epsilon = 0.2$ (solid), $\epsilon = 0.02$ (dash), $\epsilon = 0.002$ (dot).

can be replaced by the continuum transaction equation:

$$\omega = N(p,t) = \int_0^p n(\tilde{p}, t)d\tilde{p}. \qquad (3)$$

This equation makes it clear that at any fixed t the price impact can be regarded as the inverse of the cumulative depth profile $N(p,t)$. When the fluctuations are sufficiently small we can replace $n(p,t)$ by its mean value $n(p) = \langle n(p,t) \rangle$. In general, however, the fluctuations can be large, and the average of the inverse is not equal to the inverse of the average. There are corrections based on higher order moments of the depth profile, as given in the moment expansion derived in Smith et al. [26]. Nonetheless, the inverse of the mean-cumulative depth provides a qualitative approximation that gives insight into the behavior of the price impact function. Mean price impact functions are shown in figure 6 and the standard deviation of the price impact is shown in figure 7. The price impact exhibits very large fluctuations for all values of ϵ: The standard deviation has the same order of magnitude as the mean, or larger for small $N\epsilon/\sigma$ values. Note that these are actually *virtual price impact* functions. That is, to explore the behavior of the instantaneous price impact for a wide range of order sizes, we periodically compute the price impact that an order of a given size would have caused at that instant, if it had been submitted. We have checked that real price impact curves are the same, but they require a much longer time to accumulate reasonable statistics.

One of the interesting results in figure 6 is the scale of the price impact. The price impact is measured relative to the characteristic price scale p_c, which as we

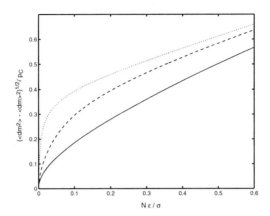

FIGURE 7 The standard deviation of the instantaneous price impact dm/p_c corresponding to the means in figure 6, as a function of normalized order size $\epsilon N/\sigma$. $\epsilon = 0.2$ (solid), $\epsilon = 0.02$ (dash), $\epsilon = 0.002$ (dot).

have mentioned earlier is roughly equal to the mean spread. As we will argue in relation to figure 8, the range of nondimensional shares shown on the horizontal axis spans the range of reasonable order sizes. This figure demonstrates that throughout this range the price is the order of magnitude (and typically less than) the mean-spread size.

Due to the accumulation of orders at the ask in the large ϵ regime, for small p the mean-price impact is roughly linear. This follows from eq. (3) under the assumption that $n(p)$ is constant. In the medium ϵ regime, under the assumption that the variance in depth can be neglected, the mean-price impact should increase as roughly $w^{1/2}$. This follows from eq. (3) under the assumption that $n(0)$ is linearly increasing and $n(0) \approx 0$. (Note that we see this as a crude approximation, but there can be substantial corrections caused by the variance of the depth profile.) Finally, in the small ϵ regime the price impact is highly concave, increasing much slower than $w^{1/2}$. This follows because $n(0) \approx 0$ and the depth profile $n(p)$ is convex.

To get a better feel for the functional form of the price impact function, in figure 8 we numerically differentiate it versus log order size, and plot the result as a function of the appropriately scaled order size. (Note that because our prices are logarithmic, the vertical axis already incorporates the logarithm.) If we were to fit a local power law approximation to the function at each price, this corresponds to the exponent of that power law near that price. Notice that the exponent is almost always less than one, so that the price impact is almost always concave. Making the assumption that the effect of the variance of the depth is not too large, so that eq. (3) is a good assumption, the behavior of this figure can

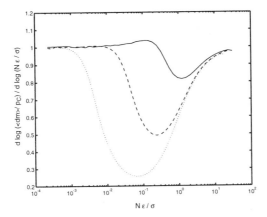

FIGURE 8   Derivative of the nondimensional mean-mid-price movement, with respect to logarithm of the nondimensional order size $N/N_c = N\epsilon/\sigma$, obtained from the price impact curves in figure 6.

be understood as follows: For $N/N_c \approx 0$ the price impact is dominated by $n(0)$ (the constant term in the average depth profile) and so the logarithmic slope of the price impact is always near to one. As N/N_c increases, the logarithmic slope is driven by the shape of the average depth profile, which is linear or convex for smaller ϵ, resulting in concave price impact. For large values of N/N_c, we reach the asymptotic region where the depth profile is flat (and where our model is invalid by design). Of course, there can be deviations to this behavior caused by the fact that the mean of the inverse depth profile is not in general the inverse of the mean, that is, $\langle N^{-1}(p) \rangle \neq \langle N(p) \rangle^{-1}$. This is discussed in more detail in Smith et al. [26].v

To compare to real data, note that $N/N_c = N\epsilon/\sigma$. N/σ is just the order size in shares in relation to the average order size, so by definition it has a typical value of one. For the London Stock Exchange, we have found that typical values of ϵ are in the range $0.001 - 0.1$. For a typical range of order sizes from $100 - 100,000$ shares, with an average size of $10,000$ shares, the meaningful range for N/N_c is therefore roughly 10^{-5} to 1. In this range, for small values of ϵ the exponent can reach values as low as 0.2. This offers a possible explanation for the previously mysterious concave nature of the price impact function, and contradicts the linear increase in price impact based on the naive argument presented in the introduction.

2.2.3 Spread.   The probability density of the spread is shown in figure 9. This shows that the probability density is substantial at $s/p_c = 0$. (Remember that

(a)

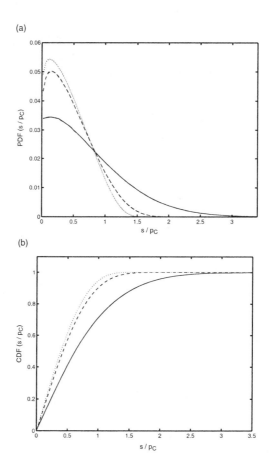

(b)

FIGURE 9   The probability density function (a), and cumulative distribution function (b) of the nondimensionalized bid-ask spread s/p_c, corresponding to the results in figure 3. $\epsilon = 0.2$ (solid), $\epsilon = 0.02$ (dash), $\epsilon = 0.002$ (dot).

this is in the limit $dp \to 0$.) The probability density reaches a maximum at a value of the spread approximately $0.2p_c$, and then decays. It might seem surprising at first that it decays more slowly for large ϵ, where there is a large accumulation of orders at the ask. However, it should be borne in mind that the characteristic price $p_c = \mu/\alpha$ depends on ϵ. Since $\epsilon = 2\delta\sigma/\mu$, by eliminating μ this can be written $p_c = 2\sigma\delta/(\alpha\epsilon)$. Thus, holding the other parameters fixed, large ϵ corresponds to small p_c, and vice versa. So in fact, the spread is very small for large ϵ, and large for small ϵ, as expected. The figure just shows the small corrections to the large effects predicted by the dimensional scaling relations.

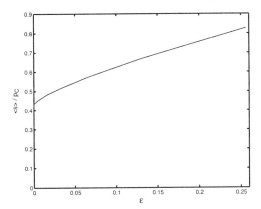

FIGURE 10   The mean value of the spread in nondimensional units $\hat{s} = s/p_c$ as a function of ϵ. This demonstrates that the spread only depends weakly on ϵ, indicating that the prediction from dimensional analysis given in table 3 is a reasonable approximation.

For large ϵ the probability density of the spread decays roughly exponentially moving away from the midpoint. This is because for large ϵ the fluctuations around the mean depth are roughly independent. Thus, the probability for a market order to penetrate to a given price level is roughly the probability that all the ticks smaller than this price level contain no orders, which gives rise to an exponential decay. This is no longer true for small ϵ. Note that for small ϵ the probability distribution of the spread becomes insensitive to ϵ, that is, the nondimensionalized distribution for $\epsilon = 0.02$ is nearly the same as that for $\epsilon = 0.002$.

It is apparent from figure 9 that in nondimensional units the mean spread increases with ϵ. This is confirmed in figure 10, which displays the mean value of the spread as a function of ϵ. The mean spread increases monotonically with ϵ. It depends on ϵ as roughly a constant (equal to approximately 0.45 in nondimensional coordinates) plus a linear term whose slope is rather small. We believe that for most financial instruments $\epsilon < 0.3$. Thus the variation in the spread caused by varying ϵ in the range $0 < \epsilon < 0.3$ is not large, and the dimensional analysis based only on rate parameters given in table 4 is a good approximation. We get an accurate prediction of the ϵ dependence across the full range of ϵ from the Independent Interval Approximation technique discussed in section 3.

2.2.4   Volatility and Price Diffusion.   The price diffusion rate, which is proportional to the square of the volatility, is important for determining risk and is a property of central interest. From dimensional analysis in terms of the order flow rates the price diffusion rate has units of $price^2/time$, and so must scale as $\mu^2 \delta/\alpha^2$. We

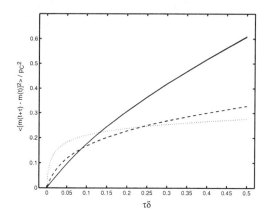

FIGURE 11 The variance of the change in the nondimensionalized midpoint price versus the nondimensional time delay interval $\tau\delta$. For a pure random walk this would be a straight line whose slope is the diffusion rate, which is proportional to the square of the volatility. The fact that the slope is steeper for short times comes from the nontrivial temporal persistence of the order book. The three cases correspond to figure 3: $\epsilon = 0.2$ (solid), $\epsilon = 0.02$ (dash), $\epsilon = 0.002$ (dot).

can also make a crude argument for this as follows: The dimensional estimate of the spread (see table 4) is $\mu/2\alpha$. Let this be the characteristic step size of a random walk, and let the step frequency be the characteristic time $1/\delta$ (which is the average lifetime for a share to be canceled). This argument also gives the above estimate for the diffusion rate. However, this is not correct in the presence of negative autocorrelations in the step sizes. The numerical results make it clear that there are important ϵ-dependent corrections to this result, as demonstrated below.

In figure 11 we plot simulation results for the variance of the change in the midpoint price at time scale τ, $\mathrm{Var}\,(m\,(t+\tau) - m\,(t))$. The slope is the diffusion rate, which at any fixed time scale is proportional to the square of the volatility. It appears that there are at least two time scales involved, with a faster diffusion rate for short time scales and a slower diffusion rate for long time scales. Such anomalous diffusion is not predicted by mean-field analysis. Simulation results show that the diffusion rate is correctly described by the product of the estimate from dimensional analysis based on order flow parameters alone, $\mu^2\delta/\alpha^2$, and a τ-dependent power of the nondimensional granularity parameter $\epsilon = 2\delta\sigma/\mu$, as summarized in table 4. We cannot currently explain why this power is $-1/2$ for short term diffusion and $1/2$ for long-term diffusion. However, a qualitative understanding can be gained based on the conservation law we discussed in section 3.

Note that the temporal structure in the diffusion process also implies non-zero autocorrelations of the midpoint price $m(t)$. This corresponds to weak negative autocorrelations in price differences $m(t) - m(t-1)$ that persist for time scales until the variance vs. τ becomes a straight line. The time scale depends on parameters, but is typically on the order of 50 market order arrival times. This temporal structure implies that there exists an arbitrage opportunity which, when exploited, would make prices more random and the structure of the order flow non-random.

2.2.5 Liquidity for Limit Orders: Probability and Time to Fill.

The liquidity for limit orders depends on the probability that they will be filled, and the time to be filled. This obviously depends on price: Limit orders close to the current transaction prices are more likely to be filled quickly, while those far away have a lower likelihood to be filled. Figure 12 plots the probability Γ of a limit order being filled versus the nondimensionalized price at which it was placed (as with all the figures in this section, this is shown in the midpoint-price centered frame). Figure 12 shows that in nondimensional coordinates the probability of filling close to the bid for sell limit orders (or the ask for buy limit orders) decreases as ϵ increases. For large ϵ, this is less than 1 even for negative prices. This says that even for sell orders that are placed close to the best bid there is a significant chance that the offer is deleted before being executed. This is not true for smaller values of ϵ, where $\Gamma(0) \approx 1$. Far away from the spread the fill probabilities as a function of ϵ are reversed, that is, the probability for filling limit orders increases as ϵ increases. The crossover point where the fill probabilities are roughly the same occurs at $p \approx p_c$. This is consistent with the depth profile in figure 3 which also shows that depth profiles for different values of ϵ cross at about $p \sim p_c$.

Similarly Figure 13 shows the average time τ taken to fill an order placed at a distance p from the instantaneous mid-price. Again we see that though the average time is larger at larger values of ϵ for small p/p_c, this behavior reverses at $p \sim p_c$.

2.3 VARYING TICK SIZE DP/P_C

The dependence on discrete tick size dp/p_c, of the cumulative distribution function for the spread, instantaneous price impact, and mid-price diffusion, are shown in figure 14. We chose an unrealistically large value of the tick size, with $dp/p_c = 1$, to show that, even with very coarse ticks, the qualitative changes in behavior are typically relatively minor.

Figure 14(a) shows the cumulative density function of the spread, comparing $dp/p_c = 0$ and $dp/p_c = 1$. It is apparent from this figure that the spread distribution for coarse ticks "effectively integrates" the distribution in the limit $dp \to 0$. That is, at integer tick values the mean-cumulative depth profiles roughly match and, in between integer tick values, for coarse ticks the probability is smaller. This happens for the obvious reason that coarse ticks quantize the possible val-

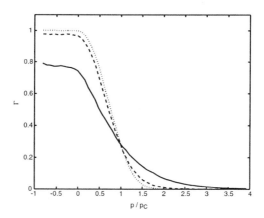

FIGURE 12   The probability Γ for filling a limit order placed at a price p/p_c where p is calculated from the instantaneous mid-price at the time of placement. The three cases correspond to figure 3: $\epsilon = 0.2$ (solid), $\epsilon = 0.02$ (dash), $\epsilon = 0.002$ (dot).

ues of the spread, and place a lower limit of one tick on the value the spread can take. The shift in the mean spread from this effect is not shown, but it is consistent with this result; there is a constant offset of roughly 1/2 tick.

The alteration in the price impact is shown in figure 14(b). Unlike the spread distribution, the average price impact varies continuously. Even though the tick size is quantized, we are averaging over many events and the probability of a price impact of each tick size is a continuous function of the order size. Large tick size consistently lowers the price impact. The price impact rises more slowly for small p, but is then similar except for a downward translation.

The effect of coarse ticks is less trivial for mid-price diffusion, as shown in figure 14(c). At $\epsilon = 0.002$, coarse ticks remove most of the rapid short-term volatility of the midpoint, which in the continuous-price case arises from price fluctuations smaller than $dp/p_c = 1$. This lessens the negative autocorrelation of midpoint price returns, and reduces the anomalous diffusion. At $\epsilon = 0.2$, where both early volatility and late negative autocorrelation are smaller, coarse ticks have less effect. The net result is that the mid-price diffusion becomes less sensitive to the value of ϵ as tick size increases, and there is less anomalous price diffusion.

3   SUMMARY OF ANALYTIC RESULTS

This section summarizes our analytic results and discusses their agreement with simulations. For a more in-depth discussion with derivations see Smith et al. [26].

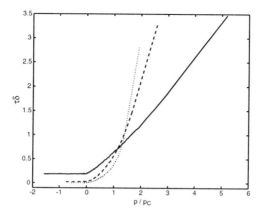

FIGURE 13   The average time τ nondimensionalized by the rate δ, to fill a limit order placed at a distance p/p_c from the instantaneous mid-price.

Below we describe three different theoretical approaches to understanding this model. A useful exact result can be derived from the requirement that all orders placed are eventually removed, which imposes global constraints on the mean-depth profile. Providing fluctuations at different prices are not too strongly correlated, an approximation to the mean-depth profile, the spread, and other properties can be obtained from an order-depth master equation. Alternatively, closed-form finite-difference expressions for the mean intervals separating orders (including the spread) may be obtained if the interval fluctuations have suitably regular distributions. These three levels of analysis are summarized in the following three subsections.

3.1   GLOBAL CONSERVATION RELATIONS

In this section we derive a useful global conservation relation. Because prices describe a random walk, in order to get stationary solutions we must use *comoving* coordinates. The resulting conservation law is slightly different depending on whether the coordinates are centered on the midpoint or on the best quote. (For convenience we derive the relation for sell orders, in which case the best quote is the best bid.)

Let $n(p,t)$ denote the number of shares in a half-closed logarithmic price interval $(p, p + dp)$ at time t, where dp is the logarithmic tick size, which may be infinitesimal. Then the share number in the bid-centered comoving frame is denoted n_b, and defined from the instantaneous bid price $b(t)$ as

$$n_b(p,t) \equiv n(p - b(t), t). \tag{4}$$

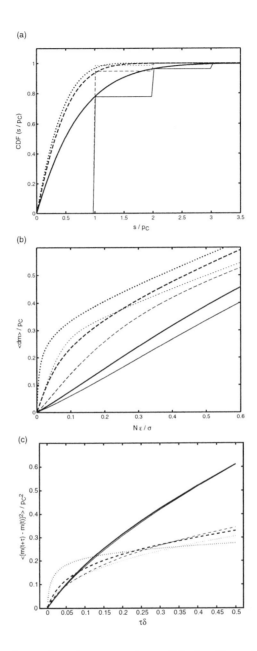

FIGURE 14   Dependence of market properties on tick size. Heavy lines are $dp/p_c \to 0$; light lines are $dp/p_c = 1$. Cases correspond to figure 3, with $\epsilon = 0.2$ (solid), $\epsilon = 0.02$ (dash), $\epsilon = 0.002$ (dot). (a) is the cumulative distribution function for the nondimensionalized spread. (b) is instantaneous nondimensionalized price impact, (c) is diffusion of the nondimensionalized midpoint shift, corresponding to figure 11.

Similarly, in a midpoint-centered frame,

$$n_m(p,t) \equiv n(p - m(t), t).$$ (5)

In bid-centered coordinates, the order-placement rate density is the constant α, and the mean-decay rate in bin p is $\delta \langle n_b(p) \rangle$, where angle brackets denote interchangeably either time or ensemble average. In addition, sell limit orders are removed by the placement of buy market orders, at the rate $\mu/2$. The fact that the number of orders placed must equal the number removed implies that

$$\frac{\mu}{2} = \sum_{p=b+dp}^{\infty} (\alpha dp - \delta \langle n_b(p) \rangle).$$ (6)

This relationship is somewhat more complicated in midpoint-centered coordinates, since orders placed below the midpoint induce a shift in the center of the coordinate system that place them above the new midpoint. This occurs whenever $0 \le p \le s/2$, where s is the spread. Thus the average additional deposition rate in midpoint-centered coordinates is $\alpha \langle s/2 \rangle$.

$$\frac{\mu}{2} = \alpha \frac{\langle s \rangle}{2} + \sum_{p=b+dp}^{\infty} (\alpha dp - \delta \langle n_m(p) \rangle).$$ (7)

Equations (6) and (7) are exact constraints on the mean-order depths, which will be respected as well by the approximate solutions below.

3.2   ORDER-DENSITY MASTER EQUATION

In this section we give an overview of a treatment based on a master equation. Instantaneous order-book configurations are one-dimensional *profiles*, which evolve stochastically under order placement and removal, as well as shifts in the origin of the comoving coordinate system when there is a change in the best quotes. The number of such profiles is too large to index tractably, but if the resulting fluctuations of the number at each price are uncorrelated, the statistical properties of the limit order book can be approximately described by the density $\pi(n, p, t)$, which gives the probability of finding n orders at price p at time t. This satisfies the conservation law

$$\sum_n \pi(n, p, t) = 1, \ \forall p, t.$$ (8)

The approximation of uncorrelated fluctuations is never satisfied in the bid-centered frame, but under appropriate conditions, discussed later, it is sometimes satisfied in the midpoint-centered frame. Therefore, n will denote n_m in the remainder of this subsection.

The master equation describing the flow of probability from individual placement, expiration, and execution events, as well as coordinate shifts, is straightforward to write down as

$$\frac{\partial}{\partial t} \pi(n,p) = \frac{\alpha(p)\, dp}{\sigma} [\pi(n-\sigma, p) - \pi(n,p)]$$

$$+ \frac{\delta}{\sigma} [(n+\sigma)\pi(n+\sigma, p) - n\pi(n,p)]$$

$$+ \frac{\mu(p)}{2\sigma} [\pi(n+\sigma, p) - \pi(n,p)]$$

$$+ \sum_{\Delta p} P_+(\Delta p) [\pi(n, p-\Delta p) - \pi(n,p)]$$

$$+ \sum_{\Delta p} P_-(\Delta p) [\pi(n, p+\Delta p) - \pi(n,p)] .$$

$$(9)$$

We are assuming time increments are sufficiently small that the time difference is well approximated by a continuous derivative, and have neglected to write the variable t that appears in every term on the right side. Here $P_\pm(\Delta p)$ are the rate densities for upward and downward shifts of the frame by Δp. They will be assumed equal for simplicity, and must be found self-consistently with the solution for mean n. To do this we assume that the shift events are otherwise uncorrelated with placement and removal events. In comoving coordinates the order placement rates are now functions of price, $\mu(p)$ and $\alpha(p)$. $\mu(p)$ represents the average rate at which market orders remove limit orders at price p. Similarly, the average rate of limit order deposition $\alpha(p)$ is affected by the fact that the best bid and ask prices are often changing. Far from the midpoint the deposition rate is unaffected, so that $\alpha(\infty) = \alpha$. These functions must be solved self-consistently.

For the analytic treatment we assume that all orders are of the same size (σ shares). In the limit $dp \to 0$ the number of orders within any given price bin of width dp is either zero or one. A solution for the mean-depth profile $\langle n(p) \rangle$ can be obtained by multiplying eq. (9) by n, summing over n, and setting the time dependence to zero. Differences of π at adjacent prices are replaced by derivatives with respect to p, and the finite-Δp shifts are expanded in Taylor's series. Two transport parameters are defined: a diffusivity

$$D \equiv \sum_{\Delta p} P(\Delta p)\, \Delta p^2, \tag{10}$$

and a mean-absolute price shift

$$\langle \Delta p \rangle \equiv \frac{\sum_{\Delta p} P(\Delta p)\, \Delta p}{\sum_{\Delta p} P(\Delta p)}. \tag{11}$$

It is convenient to express the mean-share density nondimensionally, defining

$$\psi(\hat{p}) \equiv \frac{1}{\epsilon} \frac{\delta \langle n(p) \rangle}{\alpha(\infty) dp}, \tag{12}$$

and similarly to introduce nondimensionalized transport parameters $\beta \equiv D/(p_C^2 \delta)$ and $\langle \Delta \hat{p} \rangle \equiv \langle \Delta p \rangle / p_C$.

Under the mean-field approximation of independent fluctuations, it is convenient to think of buy market orders as being deposited at logarithmic price $p = 0$, and moving to the right until they are annihilated by a sell limit order. (Recall that by definition in midpoint coordinates there are never any limit orders stored at $p < 0$.) Using non-dimensional price coordinates $\hat{p}$, the fraction of market orders surviving to price p, which is by definition also the cumulative distribution function for $\hat{s}/2$, has a simple expression in terms of the mean density:

$$\frac{\mu(\hat{p})}{\mu(0)} = \Pr(\hat{s}/2 \geq \hat{p}) = \exp\left(-\int_0^{\hat{p}} d\hat{p}' \psi(\hat{p}')\right) \equiv \varphi(\hat{p}). \tag{13}$$

Equation (13), together with the excess order-deposition relation in the midpoint-centered frame $\alpha(\hat{p})/\alpha(\hat{\infty}) = 1 + \Pr(\hat{s}/2 \geq \hat{p})$ (explained above), may be used to reduce the static first-moment (mean) solution of eq. (9) to

$$1 + \varphi = -\left[\frac{d\varphi}{d\hat{p}} + \epsilon\left(1 - \beta\frac{d^2}{d\hat{p}^2}\right)\frac{d\log\varphi}{d\hat{p}}\right]. \tag{14}$$

Direct integration over prices recovers the order-flow conservation (7), but now in nondimensional coordinates.

$$\int_0^\infty d\hat{p}(1 - \epsilon\psi) = 1 - \frac{\langle \hat{s} \rangle}{2}, \tag{15}$$

as long as $\psi \equiv 0$ at $p < 0$ and $\psi \to 1/\epsilon$ for $\hat{p} \to \infty$.

The simple fact that stored limit orders can never cross the midpoint can be used to derive an additional condition that yields a unique solution. While we cannot enforce this condition microscopically, we can at least enforce it on average. Consider the bin at $\hat{p} = 0$. The flux of orders from above is the gradient in order density times the rate of positive shifts $\langle \Delta \hat{p} \rangle$. In contrast, there is no flux of orders from below (since there are no orders below); the rate of removal is proportional to the order density. This argument can be made more formally (see Smith et al. [26]), leading to the condition

$$\langle \Delta \hat{p} \rangle \frac{d\psi}{d\hat{p}}\bigg|_0 - \psi(0) \approx 0. \tag{16}$$

The self-consistently determined parameters evaluate to

$$\beta = \frac{4}{\epsilon}\int_0^\infty d\Delta\hat{p}(\Delta\hat{p})^2 \varphi(\Delta\hat{p}), \tag{17}$$

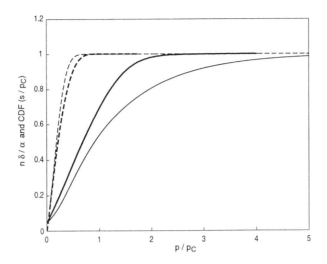

FIGURE 15 Fit of self-consistent solution to simulation results for the midpoint-centered frame, $\epsilon = 0.02$. Thin solid line is the analytic mean-number density; thick solid line is simulation. Thin dashed line is analytic $\Pr(\hat{s}/2 \leq \hat{p})$; thick dashed line is simulation.

and

$$\langle \Delta\hat{p} \rangle = \frac{\int_0^\infty d\Delta\hat{p}\, (\Delta\hat{p})\, \varphi\, (\Delta\hat{p})}{\int_0^\infty d\Delta\hat{p}\, \varphi\, (\Delta\hat{p})\,.} \tag{18}$$

Simultaneous solution of eqs. (14) and (16)–(18) produces the density and cumulative spread distribution shown in figure 3.2.

3.3 INDEPENDENT INTERVAL APPROXIMATION

An alternative to considering the share depth at $dp \to 0$ is to consider the set of price intervals x_i between orders, which in this limit are ensured to be sparse. x_0 is defined to be the spread, negative i index intervals between buy limit orders (bids), and positive i index intervals between offers. (For simplicity in defining the model, new orders are excluded from price bins containing existing orders. The resulting corrections vanish as $dp \to 0$.)

The instantaneous intervals change stochastically, by splitting when orders are added, or by joining when they are removed. For the spread, the processes and their rates are as follows:

1. $x_0 \to x_0 + x_1$, rate $(\delta + \mu/2\sigma)$ (ask removed by cancellation or market order).
2. $x_0 \to x_0 + x_{-1}$, rate $(\delta + \mu/2\sigma)$ (symmetric process for bid removal).

3. $x_0 \to x' \in (1, x_0 - 1)$, when a new offer is placed, rate $\alpha dp/\sigma$ at each unoccupied position of width dp.
4. $x_0 \to x' \in (1, x_0 - 1)$ when new bid is placed, again rate $\alpha dp/\sigma$ per bin.
5. Rate for events leaving x_0 unchanged is therefore $1 - 2\delta - \mu/\sigma - 2\alpha dp(x_0 - 1)/\sigma$.

To simplify notation in what follows σ will be set to one without loss of generality. The expected $x_0(t + dt)$, given definite $x_i(t)$, is then

$$\langle x_0(t + dt) \rangle = x_0(t)\left[1 - 2\delta - \mu_0 - 2\alpha(x_0 - 1)\right]$$
$$+ (x_0 + x_1)\left(\delta + \frac{\mu}{2}\right) + (x_0 + x_{-1})\left(\delta + \frac{\mu}{2}\right)$$
$$+ (\alpha_0 dp)x_0(x_0 - 1). \tag{19}$$

The average of eq. (19) would generate a recursion for $\langle x_0 \rangle$ from $\langle x_{\pm 1} \rangle$ if we could evaluate $\langle x_0^2 \rangle$. The mean-field approximation for independent intervals is to assume some relation $\langle x_0^2 \rangle$ by $a\langle x_0 \rangle^2$, with a to be determined self-consistently. Making this assumption, and abusing the notation by letting x_i denote the mean value of stationary solutions (and no longer the instances), gives

$$\left(\delta + \frac{\mu}{2}s\right)(x_1 + x_{-1}) = a\alpha dp x_0(x_0 - 1). \tag{20}$$

For sparse orders, the relation of mean interval to mean density depends on the fluctuation spectrum, but it is qualitatively $x_i \approx 1/\left\langle n\left(\sum_{j=0}^{i-1} x_j dp\right)\right\rangle$, becoming exact at large i. Thus, corresponding to the density solution, it is convenient to nondimensionalize the x_i as

$$\hat{x}_i \equiv \epsilon \frac{\alpha}{\delta} x_i dp = \frac{x_i dp}{p_C} \approx \frac{1}{\psi\left(\sum_{j=0}^{i-1} \hat{x}_j\right)}, \tag{21}$$

placing eq. (20) in the form

$$(1 + \epsilon)(\hat{x}_1 + \hat{x}_{-1}) = a\hat{x}_0(\hat{x}_0 - d\hat{p}). \tag{22}$$

The same sequence of steps may be followed for all x_k at $k \geq 1$, to yield the nondimensional recursion relations

$$(1 + k\epsilon)\hat{x}_k = \frac{a}{2}\hat{x}_{k-1}(\hat{x}_{k-1} - d\hat{p}) + \hat{x}_{k-1}\sum_{i=0}^{k-2}(\hat{x}_i - d\hat{p}), \tag{23}$$

which may then be solved numerically, given a convergence condition on $k \to \infty$ and the assumption of symmetry $x_i = x_{-i}$.

For asymptotically constant order placement rate density α, $\hat{x}_k$ must converge to some value $\hat{x}_\infty$ at large k. Taking $\hat{x}_{k+1} \to \hat{x}_k$ in eq. (23), it follows that $\hat{x}_\infty = \epsilon + d\hat{p}$, providing the convergence condition that constrains $\hat{x}_0$ in numerical evaluation, and agreeing with $\psi(\infty) \to 1/\epsilon$ at $dp \to 0$.

The partial sum in eq. (23) may also be evaluated in the same limit, by dividing by $\hat{x}_\infty$, to give

$$(1 + k\epsilon) = \frac{a}{2}(\hat{x}_\infty - d\hat{p}) + \sum_{i=0}^{k-2}(\hat{x}_i - d\hat{p}) \,. \tag{24}$$

Expressing $k\epsilon$ as a partial sum over $\hat{x}_\infty - d\hat{p}$, it follows that

$$1 + (1 - \frac{a}{2})\epsilon = S_\infty, \tag{25}$$

where $S_\infty \equiv \sum_{i=0}^{\infty}(\hat{x}_i - \hat{x}_\infty)$.

S_∞ may be interpreted in terms of global order flow. The rate of decay of the $k + 1$ orders in the price range $\sum_{i=0}^{k} x_i$ is $\delta(k+1)$, while the rate of market order executions is $\mu/2$. These must balance the rate of market order additions, which is $(\alpha dp)\sum_{i=0}^{k} x_i$ in the bid-centered frame (where the addition rate is not expressed directly in terms of the fluctuation spectrum of x_0). Thus, re-expressing eq. (6),

$$\frac{\mu}{2\sigma} + \delta(k+1) = \frac{\alpha dp}{\sigma}\sum_{i=0}^{k} x_i \,, \tag{26}$$

which nondimensionalized gives

$$1 = S_\infty \,. \tag{27}$$

Matching eq. (27) to eq. (25) gives the self-consistency condition $a = 2$, which would be exact if the x_k were all independent and exponentially distributed. The actual distribution obtained from simulations is approximately exponential for large k, though it is more nearly Gaussian for x_0, and has some transitional form for small k. Even so, the correspondence with the bid-centered density profile is qualitatively good across a broad range of ϵ, as shown in figure 3.3.

3.4 UTILITY OF ANALYTIC RESULTS AND AGREEMENT WITH SIMULATION

Both of the foregoing solution methods make simplifying assumptions about fluctuations: the master equation assumes that depth fluctuations are independent, while the independent interval approximation assumes that higher order interval moments have a fixed relation to mean values. Comparison to simulations has shown that both forms of approximation are good for parameter ranges $\epsilon \gtrsim 0.1$, but that they lead to progressively larger quantitative errors for smaller ϵ, so that only qualitative features of the density profile or probability distribution for the spread remain correctly predicted for $\epsilon \lesssim 0.001$.

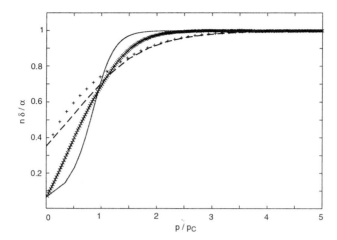

FIGURE 16   Bid-centered density profiles from Monte Carlo simulation (markers) and the Independent Interval Approximation (lines). Pluses and dash line are for $\epsilon = 0.2$, while crosses and dotted line are for $\epsilon = 0.02$.

Nevertheless, the analytic methods correctly capture the progression of the profile from concave-everywhere, to inflected, as ϵ decreases (see fig. 3.3). Qualitatively, this result allows us to understand the progression of the market impact from nearly linear, to sublinear-power dependence on order size, and shows that this relation is recovered in very different mean-field treatments, thus is not dependent at leading order, on precise properties of fluctuations.

The ϵ dependence of the mean profile, combined with the global conservation laws, also gives insight into the nature of autocorrelation of the midprice movement, and relates it to the impact through the mean order-book profile. The quantity S_∞ represents the area, in the nondimensionalized coordinates of figure 3.3, between the mean profile and a constant function with value unity. The conservation law (27) implies that this area is in fact independent of order-flow parameters. With the qualitative behavior of the book just noted, a larger market order rate (smaller ϵ) produces a lower profile near the bid, thus requiring that the profile more rapidly asymptote to one for $p/p_C \gtrsim 1$. The sparser profile near the bid indicates larger or more frequent steps in the random walk, due to shifts in the ask (and so, by symmetry, also in the bid), leading to a short-time diffusivity that should increase with decreasing ϵ. However, the exponent with which the profile asymptotes to unity at large p/p_C is inversely proportional to the late-time diffusivity, as it functions in simple diffusion models [5] indicating that this quantity must decrease with decreasing ϵ. The two are quantitatively related by the constraint (27), and in fact are shown to scale with inverse powers of $\epsilon^{1/2}$ in simulations. The physical interpretation of this relation is that, while more market orders lead to a sparser interior profile and more rapid initial price diffusion, an even greater fraction of the early steps is reversed by negatively autocorrelated later steps, reflecting the relatively greater immobility of the deeper book at large prices.

Perhaps the most quantitatively successful aspect of the analytic treatment, though, is that it motivates the nondimensionalization of the problem, by showing relatively invariant defining equations and qualitative solutions, in appropriately chosen coordinates. It shows relatively easily the existence of the continuum limit for tick size $dp/p_C \to 0$, and concurrently the nonexistence of a regular limit for order granularity $\sigma/N_C \equiv \epsilon \to 0$. It motivates parameter ranges for simulation studies, by showing that the regions of most rapid qualitative change occur over the range $\epsilon \in 0.001 - 0.1$, and gives some qualitative meaning to the order-flow values in real markets, in terms of the sensitivity to change where they occur.

4   CONCLUDING REMARKS

4.1   ONGOING WORK ON EMPIRICAL VALIDATION

This model predicts many different aspects of markets. To test these predictions quantitatively it is necesssary to measure order flow rates, which are not available in most data sets. It is nonetheless possible to compare some of the qualitative predictions of the model to those of data. For example, in a recent careful study Lillo et al. have carefully measured the price impact function for 1000 stocks traded on the New York Stock Exchange [20]. They find a price impact function that is quite concave. It does not appear to follow any simple functional form, such as a power law or logarithm, but increases roughly as the 0.5 power for small orders and the 0.2 power for larger orders. This is roughly the behavior our model generates for small values of ϵ, e.g., $\epsilon \approx 0.001$.

Members of our group are also working to test this model using data from the London Stock Exchange [11]. We have chosen this data set because it contains every order and every cancellation, which makes it possible to measure all the parameters of the model directly. It is also possible to reconstruct the order book and measure all the statistical properties we have studied in this chapter. Our empirical work so far shows that, despite its crude approximations, many of the predictions of the model are quite good. In particular, for a preliminary set of nine stocks the model explains 70% of the variance of the mean daily spread. Also, when plotted using the nondimensional coordinates defined here, the price impact function for the nine different stocks collapses rather well onto a single function. There are also some discrepancies; for example, the collapse seems to be independent of ϵ. If we somewhat arbitrarily choose $\epsilon \approx 0.001$, we get a good fit to the data. The shape of the price impact function is strikingly similar to that observed for the NYSE.

We believe that the discrepancies between the predictions of our model and the data can be dealt with by using a more sophisticated model of order flow. We summarize some of the planned improvements in the following subsection.

4.2   FUTURE ENHANCEMENTS

As we have mentioned above, the zero intelligence, IID order flow model should be regarded as just a starting point from which to add more complex behaviors. We are considering several enhancements to the order flow process whose effects we intend to discuss in future papers. Some of the enhancements include:

- *Trending of order flow.* We have demonstrated that IID order flow necessarily leads to non-IID prices. The converse is also true: Non-IID order flow is necessary for IID prices. In particular, the order flow must contain trends, i.e., if order flow has recently been skewed toward buying, it is more likely to continue to be skewed toward buying. If we assume perfect market efficiency, in the sense that prices are a random walk, this implies that there must be trends in order flow.
- *Power law placement of limit prices.* For both the London Stock Exchange and the Paris Bourse, the distribution of the limit price relative to the best bid or ask appears to decay as a power law [5, 29]. Our investigations of this show that this can have an important effect. Exponents larger than one result in order books with finite numbers of orders. In this case, depending on other parameters, there is a finite probability that a single market order can clear the entire book [26].
- *Power law or log-normal order size distribution.* A real order placement process has an order size distribution that appears to be roughly like a log-normal distribution with a power law tail [21]. This has important effects on the fluctuations in liquidity.
- *Non-Poisson order cancellation process.* When considered in real time, order placement cancellation does not appear to be Poisson [7]. However, this may not be a bad approximation in event time rather than real time.
- *Conditional order placement.* Agents may conditionally place larger market orders when the book is deeper, causing the market impact function to grow more slowly. We intend to measure this effect and incorporate it into our model.
- *Feedback between order flow and prices.* In reality, there are feedbacks between order flow and price movementss beyond the feedback in the reference point for limit order placement built into this model. This can induce bursts of trading, causing order flow rates to speed up or slow down, and give rise to clustered volatility.

The last item is just one of many examples of how one can surely improve the model by making order flow conditional on available information. However, we believe it is important to first gain an understanding of the properties of simple unconditional models, and then build on this foundation to get a fuller understanding of the problem.

4.3   COMPARISON TO STANDARD MODELS BASED ON VALUATION AND INFORMATION ARRIVAL

In the spirit of Gode and Sunder [17], we assume a simple, zero-intelligence model of agent behavior and show that the market institution exerts considerable power in shaping the properties of prices. While not disputing that agent behavior might be important, our model suggests that, at least on the short time scale, many of the properties of the market are dictated by the market institution, and, in particular, the need to store supply and demand to facilitate trading. Our model is stochastic and fully dynamic, and makes predictions that go beyond the realm of experimental economics, giving quantitative predictions about the fundamental properties of a real market. We have developed what were previously conceptual toy models in the physics literature into a model with testable explanatory power.

This raises questions about the comparison to standard models based on the response of valuations to news. The idea that news might drive changes in order flow rates is compatible with our model. That is, news can drive changes in order flow, which in turn cause the best bid or ask price to change. But notice that in our model there are no assumptions about valuations. Instead, everything depends on order flow rates. For example, the diffusion rate of prices increases as the 5/2 power of market order flow rate, and thus volatility, which depends on the square root of the diffusion rate, increases as the 5/4 power. Of course, order flow rates can respond to information; an increase in market order rate indicates added impatience, which might be driven by changes in valuation. But a change in long-term valuation could equally well cause an increase in limit order flow rate, which *decreases* volatility. Valuation *per se* does not determine whether volatility will increase or decrease. Our model says that volatility does not depend directly on valuations, but rather on the urgency with which they are felt, and the need for immediacy in responding to them.

Understanding the shape of the price impact function was one of the motivations that originally set this project into motion. The price impact function is closely related to supply and demand functions, which have been central aspects of economic theory since the 19th century. Our model suggests that the shape of price impact functions in modern markets is significantly influenced not so much by strategic thinking as by an economic fundamental: The need to store supply and demand in order to provide liquidity. *A priori* it is surprising that this requirement alone may be sufficient to dictate at least the broad outlines of the price impact curve.

Our model offers a "divide and conquer" strategy to understanding fundamental problems in economics. Rather than trying to ground our approach directly on assumptions of utility, we break the problem into two parts. We provide an understanding of how the statistical properties of prices respond to order flow rates, and leave the problem open of how order flow rates depend on more fundamental assumptions about information and utility. Order flow rates have the significant advantage that, unlike information, utility, or the cognitive powers of an agent, they are directly measurable. We hope that breaking the problem into two pieces will greatly simplify the problem of understanding markets.

ACKNOWLEDGMENTS

We would like to thank the McKinsey Corporation, Credit Suisse First Boston, the McDonnel Foundation, Bob Maxfield, and Bill Miller for supporting this research. We would also like to thank Paolo Patelli, R. Rajesh, Spyros Skouras, and Ilija Zovko for helpful discussions.

REFERENCES

[1] Bachelier, L. "Théorie de la spéculation." (Thesis) **Annales Scientifiques de Ecole Normale Superieure**, III–17, pp. 21–86, 1900. English translation in *Random Character of Stock Prices*, edited by P. H. Cootner. Cambridge, MA: MIT Press, 1964.

[2] Bak, P., M. Paczuski, and M. Shubik. "Price Variations in a Stock Market with Many Agents." *Physica A* **246** (1997): 430.

[3] Bollerslev, T., I. Domowitz, and J. Wang. "Order Flow and the Bid-Ask Spread: An Empirical Probability Model of Screen-Based Trading." *J. Econ. Dynamics & Control* **21** (1997): 1471.

[4] Bouchaud, J.-P., and R. Cont. "A Langevin Approach to Stock Market Fluctuations and Crashes." *European Phys. J. B* **6** (1998): 543.

[5] Bouchaud, J. P., M. Mézard, and M. Potters. "Statistical Properties of Stock Order Books: Empirical Results and Models." *Quant. Fin.* **2** (2002): 251.

[6] Bridgman, P. W. *Dimensional Analysis.* New Haven, CT: Yale University Press, 1922.

[7] Challet, D., and R. Stinchcombe. "Analyzing and Modeling 1+1d Markets." *Physica A* **300** (2001): 285.

[8] Challet, D., and R. Stinchcombe. "Exclusion Particle Models of Limit Order Financial Markets." *Physica A* **300** (2001): 285.

[9] Chiarella, C., and G. Iori. "A Simulation Analysis of the Microstructure of Double Auction Markets." *Quant. Fin.* **2** (2002): 346.

[10] Cohen, K. J., R. M. Conroy, and S. F. Maier. "Order Flow and the Quality of the Market." In *Market Making and the Changing Structure of the Securities Industry*, edited by Y. Amihud, T. Ho, and R. Schwartz. Lexington, MA: Lexington Books, 1985.

[11] Daniels, Marcus, J. Doyne Farmer, László Gillemot, Paolo Patelli, D. Eric Smith, and Ilija Zovko. "Predicting the Spread, Volatility, and Price Impact Based on Order Flow: The London Stock Exchange." Preliminary manuscript.

[12] Daniels, M., J. D. Farmer, G. Iori, and D. E. Smith. "How Storing Supply and Demand Affects Price Diffusion." 2001. ⟨http://xxx.lanl.gov/cond-mat/0112422⟩.

[13] Domowitz, I., and Jianxin Wang. "Auctions as Algorithms." *J. Econ. Dynamics & Control* **18** (1994): 29.

[14] Eliezer, D., and I. I. Kogan. "Scaling Laws for the Market Microstructure of the Interdealer Broker Markets." ⟨http://xxx.lanl.gov/cond-mat/9808240⟩.

[15] Farmer, J. D. "Market Force, Ecology, and Evolution." *J. Ind. & Corporate Change* **11(5)** (2002): 895–953.

[16] Farmer, J. D. "Slippage 1996." Technical Report, Prediction Company, Santa Fe, NM, 1996. ⟨http://www.predict.com⟩

[17] Gode, D., and S. Sunder. "Allocative Efficiency of Markets with Zero Intelligence Traders: Markets as a Partial Substitute for Individual Rationality." *J. Pol. Econ.* **101** (1993): 119.

[18] Hausman, J. A., and A. W. Lo. "An Ordered Probit Analysis of Transaction Stock Prices." *J. Fin. Econ.* **31** (1992): 319–379.

[19] Kempf, A., and O. Korn. "Market Depth and Order Size." *J. Fin. Markets* **2** (1999): 29.

[20] Lillo, F., J. D. Farmer, and R. Mantegna. "Single Curve Collapse of the Price Impact Function." *Nature* (2002): to appear.

[21] Maslov, S., and M. Mills. "Price Fluctuations from the Order Book Perspective—Empirical Facts and a Simple Model." *Physica A* **299** (2001): 234.

[22] Maslov, S. "Simple Model of a Limit Order-Driven Market." *Physica A* **278** (2000): 571.

[23] Mendelson, H. "Market Behavior in a Clearing House." *Econometrica* **50** (1982): 1505–1524.

[24] Plerou, V., P. Gopikrishnan, X. Gabaix, and H. E. Stanley. "Quantifying Stock Price Response to Demand Fluctuations." *Phys. Rev. E* **66** (2002): 027104.

[25] Slanina, F. "Mean-Field Approximation for a Limit Order Driven Market Model." *Phys. Rev. E* **64** (2001): 056136.

[26] Smith, Eric, J. Doyne Farmer, László Gillemot, and Supriya Krishnamurthy. "Statistical Theory of the Continuous Double Auction." ⟨http://xxx.lanl.gov/cond-mat/0210475⟩.

[27] Tang, L.-H., and G.-S. Tian. " Reaction-Diffusion-Branching Models of Stock Price Fluctuations." *Physica A* **264** (1999): 543.

[28] Torre, N. *BARRA Market Impact Model Handbook*. BARRA Inc, Berkeley CA, 1997. ⟨http://www.barra.com⟩.

[29] Zovko, I. I., and J. D. Farmer. "The Power of Patience: A Behavioral Regularity in Limit Order Placement." *Quant. Fin.* **2** (2002): 387.

Multinomial Choice with Social Interactions

William A. Brock
Steven N. Durlauf

For if anyone, no matter who, were given the opportunity of choosing amongst all the nations of the world the beliefs he thought best, he would inevitably, after careful consideration of their relative merits, choose those of his own country. Everyone without exception believes his own native customs, and the religion he was brought up in, to be the best.... There is abundant evidence that this is the universal feeling about the ancient customs of one's country. One might recall...an account told of Darius. When he was King of Persia, he summoned the Greeks who happened to be at his court and asked them what they would take to eat the dead bodies of their fathers. They replied that they would not do it for any money in the world. Later, in the presence of the Greeks...he asked some Indians...who do in fact eat their parents' dead bodies, what they would take to burn them. They uttered a cry of horror and forbade him to mention such a dreadful thing. One can see by this what custom can do and Pindar, in my opinion, was right when he called it "king of all."

Herodotus, The Histories (3.38)[1]

This chapter provides a model of individual decisionmaking in the presence of social interactions. By social interactions, we refer to interdependencies between individual decisions and the decisions and characteristics of others within a common group. In virtually any economic model, the decisions of one agent will be influenced by the behaviors and characteristics of others; what distinguishes the perspective we adopt is that the interdependences we study directly link individuals. By way of contrast, agents in a market are influenced by a common price that reflects the participation of each individual in the market. The sorts of phenomena we study are different as these describe ways to formalize ideas such as peer group influences, whereby behaviors of one agent alter the preferences of others and are not mediated by how individuals affect prices in a market equilibrium. As such, social interactions constitute an example of the type of externalities described in Arrow and Hahn [7, ch. 6, sec. 2].

Within economics, there has developed an increasing recognition that social interactions may play a major role in explaining a range of individual behaviors. In many respects, the new literature on social interactions addresses a famous criticism of economics made in Granovetter [40]:

Classical and neoclassical economics operates...with an atomized and *under*socialized conception of human action.... The theoretical arguments disallow by hypothesis any impact of social structure and social relations.... (p. 55)

In fact, one of the appealing aspects of the new literature on social interactions is that it has facilitated the introduction of sociological concepts and perspectives into economic modeling. In turn, the economics literature on social interactions has shown how these ideas may be formalized and extended using the formal rigor of economic theory. More important, the approach we take represents a first step in an integration of individual-based and social-based explanations, a perspective whose importance is well described in Arrow [6]:

It is clear that the individualist perspective does play an essential role in understanding social phenomena. Particularly striking is the *emergent* nature of social phenomena, which may be very far from the motives of the individual interactions. (p. 3)

As such, we regard the social interactions literature as a successful example of how social science benefits from the breaking down of disciplinary barriers.

---

[1] Taken from *Herodotus, The Histories* [28].

There is now a large body of theoretical and empirical studies of social inter-actions. In terms of theory, two main approaches have been taken. One strand of the social interactions literature has focused on the implications of social inter-actions in predetermined groups. Akerlof [2] and Brock and Durlauf [17, 18, 19], for example, consider the role of the interactions structure within a group on individual and group-level outcomes. Models such as those of Loury [48] and Lundberg and Startz [49] focus on the effects of social interactions within eth-nic groups with specific attention to how differences in initial conditions have long run effects. In contrast, work by Bénabou [10, 11], Durlauf [30, 31], and Hoff and Sen [42] has primarily focused on the implications of social interactions for group formation, specifically in the context of residential neighborhoods. In these models, children are influenced by the neighborhoods in which they grow up through factors such as the local tax base, the types of role models that are present, and via peer groups. Models of this type can produce poverty traps as poverty among parents is transmitted to children when children are consigned to neighborhoods whose characteristics adversely affect their subsequent economic status; poverty among parents, because of its effect on children's neighborhoods, thus transmits economic status across generations. One limitation of the exist-ing theoretical models of social interactions is the relatively weak connections between these two approaches.[2]

The empirical literature on social interactions has been dominated by atten-tion to the effects of residential neighborhoods. A wide range of analyses have produced regression evidence that links individual outcomes with neighborhood characteristics (i.e., groups defined by geographic proximity). Examples include Aizer and Currie [1], Brooks-Gunn et al. [21], Corcoran et al. [24], Brewster [15], Datcher [27], Ginther, Haveman, and Wolfe [37], Ioannides and Zabel [44, 43], Nigmatullin [58], Plotnik and Hoffman [59], Sirakaya [66], South and Baumer [67], and South and Crowder [68]. Alternative strategies for uncovering neighborhood effects using aggregated data have been developed by Glaeser, Sacerdote, and Scheinkman [38] and Topa [69]. In addition, there is now a literature that moves beyond the assumption that geographic proximity determines interactions and attempts to identify which sorts of groups in fact produce social interactions. Aizer and Currie [1] and Conley and Topa [22] are interesting empirical analyses that compare alternative groups (e.g., groups defined by geographic proximity versus common ethnicity) in terms of the social interactions with which they are associated.

Empirical work on neighborhood effects has been buttressed by two recent developments. The first is the use of "quasi-experimental" data produced by government interventions that alter the neighborhood choices of certain fami-lies. Examples of such programs include the Gautreaux program [61, 62] and the Moving to Opportunity Demonstration [45, 50]. Each of these programs is

---

[2]See Becker and Murphy [9] for a synthesis of various theoretical strands of the social interactions literature as well as for a valuable analysis of links between the two strands we have described.

interesting because each constitutes a government intervention in which a set of poor families is given incentives to move to more affluent neighborhoods, thereby permitting comparison with similar families who did not receive such incentives. These studies generally find improved outcomes, especially for children, among families who move.

The second is the development of a detailed data set that measures attitudes and beliefs across neighborhoods, called the Project on Human Development in Chicago Neighborhoods. As illustrated in Sampson, Morenoff, and Earls [63] and Sampson, Raudenbush, and Earls [64], this data can illuminate some of the structural relationships that underlie the correlations that are found in other studies between neighborhood attributes and individual outcomes. For example, these studies find that "collective efficacy," by which they mean the willingness of neighborhood members to provide public goods that contribute to social order (one example is monitoring the children of neighbors), appears strongly associated with lower crime rates.

A major weakness of the social interactions literature as it is currently constituted is the absence of strong connections between theory and empirics. By this, we mean that there has been little effort to employ theoretical models of social interactions in structural estimation. Our previous work on social interactions, Brock and Durlauf [18, 19] has attempted to address this limitation by developing models of binary choice that are directly econometrically implementable. This chapter extends that work to account for multinomial choice. This generalization leads to a number of new methodological insights as well as allows for the application of theoretical models of social interactions to a broader range of phenomena than was previously possible.

Section 1 outlines a basic choice model with social interactions. Section 2 analyzes a version of this general framework in which individual choices follow a multinomial logit structure. Section 3 considers the econometric implementation of the multinomial logit model we have developed with specific attention to identification problems that may arise when social interactions are present. Section 4 discusses how to extend our basic framework to account for alternative error specifications. We show that the basic theoretical and econometric features of the multinomial logit model apply quite generally. Section 5 considers how to integrate decisions on behaviors with decisions on group memberships. Section 6 contains summary and conclusions. A Technical Appendix contains all proofs.

1   MODELING SOCIAL INTERACTIONS

We consider i individuals who are members of a common group g. Our objective is to probabilistically describe the individual choices of each i, ω_i (a choice that is taken from the elements of some set of possible behaviors Ω_i) and thereby characterize the vector of choices of all members of the group, ω.

From the perspective of theoretical modeling, it is useful to distinguish between three sorts of influences on individual choices. These influences have different implications for how one models the choice problem. These components are:

1. h_i, a vector of deterministic (to the modeler) individual-specific characteristics associated with individual i,
2. ε_i, a vector of random individual-specific characteristics associated with i, and
3. $\mu_i^e(\omega)$, the subjective beliefs individual i possesses about behaviors in the group, expressed as a probability measure over those behaviors.

Each of these components will be treated as a distinct argument in the payoff function that determines individual choices. As we shall see, each plays a distinct role in the analysis.

The deterministic and random individual-specific characteristics capture the "standard" determinants of individual choices that one finds in economic models. Hence, if ω_i represents whether one is deciding between college and employment, or military enlistment, h_i may include variables such as the educational attainment of one's parents, or the quality of one's high school; the ε_i vector may include unobservable variables such as "true" intellectual ability or tastes. The distinction between deterministic and random characteristics will play an important role in both the theoretical and the econometric analysis of the model.

From the perspective of individual decisionmaking, what distinguishes our framework from the standard discrete choice approach is the possibility that individual choices are affected by $\mu_i^e(\omega)$, the beliefs an individual has about others. This interdependence in fact lies at the heart of the new literature on social interactions. In modeling social interactions across individuals, we assume that these interactions are mediated by beliefs; that is, individual i is influenced by what he thinks others are doing, not by their actual behavior per se. This assumption provides a great deal of analytical convenience. Its appropriateness will depend on the context under study, and in particular on the size of the group in which interactions occur. So, while the assumption seems relatively natural when one is interested in social interactions at an ethnic group level, it is clearly problematic in describing interactions between a pair of best friends.

Individual choices ω_i are characterized as representing the maximization of some payoff function V,

$$\omega_i = \arg\max_{\lambda \in \Omega_i} V(\lambda, h_i, \mu_i^e(\omega), \varepsilon_i). \tag{1}$$

Thus, we treat the decision problem facing an individual as a function of preferences (embodied in the specification of V), constraints (embodied in the specification of Ω_i), and beliefs (embodied in the specification of $\mu_i^e(\omega)$). As such, our analysis is based on completely standard microeconomic reasoning to describe individual decisions.

This basic choice model is closed by imposing self-consistency between subjective beliefs $\mu_i^e(\omega)$ and the objective conditional probabilities $\mu(\omega|F_i)$, where F_i denotes the information available to agent i. We assume that agents know the deterministic characteristics of others as well as their own and also understand the structure of the individual choice problems that are being solved. This means that subjective beliefs must obey

$$\mu_i^e(\omega) = \mu(\omega|h_j, \mu_j^e(\omega)) \quad \forall j \tag{2}$$

where the right hand of this equation is the objective conditional probability measure generated by the model; self-consistency is equivalent to rational expectations in the usual sense. From the perspective of modeling individual behaviors, it is typically assumed that agents do not account for the effect of their choices on the decisions of others via expectations formation. In this sense, this framework embodies an expectations-based version of a Nash equilibrium.

This general structure illustrates how social interactions models preserve the individual choice-based logic of microeconomics. Their novelty lies in the interdependences in choices that are induced by including $\mu_i^e(\omega)$ as an argument in individual payoffs and imposing self-consistency. From the perspective of economic theory, the interesting properties of these models emerge as a result of this interdependence.

2   A MULTINOMIAL LOGIT APPROACH TO SOCIAL INTERACTIONS

2.1   BASIC SETUP

In order to understand the implications of social interactions for the equilibrium distribution of choices within a population, it is necessary to specialize this general behavioral description. We do this in three steps.

First, we assume that each agent faces a common choice set with L discrete possibilities, such as, $\Omega_i = \{0, 1, \ldots, L-1\}$. The common choice set assumption is without loss of generality, since if agents face different choice sets, one can always assume their union is the common set and then specify that certain choices have payoffs of $-\infty$ for certain agents.

Second, we assume that each choice l produces utility for i according to:

$$V_{i,l} = h_{i,l} - Jp_{i,l}^e + \varepsilon_{i,l}. \tag{3}$$

Following the notation of the previous section, $h_{i,l}$ denotes the deterministic private utility agent i receives from the choice, $Jp_{i,l}^e$ denotes the social utility from the choice, and $\varepsilon_{i,l}$ denotes random private utility from the choice. The social utility term contains both a measure of the strength of social utility, J, and the agent's subjective expectation of the percentage of agents in the neighborhood who make the same choice $p^e_{i,l}$. This is the natural generalization of the conformity effect model developed in Brock and Durlauf [18, 19] and is also employed in Bayer and Timmins [8].

Third, we assume that the errors $\varepsilon_{i,l}$ are independent across i and l and are doubly exponentially distributed with index parameter β, i.e.,

$$\mu(\varepsilon_{i,l} \leq \varsigma) = \exp(-\exp(-\beta\varsigma + \gamma)), \tag{4}$$

where γ is Euler's constant. This assumption is, of course, standard in the discrete choice literature and is the basis of multinomial logit specifications (see Anderson, de Palma, and Thisse [4] for a discussion of the substantive behavioral restrictions that this specification imposes). The parameter β measures the dispersion in the random utility terms; higher β implies lower dispersion.

These assumptions may be combined to produce a full description of the choice probabilities for each individual, $\mu(\omega_i = l|h_{i,j}, p^e_{i,j}\forall j)$. The probability that agent i chooses l equals the probability that the payoff associated with this choice is maximal among all payoffs available to the agent, for example,

$$\mu(\omega_i = l|h_{i,j}, p^e_{i,j}\forall j) = \mu(\arg\max_{j\in\{0...L-1\}} h_{i,j} + Jp^e_{i,j} + \varepsilon_{i,j} = l|h_{i,j}, p^e_{i,j}\forall j). \tag{5}$$

This is a standard calculation under the double exponential assumption for the random payoff terms and leads to the canonical multinomial logit probability structure (cf. Anderson, dePalma, and Thisse [4, sec. 2.6]):

$$\mu(\omega_i = l|h_{i,j}, p^e_{i,j}\forall j) = \frac{\exp(\beta h_{i,l} + \beta Jp^e_{i,l})}{\sum_{j=0}^{L-1} \exp(\beta h_{i,j} + \beta Jp^e_{i,j})}. \tag{6}$$

When there are only two choices, this is the model studied in Brock and Durlauf [18, 19]. Since the random payoff terms are independent across agents, the joint choice probabilities may be written as

$$\mu(\omega_1 = l_1, \ldots, \omega_I = l_I|h_{i,j}, p^e_{i,j}\forall i, j) = \prod_i \frac{\exp(\beta h_{i,l_i} + \beta Jp^e_{i,l_i})}{\sum_{j=0}^{L-1} \exp(\beta h_{i,j} + \beta Jp^e_{i,j})}. \tag{7}$$

Finally, we characterize self-consistency as defined by eq. (2). We assume that the information set of each agent includes both the empirical distribution of deterministic payoff terms across choices and agents as well as the probability distribution from which random utility terms are drawn. We also assume that the number of agents is sufficiently large that each agent ignores the effect of his own choice on the average.[3] As self-consistent beliefs imply that the subjective

---

[3]In cases where the number of agents is small, it is perhaps more natural to express an individual's payoff as depending on the actual choices of others. There are subtle issues that

choice probabilities p_l^e equal the objective expected values of the percentage of agents in the group who choose l, p_l, the structure of the model implies that

$$p_{i,l}^e = p_l = \int \frac{\exp(\beta h_{i,l} + \beta J p_l)}{\sum_{j=0}^{L-1} \exp(\beta h_{i,j} + \beta J p_j)} dF_h \tag{8}$$

where F_h is the empirical probability distribution for the vector of deterministic terms $h_{i,l}$. It is straightforward to verify that under the Brouwer fixed-point theorem, at least one such fixed point exists, so this model always has at least one equilibrium set of self-consistent aggregate choice probabilities.

2.2 PROPERTIES

To understand the properties of this model, it is useful to focus on the special case where $h_{i,l} = 0 \; \forall i, l$. For this special case, the choice probabilities (and hence the expected distribution of choices within a neighborhood) are completely determined by the compound parameter βJ. An important question is whether and how the presence of interdependencies produces multiple equilibria for the choice probabilities in a neighborhood. In order to develop some intuition as to why the number of equilibria is connected to the magnitude of βJ, it is helpful to consider two extreme cases for the compound parameter, namely $\beta J = 0$ and $\beta J = \infty$. We consider each case in turn.

For the case $\beta J = 0$, one can immediately verify that there exists a unique equilibrium for the aggregate choice probabilities such that $p_l = 1/L \; \forall l$. This follows from the fact that under the assumption that $h_{i,l} = 0 \; \forall i, l$, all individual heterogeneity in choices comes from the realizations of $\varepsilon_{i,l}$, a process whose elements are independent and identically distributed across choices and individuals. Since all agents are *ex ante* identical, the aggregate choice probabilities must be equal.

The case $\beta J = \infty$ is more complicated. The set of aggregate choice probabilities $p_l = 1/L$ is also an equilibrium if $\beta J = \infty$, since conditional on these probabilities, the symmetries in payoffs associated with each choice that led to this equilibrium when $\beta J = 0$ are preserved as there is no difference in social utility across choices. However, this is not the only equilibrium. To see why this is so, observe that for any pair of choices l and l' for which the aggregate choice probabilities are nonzero, it must be the case that

$$\frac{p_l}{p_l'} = \frac{\exp(\beta J p_l)}{\exp(\beta J p_{l'})} \tag{9}$$

for any βJ. This follows from the fact that each agent is *ex ante* identical. Thus, it is immediate that any set of equilibrium probabilities that are bounded away

---

need to be dealt with in the small numbers case as this essentially means that agents know the $\varepsilon_{i,l}$'s for others in the group; see Kooreman and Soetevent [46]. Nevertheless, a small group approach is closely related to our framework.

from 0 will become equal, as $\beta J \Rightarrow \infty$. This condition is necessary as well as sufficient, so any configuration such that $p_l = 1/b$ for some subset of b choices and $p_l = 0$ for the other $L-b$ choices is an equilibrium. Hence, for the case where $J = \infty$, there exist $\sum_{b=1}^{L}\binom{L}{b} = 2^L - 1$ different equilibrium probability configurations. Recalling that β indexes the density of random utility and J measures the strength of interdependence between decisions, this case, when contrasted with $\beta J = 0$, illustrates why the strength of these interdependences and the degree of heterogeneity in random utility interact to determine the number of equilibria.

These extreme cases may be refined to produce a more precise characterization of the relationship between the number of equilibria and the value of βJ. In general, this relationship is highly complex, as it is necessary to account for the distribution of $h_{i,l}$ across i and l within a given group in order to develop precise statements as to how the model parameters determine the number of equilibria. Theorem 2.1 characterizes how the magnitude of βJ determines the number of equilibria in this case.

Theorem 2.1. *Multiple equilibria in the multinomial logit model with social interactions.*

Suppose that individual choices are characterized by eq. (6) with self-consistent beliefs, i.e., that beliefs are consistent with eq. (8). Assume that $h_{i,l} = k$ $\forall i, l$. Then there will exist at least three self-consistent choice probabilities if $\beta J/L > 1$.

When $L = 2$, this theorem reduces to the characterization of multiple equilibria with binary choices in Brock and Durlauf [18].[4]

In general, it is difficult to extend Theorem 2.1 to account for cases where $h_{i,l}$ is nonconstant. The reason for this is that the equilibrium aggregate choice probabilities induced by the interaction of private incentives and social incentives will in general depend on the complete distribution of $h_{i,l}$ across choices and individuals. There are some special cases where one can establish precise results. For example, suppose that $h_{il} - h_{i0} = g$ $\forall l \in \{1 \ldots L - 1\}$. In this case, the private deterministic utility of choice 0 differs from that of the other choices. In this case, the proof of Proposition 2 in Brock and Durlauf [19] implies that if $\beta J/L > 1$, there exists a threshold T for g such that if $0 < g < T$ there are multiple equilibria, whereas if $g > T$ the equilibrium is unique.

There is a common basic intuition for Theorem 2.1 and similar results in Brock and Durlauf [18, 19] that relate the number of choice equilibria to the interplay between the strength of social utility, J, the levels of deterministic private

---

[4]Brock and Durlauf [18, 19] use slightly different normalizations for the analysis of binary choice. Specifically, choices are indexed -1 and 1, and the social utility component is written as Jm, where m is the expected value of the choices in the group. For this reason, the threshold theorem in Brock and Durlauf [18, 19] is stated in terms of whether or not $\beta J > 1$ rather than $\beta J/2 > 1$ as is done here.

payoffs, $h_{i,l}$, and the parameter that indexes the degree of dispersion in random private utility, β. Multiple equilibria arise when the social utility effects on individual behavior can induce self-consistent bunching on a subset of choices. A positive J induces a tendency toward self-consistent bunching. Such a tendency is counteracted by the private utility components. One way in which this tendency toward self-consistent bunching may be countered is via the distribution of $h_{i,l}$; these private deterministic payoff components can, if sufficiently skewed, render the aggregate choice probabilities unique. A similar effect can occur via the realizations of the random payoff terms $\varepsilon_{i,l}$. With respect to Theorem 2.1, if the random utility components are sufficiently dispersed (i.e., β is small), then a sufficient percentage of agents will have draws of random utility such that their choices are dominated by one of the $\varepsilon_{i,l}$'s regardless of the strength of social utility, leaving too small a percentage of agents to engage in self-consistent bunching, as the social utility associated with the bunching depends on the percentage of agents that make the choice. Put differently, the presence of social utility effects, considered in isolation, do not identify what choices an individual makes, only that choices across individuals will be correlated. This induces a degree of freedom in the determination of what choices are actually made. (This is the same intuition that underlies the presence of multiple equilbria in various coordination failure models; see Cooper [23] for a survey.) The individual-specific deterministic and random terms, considered in isolation, do produce unique choices for the population. The interplay between the strength of these influences determines the number of equilibrium choice configurations.

An interesting feature of Theorem 2.1 is the fact that the condition for multiple equilibria depends on the number of choices. As such, the theorem explains simulation evidence in Bayer and Timmins [8] which indicated that multiple equilibria seem less likely in models when more choices are involved. This theorem makes their findings precise and provides some insight as to why they occur. Intuitively, the reason that the number of choices raises the threshold value of βJ necessary for multiple equilibria is the assumption that the random utility terms are independent. This independence means that the percentage of individuals in a population whose behavior is determined by their random utility (because of an extremely large draw for one of the choices relative to the others) increases in the number of choices, leaving a smaller percentage of the population susceptible to self-consistent bunching due to the influence of $J p_l$. Higher percentages of agents whose behavior is determined by the random utility draws will reduce the potential for social utility to produce multiple self-consistent equilibria.

2.3 COOPERATIVE EQUILIBRIA

In this section, we consider the formulation of a cooperative analog to the noncooperative model we have studied in section 2.2. The welfare properties of the noncooperative equilibria are best understood when explicitly contrasted with the equilibria that would occur under some sort of cooperation. One way to do this is to develop an analogous social planner's problem for the set of choices under consideration. Such an approach requires the use of relatively sophisticated models and techniques from the statistical mechanics literature. Following ideas originally developed in Brock [16] and subsequently elaborated in the present context in Brock and Durlauf [18], Brock and Durlauf [20] proposed a way of formulating the behavior of a particular benign social planner (i.e., one whose objective function includes the sum of the deterministic payoff components of the individual agents) in such a way that the social planner's choice of configuration ω is given by a probability measure $\mu(\omega)$ of the form

$$\mu(\omega) = Z_I^{-1} \exp\left(\sum_{i=1}^{I}\sum_{l=0}^{L-1}(\beta h_{i,l}1(\omega_i = l)) + I\beta J\sum_{l=0}^{L-1}\hat{p}_l^2\right). \tag{10}$$

In this expression, Z_I is a normalization and the $\hat{p}_l$'s are the empirical percentages of choices in the group, for example,

$$\hat{p}_l = I^{-1}\sum_{i=1}^{I}1(\omega_i = l) \tag{11}$$

where $1(\omega_i = l)$ denotes the indicator function for the choice of l by agent i.

In comparison with the probability measure that characterizes choices for noncooperative equilibrium (eq. (7)), the important difference is that the social planner's problem uses empirical probabilities in modeling the interdependence of individual choices, whereas the noncooperative equilibrium is based on population probabilities (i.e., the agents' rational expectations concerning the choices of others). This difference is to be expected, since a planner will account for how the choices of one actor affect others in ways that are ruled out in the noncooperative case. This feature makes the probability structure much more difficult to analyze. For example, the joint probability measure for the planner does not factor into a product of marginal probabilities (each representing one individual's choice) as it does in the noncooperative case. This means that there is a direct channel by which each agent's choice becomes correlated with the choices of others. The nature of this direct dependence as $I \Rightarrow \infty$ plays a key role in determining the aggregate behavior of the population.

We conjecture that as $I \Rightarrow \infty$, $\hat{p}_l \Rightarrow_w p_l^*$ $\forall l$ (w denotes weak convergence), the vector p^* with typical element p_l^* solves

$$p^* = \arg\max_{p} \lim_{I \Rightarrow \infty} I^{-1}\ln Z_I. \tag{12}$$

The Brock and Durlauf [20] assertion (their eq. (12)) that eq. (12) holds is incorrect as stated because the sufficient conditions for eq. (12) to hold are left out. For example,s when $L = 2$ and $h_{i,l} = 0$, if $(\beta J/2) > 1$, then there are two global maxima to eq. (12) which means that the limit of the sample mean

$\hat{p}$ is a mixture with a two point support; Ellis [34, p. 100] provides a complete analysis of the binary case when $h_{i,l} = h$. For the binary case with random $h_{i,l}$, results by Amaro de Matos and Perez [3] may be adapted to locate sufficient conditions for a result such as (12) to hold. In fact, for the binary choice case, these results suggest that the usual central limit theory for suitably normalized sums such as $\sum_i (\omega_i - E(\omega_i))$ needs to be modified. Although the usual central limit theorem results hold as long as (1) the value of βJ does not equal the critical value around which multiple equilibria emerge and (2) $h_{i,l}$ is constant (Ellis [34, Theorem V.9.4]), the situation changes when the variance of $h_{i,l}$ is positive, even when the global maximum of eq. (10) is unique and various regularity conditions are imposed (Amaro de Matos and Perez [3, Theorem 2.8, (a)]). More precisely, the appropriately normalized sum of deviations around the mean will converge to a mixture of normals, not a normal distribution as occurs in standard cases. Further, small changes in the distribution of $h_{i,l}$ can lead to large differences in the global maximum of eq. (12).

We do not know whether a result such as eq. (12) holds for the multinomial case with general $h_{i,l}$. For the case where the global maximum to eq. (10) is unique, there are a number of existing results that suggest that our conjecture is true. For example, Ellis and Wang [35] analyze the model eq. (10) where $h_{i,l} = 0$ $\forall i, l$ and show there is a threshold J_T such that if $J < J_T$, then $\hat{p}_l$ converges weakly to $1/L$. We will pursue a full analysis of eq. (12) in subsequent work.

3   ECONOMETRIC IMPLEMENTATION

3.1   BASIC FRAMEWORK

An important feature of the theoretical framework is that it can also be used for econometric analysis.[5] The multinomial logit property for the individual choices allows one to construct a likelihood function for data taken for I individuals who are sampled across groups. Since a typical data set will contain observations on individuals in different groups, we generalize our notation so that $g(i)$ denotes the group of agent i; ω is now the vector of choices in a given cross-group sample of individuals. Finally, each individual within a group is modeled as possessing identical beliefs about the percentage of choices within the group, so that for choice l within group $g(i)$ each group member shares a common belief concerning the expected percentage of group members that are choosing l, $p_{g(i),l}^e$. Following Manski [52], the dependence of individual behavior on $p_{g(i),l}^e$ is known as an endogenous effect, in order to highlight the notion that the (expected) choices of one agent influence the choices of another.

---

[5] A range of econometric issues that arise for models of social interactions have been studied in Brock and Durlauf [18, 19], Manski [52], and Moffitt [57]. Brock and Durlauf [19] is the study that most closely focuses on issues concerning discrete choice models, also extending the analysis of identification to duration data.

In empirical work on neighborhood effects the generic deterministic private incentive $h_{i,l}$ is usually assumed to depend on two types of observables: an r-dimension vector of individual characteristics X_i and an s-dimension vector of neighborhood characteristics $Y_{g(i)}$, also known as contextual effects. Manski [52] provides the first formal discussion of this dichotomy, which is irrelevant to the development of the theory of social interactions but has important implications for econometric analysis. Operationally, it is standard to assume

$$h_{i,l} = k_l + c_l'X_i + d_l'Y_{g(i)} . \tag{13}$$

There is no necessary reason why the same elements of X_i and $Y_{g(i)}$ should affect the payoff of each choice; one can allow for this by setting particular elements of c_l and d_l to zero.

Under the assumption that $\varepsilon_{i,l}$ is independent of X_i and $Y_{g(i)}$ $\forall i, l$, the likelihood function for a collection of choices ω will equal

$$Z_I^{-1} \prod_i \left(\sum_l \exp(\beta k_l + \beta c_l'X_i + \beta d_l'Y_{g(i)} + \beta J_l p_{g(i),l}^e) 1(\omega_i = l) \right) \tag{14}$$

where Z_I is the normalization

$$Z_I \prod_i \left(\sum_l \exp(\beta k_l + \beta c_l'X_i + \beta d_l'Y_{g(i)} + \beta J_l p_{g(i),l}^e) \right) \tag{15}$$

and beliefs are subject to a set of constraints on the subjective beliefs for members of each group $g(i)$,

$$p_{g(i),l}^e = E(p_{g(i),l} | F_{X_{g(i)}}, Y_{g(i)}, p_{g(i),l}^e \forall l) \tag{16}$$

where $F_{X_{g(i)}}$ is the empirical distribution of X_i within group $g(i)$ and expectations are formed on the basis of the probabilities defined by eq. (15). This set of constraints imposes self-consistency in expected choice probabilities across groups and choices in the way that corresponds to the analysis in section 2.

As is standard for multinomial logit models, the complete set of model parameters is not identified. It is therefore necessary to impose some normalizations; we follow McFadden [55, p. 1413] and impose the normalizations that $k_0 = 0, c_0 = 0, d_0 = 0, J_0 = 0$, and $\beta = 1$.

3.2 IDENTIFICATION

As originally recognized and analyzed in Manski [52] and further analyzed in Brock and Durlauf [19], Minkin [56], and Moffitt [57], there are possible identification problems in social interactions models due to the relationship between contextual effects $Y_{g(i)}$ and the equilibrium expected group choice probabilities $p_{g(i),l}$. Specifically, Manski [52] shows how for a class of linear models of group effects, collinearity between particular contextual effects and endogenous effects (in our context, the $p_{g(i),l}$'s) that represent self-consistent beliefs about aspects of behaviors in the group can induce nonidentification. However, in contrast to the linear case, identification can hold for our model, as described in the following theorem.

Theorem 3.1. *Identification of the multinomial choice model with social interactions.*

Let the true data generating process be given by eqs. (14)–(16) with the normalization $k_0 = 0, c_0 = 0, d_0 = 0, J_0 = 0,$ and $\beta = 1$. Assume

1. *the joint support of $X_i, Y_{g(i)}$ is not contained in a proper linear subspace of R^{r+s},*
2. *the support of $Y_{g(i)}$ is not contained in a proper linear subspace of R^s,*
3. *no linear combination of elements of X_i and $Y_{g(i)}$ is constant,*
4. *for each choice l, there exists at least one group g_l such that conditional on Y_{g_l}, X_i is not contained in a proper linear subspace of R^r,*
5. *none of the elements of $Y_{g(i)}$ possesses bounded support,*
6. *$p_{g(i),l}$ is not constant across neighborhoods, and*
7. *$\varepsilon_{i,l}$, the random utility terms for each individual, are independent of his associated X_i and $Y_{g(i)}$ and independent and identically distributed across choices and individuals.*

Then the true set of model parameters $k_1, c_1, d_1, J_1, \ldots, k_{L-1}, c_{L-1}, d_{L-1}, J_{L-1}$ is identified relative to any distinct alternative.

The proof of this theorem may be found in the appendix and is a generalization of a theorem on identification of neighborhood effects for binary choices found in Brock and Durlauf [18, 19]. The key to identification in this model is that, because models of discrete choice are inherently nonlinear in the various control variables (since choice probabilities are bounded), contextual effects and endogenous effects (in this case, the choice probabilities) cannot be linearly dependent. What the theorem in essence requires is three things. First, it is necessary that the data contain sufficient intraneighborhood variation within at least one neighborhood to ensure that k_l and c_l are identified $\forall l$. Second, there must be enough interneighborhood variation in $Y_{g(i)}$ to ensure that d_l and J_l are identified $\forall l$ because of the nonlinear relationship between contextual effects and endogenous effects. Third, there cannot be collinearity between the regressors contained in X_i and $Y_{g(i)}$, so that individual and contextual effects may be distinguished.

The conditions of the Theorem are sufficient, and clearly one could find weaker ones than those we have employed.[6] An advantage of the conditions we have used is that they make clear what underlying properties are needed for identification and so should provide a guide to developing weaker conditions if needed in a particular context.

The identification theorem applies to more general models than that studied in section 3.2 as the econometric model allows for a distinct J_l for each choice. This is appealing as one can easily imagine cases where the payoff from conforming to the behavior of others depends on the nature of the choice. For example, if one is choosing between a solitary and a group activity, one would intuitively expect the value of J_l to depend on the choice.

3.3 EXTENSIONS

Identification may also be established for the case where individual decisions depend on the expected percentages of individuals making each of the other choices as well as on the expected percentage of individuals making that choice. Formally, this means replacing eqs. (14) and (15) with

$$Z_I^{-1} \prod_i \left(\sum_l \exp(\beta k_l + \beta c_l' X_i + \beta d_l' Y_{g(i)} + \beta J_l' p_{g(i)}^e) 1(\omega_i = l) \right) \qquad (17)$$

and

$$Z_I \prod_i \left(\sum_l \exp(\beta k_l + \beta c_l' X_i + \beta d_l' Y_{g(i)} + \beta J_l' p_{g(i)}^e) \right). \qquad (18)$$

For eqs. (17) and (18), J_l is a vector $(J_{1,l} \ldots J_{L-1,l})$ and represents the weights, conditional on choice l that agent i assigns to the percentage of the population making each of the choices; $p_{g(i)}^e$ is the vector of expected choice percentages. Such a generalization is also appealing in various contexts. Suppose one is making a choice of religious affiliation in a population. It might be the case that the adherence to one affiliation is affected by the percentages of the population that adhere to certain other denominations For example, adherence to a particular affiliation that believes in creationism may be affected by the percentage of adherents to other Christian denominations that possess similar beliefs.[7] This generalization is also interesting because it allows for the possibility that there is negative social utility associated with particular cross-choice effects.[8] Hence, the expected percentage of the population making one choice

---

[6]We should also note that the assumptions are exposited in a way to facilitate understanding the proof of the Theorem in the Technical Appendix. Assumption 2 may be shown to derive from assumption 1.

[7]The existence of self-consistent equilibria under these more general forms of endogenous social interactions is a consequence of Brouwer's fixed theorem in the same way as was the case for the initial multinomial logit model.

[8]In the previous models we have analyzed, J and J_l are allowed to take on negative values, but no cross-choice effects are present.

can negatively affect the payoff for other choices. To extend our earlier example, this would allow for the expected percentage of religious believers in a population to reduce the payoffs associated with agnosticism or atheism, whereas no cross-choice effects exist between these two possibilities.

The conditions for identification for the model defined by eqs. (17) and (18) with expectations described by eq. (16) is very similar to that of Theorem 3.1. Formally, we have the following corollary.

Corollary 3.1. *Identification for generalized multinomial logit model with social interactions.*

Suppose that individual choice is described by eq. (17) with self-consistent beliefs defined by eq. (16). Denote $m_{g(i),l} = p_{g(i),l} - p_{g(i),0}$. If, in addition to the assumptions found in Theorem 3.1, the support of the set of vectors $m_{g(i)} = (m_{g(i),1}, \ldots, m_{g(i),L-1})$ does not lie in a proper linear subspace of R^{L-1}, then the true set of model parameters $(k_1, c_1, d_1, J_1, \ldots, k_{L-1}, c_{L-1}, d_{L-1}, J_{L-1})$ is identified relative to any distinct alternative.

Intuitively, the additional condition in the corollary adds sufficient variability in aggregate choice probabilities to allow for identification of the individual elements of J_l. This additional variability allows us to mimic the proof of Theorem 3.1 and apply it to Corollary 3.1 as shown in the Technical Appendix.

Finally, it is worth noting that the multinomial and binary choice models contain an interesting difference with respect to the presence of zero restrictions on the model parameters. Unlike the binary choice model, for the multinomial choice model there may be zero restrictions on particular elements of k_l, c_l, d_l, J_l that apply to one choice but not another. This means, for example, that a variable that is relevant for two of the choices may be known to be irrelevant for the others. However, since choices are determined by payoff maximization as in eq. (1), the absence of a regressor in the payoff for a given possibility does not mean that it is irrelevant to whether that possibility is chosen. This reasoning suggests that there may be ways to employ regressors that are omitted from given choice-specific payoffs to identify those choice parameters. This may also prove to be a route for finding choice-specific instrumental variables as needed in various forms of the model.

4   MULTINOMIAL CHOICE UNDER ALTERNATIVE ERROR ASSUMPTIONS

Generalizing the basic logic of the multinomial model is straightforward. This can be seen if one considers the preference structure

$$V_{i,l} = h_{i,l} + J p_{i,l}^e + \beta^{-1} \varepsilon_{i,l} . \tag{19}$$

This is the same preference structure we worked with earlier, except that β is now explicitly used to index the intensity of choice (in the McFadden sense) rather than as a parameter of the distribution of the random payoff term $\varepsilon_{i,l}$. We assume that these unobserved utility terms are independent and identically distributed with a common distribution function $F_\varepsilon(\cdot)$.

For this model, the probability that agent i makes choice l is

$$\mu\left(\begin{array}{c} \varepsilon_{i,0} - \varepsilon_{i,l} \leq \beta(h_{i,l} - h_{i,0}) + \beta J(p^e_{i,l} - p^e_{i,0}), \ldots, \\ \varepsilon_{i,L-1} - \varepsilon_{i,l} \leq \beta(h_{i,l} - h_{i,L-1}) + \beta J(p^e_{i,l} - p^e_{i,L-1}) \end{array}\right). \tag{20}$$

Following Anderson, dePalma, and Thisse [4, p. 36], conditional on a realization of $\varepsilon_{i,l}$, the probability that l is chosen is

$$\prod_{j \neq i} F_\varepsilon(\beta h_{i,l} - \beta h_{i,j} + \beta J p^e_{i,l} - \beta J p^e_{i,j} + \varepsilon_{i,l}) \tag{21}$$

which immediately implies that the probability of the choice l without conditioning on the realization of $\varepsilon_{i,l}$ is

$$p_{i,l} = \int \prod_{j \neq l} F_\varepsilon(\beta h_{i,l} - \beta h_{i,j} + \beta J p^e_{i,l} - \beta J p^e_{i,j} + \varepsilon)dF_\varepsilon. \tag{22}$$

Equation (22) provides a multinomial choice model whose structure is fully analogous to the multinomial logit structure developed in sections 2 and 3. Under self-consistency, the aggregate choice probabilities of this general multinomial choice model are the solutions to

$$p_l = \int \int \prod_{j \neq l} F_\varepsilon(\beta h_l - \beta h_j + \beta J p_l - \beta J p_j + \varepsilon)dF_\varepsilon dF_h. \tag{23}$$

As in the multinomial logit case, the compound parameter βJ plays a critical role in determining the number of self-consistent equilibrium choice probabilities p_l. This finding is formalized in Theorem 4.1.

Theorem 4.1. *Uniqueness versus multiplicity of self-consistent equilibria in multinomial choice models with social interactions.*

Suppose that individual choices and associated self-consistent equilibria are described by eqs. (22) and (23). Assume that $h_{i,l} = 0 \; \forall i, l$ and $\varepsilon_{i,l}$ are independent across i and l. There exists a threshold T such that if $\beta J < T$, then there is a unique self-consistent equilibrium, whereas if $\beta J > T$ there exist at least three self-consistent equilibria.

The relationship between βJ and the number of equilibria is less precise than was found in Theorem 2.1, the multinomial logit case, as Theorem 4.1 does not specify anything about the way in which L, the number of available choices, affects the number of equilibria. This lack of precision is to be expected since we did not specify the distribution of the errors.

One can also develop an analog to the identification results we have obtained for the multinomial logit model. We will work with the same normalizations as used in the multinomial logit case and will again assume that $\varepsilon_{i,l}$ is independent of X_i and $Y_{g(i)} \,\forall i, l$. Under self-consistency, eq. (22) defines a continuous mapping eq. (23) from the simplex

$$S =_{def} \left\{ (p_0, \ldots, p_{L-1}) | p_l \geq 0, j = 0, \ldots, L-1, \sum_l p_l = 1 \right\} \qquad (24)$$

into itself. Assume that this mapping is globally one-to-one. This is a "high level" assumption in the sense that it is an assumption that is imposed on the choice probabilities; ideally it is preferable to place assumptions on the payoff function and show that such a condition holds. However, for our purposes, the assumption should not be regarded as too extreme as it holds for standard cases such as the multinomial logit.

Global invertibility provides a route to identification. Recall that nonidentification means that there exist two sets of parameters that produce the same choice probabilities $p_{i,l}$ and hence the same choice probability differences $p_{i,l} - p_{i,0}$. It is immediate that this invariance requires that if there exist two distinct sets of parameters $(k_1, c_1, d_1, J_1, \ldots, k_{L-1}, c_{L-1}, d_{L-1}, J_{L-1})$ and $(\overline{k}_1, \overline{c}_1, \overline{d}_1, \overline{J}_1, \ldots, \overline{k}_{L-1}, \overline{c}_{L-1}, \overline{d}_{L-1}, \overline{J}_{L-1})$ that are observationally equivalent in the sense that the individuals choice probabilities they induce are equal, that

$$k_l + c_l' X_{i,l} + d_l' Y_{g(i),l} + J(p_l - p_0) = \overline{k}_l + \overline{c}_l' X_{i,l} + \overline{d}_l' Y_{g(i),l} + \overline{J}(p_l - p_0). \qquad (25)$$

Equation (25) is the same condition that was analyzed in the proof of Theorem 3.1 (compare with (A.7) in the Technical Appendix). The proof of Theorem 3.1 can, therefore, be adapted step by step to this case, allowing us to state Theorem 4.2.

Theorem 4.2. *General parametric identification for the multinomial choice model with social interactions.*

Let the true data generating process be given by eqs. (17)–(21) with the normalization $k_0 = 0, c_0 = 0, d_0 = 0, J_0 = 0$, and $\beta = 1$. Assume that the error distribution F_ε is known. Assume that the mapping defined by eq. (23) is globally one-to-one. Then the true set of model parameters $(k_1, c_1, d_1, J_1, \ldots, k_{L-1}, c_{L-1}, d_{L-1}, J_{L-1})$ is identified relative to any distinct alternative under the same assumptions 1 ... 7 as found in Theorem 3.1.

Taken together, Theorems 3 and 4 show that our basic analysis of social interactions using the multinomial logit model are not driven by the specific random payoff distribution that is assumed but rather stem from the underlying logic of the model.[9]

5 GROUP CHOICE AND BEHAVIOR CHOICE

Our analysis so far has treated groups as predetermined. For contexts such as ethnicity or gender this is presumably appropriate. However, in other contexts, such as residential neighborhoods, group memberships are themselves presumably influenced by the presence of social interactions effects. Hence a complete model of the role of social interactions on individual and group outcomes requires a joint description of both the process by which groups are formed and the subsequent behaviors they induce. As yet, the literature on social interactions has not fully developed this joint approach. In particular, analyses such as Glaeser, Sacerdote, and Scheinkman [38] and Brock and Durlauf [18, 19] that focus on the microstructure of social interactions using interacting particle systems methods, have treated the interaction structures under study as exogenous. In contrast, models such as Bénabou [10, 11], and Durlauf [30, 31] that have focused on the determinants of groups (in both cases neighborhoods) have been less concerned with the modeling of the structure of social interactions.

Further, the failure to account for the way groups form may have important econometric implications. As discussed in Brock and Durlauf [19], and Manski [53], and Moffitt [57], endogenous neighborhood choice has important implications for econometric implementation of models of neighborhood effects. Yet endogeneity of neighborhood memberships need not be an impediment to identifying neighborhood effects. Brock and Durlauf [19] show that self-selection into neighborhoods, when correctly specified, can facilitate identification via the creation of additional determinants of individual behavior in linear models and/or by inducing nonlinearities in individual behavior, each of which eliminates possible collinearity between contextual effects and endogenous effects.

In this section, we outline two approaches for the integration of group determination and individual choice in the presence of social interactions. First, we consider the integration of group choices into a linear model of behavior. Second, we integrate group and behavioral choices into a common multinomial choice framework.[10] We will not derive these models from an explicit formulation of preferences as our goal is to characterize the probability structure of behavioral choices in the presence of endogenous group memberships.

---

[9]One limitation of Theorem 4.1 is that it assumes that the distribution function F_ε is known. We are currently exploring identification in the case where F_ε is unknown.

[10]Other approaches also appear promising in terms of understanding the interplay between social interactions and group formation for particular environments. For example, Ekelund, Heckman, and Nesheim [33] show how prices associated with residential neighborhood memberships contain important information that may be used to uncover social interaction effects. Another important approach is due to Epple and Sieg [36] who show how to develop implications for the distribution of families across communities in Tiebout-type environments.

5.1 LINEAR-IN-MEANS MODELS AND ENDOGENOUS GROUP MEMBERSHIP

One approach to integrating group choice and behavioral decisions may be developed by integrating group choice into a model in which the behavior obeys a linear model. Such models are quite common in the empirical literature on social interactions and have been studied by Brock and Durlauf [18, 19], Manski [52], and Moffitt [57]. Following the formulation in Brock and Durlauf [18, 19], behavioral choices ω_i are continuous and are described by

$$\omega_i = k + c'X_i + d'Y_{g(i)} + Jm_{g(i)} + \varepsilon_i. \tag{26}$$

Relative to the multinomial choice model of behaviors, a key difference in this specification is that the possible ω_i values are ordered. Suppose that each individual assigns to each group an overall "quality" measure

$$I^*_{i,g} = \gamma'Z_{i,g} + \nu_{i,g} \tag{27}$$

where $Z_{i,g}$ denotes those observable characteristics of i that influence his evaluation of group g and $\nu_{i,g}$ denotes an unobservable individual-specific quality term. Individual i is assumed to be a member of the group with the highest $I^*_{i,g}$. We assume that $E(\varepsilon_i|X_i, Y_g, Z_{i,g}) = 0$ and $E(\nu_{i,g}|X_i, Y_g, Z_{i,g}) = 0$, $\forall i, g$. Also, we assume that the variance of ε_i, σ^2_ε, and the correlation between ε_i and $\nu_{i,g}$, ρ, are independent of group membership. This is more restrictive than the assumptions made in Lee [47]; we make this stronger assumption in order to avoid unnecessary complications.

The formulation we have described raises interesting econometric issues. First, eq. (26), known as the linear-in-means-model, has been shown to suffer from serious identification problems in the absence of endogenous group membership. Specifically, Manski [52] has shown that if there is a one-to-one correspondence between X_i and $Y_{g(i)}$ among the independent variables that appear in eq. (26), (i.e., $Y_{g(i)}$ is the average value of X_i within group g), the parameters in eq. (26) are not identified. The reason for this is that under the Manski assumption, $m_{g(i)}$ is linearly dependent on $Y_{g(i)}$. Second, linear models with self-selection into groups have received a great deal of attention in the econometric literature because of the inconsistency of ordinary least squares estimates of eq. (26). The basic problem with self-selection is that in such cases one needs to account for the possibility that $E(\varepsilon_i|i \in g) \neq 0$, a property that will hold if ε_i and $\nu_{i,g}$ are correlated.

Our goal in the subsequent discussion is to show how one can identify the parameters of the model we have described. The identification problem will be shown to revolve around the explicit incorporation of a self-selection correction into the behavioral eq. (26). Heckman [41] represents the seminal work in how to address the effects of this type of sample selection. Lee [47] has developed an approach to dealing with self-selection that we employ here. We emphasize that our purpose is illustrative in that we demonstrate identifiability only under a particular set of parametric assumptions. However, the logic of our argument is more general than the case we study and can be adapted to alternative sets of assumptions. Also, it is important to note that Ioannides and Zabel [43] recognized previously that an argument in Brock and Durlauf [19] on the use of self-selection correction to achieve identification in models with two groups could be extended to multiple groups when group membership follows a multinomial logit framework. Our derivation differs from theirs in two respects. First, we employ an approach to selection correction developed by Lee [47] rather than that due to Dubin and McFadden [29]; the relative merits of the two are discussed in Schmertmann [65] and Vella [70]. Second, we analyze how the nonlinearity of a selection correction affects identification.[11]

We require two assumptions. First we assume $\nu_{i,g}$ is double exponentially distributed as in eq. (4). Then, following Lee [47, pg. 511, eq. (3.6)] the distribution function $\Lambda_g(\cdot)$ is defined as

$$\Lambda_g(v) = \frac{\exp(v)}{\exp(v) + \sum_{j \neq g} \exp(\gamma' Z_{i,j})} \tag{28}$$

where relative to eq. (4) parameter β is normalized to equal 1. This is the function that appears in eq. (30) below. This assumption, therefore, means that the group choices obey the multinomial logit model we have already developed. Second, we assume that $\varepsilon_{i,g}$ is normally distributed; we denote the density and distributions of the standardized normal, $N(0,1)$ as $\phi(\cdot)$ and $\Phi(\cdot)$, respectively.

These assumptions allow one to transform eq. (26) in such a way as to produce a model that accounts for $E(\varepsilon_i | i \in g) \neq 0$. Following Lee [47, pg. 511, eq. (3.7)], whose analysis extends the argument that underlies Heckman [41], one may rewrite eq. (26) as

$$\omega_i = k + c'X_i + d'Y_{g(i)} + Jm_{g(i)} - \rho\sigma_\varepsilon \varphi_{g(i)}(\gamma' Z_{i,g(i)}) + \xi_{i,g(i)} \tag{29}$$

where

$$\varphi_{g(i)}(v) = \phi\left(\frac{\Phi^{-1}(\Lambda_{g(i)}(v))}{\Lambda_{g(i)}(v)}\right). \tag{30}$$

The function $\varphi_{g(i)}$ is ungainly, but is invaluable in terms of identification. In fact, there are two routes to identification in the model that are facilitated by the selection correction. To see this, it is easiest to follow Manski's assumption on the relationship between X_i and $Y_{g(i)}$ and consider

$$\omega_i = k + c'X_{i,g(i)} + d'X_{g(i)} + Jm_{g(i)} - \rho\sigma_\varepsilon \varphi_{g(i)}(\gamma' Z_{i,g(i)}) + \xi_{i,g(i)}. \tag{31}$$

---

[11]One may also consider issues raised by unobservables which do not involve self-selection for the linear-in-means model. For example, Graham and Hahn [39] study a version of eq. (26) where k is replaced by k_g. They explore alternative GMM and instrumental variables methods to identify the parameters of (26). Brock and Durlauf [19] discuss routes to identification that, for example, use differencing within groups to eliminate k_g for this context.

If $\rho = 0$, then this model is not identified. In contrast, suppose that $\rho \neq 0$ and that $m_{g(i)}$ is not an element of $Z_{i,g(i)}$. In this case $\varphi_{g(i)}(\gamma' Z_{i,g(i)})$ is an individual-specific variable whose group level average does not appear in (30). As shown in Brock and Durlauf [18, Theorem 6], the presence of such a regressor means that identification of the regression parameters in eq. (30) is possible.[12] Alternatively, suppose that $Z_{i,g(i)} = m_{i,g(i)}$, so that (outside unobserved heterogeneity), the only variable that influences group choices is the expected average behavior within the neighborhood. In this case, (30) is now a nonlinear-in-means model, in the sense that ω_i is linearly related to $J m_{g(i)} - \rho \sigma_\varepsilon \varphi_{g(i)}(\gamma m_{g(i)})$. Brock and Durlauf [19, Theorem 7] show that nonlinear in means models of this type are locally identified, except for "hairline" cases. Intuitively, the nonlinear relationship between ω_i and $m_{g(i)}$ precludes $m_{g(i)}$ from being linearly dependent when $Y_{g(i)} = X_{g(i)}$.[13]

This argument thus generalizes the analysis of identification and self-selection found in Brock and Durlauf [19, pp. 3328–3331]. The key message for empirical work is that self-selection, if properly accounted for, can facilitate the identification of social interactions.

5.2 A NESTED CHOICE APPROACH TO INTEGRATION BEHAVIORS AND GROUP MEMBERSHIPS

A second approach to endogenizing group memberships may be developed using the nested logit framework originated by Ben Akiva [12] and McFadden [54]. The basic idea of this framework is the following. An individual is assumed to make a joint decision of a group $g \in \{0, \ldots, G-1\}$ and a behavior $l \in \{0, \ldots, L-1\}$. We will denote the group choice of i as δ_i. The structure of this joint decision is nested in the sense that the choices are assumed to have a structure that allows one to decompose the decisions as occurring in two stages: first, the group is chosen and then the behavior.

The key feature of this type of model is the assumption that choices at each stage obey a multinomial logit probability structure. For the behavioral choice, this means that

$$\mu(\omega_i = l | h_{i,l,g}, p_{i,l,g}^e, \delta_i = g) = \frac{\exp \beta(h_{i,l,g} + J p_{i,l,g}^e)}{\sum_{j=0}^{L-1} \exp \beta(h_{i,l,g} + J p_{i,l,g}^e)} \qquad (32)$$

---

[12]The condition is necessary, rather than sufficient, but the presence of the variable breaks the necessary linear dependence of $m_{g(i)}$ on $Y_{g(i)}$.

[13]While this nonlinearity argument holds in principle, a common concern in empirical work with selection corrections is the "quality" of the identification for the range of observed data when identification is based on a nonlinearity argument, cf. Vella [70, pg. 135]. Hence, for the model we have described, the presence of an additional z_i that is not linearly dependent on X_i or $Y_{g(i)}$ may be very helpful in practice.

which is the same behavioral specification as eq. (6). Group choices are somewhat more complicated. In the nested logit model, group choices are assumed to obey

$$\mu(i = g | h_{i,l,g}, p^e_{i,l,g} \forall l, g) = \frac{\exp(\beta_g Z_{i,g})}{\sum_g \exp(\beta_g Z_{i,g})} \tag{33}$$

where

$$Z_{i,g} = E(\max_l h_{i,l,g} + J p^e_{i,l,g} + \varepsilon_{i,l,g}) \tag{34}$$

with $\varepsilon_{i,l,g}$ independent and doubly exponentially distributed random variables across i and l for a given g. A standard result (e.g. Anderson, de Palma, and Thisse [4, pg. 46]) is that

$$E\big(\max(h_{i,l,g} + J p^e_{i,l} + \varepsilon_{i,l,g} | h_{i,l,g}, p^e_{i,l,g} \forall l, g)\big)$$
$$= \beta^{-1} \log \left(\sum_l \exp \beta(h_{i,l,g} + J p^e_{i,l,g}) \right). \tag{35}$$

Combining, eqs. (32)–(35), the joint group membership and behavior probabilities for an individual are thus described by

$$\mu(\omega_i = l, \delta_i = g | h_{i,l,g}, p^e_{i,l,g} \forall l, g)$$
$$= \frac{\exp \left(\beta_g \beta^{-1} \log \left(\sum_l \exp \beta(h_{i,l,g} + J p^e_{i,l,g}) \right) \right)}{\sum_g \exp \left(\beta_g \beta^{-1} \log \left(\sum_l \exp \beta(h_{i,l,g} + J p^e_{i,l,g}) \right) \right)}$$
$$\cdot \frac{\exp \beta(h_{i,l,g} + J p^e_{i,l,g})}{\sum_{j=0}^{L-1} \exp \beta(h_{i,l,g} + J p^e_{i,l,g})}. \tag{36}$$

This probabilistic description may be faulted in that eq. (35) is not directly derived from a utility maximization problem. In fact, a number of papers have identified conditions under which eq. (35) is consistent with utility maximization (cf. McFadden [54] and Borsch-Supan [14] for discussion). A simple condition (cf. Anderson, dePalma, and Thisse [4, pg. 48]) that renders eq. (35) compatible with a well posed utility maximization problem is $\beta_g \leq \beta$, which in essence requires that the dispersion of random payoff terms across groups is lower than the dispersion in random payoff terms across behavioral choices within a group.

There has yet to be any analysis of models such as eq. (36) when self-consistency is imposed on the expected group choice percentages $p^e_{i,l,g}$. Such an analysis should provide a number of interesting results. For example, a nested structure of this type introduces a new mechanism by which multiple equilibria may emerge, namely the influence of beliefs about group behaviors on group memberships, which reciprocally will affect behaviors. This additional channel for social interactions, in turn, raises new identification questions.

6   CONCLUSIONS

This chapter has described an approach to modeling social interactions that extends standard tools in the discrete choice literature, namely logit models of choice. The approach allows for the incorporation of a range of alternative types of social interactions into individual decisionmaking in a way that retains the logic of economic behavior while at the same time provides additional richness to the determinants of individual behavior. A virtue of the approach is that the theoretical model can be directly taken to data, both in the sense that the description of equilibrium choices is simultaneously a likelihood function and because the various group influences embedded in the model are identifiable under intuitive and reasonably weak conditions. This has been demonstrated through the analysis of a leading case, namely, a multinomial logit version of the model. We have also shown that the qualitative theoretical and econometric features of our leading case, the multinomial logit model, also apply to alternative formulations of the random payoff process. Finally, we have illustrated how one can integrate choices about group memberships with choices on behaviors using a nested multinomial logit model.

More generally, we believe that there is wide scope for the better integration of sociological ideas and economic reasoning to provide a deeper understanding of the various phenomena that engage both disciplines. An important feature of the new social economics [32] is that it attempts to explain phenomena ranging from crime to fertility to education where sociological factors would seem to play a key role. Economists have long understood the importance of addressing such factors. Arrow [5], for example, remarks

> ...there are profound difficulties with the price system, even, so to speak, within its own logic, and these strengthen the view that, valuable though it is in certain realms, it cannot be made the arbiter of social life. (p. 21–22)

The models we analyze address one aspect of the general issues raised by Arrow and others by embedding individual choice in contexts where social factors exist outside the realm of markets or prices. In turn, we believe that the choice-based approach we have developed is valuable in terms of providing a logical structure to sociological-style arguments. One reason for this judgment is that social explanations of aggregate phenomena are most useful when the implied rules for individual behavior are interpretable as purposeful decisions. Arrow [6] makes precisely this argument:

> It is a salutary check on any theory of the economy or any other part of society that the explanations make sense on the basis of the individuals involved. (p. 3)

The theoretical and econometric approach we advocate is inspired by and attempts to implement Arrow's vision.

TECHNICAL APPENDIX

Proof of Theorem 2.1.
In verifying this theorem, it is convenient to rewrite eq. (8) so as to measure the deviation of choice probabilities from $l = 0$; i.e., we work with $m_l = p_l - p_0$ and $g_{i,l} = h_{i,l} - h_{i,0}, l = 1, \ldots, L - 1$. The probability differences m_l may be written as

$$m_l = \int \frac{\exp(\beta g_{i,l} + \beta J m_l) - 1}{W_i dF_h} \tag{1}$$

where

$$W_i = \sum_{l=1}^{L-1} \exp(\beta g_{i,l} + \beta J m_l) + 1. \tag{2}$$

Letting $m = (m_1, \ldots, m_{L-1})$ and $g = (g_1, \ldots, g_{L-1})$, the $L - 1$ equations defined by (A.1) and (A.2) constitute a mapping from $[-1, 1]^{L-1}$ to $[-1, 1]^{L-1}$ which we denote as $\psi(m, \beta J, g)$. Fixed points of the mapping are defined by $m = \psi(m, \beta J, g)$ and constitute the self-consistent equilibria of the model. The question of the relationship between the behavioral parameters of the model and the number of equilibria may be answered by determining how this mapping changes as βJ changes under the assumptions of the theorem. Under the assumption that $h_{i,l} = k \; \forall i, l$, it is of course the case that $g = 0$, since there are no differences in the private deterministic utility differences between choices. This assumption allows the analysis to focus entirely on the effect of βJ. Under this assumption, there exists a fixed point $m = 0$ for any value of βJ. To see whether other fixed points exist, we compute the derivative of $\psi(m, \beta J, 0)$ with respect to m at the fixed point $m = 0$. The Jacobian matrix of derivatives of $\psi(m, \beta J, 0)$ taken with respect to elements of m contains diagonal elements

$$\frac{\partial \psi_l(m, \beta J, 0)}{\partial m_l} = \frac{\beta J \exp(\beta j m_l)}{\left(\sum_{i=1}^{L-1} \exp(\beta J m_j) \right) + 1} - \frac{\beta J (\exp(\beta J m_l) - 1)(\exp(\beta J m_l))}{\left(\left(\sum_{i=1}^{L-1} \exp(\beta J m_j) \right) + 1 \right)^2} \tag{3}$$

and off-diagonal elements

$$\frac{\partial \psi_l(m, \beta J, 0)}{\partial m_j} = -\frac{\beta J (\exp(\beta J m_l) - 1)(\exp(\beta J m_j))}{\left(\left(\sum_{i=1}^{L-1} \exp(\beta J m_i) \right) + 1 \right)^2} \tag{4}$$

so for $m = 0$,

$$\frac{\partial \psi_l(0, \beta J, 0)}{\partial m_k} = \frac{\beta J}{L} \text{if } l = k, 0 \text{ otherwise}. \tag{5}$$

Consider the set of vectors m of the form $(m_1, 0)$, i.e., vectors with zero components except for the first element. Denote the set of all such vectors by Γ_1. Observe that Γ_1, which lies in R^{L-1}, is an invariant set with respect to $\psi(m, \beta J, 0)$ as each element of Γ_1 maps onto an element of Γ_1. We now focus on the first component of the ψ map, ψ_1, which can always be written as a one-dimensional map on R, denote this as $\rho(m_1, \beta J)$.

Finally, consider fixed points for the mapping $\rho(m_1, \beta J)$. One fixed point exists, as previously observed, at $m_1 = 0$. Further, recall that by (A.5),

$$\frac{\partial \rho(0, \beta J)}{\partial m_1} = \frac{\beta J}{L}. \tag{6}$$

It is easy to verify that ρ is a convexo-concave function with respect to its first argument. This means that as $\beta J / L$ becomes greater than 1, two new fixed points must emerge. This argument is sufficient to verify Theorem 2.1. ∎

Proof of Theorem 3.1.

This proof is a generalization of the proof for identification for a binary choice model in Brock and Durlauf [18, 19] which, in turn, develops a mode of argument found in Manski [51]. Suppose that for $(k_1, c_1, d_1, J_1, \ldots, k_{L-1}, c_{L-1}, d_{L-1}, J_{L-1})$, the set of true parameters for the multinomial choice model, there exists another vector $(\overline{k}_1, \overline{c}_1, \overline{d}_1, \overline{J}_1, \ldots, \overline{k}_{L-1}, \overline{c}_{L-1}, \overline{d}_{L-1}, \overline{J}_{L-1})$ that generates the same observed data. If both sets of parameters generate the same probabilities for the observables, this implies,

$$\ln \frac{p_{li}}{p_{0i}} = k_l + c'_l X_{i,l} + d'_l Y_{g(i),l} + J_l(p_l - p_0) = \overline{k}_l + \overline{c}'_l X_{i,l} + \overline{d}'_l Y_{g(i),l} + \overline{J}_l(p_l - p_0) \tag{7}$$

for $l = 1, \ldots, L - 1$. From assumption 4 of the Theorem, there is at least one neighborhood for each choice l such that within that neighborhood, $X_{i,l}$ is not contained in a proper linear subspace of R^r. Hence, (A.7) can hold if and only if $c_l = \overline{c}_l$. This argument applies to each of the possible choices, so $c_1, \ldots, c_{L-1}$ are identified.

Given that $c_1, \ldots, c_{L-1}$ are identified, it must be the case that the Theorem is true if $J = \overline{J}$; lack of identification would imply that either (1) $(X_{i,l}, Y_{g(i),l})$ lies in a proper linear subspace of R^{r+s}, which would violate assumption 1 of the theorem or (2) that some linear combination of elements in $(X_{i,l}, Y_{g(i),l})$ is constant, which would violate assumption 3. We can, therefore, restrict attention to the case $J \neq \overline{J}$. Define $m_{g(i),l} = p_{g(i),l} - p_{g(i),0}$. Notice that $m_{g(i),l}$ is bounded between -1 and 1. Since $c_1, \ldots, c_{L-1}$ are identified, (A.7) requires that

$$k_l - \overline{k}_l + (d'_l - \overline{d}'_l)Y_{g(i),l} = (\overline{J}_l - J_l)m_{g(i),l} \tag{8}$$

since $c_l = \overline{c}_l \forall l$. Since $m_{l,g(i)}$ cannot be zero for all $g(i)$ by assumption 6 and since assumption 5 implies that $(d'_l - \overline{d}'_l)Y_{g(i),l}$ is unbounded if $d_l \neq \overline{d}_l$, we have a contradiction to the boundedness of $(\overline{J}_l - J_l)m_{g(i),l}$ unless $d_l = \overline{d}_l$. Failure of identification now requires that

$$k_l - \overline{k}_l = (\overline{J}_l - J_l)m_{g(i),l} \tag{9}$$

holds across all groups. Given assumption 6, the nonconstancy of $p_{l,g(i)}$ (and thus $m_{g(i),l}$) across groups, can only hold across neighborhoods if $J_l = \overline{J}_l$. Substituting this into (A.7), it is obvious that $k_l = \overline{k}_l$ which completes the proof. ∎

Proof of Corollary 3.1.
Following the proof of Theorem 3.1, Corollary 3.1 will be proved if one can show that

$$\ln \frac{p_{li}}{p_{0i}} = k_l + c_l' X_{i,l} + d_l' Y_{g(i),l} + J_l'(p_l - p_0) = \overline{k}_l + \overline{c}_l' X_{i,l} + \overline{d}_l' Y_{g(i),l} + \overline{J}_l'(p_l - p_0) \tag{10}$$

cannot hold for any $(\overline{k}_1, \overline{c}_1, \overline{d}_1, \overline{J}_1, \ldots, \overline{k}_{L-1}, \overline{c}_{L-1}, \overline{d}_{L-1}, \overline{J}_{L-1})$, distinct from $(k_1, c_1, d_1, J_1, \ldots, k_{L-1}, c_{L-1}, d_{L-1}, J_{L-1})$. The argument made immediately after (A.7) applies to (A.10) as well, which means that $c_1, \ldots, c_{L-1}$ are identified. Similarly, the argument made after (A.8) applies to (A.10) which implies that $d_1, \ldots, d_{L-1}$ are identified. Hence, we can restrict our attention to

$$k_l - \overline{k}_l = (\overline{J}_l - J_l)' m_{g(i)} . \tag{11}$$

Given the assumption of the Corollary that the support of $m_g(i)$ does not lie in a proper linear subspace of R^{L-1}, (A.11) can only hold if $\overline{J}_l = J_l$. This implies $k_l = \overline{k}_l$ which verifies the Corollary. ∎

Proof of Theorem 4.1.
To verify Theorem 4.1, we follow the same logic as the proof for Theorem 2.1. Define the mapping

$$m_l = \int (p_{i,l} - p_{i,0}) dF_h \tag{12}$$

$l = 1 \ldots L - 1$. By eq. (23) in the text, this defines a mapping $\psi(m_1, 0, \beta J, \beta)$ from m to m. Under the assumption that $h_{i,l} = 0 \; \forall i, l$, it is straightforward to verify that $\Gamma_1 = (m_1, 0)$ is an invariant set under this mapping. Hence, in parallel to the proof of Theorem 2.1, there is a mapping $\rho(m_1, \beta J, \beta)$ from R to R such that

$$\rho(m_1, \beta J, \beta) = \psi_1(m_1, 0, \beta J, \beta) . \tag{13}$$

Under the assumptions that $h_{i,l} = 0 \; \forall i, l$ and $\varepsilon_{i,l}$ are independent across i and l, it is immediate that $m_1 = 0$ must be a fixed point of this mapping.

The existence of other fixed points will depend on the derivative of $\rho(\cdot, \cdot, \cdot)$ at $m_1 = 0$. To analyze this derivative, note that

$$p_{i,1} - p_{i,0} = \int \prod_{j \neq 1} F_\varepsilon(\beta J m_1 - \beta J m_j + \varepsilon) dF_\varepsilon$$

$$- \int \prod_{j \neq 0} F_\varepsilon(\beta J m_0 - \beta J m_j + \varepsilon) dF_\varepsilon = \int \prod_{j \neq 1} F_\varepsilon(\beta J m_1 + \varepsilon) dF_\varepsilon$$

$$- \int \prod_{j \neq 0} F_\varepsilon(-\beta J m_1 + \varepsilon) dF_\varepsilon \qquad (14)$$

since $m_l = 0$ for $l = 2, \ldots, L-1$. Further, given the assumptions that $h_{i,l} = 0$ $\forall i, l$ and $\varepsilon_{i,l}$ are independent across i and l, $p_{i,1} - p_{i,0} = m_1$. Therefore, we can define a map A from m_1 to itself such that

$$m_1 = A(\beta J m_1, L, \beta). \qquad (15)$$

This function, which is clearly monotonic and bounded between -1 and 1, depends on L through the products in (A.12) via (A.14). The derivative of this function is $\beta J A'(\beta J m_1, L, \beta)$. Consider $\beta J A'(0, L, \beta)$, the derivative of the function at the fixed point $m_1 = 0$. Following the same argument in the proof of Theorem 2.1, if $\beta J A'(0, L, \beta) < 1$, then the fixed point $m_1 = 0$ is unique, whereas if $\beta J A'(0, L, \beta) > 1$ then at least two additional fixed points must exist. Hence the magnitude of βJ can be varied so as to move from a unique to multiple (at least three) equilibria. This verifies Theorem 4.1. ■

ACKNOWLEDGMENTS

We thank the John D. and Catherine T. MacArthur Foundation, National Science Foundation, University of Wisconsin Graduate School, and Vilas Trust for financial support. Artur Minkin, Eldar Nigmatullin, and Chih Ming Tan have provided outstanding research assistance. The research presented here is part of the Santa Fe Institute Economics Program. This chapter is written in honor of Kenneth Arrow.

REFERENCES

[1] Aizer, A., and J. Currie. "Networks or Neighborhood? Correlations in the Use of Publicly-Funded Maternity Care in California." Working Paper no. 9209, National Bureau of Economic Research, Cambridge, MA, 2002.

[2] Akerlof, G. "Social Distance and Social Decisions." *Econometrica* **65** (1997): 10005–10027.

[3] Amaro de Matos, J., and J. Perez. "Fluctuations in the Curie-Weiss Version of the Random Field Ising Model." *J. Stat. Phys.* **62** (1991): 587–608.

[4] Anderson, S., A. de Palma, and J. Thisse. *Discrete Choice Theory of Product Differentiation.* Cambridge, MA: MIT Press, 1992.

[5] Arrow, K. *The Limits of Organization.* New York: W. W. Norton, 1974.

[6] Arrow, K. "Methodological Individualism and Social Knowledge." *Am. Econ. Rev.* **84(2)** (1994): 1–9.

[7] Arrow, K., and F. Hahn. *General Competitive Analysis.* Amsterdam: North Holland, 1971.

[8] Bayer, P., and C. Timmins. "Identifying Social Interactions in Endogenous Sorting Models." Mimeo, Yale University, New Haven, CT, 2001.

[9] Becker, G., and K. Murphy. *Social Economics.* Cambridge, MA: Harvard University Press, 2000.

[10] Bénabou, R. "Workings of a City: Location, Education, and Production." *Quart. J. Econ.* **CVIII** (1993): 619–652.

[11] Bénabou, R. "Equity and Efficiency in Human Capital Investment: The Local Connection." *Rev. Econ. Stud.* **62** (1996): 237–264.

[12] Ben Akiva, M. "Structure of Passenger Travel Demand Models." Ph.D diss., Department of Civil Engineering, MIT, 1973.

[13] Ben Akiva, M., and S. Lerman. *Discrete Choice Analysis: Theory and Application to Travel Demand.* Cambridge, MA: MIT Press, 1985.

[14] Borsch-Supan, A. "On the Compatibility of Nested Logit Models with Utility Maximization." *J. Econ.* **43** (1990): 373–388.

[15] Brewster, K. "Race Differences in Sexual Activity Among Adolescent Women: The Role of Neighborhood Characteristics." *Am. Socio. Rev.* **59** (1994): 408–424.

[16] Brock, W. "Pathways to Randomness in the Economy: Emergent Nonlinearity and Chaos in Economics and Finance." *Estudios Economicos* **8** (1993): 3–55.

[17] Brock, W., and S. Durlauf. "A Formal Model of Theory Choice in Science." *Economic Theory* **14** (1999): 113–130.

[18] Brock, W., and S. Durlauf. "Discrete Choice with Social Interactions." *Rev. Econ. Stud.* **68** (2001): 235–260.

[19] Brock, W., and S. Durlauf. "Interactions-Based Models." In *Handbook of Econometrics 5*, edited by J. Heckman and E. Leamer. Amsterdam: North-Holland, 2001.

[20] Brock, W., and S. Durlauf. "A Multinomial Choice Model of Neighborhood Effects." *Am. Econ. Rev.* **92** (2002): 298–303.

[21] Brooks-Gunn, J., G. Duncan, P. Klebanov, and N. Sealand. "Do Neighborhoods Affect Child and Adolescent Development?." *Am. J. Socio.* **99(2)** (1993): 353–395.

[22] Conley, T., and G. Topa. "Socio-Economic Distance and Spatial Patterns in Unemployment." *J. Applied Econ.* **17** (2002): 303–327.

[23] Cooper, R. *Coordination Games*. New York: Cambridge University Press, 1999.

[24] Corcoran, M., R. Gordon, D. Laren, and G. Solon. "The Association between Men's Economic Status and Their Family and Community Origins." *J. Human Res.* **27** (1992): 575–601.

[25] Costa, D., and M. Kahn. "Cowards and Heroes: Group Loyalty in the Civil War." Working Paper 8627, National Bureau of Economic Research, Cambridge, MA, 2001.

[26] Crane, J. "The Epidemic Theory of Ghettos and Neighborhood Effects on Dropping Out and Teenage Childbearing." *Am. J. Socio.* **96** (1991): 1226–1259.

[27] Datcher, L. "Effects of Community and Family Background on Achievement." *Rev. Econ. & Stat.* **64** (1982): 32–41.

[28] de Selincourt, A. *Herodotus, The Histories*. New York: Penguin, 1996

[29] Dubin, J., and D. McFadden. "An Econometric Analysis of Residential Electric Appliance Holdings and Consumption." *Econometrica* **52** (1984): 345–362.

[30] Durlauf S. "A Theory of Persistent Income Inequality." *J. Econ. Growth* **1** (1996): 75–93.

[31] Durlauf, S. "Neighborhood Feedbacks, Endogenous Stratification, and Income Inequality." In *Dynamic Disequilibrium Modelling*, edited by W. Barnett, G. Gandolfo, and C. Hillinger. Cambridge, MA: Cambridge University Press, 1996.

[32] Durlauf, S., and H. P. Young. "The New Social Economics." In *Social Dynamics*, edited by S. Durlauf and H. P. Young, 1–14. Cambridge, MA: MIT Press, 2001.

[33] Ekelund, I., J. Heckman, and L. Nesheim. "Identification and Estimation of Hedonic Price Models." Mimeo, Department of Economics, University of Chicago, 2001.

[34] Ellis, R. *Entropy, Large Deviations, and Statistical Mechanics*. New York: Springer-Verlag, 1985.

[35] Ellis, R., and K. Wang. "Limit Theorems for the Empirical Vector of the Cuire-Weiss-Potts Model." *Stochastic Processes and Their Applications* **40** (1990): 251–288.

[36] Epple, D., and H. Sieg. "Estimation Equilibrium Models of Local Jurisdictions." *J. Pol. Econ.* **107** (1999): 645–681.

[37] Ginther, D., R. Haveman, and B. Wolfe. "Neighborhood Attributes as Determinants of Children's Outcomes: How Robust are the Relationships?" *J. Human Res.* **35(4)** (2000): 603–642.

[38] Glaeser, E., B. Sacerdote, and J. Scheinkman. "Crime and Social Interactions." *Quart. J. Econ.* **CXI** (1996): 507–548.

[39] Graham, B., and J. Hahn. "Identification and Estimation of Linear-in-Means Models." Mimeo, Department of Economics, Harvard University, 2003.

[40] Granovetter, M. "Economic Action and Social Structure: The Problem of Embeddedness." *Am. J. Soc.* **91(3)** (1985): 481–510.

[41] Heckman, J. "Sample Selection Bias as a Specification Error." *Econometrica* **47** (1979): 153–161.

[42] Hoff, K., and A. Sen. "Home-Ownership, Community Interactions, and Segregation." Mimeo, World Bank, 2000.

[43] Ioannides, Y., and J. Zabel. "Interactions, Neighborhood Selection, and Housing Demand." Mimeo, Department of Economics, Tufts University, 2002.

[44] Ioannides, Y., and J. Zabel. "Neighborhood Effects and Housing Demand." Mimeo, Tufts University, 2002.

[45] Katz, L., J. Kling, and J. Liebman. "Moving to Opportunity in Boston: Early Results of a Randomized Mobility Experiment." *Quart. J. Econ.* **CXVI** (2001): 607–654.

[46] Kooreman, P., and A. Soetevent. "A Discrete Choice Model with Social Interactions: An Analysis of High School Teen Behavior." Mimeo, Department of Economics, University of Groningen, 2002.

[47] Lee, L.-F. "Generalized Econometric Models with Selectivity." *Econometrica* **51** (1983): 507–512.

[48] Loury, G. "A Dynamic Theory of Racial Income Differences." In *Women, Minorities, and Employment Discrimination*, edited by P. Wallace and A. Lamond. Lexington MA: Lexington Books, 1977.

[49] Lundberg, S., and R. Startz. "On the Persistence of Racial Inequality." *J. Labor Econ.* **16(2)** (1998): 292–323.

[50] Ludwig, J., G. Duncan, and P. Hirschfield. "Urban Poverty and Juvenile Crime: Evidence from a Randomized Housing-Mobility Experiment." *Quart. J. Econ.* **116(2)** (2001): 655–680.

[51] Manski, C. "Identification of Binary Choice Models." *J. Am. Stat. Assoc.* **83(403)** (1988): 729–738.

[52] Manski, C. "Identification of Endogenous Social Effects: The Reflection Problem." *Rev. Econ. Stud.* **60** (1993): 531–542.

[53] Manski, C. "Economic Analysis of Social Interactions." *J. Econ. Perspectives* **14** (2000): 115–136.

[54] McFadden, D. "Modelling the Choice of Residential Location." In *Spatial Interaction Theory and Planning Models*, edited by A. Karlvist, L. Lunqvuist, F. Snickars, and J. Weibull, 75–96. Amsterdam: North Holland, 1978.

[55] McFadden, D. "Qualitative Response Models." In *Handbook of Econometrics 2*, edited by Z. Griliches and M. Intriligator, 1395–1457. Amsterdam: North Holland, 1984.

[56] Minkin, A. "Heterogeneous Social Interactions." Mimeo, Department of Economics, University of Wisconsin, 2002.

[57] Moffitt, R. "Policy Interventions, Low-Level Equilibria, and Social Interactions." In *Social Dynamics*, edited by S. Durlauf and H. P. Young, 45–82. Cambridge, MA: MIT Press, 2001.

[58] Nigmatullin, E. "Neighborhood Interactions and Fertility Dynamics." Mimeo, Department of Economics, University of Wisconsin, 2002.

[59] Plotnick, R., and S. Hoffman. "The Effect of Neighborhood Characteristics on Young Adult Outcomes: Alternative Estimates." *Soc. Sci. Quart.* **80** (1999): 1–18.

[60] Rosenbaum, E., and L. Harris. "Residential Mobility and Opportunities: Early Impacts of the Moving to Opportunity Demonstration in Chicago." *Housing Policy Debate* **12** (2001): 321–346.

[61] Rosenbaum, J. "Changing the Geography of Opportunity by Expanding Residential Choice: Lessons from the Gautreaux Program." *Housing Policy Debate* **6** (1995): 231–269.

[62] Rosenbaum, J., and S. Popkin. "Employment and Earnings of Low-Income Blacks Who Move to Middle Class Suburbs." In *The Urban Underclass*, edited by C. Jencks and P. Peterson. Washington, DC: Brookings Institution Press, 1991.

[63] Sampson, R., J. Morenoff, and F. Earls. "Beyond Social Capital: Collective Efficacy for Children." *Am. Socio. Rev.* **64** (1999): 633–660.

[64] Sampson, R., S. Raudenbush, and F. Earls. "Neighborhoods and Violent Crime: A Study of Collective Efficacy." *Science* **277** (1997): 918–924.

[65] Schmertmann, C. "Selectivity Bias Correction Methods in Polychotomous Sample Selection Models." *J. Econ.* **60** (1994): 101–132.

[66] Sirakaya, S. "Recidivism and Social Interactions." Mimeo, Department of Economics, University of Wisconsin, 2002.

[67] South, S., and E. Baumer. "Deciphering Community and Race Effects on Adolescent Premarital Childbearing." *Social Forces* **78(4)** (2000): 1379–1408.

[68] South, S., and K. Crowder. "Neighborhood Effects on Family Formation: Concentrated Poverty and Beyond." *Am. Socio. Rev.* **64** (1999): 113–132.

[69] Topa, G. "Social Interactions, Local Spillovers, and Unemployment." *Rev. Econ. Stud.* **68(2)** (2001): 261–295.

[70] Vella, F. "Estimating Models with Sample Selection Bias: A Survey." *J. Human Res.* **33(1)** (1998): 127–169.

Heterogeneity and Uniqueness in Interaction Games

Stephen Morris
Hyun Song Shin

Incomplete information games, local interaction games, and random matching games are all special cases of a general class of interaction games [22]. In this chapter, we use this equivalence to present a unified treatment of arguments generating uniqueness in games with strategic complementarities by introducing heterogeneity in these different settings. We also report on the relationship between local and global heterogeneity, on the role of strategic multipliers, and on purification in the three types of interaction game.

1 INTRODUCTION

In an incomplete information game, players are uncertain about the environment that they are in. We can represent their uncertainty by saying that each player is one of a large set of possible types, and the type profile for all players is drawn

The Economy as an Evolving Complex System III,
edited by Lawrence E. Blume and Steven N. Durlauf, Oxford University Press

from some distribution. In random matching games, a large population of players are interacting; which player is randomly matched with which other player is determined by a random draw. In a local interaction game, a large number of players are located either physically or socially in a network of relations with other players; a player's payoff depends on his own actions and the actions of players who are close to him in the network. These three classes of games share the feature that each player/type of a player will want to choose an action that is a best response to a distribution of his opponents' actions. In the incomplete information case, one type of one player is uncertain which type(s) of his (known) opponent(s) he is facing. In the random matching case, each player is uncertain which opponent he is facing. In the local interaction case, each player is facing a distribution of actions by nearby players. In fact, all these classes of games can be shown to be special cases of a class of *interaction games* [22]. This equivalence throws new light on old problems by drawing out the analogies between different categories of models and suggesting new directions in which to take the analysis.[1] By highlighting the common elements in the structure of the arguments, it allows us to identify the essential elements in the arguments.

In this chapter, we focus on one particular set of issues and see how they translate across different types of interaction games. Complete information games with strategic complementarities often have multiple equilibria. Introducing heterogeneity often reduces the amount of multiplicity. A simple intuition for why this might be the case comes from thinking about a symmetric payoff game with continuous actions. In this case, we can look for (symmetric) equilibria by looking at the best response function of the game. In a game with strategic complementarities, this best response function will be increasing. The set of equilibria will correspond to the set of points where the best response function $b(.)$ crosses the 45° line, as illustrated in figure 1.

Now suppose that we introduce heterogeneity of some kind, so that a player is no longer sure that his opponent is choosing the same action, but instead has a diffuse belief over his opponents' actions. This will tend to smooth out the best response function, perhaps generating uniqueness. Such heterogeneity can be generated by incomplete information, local interaction, or random matching. Various papers in the literature generate uniqueness by adding heterogeneity, including (1) for incomplete information, the global games analysis of Carlsson and van Damme [6] and Morris and Shin [24, 28], quantal response equilibria of McKelvey and Palfrey [16] and the arms race game of Baliga and Sjöström [3]; and (2) for random matching, Herrendorf, Valentinyi, and Waldmann [15]. We will describe a formal model that will translate naturally from incomplete information to random matching to local interaction settings where we can see how

---

[1]For example, the results in Morris [20] were obtained by translating results about approximate common knowledge in incomplete information games into a local interaction setting: the local interaction analogue of almost common knowledge events is cohesive neighborhoods, where *all* players have most of their neighbors within the neighborhood.

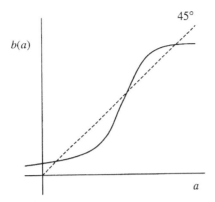

FIGURE 1   Best response function.

the "heterogeneity implies uniqueness" argument works in general (in sections 2 and 3).

One immediate benefit of our exercise is the reconciliation of two themes in the literature that are apparently at odds with each other. On the one hand, there are arguments that show how very small but highly correlated heterogeneity generates uniqueness (e.g., the global games papers above). Such arguments often require sufficiently *small* heterogeneity to guarantee uniqueness. On the other hand, there are some arguments where *large* independent heterogeneity is required for uniqueness (e.g., among the papers listed above, McKelvey and Palfrey [16], Baliga and Sjöström [3] and Herrendorf, Valentinyi, and Waldmann [15]).

On the surface, these apparently contradictory results present a confused picture of this field. However, this appearance is deceptive. When the underlying nature of the strategic uncertainty is formalized properly, there is a common framework that ties together these disparate results in the literature. That framework is one where we can separate out the uncertainty concerning the underlying *fundamentals* of the game (such as uncertainty over payoff parameters), from the *strategic uncertainty* facing the players, which has to do with the uncertainty over the actions of the other players. Stated loosely, what matters for uniqueness is that the strategic uncertainty be quite insensitive to a player's type. Thus, when taken to extreme, the conditions that are most conducive for uniqueness are those in which strategic uncertainty is *invariant* to a player's type. In some cases, such invariance is best achieved by having very small noise, but in other cases, invariance results from very large noise. From these insights, we can provide a sufficient condition for uniqueness that naturally embeds both cases. We do this in section 4.

Another theme explored here is the idea of strategic *multipliers* (section 5). Cooper and John [8] noted that, in games with strategic complementarities, it is useful to distinguish two mechanisms by which an increased desirability of an action translates into higher equilibrium actions. First, given the actions of one's opponents, each player has a private incentive to increase his own action. Second, each player anticipates that others will also raise their actions, giving rise to a multiplier effect. Versions of this effect are labelled the social multiplier in the local interaction literature (see, e.g., Glaeser and Scheinkman [12]). In an incomplete information context, Morris and Shin [24, sec. 3] have noted how private information about the desirability of raising one's action has less impact than equally informative public information. Intuitively, public information tells you not only that it is desirable for you to raise your action, but also that others will be doing so. There is a *publicity multiplier* that is the analogue of the social multiplier in the local interaction literature.[2] In the case where small heterogeneity generates uniqueness (e.g., the global games case), it is also useful to distinguish a third mechanism by which an increased desirability of an action translates into higher equilibrium actions. The strategic multiplier of Cooper and John [8] is a comparative statics concept applied to a particular equilibrium. It is an *intra*-equilibrium notion, identifying how a complete information Nash equilibrium varies as a payoff parameter favoring higher actions increases. In global games, we also identify a point at which there is a jump from one equilibrium to another of the complete information game. This *inter*-equilibrium effect will locally be much larger than the intra-equilibrium effect and it is useful to distinguish them. Of course, this combination of effects arises in local interaction and random matching games, as well as in incomplete information games.

A final issue that we touch on is the *purification* of mixed strategy equilibria (in section 6). The classical interpretation of mixed strategies is that players are deliberately randomizing. The Bayesian interpretation of mixed strategies says that players do not deliberately randomize; rather, a player's mixed strategy represents other players' uncertainty about that player's pure strategy. Harsanyi [13] showed that for any mixed strategy equilibrium of a complete information game, if we added a small amount of independent payoff shocks to each player's payoffs, the induced incomplete information game would have a pure strategy equilibrium that converged—in average behavior—to the original mixed strategy equilibrium as noise goes to zero. In his 1950 thesis (reprinted in Nash [32]), Nash gave a large population analogue of the Bayesian view of mixed strategies: in a large population, each player may follow a pure strategy but will have a non-degenerate distribution over the play of his opponent. Average play in the population will correspond to a mixed strategy of the underlying game. Of course, in the interaction game interpretation, these arguments are one and the same.

---

[2]Morris and Shin [27] investigate this publicity multiplier in more detail.

Another class of games in which heterogeneity generates uniqueness is dynamic games. If a large number of players are unable to adjust their behavior at identical times, they will similarly face non-degenerate beliefs about the population's play, again leading to uniqueness (e.g., Matsui and Matsuyama [17], Morris [21], Frankel, and Pauzner [10], and Burdzy, Frankel, and Pauzner [5]). However, the connection of such games to interaction games is not direct. We will also discuss a (slightly contrived) dynamic interpretation of interaction games that may help understand the relation to the dynamic uniqueness results, by analogy.

Our main purpose in this chapter is to relate some existing work by ourselves and others in a way that sheds light on both the original results and on the relationship between different classes of interaction games. In our survey of the theory and applications of global games, Morris and Shin [26], a section called "Related Models: Local Heterogeneity and Uniqueness" touched on the issues raised in this chapter. This chapter can thus be seen as a detailed elaboration of the argument there. The main results reported here are straightforward applications of the type of argument used in Frankel, Morris, and Pauzner [11]. Ui [33] discussed a class of games with *correlated quantal responses*, noting how global games and McKelvey and Palfrey's [16] quantal response equilibria could be understood as special cases of the same class of games, with different correlation assumptions. That paper introduced the very valuable parameterization of global games using the correlation described in section 2. The relation between global games and Harsanyi's [13] purification result was the subject of appendix B of Carlsson and van Damme [6].

2   BINARY ACTION LEADING EXAMPLE

In this section, we first introduce a simple binary action example with a random matching interpretation. Then we discuss alternative—incomplete information, local interaction, and dynamic—interpretations. We also note how the correlation structure of players' types could be related back to properties of private and public signals. We also discuss the origins of this example and its relationship to the literature.

2.1   EXAMPLE

Consider the following random matching game. Two players are randomly chosen from a population. Each player i is characterized by a payoff parameter x_i. The payoffs from their interaction are given by:

		Player 2	
		0	1
Player 1	0	$1, 1$	$0, x_2$
	1	$x_1, 0$	x_1, x_2

We assume that the payoff parameter is normally distributed in the population with mean y and standard deviation σ. However, the draws from the population are not independent: two players are more likely to be chosen to interact if they have similar payoff parameters. Thus, x_1 and x_2 are jointly normally distributed with correlation coefficient ρ (and each has mean y and standard deviation σ). A pure strategy in this game is a mapping $s : \mathbb{R} \to \{0, 1\}$.

This is a *private values* game in which a player knows the payoff to action 1. In this sense, there is no fundamental uncertainty. The only type of uncertainty facing a player is the strategic uncertainty over the opponent's action, which in turn is attributable to the uncertainty over the opponent's payoff parameter. When x_i is either very high (greater than one) or very low (less than zero), player i has a dominant action. Thus, strategic uncertainty is relevant for player i only when x_i lies between zero and one.

As a first step to solving this game, let us first look for equilibria in switching strategies in which there is a threshold value $\hat{x}$ below which a player chooses action 0, but above which he takes action 1. Since the game is symmetric, let us start by looking for equilibria where this threshold value $\hat{x}$ is common to both players.

The expected payoff to player 1 from taking action 0 when his own payoff parameter is x_1 is given by

$$\text{Prob}\,(x_2 < \hat{x}|x_1)\ .$$

His payoff to action 1 is x_1 itself, and so action 1 is preferred when

$$x_1 - \text{Prob}\,(x_2 < \hat{x}|x_1) > 0\ .$$

Action 0 is preferred if this inequality is reversed. At any switching point $\hat{x}$, a player is indifferent between the two actions, so that

$$\hat{x} - \text{Prob}\,(x_2 < \hat{x}|\hat{x}) = 0\ . \tag{1}$$

How many solutions are there of this equation? If there is more than one solution, then we can construct more than one switching equilibrium. The question boils down to how sensitive the conditional probability $(\text{Prob}(x_2 < \hat{x}|\hat{x}))$ is with respect to shifts in the switching point $\hat{x}$. If this probability were invariant to shifts in $\hat{x}$, then (1) would imply that $\hat{x} = c$ for some constant c, and we would have a unique solution for $\hat{x}$.

In our case, since x_1 and x_2 are jointly normal with equal variances, if player 1 has payoff parameter x_1, he will believe that x_2 is distributed normally with mean

$$\rho x_1 + (1 - \rho) y \tag{2}$$

and variance $\sigma^2 (1 - \rho^2)$. Thus,

$$\text{Prob}\, (x_2 < \hat{x}|x_1) = \Phi \left(\frac{\hat{x} - \rho x_1 - (1 - \rho)\, y}{\sigma \sqrt{1 - \rho^2}} \right) \tag{3}$$

where $\Phi\,(.)$ is the cumulative distribution function of the standard normal. In particular, when $x_1 = \hat{x}$,

$$\text{Prob}\, (x_2 < \hat{x}|\hat{x}) = \Phi \left(\frac{(1 - \rho)\, \hat{x} - (1 - \rho)\, y}{\sigma \sqrt{1 - \rho^2}} \right)$$

$$= \Phi \left(\frac{\hat{x} - y}{\sigma} \cdot \sqrt{\frac{1 - \rho}{1 + \rho}} \right). \tag{4}$$

Note two special cases of this conditional probability. First, when σ becomes large, the expression inside the brackets in (4) goes to zero, so that $\text{Prob}(x_2 < \hat{x}|\hat{x})$ tends to the constant $1/2$. In this limit, there is a unique solution to (1) given by $\hat{x} = 1/2$. However, there is a second special case that yields the same solution. This is when $\rho \to 1$. When x_1 and x_2 become more and more highly correlated, the conditional probability $\text{Prob}(x_2 < \hat{x}|\hat{x})$ again tends to the constant $1/2$.

The two special cases ($\sigma \to \infty$ and $\rho \to 1$) are instances where the strategic uncertainty becomes invariant to a player's type. Conditional on $\hat{x}$, the probability that my opponent's payoff parameter is less than $\hat{x}$ does not depend on $\hat{x}$ itself. The intuition for each case is easy to grasp. When σ becomes larger and larger, the density over x approaches the uniform density, and so the area to the left of any point $\hat{x}$ tends to $1/2$. The intuition for the case where ρ is close to 1 is quite different. When ρ is close to 1, the predictive value of knowing the *ex ante* density over my opponent's payoff parameter becomes small, since this is swamped by my own signal. From (2), it is as likely for my opponent's payoff parameter to be "above" my own, as it is for it to be "below" my own.

Even away from this limit, when σ is large, or when ρ is close to one, the strategic uncertainty is quite insensitive to a player's type, in the sense that the conditional probability ($\text{Prob}(x_2 < \hat{x}|\hat{x})$) does not vary much with respect to shifts in $\hat{x}$. If strategic uncertainty is sufficiently "sticky" with respect to shifts in a player's type, there is a unique solution to (1).

With this insight, we can characterize the conditions that are necessary and sufficient for uniqueness of equilibrium. The following argument follows Morris and Shin [26]. Let $u\,(x, \hat{x})$ be the payoff gain to choosing action 1 rather than action 0 for type x when the opponent is following a switching strategy around

$\widehat{x}$. Thus,

$$u\left(x,\widehat{x}\right) = x - \Phi\left(\frac{\widehat{x} - \rho x_1 - (1-\rho)\,y}{\sigma\sqrt{1-\rho^2}}\right).$$

Observe that

$$U(x) = u\left(x,x\right)$$

$$= x - \Phi\left(\frac{(1-\rho)\,(x-y)}{\sigma\sqrt{1-\rho^2}}\right).$$

If $U\left(\widehat{x}\right) = 0$, then there is an equilibrium of this game where each player chooses action 0 if his signal is below $\widehat{x}$ and chooses action 1 if his signal is above $\widehat{x}$. If we let $\underline{x}$ and $\overline{x}$ be the smallest and largest solutions to the equation $U\left(x\right) = 0$, then action 1 is rationalizable for player i if and only if $x_i \geq \underline{x}$ and action 0 is rationalizable if and only if $x_i \leq \overline{x}$.

Thus, there is a unique rationalizable action for (almost) all types if the equation $U\left(x\right) = 0$ has a unique solution. Observe that $U\left(x\right) \to -\infty$ as $x \to -\infty$ and $U\left(x\right) \to \infty$ as $x \to \infty$. So, a sufficient condition for the equation to have a unique solution is that $U'\left(x\right) \geq 0$ for all x. But if $U'\left(x\right) < 0$ for some x and y, then for some other value of y, $U\left(x\right) = 0$ will have multiple solutions. So, there is a unique rationalizable action for (almost) all types and for *all* y if and only if the equation $U'\left(x\right) \geq 0$ for all x.

$$U'\left(x\right) = 1 - \frac{1-\rho}{\sigma\sqrt{1-\rho^2}}\phi\left(\frac{(1-\rho)\,(x-y)}{\sigma\sqrt{1-\rho^2}}\right)$$

$$= 1 - \frac{1}{\sigma}\sqrt{\frac{1-\rho}{1+\rho}}\phi\left(\frac{(1-\rho)\,(x-y)}{\sigma\sqrt{1-\rho^2}}\right).$$

Thus for uniqueness, we must have

$$1 - \frac{1}{\sigma}\sqrt{\frac{1-\rho}{1+\rho}}\frac{1}{\sqrt{2\pi}} \geq 0.$$

Re-writing, this gives

$$\sigma^2 \geq \frac{1}{2\pi}\left(\frac{1-\rho}{1+\rho}\right). \tag{5}$$

We will refer to this as the uniqueness condition. There is a unique equilibrium either if there is sufficient variance of players' private values or if those private values are sufficiently closely (but not perfectly) correlated.[3]

---

[3]If private values are perfectly correlated (i.e., $\rho = 1$), there will be multiple equilibria whenever the players in a match have a (common) private value between 0 and 1.

2.2 ALTERNATIVE INTERPRETATIONS OF THE EXAMPLE

2.2.1 An Incomplete Information Interpretation.

Let there be two players who will interact with each other for sure. But each player $i = 1, 2$ is unsure of the other player's private value (or type) x_i. Suppose that their private values are *ex ante* symmetrically and normally distributed. Then the prior distribution over their private values/types is characterized by the unconditional mean y, the unconditional variance σ^2 and the correlation coefficient ρ. The uniqueness result says that if condition (5) is satisfied, there will be a unique equilibrium where each player chooses action 1 only if his type is above some threshold. Note that if ρ were identically equal to one, in other words, players' types were perfectly correlated so that there was complete information, there would be multiple equilibria whenever the players' common type was between 0 and 1.

2.2.2 A Local Interaction Interpretation.

Let a continuum of players be situated on the real line. Let the density of players be normal with mean y and variance σ^2. Thus players are concentrated around a location y, with a few players out at the tails. Suppose that a player's private value x_i is identically equal to his location. If players interacted equally with the whole population, that is, there was uniform interaction, then a player would be equally concerned about the actions of all players in the population, and he would weight the action of players at a given location by the mass of players at that location. But we would like to capture the possibility that a player is more likely to interact with players of a similar type himself—a feature of many real interaction structures. This can be captured by letting the weights he puts on his neighbors' actions also depend on how close they are to him. If we assume that his weights are generated by the conditional density of the bivariate normal with common mean y, variance σ^2 and correlation coefficient ρ based on his own location x, then the analysis of this problem is identical to the random matching model above. The uniqueness result says that if condition (5) is satisfied, there will be a unique equilibrium where each player chooses action 1 only if he is located to the right of some point. Note that if ρ were identically equal to one, that is, players interacted only with players at the same location, there would be multiple equilibria for all players located between 0 and 1.

2.2.3 A Dynamic Interpretation.

Let a continuum of players each live for one instant. We write x for a player who lives at date x. Let players' birthdates be normally distributed with mean y and variance σ^2. Thus players are concentrated around date y, with a few players out at the tails. A player's private value x_i is identically equal to the date at which he lives, so action 1 is becoming deterministically more desirable through time. In particular, there is a date beyond which action 1 is dominant.

A player's payoff depends on his own action, his payoff parameter, and the actions of others at different dates, both in the past and in the future. The fact that payoffs depend on actions of as yet unborn individuals is somewhat unconventional, but provided that the actions in the future can be anticipated (as will be the case here) institutions such as securities markets will enable players living today to consume today.

If players interacted equally with the whole population, in other words, there was uniform interaction, then a player would be equally concerned about the actions of all players at all dates. But we would like to capture the possibility that a player is more concerned about the actions of players choosing at around the same time. This can be captured by letting the weights he puts on his neighbors' actions also depend on how close in time they live to him. If we assume that his weights are generated by the conditional density of the bivariate normal with common mean y, variance σ^2, and correlation coefficient ρ, then the analysis of this problem is identical to the random matching model above. The uniqueness result says that if condition (5) is satisfied, there will be a unique equilibrium where each player chooses action 1 only if he lives after some cutoff date. Note that if ρ were identically equal to one, that is, players interacted only with players with whom they interacted simultaneously, there would be multiple equilibria for all players living between dates 0 and 1.

2.3 INTERPRETING THE CORRELATION FROM COMMON AND IDIOSYNCRATIC COMPONENTS

In the incomplete information interpretation of the above example, one very natural reason why private values are correlated is that there is a common and an idiosyncratic component in their private valuations. In particular, suppose that the distribution of private values x_i is derived in the following way. An unknown θ is normal with mean y and precision α. Each $x_i = \theta + \varepsilon_i$, where each ε_i is independently normally distributed with mean 0 and precision β. This setting is equivalent to the setting studied above, where we set

$$\sigma^2 = \frac{1}{\alpha} + \frac{1}{\beta},$$

$$\rho = \frac{\beta}{\alpha + \beta}.$$

Observe that with this reinterpretation, condition (5) becomes:

$$\frac{1}{\alpha} + \frac{1}{\beta} \geq \frac{1}{2\pi} \left(\frac{\alpha}{\alpha + 2\beta} \right)$$

or

$$\frac{\alpha^2 \beta}{(\alpha + \beta)(\alpha + 2\beta)} \leq 2\pi. \tag{6}$$

This reparameterization can also be applied to the random matching, local interaction, and dynamic interpretations discussed above.

Equation (6) nicely points to the two kinds of uniqueness arguments (correlated and independent heterogeneity) alluded to in the introduction. Note that condition (6) is satisfied *either* if α is sufficiently large and $\beta < 2\pi$ *or* if β is sufficiently large for any given α.[4] In the former case, as $\alpha \to \infty$, players' types are independent and the requirement that $\beta < 2\pi$, implies that there must be a minimum amount of heterogeneity to get uniqueness. But in the latter case, as β becomes large for any fixed α, players' types become more and more closely correlated and very small heterogeneity (i.e., large β) is required for uniqueness. Note that as $\beta \to \infty$, the variance of private values is reduced, which is bad according to condition (5). But the increased correlation more than compensates.

2.4 BACKGROUND AND RELATED LITERATURE

Let us start with incomplete information. The above example was discussed in Carlsson and van Damme [6] (appendix B), with the common and idiosyncratic components interpretation of section 2.3. Morris and Shin [24] used a special case of this example to illustrate the connection between different types of interaction games. Note that in the interpretation of section 2.3, the prior mean y is a public signal of the common component θ, while private value x_i is a private signal of θ. In Morris and Shin [24, 25], we have examined the contrasting roles of public and private signals in *common value global games* in which players care only about the value of θ. In the appendix, we briefly contrast the private value global games analyzed in this chapter with common value global games (which is the case more generally studied in the literature).

Ui [33] was the first to combine the global games analysis with the very useful parameterization in terms of the correlation of players' signals. In the normal case that has been much analyzed, this is a very fruitful way of understanding what is driving various uniqueness results. Ui used his global games with correlated private values to explain the connection between global game uniqueness results (where *small* noise is required for uniqueness) and quantal response equilibria (where *large* noise is required for uniqueness).

A number of papers have examined how sufficient independent heterogeneity gives rise to uniqueness in incomplete information games. McKelvey and Palfrey [16] introduced the idea of quantal response equilibria as a way of analyzing experimental results on games, exploiting existing discrete choice models employed in econometrics. They assumed that each player has a payoff shock with a logistic distribution. They noted that if the shocks were sufficiently large, a player will simply have a uniform distribution over his opponent's actions, and thus will have a unique best response. Thus uniqueness is a consequence of sufficiently large heterogeneity. Myatt and Wallace [31] consider a two-player two-action coordination game with independent normal payoff shocks. Their prime focus is on what happens with small shocks with an evolutionary dynamic. However, they also note that uniqueness also arises automatically, even

---

[4]There is a more detailed discussion of this condition in the appendix.

without the evolutionary dynamic, if the heterogeneity is sufficiently large. Baliga and Sjöström [3] analyze a two-player two-action coordination game with independent heterogeneous payoffs, and give a necessary and sufficient condition for uniqueness.[5]

Herrendorf, Valentinyi, and Waldmann [15] give a random matching argument showing that sufficient heterogeneity implies uniqueness. Their argument is embedded in a dynamic model that is not directly comparable; however, the underlying logic is very close to the uniqueness result in the random matching interpretation of the model described here.[6] Ciccone and Costain [7] have criticized the argument of Herrendorf, Valentinyi, and Waldmann [15] on the grounds that sufficient heterogeneity incidentally implies that a high proportion of the population has a dominant strategy to play one action, or the other. Their critique applies equally well to other interpretations of the model. Note, however, that when local heterogeneity generates uniqueness, the same criticism is not valid.

In a local interaction setting, a number of papers have shown that local interaction allows the risk dominant action to spread contagiously by best response dynamics alone (e.g., Blume [4] and Ellison [9]). These arguments have been used to show fast convergence to the risk dominant outcome in evolutionary settings. Small variations on the original contagion arguments can be used to establish that a small amount of heterogeneity can pin down equilibrium, even without dynamic/evolutionary considerations (see Morris [22]). The local interaction interpretation of the above example is a continuum population formalization of such arguments (for this, consider the case where $\alpha \to 0$).

In the dynamic interpretation of the above example, we assumed that each individual lived for an instant but cared about the actions of people making choices at different (but—in the correlated case—nearby) times. We also assumed that payoffs depended on the time at which you were choosing. This introduced correlated heterogeneity: each player with a given payoff parameter understood that he was interacting with players with different payoff parameters. A number of related ways of introducing correlated heterogeneity have been employed in the literature. Closest to the story we just told, Adsera and Ray [2] assume that a player's payoff depends on his own current action and lagged actions of others, for technological reasons. Morris [21] and Abreu and Brunnermeier [1] assume that players have asynchronized timing devices, so that while their payoffs may depend on contemporaneous actions, they care about actions of others choosing at (slightly) different clock times. Matsui and Matsuyama [17], Frankel and

---

[5]Baliga and Sjöström's [3] sufficient condition applies to a two-player two-action coordination game with independent private values, and thus corresponds to the model of this section in the case where $\rho = 0$. They consider a case where there is only one "dominance region" and a slightly different parameterization of payoffs. However, adapted to the setting of this chapter, their uniqueness condition reduces to (5)—with $\rho = 0$—in the special case of the normal distribution. We are grateful to Sandeep Baliga for helping us clarify the relation.

[6]In a private communication, Valentinyi has suggested that the underlying logic of their paper is well captured by the above example in the special case where $\alpha \to \infty$.

Pauzner [10], and Burdzy, Frankel, and Pauzner [5] assume that players' payoffs depend on contemporaneous actions, but each player can only occasionally revise his action choice. Thus his payoff depends on his action choice and the action choices of others at (slightly) different real times. All these dynamic stories have other significant differences from the dynamic interpretation we offered of the above example. However, highly but not perfectly correlated heterogeneity is playing an analogous role.

3   A MORE GENERAL MODEL

We will build on the insights from the leading example to identify a set of conditions that are jointly sufficient for uniqueness of equilibrium. The main theme is that uniqueness follows from the insensitivity of strategic uncertainty with respect to shifts in a player's own type.

In general, shifts in strategic uncertainty flow from shifts in the conditional density over my opponent's types as my own type changes. However, the very simple nature of the payoffs in the leading example meant we needed only to keep track of one summary statistic of this conditional density over the opponent's type—namely the probability that my opponent's type is lower than my own. With more general payoffs, strategic uncertainty will depend on the whole density, and so when we attempt to define the notion of the insensitivity of strategic uncertainty with respect to one's own type, the condition must be sufficiently restrictive so that it applies to the whole of the conditional density. Denoting by $F_i(x_j | x_i)$ the conditional c.d.f. of x_j given x_i, the key property used in our argument is that there exists $\delta > 0$ such that for all x_j and all Δ,

$$\frac{d}{dx_i} F_i(x_i + \Delta | x_i) \le \delta. \tag{7}$$

This is a strong requirement, since δ has to satisfy this inequality for all x_i and Δ. We dub this the condition of *uniformly bounded marginals on differences*. However, we will show that many standard formulations of strategic uncertainty accommodate special cases where this condition holds.

We will develop the general model in terms of a random matching problem, and show later how the same framework can be given alternative interpretations. A match consists of a player in role 1 and a player in role 2. Let $x_i \in \mathbb{R}$ be the payoff relevant type of the player in role i. Let $f \in \Delta(\mathbb{R}^2)$ be a probability density over possible pairs of payoff relevant types. The action set A of each player is a subset of the closed unit interval that contains 0 and 1. That is, $\{0, 1\} \subseteq A \subseteq [0, 1]$. The choice of 0 and 1 is not important *per se*, but our argument depends on the action set being bounded and closed.

Let $u_i(a_i, \Gamma, x)$ be a player's payoff if he has role i, he chooses action a_i, his belief about his opponent's action is Γ, and his payoff relevant type is x. We assume that u_i is continuous in a_i. The action distribution Γ is a c.d.f. on A, where $\Gamma\left(a\right)$ is the probability that the action is less than a. A strategy for players in role i is a mapping $s_i : \mathbb{R} \to A$. Write

$$\widehat{\Gamma}_i\left(s_j, x_i\right)$$

for a role i player's induced belief over his opponent's actions when he has observed signal x_i and believes his opponent is following strategy s_j. Thus

$$\widehat{\Gamma}_i\left(s_j, x_i\right)[a] = \int_{x_j} f\left(x_j \mid x_i\right) I_{s_j(\cdot)\leq a}\left(x_j\right) dx_j \, ,$$

where

$$I_{s_j(\cdot)\leq a}\left(x_j\right) = \left\{ \begin{array}{l} 1 \, , \text{if } s_j\left(x_j\right) \leq a \\ 0 \, , \text{if } s_j\left(x_j\right) > a \end{array} \right. .$$

Now a player's payoff if he chooses action a_i, his opponents follow strategy s_j, and his payoff relevant type is x_i, is

$$u_i\left(a_i, \widehat{\Gamma}_i\left(s_j, x_i\right), x_i\right) \, .$$

A strategy profile is a pair $s = \left(s_1, s_2\right)$. Now s is a population equilibrium if and only if

$$s_i\left(x_i\right) \in \arg \max_{a_i \in A} u_i\left(a_i, \widehat{\Gamma}\left(s_j, x_i\right), x_i\right)$$

for all i and x_i.

3.1   SPECIAL PROPERTIES OF THE PAYOFF FUNCTION

There are two important special cases to bear in mind. We say that u_i has the *average action property* if there exists $u_i^* : A^2 \times \mathbb{R} \to \mathbb{R}$ such that

$$u_i\left(a_i, \Gamma, x_i\right) = u_i^*\left(a_i, \int_{a_j \in A} a_j d\Gamma\left(a_j\right), x_i\right) \, .$$

In this case, a player cares only about the expected action of his opponents.

We say that u_i has the *average utility property* if there exists $u_i^{**} : A^2 \times \mathbb{R} \to \mathbb{R}$ such that

$$u_i\left(a_i, \Gamma, x\right) = \int_{a_j \in A} u_i^{**}\left(a_i, a_j, x\right) d\Gamma\left(a_j\right) \, .$$

In this case, there is a utility associated with each possible action of the opponent; thus $u_i^{**}\left(a_i, a_j, x_i\right)$ is a player's utility if he chooses action a_i, his opponent chooses action a_j, and his payoff relevant type is x_i. Now $u_i(a_i, \Gamma, x_i)$ is just the expected value of $u_i^{**}(a_i, a_j, x_i)$ if a_j is drawn according to Γ.

In some very special cases, a game may satisfy both the average action property and the average utility property. For example, if there exist $g_i : A \times \mathbb{R} \to \mathbb{R}$ and $h_i : A \times \mathbb{R} \to \mathbb{R}$ such that

$$u_i(a_i, \Gamma, x_i) = g_i(a_i, x_i) \left[\int_{a_j \in A} a_j d\Gamma(a_j) \right] + h_i(a_i, x_i) ,$$

then u_i has the average action property, by setting

$$u_i^*(a_i, a_j, x_i) = g_i(a_i, x_i) a_j + h_i(a_i, x_i)$$

and u_i also has the average utility property by setting

$$u_i^{**}(a_i, a_j, x_i) = g_i(a_i, x_i) a_j + h_i(a_i, x_i) .$$

In the random matching interpretation, it is natural to assume the average utility property: this is simply the standard expected utility assumption for this interpretation. On the other hand, if the average utility property fails, the model still makes sense. The decision maker just has non-expected utility preferences over the opponent's actions.

We will see that the average utility property may be less compelling in other interpretations.

3.2   ALTERNATIVE INTERPRETATIONS OF THE GENERAL MODEL

3.2.1   An Incomplete Information Interpretation.
Now let there be two players, 1 and 2. Each player i has a type x_i; $f(\cdot)$ is the probability distribution over players' possible types; $u_i(a_i, \Gamma, x_i)$ is player i's payoff if he chooses action a_i, his belief about his opponent's action is Γ and his payoff relevant type is x_i. If the average utility property is satisfied, we have a standard game of incomplete information, where $u_i^{**}(a_i, a_j, x_i)$ is player i's payoff if he chooses action a_i, his opponent chooses action a_j, and his payoff relevant type is x_i.

3.2.2   A Local Interaction Interpretation.
Now let there be two roles, 1 and 2. Players in role 1 are connected to players in role 2, and vice-versa, in an interaction network. Thus we have a *bipartite* graph with two continua of vertices. Each player in each role has a payoff relevant type x_i. We assign a weight to each connection and we normalize the sum of weights to 1. Thus $f \in \Delta(\mathbb{R}^2)$ is now a weighting function for the interaction graph. A player's utility depends on the weighted distribution of opponents' actions.

While we will maintain the "roles" assumption in the analysis that follows, all the results go through unchanged if we allow there to be only one role and, therefore, drop the bipartite graph assumption.

In this interpretation, the average action property is more natural. It is a maintained assumption, for example, in the analysis of Glaeser and Scheinkman [12].

3.3 ASSUMPTIONS

We will be concerned with the following properties of the payoff functions:

A1 Strategic Complementarities: $u_i(a_i, \Gamma, x_i) - u_i(a_i', \Gamma, x_i) \geq u_i(a_i, \Gamma', x_i) - u_i(a_i', \Gamma', x_i)$ if $a_i \geq a_i'$ and Γ dominates Γ' in the sense of first degree stochastic dominance.

A2 Limit Dominance I: There exist $\underline{x}_i$ and $\overline{x}_i$ such that $u_i(0, \Gamma, x_i) > u(a_i, \Gamma, x_i)$ for all $a_i \neq 0$, Γ, and $x_i \leq \underline{x}_i$; and $u_i(1, \Gamma, x_i) > u_i(a_i, \Gamma, x_i)$ for all $a_i \neq 1$, Γ, and $x_i \geq \overline{x}_i$.

A3 State Monotonicity: $u_i(a_i, \Gamma, x_i) - u(a_i', \Gamma, x_i)$ is increasing in x_i if $a_i \geq a_i'$.

A4 Uniformly Positive ($\underline{\kappa}$) Sensitivity to the State: There exists $\underline{\kappa}$ such that if $a \geq a'$ and $x \geq x'$,

$$[u(a, \Gamma, x) - u(a', \Gamma, x)] - [u(a, \Gamma, x') - u(a', \Gamma, x')] \geq \underline{\kappa}(a - a')(x - x').$$

A5 Uniformly Bounded ($\overline{\kappa}$) Sensitivity to Opponents' Actions: There exists $\overline{\kappa}$ such that if

$$[u(a, \Gamma, x) - u(a', \Gamma, x)] - [u(a, \Gamma', x) - u(a', \Gamma', x)] \leq \overline{\kappa}(a - a')|\Gamma - \Gamma'|,$$

where

$$|\Gamma - \Gamma'| = \sup_{a \in A} |\Gamma(a) - \Gamma'(a)|.$$

Note that A4 thus implies A3.

We will be concerned with the following properties of the probability distribution (or weighting function) f. We assume throughout that f is a non-atomic density. We write $f_i(x_j | x_i)$ for the conditional density over on x_j given x_i and $F_i(x_j | x_i)$ for the corresponding c.d.f.

A6 Limit Dominance II: f has support including $[\underline{x}, \overline{x}]^2$.

A7 Stochastically Ordered Marginals: $F_i(x_j | x_i)$ is increasing in x_i for all x_j.

A8 Uniformly Bounded (δ) Marginals on Differences: there is $\delta > 0$ such that for all x and Δ,

$$\frac{d}{dx} F_i(x_i + \Delta | x_i) \leq \delta.$$

3.4 EXAMPLES

3.4.1 The Binary Action Example Revisited.
The binary action example of section 2 satisfies all the assumptions of the general model. In particular, one can check that A4 is satisfied with $\underline{\kappa} = 1$ (and this is the highest value such that A4 holds); A5 is satisfied with $\overline{\kappa} = 1$ (and this is the lowest value such that A5 holds); and A8 is satisfied with

$$\delta = \sqrt{\frac{1-\rho}{2\pi\sigma^2\,(1+\rho)}}$$

(and this is the lowest value such that A8 holds). To show the last claim, note that arguments in section 2 show that

$$F_i\,(x + \Delta|\,x) = \Phi\left(\frac{\Delta + (1-\rho)\,(x-y)}{\sigma\sqrt{1-\rho^2}}\right)$$

so that

$$\begin{aligned}
\frac{d}{dx} F_i\,(x_i + \Delta|\,x_i) &= \frac{(1-\rho)}{\sigma\sqrt{1-\rho^2}}\phi\left(\frac{\Delta + (1-\rho)\,(x-y)}{\sigma\sqrt{1-\rho^2}}\right) \\
&\leq \frac{(1-\rho)}{\sigma\sqrt{1-\rho^2}}\frac{1}{\sqrt{2\pi}} \\
&= \sqrt{\frac{1-\rho}{2\pi\sigma^2\,(1+\rho)}}.
\end{aligned}$$

3.4.2 The Smooth Symmetric Case.
A smooth example in the spirit of Cooper and John [8] will be used in a number of the results that follow. Let there be a continuum of actions ($A = [0,1]$); symmetric payoffs (i.e., no roles); and the average action property. Thus $u^*\,(a,\overline{a},x)$ will be any player's payoff if he takes action a, the average action of his opponents is $\overline{a}$, and his payoff relevant type is x. Assume that u^* is twice differentiable and strictly concave in a ($(\partial^2 u^*)/(\partial a^2) < 0$). The latter assumption implies that each player has a continuous best response to his opponents' average action.

In the setting, the above assumptions translate as follows:

A1: $(\partial^2 u^*)/(\partial a\partial\overline{a}) > 0$.

A3: $(\partial^2 u^*)/(\partial a\partial x) > 0$.

A4: $(\partial^2 u^*)/(\partial a\partial x) \geq \underline{\kappa}$.

A5: $(\partial^2 u^*)/(\partial a\partial\overline{a}) \leq \overline{\kappa}$.

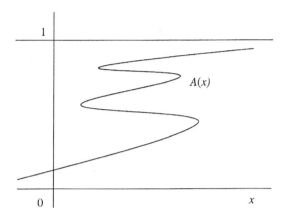

FIGURE 2   Complete information equilibria.

Note that in this setting, if we write $b(\bar{a}, x)$ for a player's best response if the average action of his opponents is $\bar{a}$ and he is type x, then b is well-defined and is strictly increasing in $\bar{a}$ at any interior solution. The set of equilibria in the case of complete information (common knowledge of a common private value x) will look as in figure 2.

4   UNIQUENESS

4.1   UNIQUENESS FROM PAYOFFS ALONE

We first note that there are conditions ensuring uniqueness in interaction games with strategic complementarities that do not exploit any properties of the interaction structure. Consider the smooth example discussed in the section 3.4.2 but assume only A1 from the assumptions described in section 3.3. Note that the slope of the best response function b will be:

$$\frac{db}{d\bar{a}} = -\frac{\frac{\partial^2 u^*}{\partial a \partial \bar{a}}}{\frac{\partial^2 u^*}{\partial a^2}}.$$

A sufficient condition for uniqueness in the complete information game is that $(db)/(d\bar{a}) < 1$, that is,

$$\left| \frac{\frac{\partial^2 u^*}{\partial a \partial \bar{a}}}{\frac{\partial^2 u^*}{\partial a^2}} \right| < 1.$$

This will also be a sufficient condition for uniqueness in the interaction game for any f. Glaeser and Scheinkman [12] have noted this sufficient condition for uniqueness (they call it *marginal social influence*) in a related interaction game (they have discrete types). Cooper and John [8] pointed out that a similar condition was sufficient with uniform interaction.

4.2   UNIQUENESS FROM HETEROGENEITY: A UNIFIED RESULT

Often, then, there is multiplicity in the underlying complete information game. Adding heterogeneity sometimes removes that multiplicity. As we discussed in the introduction, two alternative approaches in the literature involve (1) global heterogeneity (where a minimum amount of heterogeneity is required) and (2) local heterogeneity (where a maximum amount of heterogeneity is sometimes required). Here we give a unified treatment to clarify the relationship.

Proposition 4.1. *If A1 through A8 are satisfied, with $\delta\overline{\kappa} < \underline{\kappa}$ (where $\underline{\kappa}$, $\overline{\kappa}$ and δ are defined in A4, A5, and A8, respectively), then the interaction game has a unique strategy profile surviving iterated deletion of strictly dominated strategies.*

Thus for any given $\overline{\kappa}$ and $\underline{\kappa}$, there will be uniqueness if δ is low enough, that is, if players' beliefs about how other players' types differ from their own are not too sensitive to their own type. The sufficient condition of the proposition is tight: recall (from section 3.4.1) that in the binary action example of section 2, we had $\overline{\kappa} = \underline{\kappa} = 1$ and

$$\delta = \sqrt{\frac{1-\rho}{2\pi\sigma^2\,(1+\rho)}}\,.$$

Thus, the requirement that $\delta\overline{\kappa} < \underline{\kappa}$ is equivalent (up to the inequality) to the tight uniqueness condition (5) for the example.

This proposition is a variant of Theorem 1 of Frankel, Morris, and Pauzner [11]. We will sketch the argument and then highlight afterwards the small differences required for this setting. The proposition follows from two lemmas.

Lemma 4.1   *If A1 (strategic complementarities), A3 (state monotonicity) and A7 (stochastically ordered marginals) are satisfied, then the interaction game has a largest and smallest pure strategy profile ($\overline{s}$ and $\underline{s}$) satisfying iterated deletion of dominated strategies. Moreover, these strategy profiles are monotonic and are equilibria of the interaction game.*

This is a consequence of standard arguments concerning supermodular games, following Vives [34] and Milgrom and Roberts [19].

Lemma 4.2   *If A1 through A8 are satisfied, with $\delta\overline{\kappa} < \underline{\kappa}$, and $\overline{s}$ and $\underline{s}$ are monotonic equilibria of the interaction game with $\overline{s} \geq \underline{s}$, then $\overline{s} = \underline{s}$.*

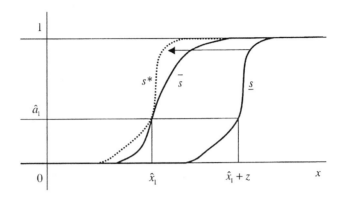

FIGURE 3 Translation argument.

Proposition 4.1 follows immediately from these two lemmas, since lemma 4.2 establishes that the largest and smallest strategy profiles surviving iterated deletion in lemma 4.2 must be the same.

Before jumping into the formal proofs, it is illuminating to sketch the outlines of the argument using figure 3.

For the purpose of this illustration, let us take the extreme case in which the strategic uncertainty is invariant with respect to a player's type in the sense that the conditional distribution $F_i(x_i + \Delta | x_i)$ is invariant to i's type x_i.

Suppose, for the sake of argument, $\underline{s} \neq \bar{s}$ (see fig. 3). Now, consider a new strategy s^* which is derived from $\underline{s}$ by translating it to the left so that two conditions are satisfied. First, s^* lies on or above $\bar{s}$ for all x. Second, there is some point $\hat{x}_1$ at which $s^* = \bar{s}$. Let z be the size of the translation (see fig. 3). We can always accomplish such a translation since the action set is bounded, and the limit dominance condition ensures that both $\bar{s}$ and $\underline{s}$ hit the top and bottom of the action set. Let

$$\tilde{a}_1$$

be the optimal action of player 1 when his own type is $\hat{x}_1$ when he believes that his opponent is playing according to s^*. Since $s^* \geq \bar{s}$, strategic complementarity implies that

$$\tilde{a}_1 \geq \bar{s}(\hat{x}_1) . \tag{8}$$

Meanwhile, our working hypothesis that the strategic uncertainty is invariant to shifts in x means that the beliefs around $\hat{x}_1$ are identical to the beliefs around $\hat{x}_1 + z$. If the opponent follows s^*, then the strategic uncertainty is identical at $\hat{x}_1$ and $\hat{x}_1 + z$. The only difference then is the higher payoff parameter at $\hat{x}_1 + z$.

By state monotonicity, we have

$$\underline{s}\left(\hat{x}_1 + z\right) > \tilde{a}_1 . \tag{9}$$

From (8) and (9), we have $\underline{s}\left(\hat{x}_1 + z\right) > \bar{s}\left(\hat{x}_1\right)$. But figure 3 tells us that they were constructed to be equal to each other. Hence, we have a contradiction. This tells us that our initial hypothesis that $\underline{s} \neq \bar{s}$ cannot be valid. We must have $\underline{s} = \bar{s}$ instead.

In the informal argument just sketched, we made heavy use of the invariance of strategic uncertainty with respect to type. The full argument has to allow for the fact that the strategic uncertainty can shift, but not shift too much.

The proof for lemma 4.2 proceeds as follows. Suppose that $\bar{s} \neq \underline{s}$. Then translate $\underline{s}$ to the left until each player's strategy in the translated profile lies above his strategy under $\bar{s}$, but such that the translated strategy just touches $\bar{s}$ for some player at some point. Let z be the amount of the translation, let player 1 (w.l.o.g.) with type $\hat{x}_1$ be taking $\hat{a}_1$ at the point where the strategies touch. Write s^* for the translated strategy profile. Thus

$$s_i^*\left(x_i\right) = \underline{s}_i\left(x_i + z\right)$$

for all i and x_i, and

$$\bar{s}_1\left(\hat{x}_1\right) = s_1^*\left(\hat{x}_1\right) .$$

Write

$$\Delta_i\left(a_i, a_i', \Gamma_i, x_i\right) = u_i\left(a_i, \Gamma_i, x_i\right) - u_i\left(a_i', \Gamma_i, x_i\right) .$$

Since s_2^* lies above $\bar{s}_2$, A1 implies that if $a_1 > \hat{a}_1$, then

$$\Delta_1\left(a_1, \hat{a}_1, \widehat{\Gamma}_1\left(s_2^*, \hat{x}_1\right), \hat{x}_1\right) \geq \Delta_1\left(a_1, \hat{a}_1, \widehat{\Gamma}_1\left(\bar{s}_2, \hat{x}_1\right), \hat{x}_1\right) . \tag{10}$$

By A8, and since s_2^* is simply a translation of $\underline{s}_2$, we have

$$d\left(\widehat{\Gamma}_1\left(s_2^*, \hat{x}_1\right), \widehat{\Gamma}_1\left(\underline{s}_2, \hat{x}_1 + z\right)\right) \leq \delta z .$$

Now if $a_1 > \hat{a}_1$, then by A5,

$$\left| \Delta_1\left(a_1, \hat{a}_1, \widehat{\Gamma}_1\left(s_2^*, \hat{x}_1\right), \hat{x}_1\right) - \Delta_1\left(a_1, \hat{a}_1, \widehat{\Gamma}_1\left(\underline{s}_2, \hat{x}_1 + z\right), \hat{x}_1\right)\right|$$
$$\leq \bar{\kappa}\left(a_1 - \hat{a}_1\right) \delta z$$

and thus

$$\Delta_1\left(a_1, \hat{a}_1, \widehat{\Gamma}_1\left(\underline{s}_2, \hat{x}_1 + z\right), \hat{x}_1\right) \geq \Delta_1\left(a_1, \hat{a}_1, \widehat{\Gamma}_1\left(s_2^*, \hat{x}_1\right), \hat{x}_1\right)$$
$$-\bar{\kappa}\left(a_1 - \hat{a}_1\right) \delta z . \tag{11}$$

Finally, observe that if $a_1 > \widehat{a}_1$, then by A4,

$$\Delta_1\left(a_1, \widehat{a}_1, \widehat{\Gamma}_1\left(\underline{s}_2, \widehat{x}_1 + z\right), \widehat{x}_1 + z\right) \geq \Delta_1\left(a_1, \widehat{a}_1, \widehat{\Gamma}_1\left(\underline{s}_2, \widehat{x}_1 + z\right), \widehat{x}_1\right)$$
$$+\underline{\kappa}\left(a_1 - \widehat{a}_1\right) z. \tag{12}$$

Now (10), (11), and (12) together imply (for all $a_1 > \widehat{a}_1$)

$$\Delta_1\left(a_1, \widehat{a}_1, \widehat{\Gamma}_1\left(\underline{s}_2, \widehat{x}_1 + z\right), \widehat{x}_1 + z\right) \geq \left\{\begin{array}{l} \Delta_1\left(a_1, \widehat{a}_1, \widehat{\Gamma}_1\left(\overline{s}_2, \widehat{x}_1\right), \widehat{x}_1\right) \\ +\underline{\kappa}\left(a_1 - \widehat{a}_1\right) z - \overline{\kappa}\left(a_1 - \widehat{a}_1\right) \delta z \end{array}\right\} \tag{13}$$
$$= \left\{\begin{array}{l} \Delta_1\left(a_1, \widehat{a}_1, \widehat{\Gamma}_1\left(\overline{s}_2, \widehat{x}_1\right), \widehat{x}_1\right) \\ +\left(\underline{\kappa} - \overline{\kappa}\delta\right)\left(a_1 - \widehat{a}_1\right) z \end{array}\right\}. \tag{14}$$

Now observe that if A is a discrete set, then there exists $a_1 > \widehat{a}_1$, such that

$$\Delta_1\left(a_1, \widehat{a}_1, \widehat{\Gamma}_1\left(\overline{s}_2, \widehat{x}_1\right), \widehat{x}_1\right) = 0.$$

If this were not true, $\widehat{a}_1$ would be optimal against $\overline{s}_2$ for types strictly greater than $\widehat{x}_1$, contradicting our construction. But now we must have

$$\Delta_1\left(a_1, \widehat{a}_1, \widehat{\Gamma}_1\left(\underline{s}_2, \widehat{x}_1 + z\right), \widehat{x}_1 + z\right) > 0$$

for some $a_1 > \widehat{a}_1$, contradicting our assumption that $\underline{s}$ is an equilibrium. If A is continuous, then we must have

$$\frac{\Delta_1\left(a_1, \widehat{a}_1, \widehat{\Gamma}_1\left(\overline{s}_2, \widehat{x}_1\right), \widehat{x}_1\right)}{a_1 - \widehat{a}_1} \to 0$$

as $a_1 \downarrow \widehat{a}_1$. This implies that

$$\frac{\Delta_1\left(a_1, \widehat{a}_1, \widehat{\Gamma}_1\left(\underline{s}_2, \widehat{x}_1 + z\right), \widehat{x}_1 + z\right)}{a_1 - \widehat{a}_1} = \left(\underline{\kappa} - \overline{\kappa}\delta\right) z + \frac{\Delta_1\left(a_1, \widehat{a}_1, \widehat{\Gamma}_1\left(\overline{s}_2, \widehat{x}_1\right), \widehat{x}_1\right)}{a_1 - \widehat{a}_1}$$
$$\to \left(\underline{\kappa} - \overline{\kappa}\delta\right) z,$$

so that some sufficiently small $a_1 > \widehat{a}_1$ is a better response than $\widehat{a}_1$, again contradicting our assumption that $\underline{s}$ is an equilibrium.

As already noted, our argument follows that in Frankel, Morris, and Pauzner [11]. Two features of the current environment simplify the argument. First, with an incomplete information interpretation, we have a *private value* global game, where a player knows his own payoff function; in Frankel et al. [11], a player's type was a signal of a common type; as noise goes to zero, this distinction is not important but requires extra technical work. Second, here we assumed A7 (stochastically ordered marginals) and A8 (uniformly bounded marginals on differences), whereas Frankel et al. [11] assumed only that each player observed a noisy signal of a common type, and showed that A7 and A8 held in the limit as noise goes to zero, under quite general assumptions. However, with our extra assumptions, proposition 4.1 offers two small improvements (using the same argument). First, there is a uniqueness result that can be applied away from the limit. Second, the above theorem applies to the more general class of interaction games, not just to average utility games. Of course, the latter assumption is standard and natural for the incomplete information interpretation.

The uniformly bounded marginal on differences condition is key to the uniqueness result. We now note how this condition is automatically satisfied in the two settings outlined in the introduction: when there is sufficiently large independent heterogeneity (the global heterogeneity case) and sufficiently small correlated heterogeneity (the local heterogeneity case).

4.2.1 Global Heterogeneity Sufficient Condition. Let

$$f(x_1, x_2) = h\left(\frac{x_1 - y}{\sigma}\right) h\left(\frac{x_2 - y}{\sigma}\right)$$

where $h(\cdot)$ is a bounded density with zero mean (with c.d.f. H). Thus x_1 and x_2 are iid from a distribution with mean y and scaling parameter σ. Observe that f automatically satisfies stochastically ordered marginals. Now

$$F_i(x_i + \Delta \mid x_i) = H\left(\frac{x_i + \Delta - y}{\sigma}\right)$$

$$\text{and} \quad \frac{dF_i}{dx_i}(x_i + \Delta \mid x_i) = \frac{1}{\sigma} h\left(\frac{x_i + \Delta - y}{\sigma}\right);$$

thus f has δ-bounded marginals on differences if and only if

$$\frac{1}{\sigma} h(\eta) \leq \delta$$

for all η, that is,

$$\sigma \geq \frac{\sup_\eta h(\eta)}{\delta}.$$

Thus for any δ and bounded h, f satisfies δ-bounded marginals on differences for sufficiently large σ. Thus sufficient independent heterogeneity guarantees uniqueness.

4.2.2 Local Heterogeneity Sufficient Condition. Let

$$f(x_1, x_2) = \int_{\theta = -\infty}^{\infty} g\left(\frac{\theta - y}{\tau}\right) h\left(\frac{x_1 - \theta}{\sigma}\right) h\left(\frac{x_2 - \theta}{\sigma}\right) d\theta$$

where $h(\cdot)$ and $g(\cdot)$ are densities with zero mean.[7] Thus x_1 and x_2 can be thought of as conditionally independent signals of an unknown θ. Thus each player i's payoff has a common term θ and an idiosyncratic term $x_i - \theta$ that player i cannot distinguish. This has the private value global game interpretation. The argument of Frankel, Morris, and Pauzner [11] shows that for sufficiently small σ and/or sufficiently large τ, this f will satisfy the *δ-bounded marginals on differences* for any given δ.

5 MULTIPLIERS

We now discuss the strategic multipliers in this setting. We focus on the smooth symmetric case described in section 3.4.2, where $b\,(\overline{a}, x)$ describes any player's best response if the average action of his opponents is $\overline{a}$ and his type is x. We will maintain assumptions A1 through A8 throughout this section.

5.1 COMPLETE INFORMATION ANALYSIS

Cooper and John [8] analyze essentially this model under the assumption that x is common across players and common knowledge, so that the players are involved in a symmetric complete information game. We define $A^*\,(x)$ to be the set of Nash equilibrium actions of that complete information game, that is,

$$A^*\,(x) \equiv \{a : a = b\,(a, x)\} \ .$$

Under our maintained assumptions, this set will typically look as plotted in figure 2. Now we can ask what happens as x is varied. Let $\widetilde{a}\,(x)$ describe an equilibrium in the neighborhood of x. Totally differentiating,

$$\frac{d\widetilde{a}}{dx} = \frac{\partial b}{\partial a}\frac{d\widetilde{a}}{dx} + \frac{\partial b}{\partial x} \ .$$

Rearranging gives

$$\frac{d\widetilde{a}}{dx} = \frac{\frac{\partial b}{\partial x}}{1 - \frac{\partial b}{\partial a}} \ .$$

At the largest or smallest equilibrium (and at any locally stable equilibrium) we have $0 < (\partial b)/(\partial a) < 1$. Thus we have the following natural interpretation. The *direct* effect of changing x on a player's action is

$$\frac{\partial b}{\partial x} \ .$$

---

[7]Note that this example may fail assumption A7 (stochastically ordered marginals), but as noted above, FMP showed that this assumption is automatically satisfied for sufficiently small σ.

But via the strategic complementarities, increasing x will also increase your expectations of others' actions. Thus, there is a complete information multiplier

$$\frac{1}{1 - \frac{\partial b}{\partial a}} \cdot$$

Thus the extra strategic effect (or *intra-equilibrium effect*) is

$$\left[\frac{\frac{\partial b}{\partial a}}{1 - \frac{\partial b}{\partial a}} \right] \frac{\partial b}{\partial x} \cdot$$

Roughly speaking, this is Cooper and John's formalization of why small actions by, say, the government can have a large effect on outcomes. This multiplier exists whether there are multiple equilibria (and we examine the local comparative statics of stable equilibria) or there is a unique equilibrium (because $(\partial b)/(\partial a) < 1$ everywhere).

5.2   ANALYSIS WITH LOCAL HETEROGENEITY

Now suppose that the population is heterogeneous. We will study an interaction game, with the local interaction interpretation, so f is the distribution of weights. Suppose that

$$f(x_1, x_2) = \int\limits_{\theta = -\infty}^{\infty} g\left(\frac{\theta - y}{\tau}\right) h\left(\frac{x_1 - \theta}{\sigma}\right) h\left(\frac{x_2 - \theta}{\sigma}\right) d\theta.$$

We noted in section 4.2.2 that as $\sigma \to 0$, the uniformly bounded marginals of differences condition is satisfied for arbitrarily small δ. Thus proposition 4.1 holds and there is a unique equilibrium. In fact, games with the average action property turn out to satisfy a *limit uniqueness property* studied in FMP: not only is there a unique equilibrium, but we can characterize the unique equilibrium independent of the shape of f.[8] In particular, for any x, let $a^*(x)$ be the element in $A^*(x)$ that maximizes the area between the best response function and the 45° line. Thus

$$a^*(x) = \arg\max_a \int\limits_{a'=0}^{a} (b(a', x) - a') \, da'.$$

Thus in the example depicted in figure 4, $a^*(x)$ would be equal to the smallest equilibrium, since area A in figure 4 is less than area B.

At some point x^*, these areas will be equal, and $a^*(\theta)$ will jump to the largest equilibrium (see fig. 5).[9]

---

[8]Morris and Shin [26] investigate this publicity multiplier in more detail.

[9]These limit uniqueness properties of expected action games were proved in early versions of Frankel, Morris, and Pauzner [11] using the sufficient conditions that are contained in the forthcoming version of the paper.

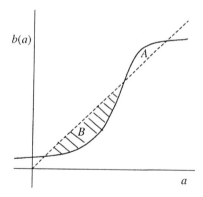

FIGURE 4   Selection criterion.

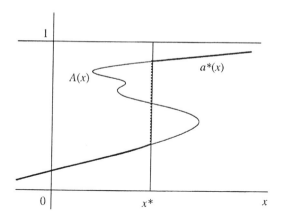

FIGURE 5   Selected equilibrium in limit.

A strategy in the interaction game parameterized by σ is a function $s : \mathbb{R} \to \mathbb{R}$, where $s(x)$ is the action chosen under that strategy by a player who observes signal x. The arguments of Frankel, Morris, and Pauzner [11] imply that for each σ sufficiently small, there exists a unique strategy s_σ surviving iterated deletion of strictly dominated strategies; and as $\sigma \to 0$, $s_\sigma(x) \to a^*(x)$. Thus, for small σ, s_σ will be shaped as in figure 6.

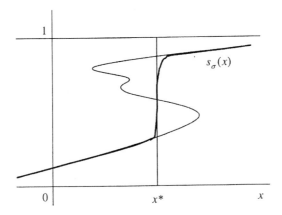

FIGURE 6   Unique equilibrium for small σ.

Now consider the sensitivity of a player's action in the unique equilibrium to his type x. We will clearly have

$$\frac{ds_\sigma}{dx} > 0$$

always. If σ is small and $\widehat{x}$ is not close to x^*, then we will have

$$\left.\frac{ds_\sigma}{dx}\right|_{x=\widehat{x}} \approx \frac{\left.\frac{\partial b}{\partial x}\right|_{x=\widehat{x},a=a^*(\widehat{x})}}{1 - \left.\frac{\partial b}{\partial a}\right|_{x=\widehat{x},a=a^*(\widehat{x})}}.$$

This effect consists of the direct effect and the intra-equilibrium strategic effect. But as $\sigma \to 0$,

$$\left.\frac{ds_\sigma}{dx}\right|_{x=x^*} \to \infty.$$

In particular, it tends to ∞ at the same rate as $1/\sigma$, that is, there exists a constant c such that

$$\sigma\left(\left.\frac{ds_\sigma}{dx}\right|_{x=x^*}\right) \to c.$$

Thus there is an *inter-equilibrium strategic effect* that operates only in the neighborhood of x^* and is (locally) orders of magnitude larger than the complete information multiplier.

Formally, then, for any fixed σ, we would define the three effects as follows:

$$\text{Direct Effect } D(\widehat{x}) = \frac{\partial b(s_\sigma(\widehat{x}),\widehat{x})}{\partial x}$$

$$\text{Intra-Equilibrium Multiplier Effect } M_1\left(\widehat{x}\right) = \left[\frac{1}{1 - \frac{\partial b(s_\sigma(\widehat{x}),\widehat{x})}{\partial a}}\right] D\left(\widehat{x}\right) - D\left(\widehat{x}\right)$$

$$= \left[\frac{\frac{\partial b(s_\sigma(\widehat{x}),\widehat{x})}{\partial a}}{1 - \frac{\partial b(s_\sigma(\widehat{x}),\widehat{x})}{\partial a}}\right] D\left(\widehat{x}\right)$$

$$\text{Inter-Equilibrium Multiplier Effect } M_2\left(\widehat{x}\right) = \frac{ds_\sigma\left(\widehat{x}\right)}{dx} - M_1\left(\widehat{x}\right) - D\left(\widehat{x}\right).$$

This classification suggests a useful qualitative distinction between different kinds of strategic multiplier. It highlights the observation (emphasized by Michael Woodford in his discussion of Morris and Shin [26]) that the extreme sensitivity in the limit of a global game (i.e., for small σ) is closely related to the jumps between complete information equilibria that must occur if there is not common knowledge. In settings where there is a small amount of local heterogeneity, the local sensitivity is largest when heterogeneity is small.

6 PURIFICATION

Carlsson and van Damme used the binary action example presented in section 2 to illustrate the relation between purification and global games. Consider the model with common and idiosyncratic components of types in section 2.3. As the idiosyncratic component becomes small (we let $\beta \to \infty$ for any fixed α), the game has a unique equilibrium. But if $\alpha = \infty$, so that there is no common component, then we have independent types for the players. If β is low ($\beta \leq 2\pi$), there is a unique equilibrium in this case. But if β is high, so that there is a small amount of independent idiosyncratic payoff shocks, then there are multiple equilibria. This corresponds exactly to the perturbation of Harsanyi [13], where he showed that mixed strategy equilibria can be "purified." In particular, suppose that $y \in (0, 1)$ and common knowledge (i.e., $\alpha = \infty$). The underlying complete information game will then have a mixed strategy equilibrium as well as two pure strategy equilibria. For high β, there will be an equilibrium of the interaction game where most types play according to the pure strategy equilibrium. But there will also be an equilibrium where each player employs a cutoff strategy in such a way that the other player's belief about his play is close to the mixed strategy equilibrium of the complete information game (and converges to it as $\beta \to \infty$).[10]

These results have important implications for social interactions. With heterogenous populations interacting, we might expect to see mixed strategies reflected in population behavior in this way. One implication is that behavior will be well correlated with player's types, even though each player is close to indifferent between two actions.

---

[10]An early version of Hellwig [14] looked at purification in *common value* global games.

7   CONCLUSION

We have described how global games can be given incomplete information, local interaction and random matching interpretations. We have provided a sufficient condition for heterogeneous interaction generating uniqueness in games with strategic complementarities. The sufficient condition requires that a player's beliefs about how her opponent's payoffs *differ* from her payoffs not be too sensitive to the *level* of her payoffs. This sufficient condition is tight and contains as special cases the local heterogeneity arguments of global games and various global heterogeneity arguments with independent interaction. We also saw how strategic multipliers and purification can be interpreted across different interaction settings.

APPENDIX: PRIVATE VERSUS COMMON VALUE GLOBAL GAMES

The analysis of this chapter concerned a private value global game. The literature on global games focuses on common value global games. With small noise (or local heterogeneity) the distinction is unimportant, but it becomes important when there is significant heterogeneity. In this appendix, we describe a simple example that embeds both cases and explore in somewhat more detail the uniqueness condition that emerges.

Consider the following two-player, two-action game.

		Player 2	
		0	1
Player 1	0	$1,1$	$0,\theta_2$
	1	$\theta_1,0$	θ_1,θ_2

Let θ be normally distributed with mean y and precision α; y is common knowledge and can be interpreted as a public signal about θ; each player i observes a noisy signal of θ, $x_i = \theta + \varepsilon_i$, where ε_1 and ε_2 are iid normal with mean 0 and precision β. Finally, $\theta_i = q\theta + (1-q)x_i$ (although θ_i is not observed at the time of the action choice).

If $q = 0$, we have the private values model of Carlsson and van Damme [6] (appendix B) and section 2 with the common/idiosyncratic components interpretation. If $q = 1$, we have the common values model of Morris and Shin [24, 25], where each player observes a noisy signal of a common payoff parameter.[11] As

---

[11]Morris and Shin [25] analyzed the two-player case discussed here. When that paper was incorporated into Morris and Shin [24], a continuum player case was discussed, but it was noted that equilibrium characterization is identical. Morris and Shin [23, 26], Hellwig [14], and Metz [18] also discuss public and private normal signals in (common value) global games with a variety of other payoff functions.

Carlsson and van Damme [6] noted, the private and common value models will behave in very similar ways if β is large relative to α. We will see below that they behave very differently if α is large relative to β.

For completeness, we again summarize the argument generating the uniqueness condition for any $q \in [0,1]$, again paralleling well known arguments.

Player 1 will believe that x_2 is distributed normally with mean

$$\frac{\alpha y + \beta x_1}{\alpha + \beta}$$

and precision

$$\frac{\beta(\alpha + \beta)}{\alpha + 2\beta}.$$

If he believes his opponent is choosing action 0 if and only if $x_2 \leq \widehat{x}$, then his expected payoff to action 0 is

$$\Phi\left(\sqrt{\frac{\beta(\alpha + \beta)}{\alpha + 2\beta}}\left(\widehat{x} - \frac{\alpha y + \beta x_1}{\alpha + \beta}\right)\right);$$

and his expected payoff to action 1 is

$$q\left(\frac{\alpha y + \beta x_1}{\alpha + \beta}\right) + (1 - q)x_1 = \left(\frac{q\alpha}{\alpha + \beta}\right)y + \left(1 - \frac{q\alpha}{\alpha + \beta}\right)x_1.$$

Thus, the gain to choosing action 1 rather than action 0 when he has observed signal x and thinks his opponent is following a switching strategy with cutoff $\widehat{x}$ is

$$u(x, \widehat{x}) = \left(\frac{q\alpha}{\alpha + \beta}\right)y + \left(1 - \frac{q\alpha}{\alpha + \beta}\right)x - \Phi\left(\sqrt{\frac{\beta(\alpha + \beta)}{\alpha + 2\beta}}\left(\widehat{x} - \frac{\alpha y + \beta x}{\alpha + \beta}\right)\right).$$

Observe that

$$U(x) = u(x, x)$$

$$= \left(\frac{q\alpha}{\alpha + \beta}\right)y + \left(1 - \frac{q\alpha}{\alpha + \beta}\right)x - \Phi\left(\sqrt{\frac{\beta(\alpha + \beta)}{\alpha + 2\beta}}\left(x - \frac{\alpha y + \beta x}{\alpha + \beta}\right)\right)$$

$$= \left(\frac{q\alpha}{\alpha + \beta}\right)y + \left(1 - \frac{q\alpha}{\alpha + \beta}\right)x - \Phi\left(\sqrt{\frac{\beta(\alpha + \beta)}{\alpha + 2\beta}}\left(\frac{\alpha}{\alpha + \beta}\right)(x - y)\right).$$

If $U(\widehat{x}) = 0$, then there is an equilibrium of this game where each player chooses action 0 if his signal is below $\widehat{x}$ and chooses action 1 if his signal is above $\widehat{x}$. If we let $\underline{x}$ and $\overline{x}$ be the smallest and largest solutions to the equation $U(x) = 0$, then action 1 is rationalizable for player i if and only if $x_i \geq \underline{x}$ and action 0 is rationalizable if and only if $x_i \leq \overline{x}$.

Thus, there is a unique rationalizable action for (almost) all types if and only if the equation $U(x) = 0$ has a unique solution. Observe that $U(x) \to -\infty$ as $x \to -\infty$ and $U(x) \to \infty$ as $x \to \infty$. So, a sufficient condition for the equation to have a unique solution is that $U'(x) \geq 0$ for all x. If $U'(x) < 0$ for some y, we could choose y' such that $U'(x') < 0$ and $U(x') = 0$ for some x' (as argued in footnote 3). So, there is a unique rationalizable action for (almost) all types and for all y if and only if the equation $U'(x) \geq 0$ for all x.

$$U'(x) = 1 - \frac{q\alpha}{\alpha + \beta} - \sqrt{\frac{\beta(\alpha + \beta)}{\alpha + 2\beta}}\left(\frac{\alpha}{\alpha + \beta}\right)\phi\left(\sqrt{\frac{\beta(\alpha + \beta)}{\alpha + 2\beta}}\left(\frac{\alpha}{\alpha + \beta}\right)(x - y)\right).$$

Thus we must have

$$1 - \frac{q\alpha}{\alpha + \beta} - \sqrt{\frac{\beta(\alpha + \beta)}{\alpha + 2\beta}}\left(\frac{\alpha}{\alpha + \beta}\right)\frac{1}{\sqrt{2\pi}} \geq 0.$$

Rewriting, this gives

$$\tilde{\gamma}(\alpha, \beta, q) \leq 2\pi \tag{15}$$

where

$$\tilde{\gamma}(\alpha, \beta, q) = \left(\sqrt{\frac{\beta(\alpha + \beta)}{\alpha + 2\beta}}\left(\frac{\alpha}{\alpha + \beta}\right)\left(\frac{1}{1 - \frac{q\alpha}{\alpha+\beta}}\right)\right)^2$$

$$= \frac{\beta(\alpha + \beta)}{\alpha + 2\beta}\left(\frac{\alpha}{\alpha + \beta}\right)^2\left(\frac{\alpha + \beta}{\alpha(1 - q) + \beta}\right)^2$$

$$= \frac{\alpha + \beta}{\alpha + 2\beta}\left(\frac{\beta\alpha^2}{(\alpha(1 - q) + \beta)^2}\right).$$

So the necessary and sufficient condition for uniqueness is:

$$\frac{\alpha + \beta}{\alpha + 2\beta}\left(\frac{\beta\alpha^2}{(\alpha(1 - q) + \beta)^2}\right) \leq 2\pi. \tag{16}$$

In the pure common values case, where $q = 1$, this reduces to the condition of Morris and Shin [24, 25]:

$$\tilde{\gamma}(\alpha, \beta, 1) = \frac{\alpha + \beta}{\alpha + 2\beta}\left(\frac{\alpha^2}{\beta}\right). \tag{17}$$

For any fixed α, (16) will hold for all β sufficiently large and fail for all β sufficiently small. This result illustrates the equilibrium selection result of Carlsson and van Damme. More precisely, there is a unique rationalizable action if and only if

$$\beta \geq \frac{\alpha}{8\pi}\left(\alpha - 2\pi + \sqrt{(\alpha - 2\pi)^2 + 16\alpha}\right).$$

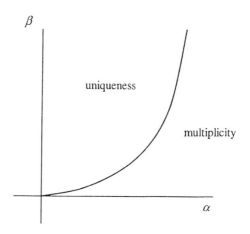

FIGURE 7   Common values uniqueness region.

For large α, requiring that $\widetilde{\gamma}(\alpha, \beta, 1) \leq 2\pi$ is equivalent to requiring that $\beta \geq (\alpha^2)/(4\pi)$ (see fig. 7).

In the special case where $q = 0$, this reduces to the case analyzed in section 2 and we have

$$\widetilde{\gamma}(\alpha, \beta, 0) = \frac{1}{\alpha + 2\beta} \left(\frac{\beta \alpha^2}{\alpha + \beta} \right).$$

Thus (16) is equivalent to (6) in the text. Recall that if we followed Ui [33] in reparameterizing the private values global game in terms of correlation and unconditional variance, we got the simple and easy to interpret uniqueness condition (5). But for comparison with the common value global game (where such a simple reparameterization is not available), we here analyze in more detail the uniqueness condition in terms of the precisions of public and private components.

Note that the cutoff values of uniqueness occur when

$$\frac{1}{\alpha + 2\beta} \left(\frac{\beta \alpha^2}{\alpha + \beta} \right) = 2\pi.$$

Re-arranging the equation, we get the quadratic

$$4\pi \beta^2 + \alpha (6\pi - \alpha) \beta + 2\pi \alpha^2 = 0.$$

This has two solutions,

$$\beta = \frac{\alpha}{8\pi} \left[\alpha - 6\pi \pm \sqrt{(\alpha - 6\pi)^2 - 32\pi^2} \right].$$

There are three cases to consider.

1. If
$$\alpha \leq 2\pi \left(3 - 2\sqrt{2}\right),$$

the quadratic has real solutions, but both are negative; in this case, $\widetilde{\gamma}(\alpha, \beta, 0) < 2\pi$ for all β.

2. If
$$2\pi \left(3 - 2\sqrt{2}\right) < \alpha < 2\pi \left(3 + 2\sqrt{2}\right),$$

then the quadratic has no real solutions; again, $\widetilde{\gamma}(\alpha, \beta, 0) < 2\pi$ for all β.

3. If $\alpha \geq 2\pi \left(3 + 2\sqrt{2}\right)$, then the quadratic has two real solutions:

$$\underline{\beta}(\alpha) = \frac{\alpha}{8\pi} \left[\alpha - 6\pi - \sqrt{(\alpha - 6\pi)^2 - 32\pi^2}\right]$$

$$\text{and } \overline{\beta}(\alpha) = \frac{\alpha}{8\pi} \left[\alpha - 6\pi + \sqrt{(\alpha - 6\pi)^2 - 32\pi^2}\right];$$

in this case, $\widetilde{\gamma}(\alpha, \beta, 0) \leq 2\pi$ for all $\beta \leq \underline{\beta}(\alpha)$ and for all $\beta \geq \overline{\beta}(\alpha)$. But $\widetilde{\gamma}(\alpha, \beta, 0) > 2\pi$ for all $\underline{\beta}(\alpha) < \beta < \overline{\beta}(\alpha)$.

Observe that $2\pi \left(3 + 2\sqrt{2}\right) \approx 36.6$ and

$$\underline{\beta}\left(2\pi \left(3 + 2\sqrt{2}\right)\right) = \overline{\beta}\left(2\pi \left(3 + 2\sqrt{2}\right)\right) = \left(4 + 3\sqrt{2}\right)\pi \approx 25.9.$$

Also observe

$$\begin{aligned}
\underline{\beta}(\alpha) &= \frac{\alpha}{8\pi} \left[\alpha - 6\pi - \sqrt{(\alpha - 6\pi)^2 - 32\pi^2}\right] \\
&= \frac{\alpha}{8\pi} \left[\sqrt{(\alpha - 6\pi)^2} - \sqrt{(\alpha - 6\pi)^2 - 32\pi^2}\right] \\
&= \frac{\alpha}{8\pi} \left[\frac{(\alpha - 6\pi)^2 - \left((\alpha - 6\pi)^2 - 32\pi^2\right)}{\sqrt{(\alpha - 6\pi)^2} + \sqrt{(\alpha - 6\pi)^2 - 32\pi^2}}\right] \\
&= \frac{\alpha}{8\pi} \left[\frac{32\pi^2}{\sqrt{(\alpha - 6\pi)^2} + \sqrt{(\alpha - 6\pi)^2 - 32\pi^2}}\right].
\end{aligned}$$

So as $\alpha \to \infty$,
$$\underline{\beta}(\alpha) \to 2\pi.$$

But also as $\alpha \to \infty$,
$$\frac{\overline{\beta}(\alpha)}{\alpha^2} = \frac{1}{4\pi}.$$

To summarize, there is multiplicity if and only if $\alpha > 2\pi \left(3 + 2\sqrt{2}\right)$ and $\underline{\beta}(\alpha) \leq \beta \leq \overline{\beta}(\alpha)$ (see fig. 8).

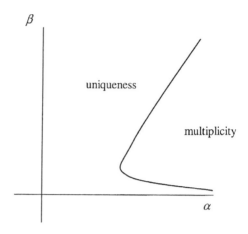

FIGURE 8   Private values uniqueness region.

What about the intermediate case, where $0 < q < 1$? While the corresponding equations are a little messier, this case behaves qualitatively like the private values case. In particular, fixing $q \in (0,1)$, we will have that for α sufficiently small, we have $\widetilde{\gamma}(\alpha, \beta, q) < 2\pi$. For larger α, we will have $\widetilde{\gamma}(\alpha, \beta, q) \leq 2\pi$ as long as β is either sufficiently small or sufficiently large. As $\alpha \to \infty$, we will get $\widetilde{\gamma}(\alpha, \beta, q) \leq 2\pi$ as long as *either*

$$\beta \leq 2\pi (1 - q)^2$$

or

$$\beta \geq \frac{\alpha^2}{4\pi}.$$

ACKNOWLEDGMENTS

This chapter incorporates our earlier notes circulated under the title "Big Noise, Little Noise." The authors are grateful for very valuable discussions with Rosa Argenziano, Sandeep Baliga, David Frankel, Atsushi Kajii, Ady Pauzner, Takashi Ui, and Akos Valentinyi.

REFERENCES

[1] Abreu, D., and M. Brunnermeier. "Bubbles and Crashes." *Econometrica* **71** (2003): 173–204.

[2] Adsera, A., and D. Ray. "History and Coordination Failure." *J. Econ. Growth* **3** (1998): 267–276.

[3] Baliga, S., and T. Sjöström. "Arms Races and Negotiations." *Rev. Econ. Stud.* **71** (2004).

[4] Blume, L. "The Statistical Mechanics of Best-Response Strategy Revision." *Games & Econ. Behav.* **11** (1995): 111–145.

[5] Burdzy, K., D. Frankel, and A. Pauzner. "Fast Equilibrium Selection by Rational Players Living in a Changing World." *Econometrica* **69** (2001): 163–189.

[6] Carlsson, H., and E. van Damme. "Global Games and Equilibrium Selection." *Econometrica* **61** (1993): 989–1018.

[7] Ciccone, A., and J. Costain. "On Payoff Heterogeneity in Games with Strategic Complementarities." 2001. Barcelona, Spain. Working paper 546, Universitat Pompeu Fabra. July 2004. ⟨http://www.econ.upf.es/docs/papers/downloads/546.pdf⟩.

[8] Cooper, R., and A. John. "Coordinating Coordination Failures in Keynesian Models." *Quart. J. Econ.* **103** (1988): 441–463.

[9] Ellison, G. "Learning, Local Interaction, and Coordination." *Econometrica* **61** (1993): 1047–1071.

[10] Frankel, D., and A. Pauzner. "Resolving Indeterminacy in Dynamic Settings: The Role of Shocks." *Quart. J. Econ.* **115** (2000): 285–304.

[11] Frankel, D., S. Morris and A. Pauzner. "Equilibrium Selection in Global Games with Strategic Complementarities." *J. Econ. Theor.* **108** (2003): 1–44.

[12] Glaeser, E., and J. Scheinkman. "Non-Market Interactions." In *Advances in Economics and Econometrics*, edited by M. Dewatripont, L. Hansen and S. Turnovsky. Proceedings of the Eighth World Congress of the Econometric Society. Cambridge, England: Cambridge University Press, 2003.

[13] Harsanyi, J. "Games with Randomly Disturbed Payoffs: A New Rationale for Mixed Strategy Equilibrium Points." *Int'l. J. Game Theor.* **2** (1973): 1–23.

[14] Hellwig, C. "Public Information, Private Information and the Multiplicity of Equilibria in Coordination Games." *J. Econ. Theor.* **107** (2002): 191–222.

[15] Herrendorf, B., A. Valentinyi, and R. Waldmann. "Ruling out Multiplicity and Indeterminacy: The Role of Heterogeneity." *Rev. Econ. Stud.* **67** (2000): 295–308

[16] McKelvey, D., and T. Palfrey. "Quantal Response Equilibria for Normal Form Games." *Games & Econ. Behav.* **10** (1995): 6–38.

[17] Matsui, A., and K. Matsuyama. "An Approach to Equilibrium Selection." *J. Econ. Theor.* **65** (1995): 415–434.

[18] Metz, C. "Private and Public Information in Self-Fulfilling Currency Crises." *J. Econ.* **76** (2002): 65–85.

[19] Milgrom, P., and J. Roberts. "Rationalizability, Learning, and Equilibrium in Games with Strategic Complementarities." *Econometrica* **58** (1990): 1255–1277.

[20] Morris, S. "Contagion." *Rev. Econ. Stud.* **67** (2000): 57–78.

[21] Morris, S. "Cooperation and Timing." 1995. CARESS Working Paper 95-05, University of Pennsylvania. July 2004. ⟨http://ssrn.com/abstract=237530⟩.

[22] Morris, S. "Interaction Games: A Unified Analysis of Incomplete Information, Local Interaction and Random Matching." 1997. Santa Fe, NM. Working Paper 97-08-072, Santa Fe Institute. ⟨http://ssrn.com/abstract=290880⟩.

[23] Morris, S., and H. S. Shin. "Coordination Risk and the Price of Debt." *Europ. Econ. Rev.* **48** (2004): 133–153.

[24] Morris, S., and H. S. Shin. "Global Games: Theory and Applications." In *Advances in Economics and Econometrics*, edited by M. Dewatripont, L. Hansen and S. Turnovsky. Proceedings of the Eighth World Congress of the Econometric Society. Cambridge, England: Cambridge University Press, 2003.

[25] Morris, S., and H. S. Shin. "Private versus Public Information in Coordination Problems." 1999. July 2004. ⟨http://www.econ.yale.edu/~tsm326/research.html⟩.

[26] Morris, S., and H. S. Shin. "Rethinking Multiple Equilibria in Macroeconomic Modelling." In *NBER Macroeconomics Annual 2000*, 139–161. Cambridge, MA: MIT Press, 2001.

[27] Morris, S., and H. S. Shin. "The Social Value of Public Information." *Am. Econ. Rev.* **92** (2002): 1521–1534.

[28] Morris, S., and H. S. Shin. "Unique Equilibrium in a Model of Self-Fulfilling Attacks." *Am. Econ. Rev.* **89** (1998): 587–597.

[29] Morris, S., and T. Ui. "Best Response Equivalence." *Games & Econ. Behav.* forthcoming.

[30] Morris, S., and T. Ui. "Generalized Potentials and Robust Sets of Equilibria." *J. Econ. Theory* frothcoming.

[31] Myatt, D., and C. Wallace. "Adaptive Play by Idiosyncratic Agents." 2002. Oxford UK. Discussion Paper 89, University of Oxford Department of Economics. July 2004. ⟨http://www.econ.ox.ac.uk/Research/WP/PaperDetails.asp?PaperID=121⟩.

[32] Nash, J. *The Essential John Nash.* Princeton NJ: Princeton University Press, 2001.

[33] Ui, T. "Correlated Quantal Responses and Equilibrium Selection." 2002. Yokohama National University, Japan. July 2004. ⟨http://www2.igss.ynu.ac.jp/~oui/correlatedqre.pdf⟩.

[34] Vives, X. "Nash Equilibrium with Strategic Complementarities." *J. Math. Econ.* **19** (1990): 305–321.

Perspectives on the Economy as an Evolving Complex System

Larry Samuelson

1 INTRODUCTION

Thinking of the economy as an evolving complex system entails two departures from the classical model of competitive equilibrium. First, *equilibrium* analysis, characterized by the absence of incentives to alter behavior, is replaced by *evolutionary* analysis, in which behavior persistently responds to constant incentives to adjust current actions. Second, the competitive-equilibrium assumption of *behavioral anonymity*, in which agents' preferences depend only on their own behavior and agents' choice sets depend only on common market prices, is replaced by an assumption of *behavioral interdependence* that allows more personal links between agents' preferences and sets of choices.

What are the advantages that have maintained equilibrium analyses as the primary analytical tool in economics? First, one might hope that the economy is "close enough" to an equilibrium "enough of the time" that equilibrium analysis provides a reasonable approximation of economic behavior. The economy itself may be a dynamic process that is never literally in equilibrium, but if one knows

The Economy as an Evolving Complex System III,
edited by Lawrence E. Blume and Steven N. Durlauf, Oxford University Press

only that the process has been running for a long time, the set of equilibria may be the best (approximate) prediction for the behavior of the system. Second, an equilibrium analysis often provides more revealing intuition than does an evolutionary analysis. The ability of prices to implicitly convey information about marginal benefits and costs is clear in an equilibrium setting, but less apparent in an evolutionary model. Third, static models are easier to analyze than dynamic ones. We have well-understood tools for establishing the existence of an equilibrium and probing its characteristics, while the analytical or simulation methods for studying dynamics are less familiar. Finally, we have a better understanding of the behavioral principles that determine equilibrium behavior than of those that respond to disequilibrium behavior.

Once we allow for the complexities of behavioral interdependence, these advantages tend to disappear. The principles guiding behavior in such situations are no longer obvious, nor are equilibria straightforward enough to characterize or interpret. Moreover, the dynamic models that have appeared in response to these difficulties have shown that equilibria are often not good predictors of behavior. The limiting outcomes of such models can be extremely sensitive to the specification of initial conditions, suggesting that an equilibrium analysis is not a good substitute for lack of knowledge concerning other aspects of the economy.

The evolving-complex-systems approach to economics has typically focused on modeling the evolutionary aspects of the problem. This chapter suggests that there are similar gains to be had from focusing on the "complexity" aspect. Doing so allows us to recover another sense in which results are sensitive to the specification of the model.

I work throughout with models simple enough to permit an equilibrium analysis, chosen for their ability to isolate key relationships. Interest then centers on the contrasting implications of various interdependencies between agents. The theme of the analysis is that the detailed specification of these interdependencies matters. If we are to understand the economic implications of complexity, we must be specific about the individual characteristics that give rise to this complexity. This theme is developed in the context of a particular type of interdependency, namely a concern for relative economic position.

2   CONCERNS FOR RELATIVE ECONOMIC POSITION

A standard economic model posits a strong form of behavioral independence. Each agent's preferences depend upon only his own consumption, regardless of the consumption or other characteristics of the remaining agents in the economy. Each agent's behavior in turn depends only upon his preferences and the constraints posed by market prices.

Though analytically convenient, this convention contrasts with a view, commonly voiced in other disciplines, that people are preoccupied with considerations of how their behavior compares to that of others (e.g., Aronson [1]).

In a psychological setting, this concern appears most obviously in an inclination to conform one's behavior to that of others, while in a social setting, it appears in the form of peer group effects (Aronson [1, ch. 2] and Cialdini [3, ch. 4]). To the extent that it has been studied in an economic setting, this concern often appears in the guise of a preference for *relative* rather than absolute economic position [7, 8]. Individual behavior appears to depend critically on the behavior of the others as people struggle to "keep up with the Joneses."

Three distinctions are in order. First, there are a number of reasons why one's actions may appear to depend upon the behavior of others. Manski [12, p. 532] identifies three ways that an individual's behavior may be apparently linked to that of a reference group, including

> *endogenous effects*, wherein the propensity of an individual to behave in some way varies with the behavior of the group...
>
> *exogenous (contextual)* effects, wherein the propensity of an individual to behave in some way varies with the exogenous characteristics of a group...
>
> *correlated* effects wherein individuals in the same group tend to behave similarly because they have similar individual characteristics or face similar institutional environments.

Correlated effects arise in the eye of the beholder. The underlying behavior is consistent with a standard model, in which an agent's behavior depends only upon his own characteristics and constraints, but the inability of the analyst to perfectly observe these characteristics and constraints gives rise to apparent links to the behavior of others. Depending upon the exogenous group characteristics which affect individual behavior, exogenous effects may also be in the eye of the beholder. One who invests in skills complementary to those of people with whom he is most likely to interact is simply responding to the relative rates of return on contending investments. Endogenous effects, in contrast, represent a significant departure from the standard model of behavior and will persist no matter how refined one's ability to observe individual characteristics and constraints.

Given that we must live with imperfect data, we must always expect to face daunting econometric problems when trying to distinguish the possible sources of apparent behavioral interdependencies (cf. Brock and Durlauf [2]). Endogenous effects are likely to pose particular difficulties. Endogenous effects posit that i's behavior is linked to j's behavior, while exogenous and contextual effects posit that i's behavior is linked to j's characteristics or to characteristics of i that are correlated with those of j. But we expect j's behavior, in turn to, be linked to j's characteristics. Distinguishing the effects may then require counterfactual observations of behavior on the part of j other than that ordinarily chosen by an agent with such characteristics.

We put these issues aside in this chapter to concentrate on endogenous effects arising out of concerns for relative economic position. Hence, we are interested in cases in which an econometrician able to identify common group characteristics or correlations in individual characteristics would still find it easiest to explain behavior by positing that i's behavior depends upon j's actions, and in our particular case, to posit that i's behavior reflects a concern with the relative economic positions of i and j.

Second, a concern for relative position and its induced endogenous effects may be either *intrinsic* or *instrumental*. We say that agent i has an intrinsic concern for relative position or relative consumption if the consumption of some agent j directly enters i's preferences. Agent i may derive pleasure from a large house, and especially from having a larger house than his neighbor. Agent i has an instrumental concern for relative position if agent i has preferences defined only over his own consumption, but the economy is so structured that the key to securing such consumption involves a comparison with agent j. For example, agent i may value the attention of certain members of the opposite sex, which may in turn be easier to secure if i has a larger house than his neighbors.

Postlewaite [13] argues that, whenever possible, economists should work with models of instrumental rather than intrinsic interdependencies. Allowing interdependencies to be intrinsic potentially removes all discipline from our modeling. There appears to be no limit to what we can build into preferences, and hence to the behavior we can rationalize with suitably defined preferences. Insisting the interdependencies be instrumental imposes some structure on what can be explained. In addition, simply inserting a preference for the behavior we observe into the utility function ensures that our model can generate the behavior, but gives us little insight beyond the statement that "people prefer to do what they do." A model of instrumental dependencies is more likely to expose the links between the structure of interactions and the resulting interdependencies. For example, a model in which people prefer exclusive neighborhoods because they have good schools is likely to make more precise predictions than a model in which people simply have a taste for exclusivity. Accordingly, we begin with an instrumental model of concerns for relative consumption.

Third, concerns for relative economic position are often interpreted as concerns for status, with status, in turn, determined by how one's consumption compares to that of others. Everyday experience suggests both that status is important and that the route to high status is a complicated one involving a variety of social as well as economic factors. Being wealthy may help one attain high status, but status may also depend upon one's family, occupation, involvement in the community, and hobbies. We consider only economic comparisons in this chapter, a focus occasionally reinforced by the use of the term "relative economic position" rather than the less cumbersome "relative position." Relative economic position is itself both difficult to define and difficult to observe. On the strength of the belief that economic considerations contribute to status (which depends at least partly on the ability to support conspicuously high consumption), we will concentrate on interdependencies that arise from a concern for relative consumption, interpreting the model as capturing a concern for status whenever doing so is convenient.

3   CONCERNS FOR RELATIVE CONSUMPTION

3.1   A BENCHMARK MODEL

It is helpful to begin with the observation that a completely standard economy gives rise to behavior that could be interpreted as reflecting instrumental concerns for relative consumption. Suppose there are two consumers who are endowed with w_1 and w_2 units of good x, whose price is normalized to one. A third consumer is endowed with one unit of good y. The utility functions of the first two consumers are given by

$$2\left(x^{\frac{1}{2}} + y^{\frac{1}{2}}\right)$$

and the third consumer's utility is simply the amount of good x consumed. The third consumer thus sells the entire endowment of good y. Letting p be the price of good y, we can solve for the demand functions of the first two consumers to obtain, for $i = 1, 2$,

$$x_i(p) = \frac{pw_i}{1 + p}$$

$$y_i(p) = \frac{w_i}{p(1 + p)}.$$

The market clearing price must balance the quantities of good y supplied and demanded, and hence must satisfy $y_1(p) + y_2(p) = 1$. The equilibrium price thus solves

$$p(1 + p) = w_1 + w_2.$$

Standard arguments show that this equilibrium outcome is efficient.

Three comments are now in order. First, suppose that an econometrician had data from many such economies, with the endowments of consumers 1 and 2 varying across economies. Suppose further that the econometrician examines the behavior of consumer 1 while neglecting to include the price p in the analysis, but including consumer 2's consumption of y. The data would show that consumer 1 consumes less x whenever consumer 2 consumes more y (and hence the price p is high). If we interpret x as leisure and y as a conspicuous consumption good, the conclusion would be that consumer 1 works harder to keep up with consumer 2 whenever consumer 2's consumption is relatively high. However, incorporating the price p in the analysis would eliminate this effect, leaving the analyst with the simple conclusion that consumer 1 has downward sloping demand curves. Once again, we see that identifying endogenous effects will often be a subtle task. Instrumentally induced concerns for relative position may sometimes rest in the eye of the beholder. In this case, it seems sufficiently obvious that prices should be incorporated in an analysis of consumption decisions so as to ensure that such confusion could not arise, but things will not always be so straightforward. And even if an appropriate model suffices to banish endogenous effects, the resulting specification may be significantly more complicated than our ordinary models.

Second, consumers 1 and 2 exert an externality on one another. If consumer 2 demands more y, the price increases, reducing consumer 1's consumption possibilities. Despite the fact that consumer 2 ignores this externality when making consumption choices, the equilibrium is efficient. This is a pecuniary externality that is precisely captured by competitive prices.

How do competitive prices internalize this externality? Assuming that utility functions have the appropriate smoothness properties, a necessary condition for equilibrium is that marginal variations in consumer 2's consumption along the frontier of 2's feasible set leave 2's utility unchanged. Otherwise, there would be a direction in which a marginal adjustment would increase 2's utility. The question of efficiency now hinges upon what effect marginal adjustments in 2's consumption have on 1's utility. In a Cournot duopoly, for example, firm 2 maximizes profits by choosing the quantity of output that sets marginal cost equal to marginal revenue, ensuring that marginal variations in output cannot increase profits. The inefficiency (from the point of view of the firms) arises out of the fact that a marginal reduction in 2's output would increase firm 1's profit rather than leave it unchanged. Intuitively, the marginal rate of substitution differs across agents, allowing adjustments that (possibly with the help of side payments) bring gains to both. A competitive equilibrium, in contrast, ensures that marginal rates of substitution are equal to price ratios and hence equal across agents. Any small movement along the frontier of 2's feasible set leaves 2's utility unchanged, and hence the compensating adjustment in 1's utility (to preserve aggregate feasibility) must also leave 1's utility unchanged. No reallocation, even with side payments, can then bring gains to both agents.

Concerns for relative position introduce a new externality into consumption decisions. Much of our interest in such concerns is motivated by the possibility that the resulting outcomes may be inefficient. This example suggests that much will hinge upon whether this quest for position is mediated by competitive prices. We shall see that it is not always straightforward to identify whether a good, such as position, is priced.

Third, Hirsch would identify good y in our example as a *positional* good, in other words, a good that is "either (1) scarce in some absolute or socially imposed sense or (2) subject to congestion or crowding through more extensive use" (Hirsch [10, p. 27]). It is common to argue that positional goods must give rise to inefficiency. For example, if there are only a few houses with the best view, then competition to outbid one's peers in order to attain the status attached to having such a house would seem to give rise to an inefficient outcome. However wasteful it may be from the point of view of the bidders, this competition is not inefficient if the houses are competitively priced. In this case, the seemingly ruinous competition for prime locations efficiently (though perhaps not equitably) enriches the sellers of these locations. Again, we see that concerns for status per se need not lead to efficiency as long as status is priced.

3.2   AN ECONOMY

When are instrumental concerns for relative consumption not reconciled by competitive prices? To address this issue, we consider a simple framework in which a series of examples can be constructed, corresponding to different specifications of the interdependencies in utility functions.

Consider an economy with two types of agents, denoted A and B. In applications, we might think of these as firms and workers or buyers and sellers or males and females. To provide a setting conducive to competitive pricing, let there be infinitely many of each type of agent, with agents corresponding to the real numbers in the unit interval, and hence with a unit measure of each type of agent. Let each A agent be endowed with a parameter $\epsilon \in [0, 1]$ identifying a characteristic of the agent. For example, ϵ may be an index of the agent's productivity. Similarly, each B agent is characterized by a parameter $\psi \in [0, 1]$ that again will often be interpreted as a productivity.

Let the distributions of the productivity parameters in the respective populations be described by strictly increasing, differentiable distribution functions F and G. Each A agent (but not B agents) is endowed with one unit of leisure.

Agents of type A first simultaneously choose how much of their endowment of leisure to consume and how much to invest in the production of an intermediate output c, with production function

$$c = f(1 - \ell, \epsilon),$$

where $f : [0, 1] \to \mathbb{R}_+$ is strictly increasing in both arguments and concave in its first argument. In some cases, we will interpret this investment as an exercise in improving one's productivity, such as acquiring education or skills, so that the intermediate output is a body of knowledge or a repertoire of abilities. In other cases, we will interpret the investment as the acquisition of conspicuous consumption goods.

After the A agents undertake production, A and B agents match with one another. We can interpret the A agents as workers being hired by firms or as males matching with females. We assume throughout that the matching process must be one-to-one, so that each firm can hire only one worker. We will allow considerable liberty in specifying how payoffs are determined as a function of the characteristics of the matched agents and investigate a series of examples that differ in their specification of these payoffs. These will give rise to differing patterns of interdependency between the agents in the economy.

3.3 JOINT CONSUMPTION

We begin with a case in which prices necessarily play no role in equating marginal rates of substitution. Assume that if an A agent of type ϵ with leisure/intermediate-output allocation (ℓ, c) matches with a B agent of type ψ, the resulting utilities are

$$u_0(\ell) + u(g(c, \epsilon), \psi)$$
$$v(g(c, \epsilon), \psi),$$

where each of the functions u_0, g, u, and v is strictly increasing. The A agent privately consumes his leisure in this case, and hence privately bears the cost of producing the intermediate output c. The payoff of the match is determined by the level of this intermediate output as well as the characteristics of the A and B workers. The key feature of this example is that there is no way to transfer utility between the two agents and hence no way to adjust the allocation of the payoff resulting from the match between the two agents. In particular, there is no provision for prices to make transfers from one agent to another.

We can think of these transfers between the agents as being impossible because the benefits of the match are jointly consumed. We accordingly refer to this as the *joint consumption economy*. Such a specification might be appropriate if we think of the agents as males and females, an interpretation we adopt throughout this section. In this case the good c is readily interpreted as consumption, which we view the male as producing before matching with the female. More realistically, the male may invest in education, which then determines the post-matching level of consumption, a process that we represent simply as the choice of c. Because the consumption level must be chosen before matching, with higher consumption leading to a more desirable match, we will often refer to the choice of consumption good as an investment. In the alternative context of firms and workers, transfers may be relatively ineffective if the firm and worker constitute a partnership whose rewards are primarily nonpecuniary, as may be the case in many creative partnerships. Here, c might be an intermediate good such as enhanced productivity.

The male's productivity parameter affects both the payoff of the match and the cost of producing the good c, which also affects the payoff of the match. Higher contributions to the joint payoff will be generated by workers of high productivity and by workers who have produced large amounts of consumption. It facilitates the interpretation of the model to collect these considerations into the function $g(c, \epsilon)$ which, in turn, appears within the functions u and v. We assume that u and v are nonnegative, so that every agent will at least weakly prefer to be matched with an agent on the other side of the market.

We will think of matches between males and females as being determined in a market. Given the presumption that utility cannot be transferred between agents, however, prices will play no role in determining matches or in affecting the distribution of the surplus between matched agents. Instead, we will think of males as "buying" values of the characteristic ψ, offering in return a value $g(c, \epsilon)$. Similarly, we can think of females as offering values of ψ in return for values of $g(c, \epsilon)$. However, there is no scope for an agent in this market to announce that "I'm willing to contribute characteristic ϵ and intermediate output c in return for a match with characteristic ψ and a transfer of p."

We will say no more about the matching process that brings firms and workers together, conditional on the amounts of consumption produced by workers, other than to assume that it produces stable matchings. The input to the matching process is the distribution of values of ψ among females, described by the function G, and a distribution of values of $g(c, \epsilon)$, determined by the function F and males' investment choices. The output is a bijection between the set of males and females with the property that there is no male-female pair who would strictly prefer to be matched to each other rather than to their current partners.

If the sets of males and females were finite, then the existence of a stable matching would be straightforward [9]. While existence is less obvious in general with infinite sets of agents, our economy is sufficiently simple that it is again straightforward to ensure stable matching exists and to identify their characteristics. In particular, all females agree that higher values of $g(c, \epsilon)$ are preferred, while males agree that higher values of ψ are preferred. It is then immediate that the matching process must be assortative, meaning that a higher value of $g(c, \epsilon)$ cannot reduce the value of ψ with which a male is matched (and vice versa). If not, we could find two matches $(g(c, \epsilon), \psi)$ and $(g(c', \epsilon'), \psi')$ with $g(c, \epsilon) > g(c', \epsilon')$ but $\psi < \psi'$. But then the $g(c, \epsilon)$ and ψ' agents would both prefer being matched to each other over their own match, ensuring that the matching is not stable.

An allocation is the result of the investment and matching processes, specifying how much consumption good each male produces and specifying which values of (c, ϵ) match with which values of ψ. A Nash equilibrium is a specification of males' investment decisions such that each investment decision is optimal, given the investment decisions of other agents and the matching process. Accordingly, we can describe an equilibrium as an increasing function $C(\epsilon)$, identifying the amount of consumption goods produced by each male, and a function $H_C : [0, 1] \rightarrow \mathbb{R}_+$, where $H_C(\Psi)$ is the set of values of $g(c, \epsilon)$ attached to those males who match with females whose consumption levels ψ are drawn from the set Ψ, given investment decisions C.

Feasibility requires that the investment choices be feasible and that the matching function be measure preserving, or

$$F(\epsilon : (g(C(\epsilon), \epsilon) \in H_C(\Psi))) = G(\Psi).$$

We can interpret $H(\psi)$ as the value of $g(c, \epsilon)$ with which a female with characteristic ψ will match, and can similarly interpret $H^{-1}(g(c, \epsilon))$ as the value of ψ with which a male whose investment decision and characteristic yields a value of g equal to $g(c, \epsilon)$ will match.

What about a value $g(c, \epsilon)$ that is not the equilibrium choice of any male? We must identify the matching consequences of such choices in order to assess the optimality of males' investment decisions. We assume that a male choosing a currently unproduced value $g(\hat{c}, \hat{\epsilon})$ matches with a value of ψ given by the supremum of the values of ψ that currently match with values $g(c, \epsilon) < g(\hat{c} + \hat{\epsilon})$. Suppose, for example, that the equilibrium configuration of males' investments is such that no values from the set $[g(c', \epsilon'), g(c'', \epsilon'')]$ are offered in the market and that an agent chooses a value $g(\hat{c}, \hat{\epsilon}) \in [g(c', \epsilon'), g(c'', \epsilon'')]$. It is clear that such a male will be preferred to their current match by every female whose current match is with a male drawn from the interval $[0, g(c', \epsilon')]$. Hence, the male in question can choose a match from any of the females currently matched with values of $g(c, \epsilon) < g(\hat{c}, \hat{\epsilon})$, and hence can command a value of ψ arbitrarily close to the supremum of the values of ψ represented in such matches. A necessary condition for equilibrium must then be that the male's current utility be at least as high as the supremum of the utilities offered by such matches, motivating our assumption.

The conditions under which an equilibrium exists in such an economy are straightforward. Our interest turns to the question of whether equilibria will be efficient. We have:

Proposition 1. *A Nash equilibrium of the joint consumption economy is efficient.*

Proof. Suppose the equilibrium is not efficient. Then there must exist a pair of agents (ϵ^*, ψ^*) and a consumption-good level $c^* = f(1 - \ell^*, \epsilon^*)$ such that the utilities $u_0(\ell^*) + u(g(c^*, \epsilon^*), \psi^*)$ and $v(g(c^*, \epsilon^*), \psi^*)$ are higher than the equilibrium utilities of agents ϵ^* and ψ^*. Let $H(\psi^*)$ be the level of $g(c,\epsilon)$ with which agent ψ^* is matched in equilibrium. Then it must be that $g(c^*, \epsilon^*) > H(\psi^*)$, since otherwise agent ψ^* would not prefer the proposed alternative match. But in equilibrium, agent ϵ^* can then choose intermediate-good level ψ^* and be assured a match with an agent with characteristics at least as high as ψ^*. The choice $C(\epsilon^*)$ is thus not an equilibrium choice, a contradiction. ∎

Three considerations lie behind this efficiency result. First, in equilibrium, each male will choose c so as to balance the utility-decreasing effects of an increase in c against the ability of an increased c to attract a match with a better female. Conditional on the characteristics of a matched male and female, an increase in consumption good c always increases the female's payoff. Together, these observations ensure that there are no efficiency gains to be obtained by adjusting values of c within a match. Second, the stability of the matching ensures that there are no efficiency gains to be obtained by adjusting matches, conditional on intermediate good production. Finally, could efficiency gains be generated by simultaneously adjusting matches and intermediate good levels? To make a female better off, a male must offer a higher $g(c, \epsilon)$ than the female achieves in equilibrium. But then the male would fare just as well by offering this higher value of $g(c, \epsilon)$ to the market, ensuring that the male would match with a female at least as desired as the one in question. However, an allocation is an equilibrium only if it is not beneficial for the male to do so, and hence only if there are no efficiency gains available.

In equilibrium, the males in the joint consumption economy will appear to exhibit relative consumption effects. Altering the consumption-good levels of other males, by altering the values of ψ that male ϵ can "buy" with various values of c, alters male ϵ's behavior. A male who observes his contemporaries consuming less leisure and working harder will typically do likewise. This inclination to work harder as others do so is identified by Frank [8] as an important source of inefficiency in our economy, as interpersonal externalities drive marginal rates of substitution away from their optimal equality with market prices.

Unlike the pecuniary externalities of the previous subsection, it will be difficult to exorcise this relative consumption effect by incorporating appropriate prices into one's analysis. The joint nature of consumption ensures that there is no counterpart of a wage or price of labor in this market. One might think of the quantity of intermediate good c brought to a match as the price a worker pays for a match, but this interpretation encounters some difficulties. Quantity c may match with characteristic ψ, but this would not ensure that another worker could secure a match at least this favorable by bidding $c' > c$. In particular, a worker with too small a value of ϵ would have such a bid rejected. The appropriate price of a match with a firm of type ψ is the value $g(c, \epsilon) = H(\psi)$, which is likely to be prohibitively difficult to observe.

Despite this lack of pricing, and in contrast to the models sketched by Frank [8], the equilibrium is efficient. Even without prices, the market drives marginal rates of substitution to equality. For each male of type ϵ, the equilibrium allocation implicitly defines a schedule $c(\psi, \epsilon)$ identifying the level of the consumption good c this male must offer a female of type ψ to just match her market utility. In equilibrium, the male optimizes against this constraint, equating the marginal rate of substitution between c and ψ in his preferences just equal to the marginal rate identified by the constraint. As a result, marginal variations in the males' choice along the frontier of his feasible set leave the male's utility unchanged, and also would not push the utilities of the females with whom he would match away from their equilibrium levels. This mimics the equality of marginal rates of substitution of a competitive economy.

Males behave optimally given the market constraint they face. This constraint is itself distorted by males' concerns for relative position, as the competition for females pushes upward the constraint $c(\psi, \epsilon)$ facing each male. But females are the beneficiary of this distortion, ensuring that it is not inefficient. The common criticism of markets in which agents exhibit a concern for relative position, that the resulting equilibria exhibit inefficiently excessive investments in position, is thus misplaced in this case. Concerns for relative position may induce males to consume more than would otherwise be the case, but this simply transfers gains to the other side of the market rather than generating inefficiency. This is the counterpart of the observation that positional goods cause no inefficiency if properly priced.

3.4   ONE-SIDED PAYOFFS

In the joint consumption economy, investments in the consumption good increase the payoffs of females. To highlight the role of this relationship in producing efficient outcomes, we examine an alternative, the *one-sided payoff economy*. The specification of the market matches that of the joint consumption economy, except that payoffs for A agents are given by

$$u_0(\ell) + u(g(c, \epsilon), \psi)$$

while payoffs for B agents are fixed at zero. It is most natural to interpret the agents as a firm and worker in this case, with c being an investment in the worker's productivity. We refer to c as an intermediate good. We assume that the production function for the intermediate good takes the form

$$c = 1 - \ell.$$

The surplus $u(g(c, \epsilon), \psi)$ is now consumed only by the worker. Intuitively, we view utility as being transferable, so that the surplus can be divided into a portion accruing to the worker and a portion accruing to the firm. This corresponds better to a more traditional view of an employment relationship, in which wage payments transfer surplus between parties, than does the previous joint consumption specification. In addition, we assume that the labor market is organized so that all of the surplus is captured by workers. For example, we might think of firms bidding in Bertrand fashion for the services of the workers. Notice, however, it is not immediately obvious how to reconcile such an outcome with the fact that firms with large values of ψ are scarce. The mechanism by which the surplus is divided is important, an issue to which we return in the next subsection.

In contrast to the joint consumption economy, we now have an additional price, set by a competitive process. Paradoxically, we find that this competitive process is an impediment to efficiency.

For a fixed value of ψ, let $c^*(\epsilon, \psi)$ be the optimal value of intermediate good c produced by a worker of type ϵ who is arbitrarily constrained to be matched with a firm of type ψ (no matter what value of c the worker produces). The first order condition for this optimal value, assuming differentiability, is

$$\frac{du_0(1 - c^*)}{d\ell} + \frac{du(g(c^*, \epsilon), \psi)}{dg} \frac{dg(c^*, \epsilon)}{dc} = 0. \tag{1}$$

The worker thus balances the production cost of the intermediate good with the surplus gains in the worker's relationship with the firm.

It is a common result that agents who must invest in the production of a surplus to be shared with other agents will choose inefficient levels for those investments. Because the surplus is shared, each investor reaps only a fraction of the rewards of their investment, while bearing all of the cost. This, in turn, ensures that they stop investing short of the point which equates the marginal costs and benefits of the investment. Notice, however, that this consideration does not arise in our one-sided payoff economy. A worker who invests in the intermediate good captures all of the return on that investment, ensuring that the worker has the correct incentives to invest efficiently. Condition (1) thus characterizes efficient investments.

We simplify the analysis by assuming:

Assumption 1. $c^*(\epsilon, \psi)$ *is differentiable and increasing.*

This assumption could easily be derived from more primitive considerations. Differentiability will hold if the functions u_0, u and g have appropriate differentiability properties. The optimal investment $c^*(\epsilon, \psi)$ will be increasing in ϵ if the utility function $u_0(1 - c) + u(g(c, \epsilon), \psi)$ satisfies the strict single-crossing condition that its second derivative in c and ϵ is positive. The investment in productivity captured by c is thus relatively more valuable for workers with relatively high characteristics. We could alternatively generate a single-crossing relationship by retaining the assumption that the production function for the intermediate good is given by $f(1 - \ell, \epsilon)$ and assuming a single-crossing condition that high-characteristic workers find it relatively less costly to undertake investments in c. Finally, $c^*(\epsilon, \psi)$ will be increasing in ψ if g and ψ are strategic complements in u, so that increasing ψ increases the marginal value of $g(c, \epsilon)$. Hence, workers must find it relatively more valuable to be more productive at more productive firms.

Once again, an equilibrium is a function $C(\epsilon)$ identifying the level of intermediate good produced by each worker type ϵ and a function $H_C(\psi)$ identifying the level $g(c, \epsilon)$ with which a firm of type ψ is matched, given the investment levels specified by C. We assume that the equilibrium matching must be assortative. Notice that this is now an assumption rather than a result. Since firms receive a zero payoff, regardless of the identity of the worker with whom they are matched, firms will be indifferent concerning their match. The assumption of assortative matching reflects an implicit view of the mechanism by which firms' payoffs are driven to zero. In particular, though firms receive zero payoffs in equilibrium, a worker offering a higher value of $g(c, \epsilon)$ should be able to bid characteristic ψ away from a worker with a lower value of $g(\psi, \epsilon)$. The equilibrium configuration should then be zero profits for firms, but with workers competing for productive firms so as to ensure assortative matching. We have not modeled this process, however, an omission that will prove important.

We now have:

Proposition 2. *Let Assumption 1 hold. Then an efficient equilibrium does not exist in the one-sided payoff economy.*

Proof. Let H be the equilibrium matching function. A necessary condition for efficiency is that, at the equilibrium allocation (cf. (1)),

$$\frac{du_0(1-c)}{d\ell} + \frac{du(g(c,\epsilon), H^{-1}(g(c,\epsilon)))}{dc} = 0 . \tag{2}$$

This is again simply the statement that workers' agents make their production decisions optimally, conditional on their equilibrium match. However, the equilibrium decision for a worker must satisfy

$$\frac{du_0(1-c)}{d\ell} + \frac{du(g(c,\epsilon), H^{-1}(g(c,\epsilon)))}{dg} \frac{dg(c,\epsilon)}{dc}$$

$$+ \frac{du(g(c,\epsilon), H^{-1}(g(c,\epsilon)))}{d\psi} \frac{dH^{-1}(g(c,\epsilon))}{dg} \frac{dg(c,\epsilon)}{dc} = 0 . \tag{3}$$

The final product of terms captures the fact that by increasing production of the intermediate good, agent ϵ can secure a match with a higher value of ψ. These terms are positive, distorting choices of c inefficiently upward. ∎

Inefficiency arises in this case because workers inefficiently increase production of the intermediate good in order to compete for matches with better firms. In equilibrium, this competition is futile—the equilibrium (assortative) matching remains unchanged when all agents increase their production levels. But the partial equilibrium effect of one agent's increased production is a better match. Equilibrium is then defined by a collection of incentive constraints that deter further competition for better matches, but that do so only with the help of inefficiently high production levels. A similar phenomenon is described by Cook and Frank [5], who argue that many professions attract entrants inefficiently in hopes of matching them with the particularly desirable jobs in those professions.

Once again, males optimize given the market constraints they face. As with the joint consumption economy, this ensures that marginal movements along the frontier of a worker's feasible space preserve the agent's utility and also the utility of the firms with which the agent is faced. There are then no efficiency gains to be found from reconfiguring matches. Instead, the efficiency gains are found in altering the value of c within a match. In the joint consumption economy, larger values of c are valued by females. Competition for females thus pushed males' values of c beyond the optimal values that would prevail in the absence of competition for females, so that conditional on the value of ψ with which a male is characterized by ϵ matches, the male is consuming too much (from his point of view). But this increased consumption can only increase the utility of the female characterized by ψ. Males and females thus have opposing preferences over c, ensuring that the equilibrium level is efficient.

In the one-sided payoff economy, competition for firms again pushes production of the intermediate good c beyond the values that males would choose in the absence of such competition. However, in equilibrium firms receive no gains from these larger values of the consumption good, begin doomed to zero payoffs. Males' investment levels are thus inefficiently high. The assumption that firms receive no surplus, regardless of the equilibrium pattern of workers' investments, is thus crucial. This, in turn, suggests that one should not leave this feature of the market as an unmodeled assumption.

We can view the inefficiency in the present model as arising from a missing market. Suppose that ψ, instead of being drawn from the unit interval, is drawn from the two-element set $\{\underline{\psi}, \overline{\psi}\}$. Think of $\underline{\psi}$ as denoting a mediocre job or a job in a mediocre firm and $\overline{\psi}$ as denoting a good job or a job in a good firm. The equilibrium incentive constraint will be that agents matched with $\overline{\psi}$ firms invest in sufficiently inefficient consumption so as to deter agents matched with $\underline{\psi}$ firms from increasing their production in hopes of winning a spot at a $\overline{\psi}$ firm.

The missing market is that for access to $\overline{\psi}$ firms. If possible, the firms themselves would sell this right, but the current model precludes this possibility by assuming that workers capture all of the surplus. The model of the previous subsection essentially allowed firms to sell this right by assuming that firms value workers' production. One could alternatively create such a market, and restore efficiency, by requiring workers to purchase an appropriately-priced license to work at a $\overline{\psi}$ firm, with the license revenues distributed to agents not involved in this market.

It is clear that an important role is played by the assumption that firms capture none of the surplus. In some cases, this is unavoidable. Suppose that ψ denotes the ability to exploit an unowned resource, such as a valuable site for mining gold on unclaimed land. Then we can expect the land to capture none of the surplus, leading to inefficiently high investment in activities designed to secure such sites. If ownership to the land can be established and mining rights sold, then efficiency may be restored.

In other cases, one might hope that market forces would allow B agents to capture some of the surplus, and that this division of the surplus might efficiently price access to ψ. We illustrate this possibility in the following subsection.

3.5 ALLOCATED SURPLUS

Let us augment the one-sided payoff economy with the assumption that there is a function $\pi(\psi)$ identifying the payment that any worker must make in order to match with a ψ firm. Instead of competition bidding firms' profits down to zero, we can now think of $\pi(\psi)$ as the equilibrium payoff to a firm of type ψ. Call the result the *allocated surplus* economy, since the surplus created by any match can be allocated between the firm and worker by the function $\pi(\psi)$. We have:

Proposition 3. *There exists a specification of $\pi(\psi)$ such that the allocated surplus economy has an efficient equilibrium.*

Proof. Let $G(\psi)$ be a function associating with each value of ψ the value of ϵ that characterizes an efficient solution. Let $c(\epsilon)$ satisfy

$$\frac{du_0(1 - c(\epsilon))}{d\ell} + \frac{du(g(c(\epsilon), \epsilon), G^{-1}(\epsilon))}{dc} = 0. \tag{4}$$

The function $c(\epsilon)$ thus identifies efficient production levels. Now let $\pi(\psi)$ satisfy

$$\frac{du(g(c, \epsilon), H^{-1}(g(c, \epsilon)))}{d\psi} \frac{dH^{-1}(g(c, \epsilon))}{dg} \frac{dg(c, \epsilon)}{dc}$$

$$+ \frac{d\pi(H^{-1}(g(c(\epsilon), \epsilon)))}{d\psi} \frac{dH^{-1}(g(c(\epsilon), \epsilon))}{dc} = 0.$$

Notice that this is well defined, since the specification $c(\epsilon)$ fixes the function H. Then the counterpart of (3) will duplicate (4), ensuring efficiency. ■

This result is reminiscent of similar findings in Cole, Mailath, and Postlewaite [4], who examine a two-sided investment-and-matching model, showing that equilibria will be efficient if the transfer function is fortuitously defined. The latter must ensure that, compared to the efficient configuration of investments and matches, the advantages to a worker of seeking a match with a higher value of ψ are precisely neutralized by the increased transfer cost of such a match. These transfers take the place of the missing market in the one-sided payoff economy by effectively pricing access to firms.

While it is straightforward to design a function $\pi(\psi)$ that ensures an efficient outcome, we would expect these transfers to arise endogenously as a result of competition in the labor market.

As Cole, Mailath, and Postlewaite observe, there is no reason to expect transfers to take precisely the form required for efficiency. The plausibility of such an equilibrium can be assessed only by carefully modeling the market process that associates transfers with matches.

3.6 CONSPICUOUS CONSUMPTION

We now again let consumption be joint, but with utility functions

$$u_0(1 - c, \epsilon) + u(\epsilon, \psi)$$
$$v(\epsilon, \psi).$$

The male's investment in good c now has no effect on the utility levels produced in a match, which depend only on the characteristics of the male and female.

Then why would the male ever undertake the investment? We assume that males' types are unobservable. The investment potentially serves as an unproductive signal of this type. We refer to this as the *conspicuous consumption economy*, since the sole purpose of the good c is to be consumed sufficiently conspicuously as to provide a reliable signal of the type of the male doing the consumption.

As is common in signaling contexts, we assume that $u_0(1 - c, \epsilon)$ is increasing in ϵ and that the male's utility function satisfies the strict single-crossing condition that the cross second derivative in c and ϵ is strictly positive. The interpretation here is that males of higher productivity find it relatively less costly to generate the signal c.

We concentrate on separating equilibria in which levels of c reveal the males' types. The matching must again be assortative in such an equilibrium. The equilibrium matching is thus given by a function $H(\psi)$ satisfying the feasibility constraint

$$F(\{\epsilon : \epsilon \in H(\Psi)\}) = G(\Psi).$$

This matching is uniquely determined (up to sets of measure zero) by the requirements that the matching be assortative and feasible.

The equilibrium investment levels of males are then determined by the incentive constraints that no male prefers to misrepresent his type. Hence, the function $c(\epsilon)$, mapping males' types into investment levels, is an equilibrium only if

$$u_0(1 - c(\epsilon)) + u(\epsilon, H(\epsilon)) \geq u_0(1 - c(\epsilon')) + u(\epsilon, H(\epsilon'))$$

for any male of type ϵ and any type ϵ' that the male might attempt to imitate. Rearranging terms, dividing by $\epsilon - \epsilon'$ and taking the limit as $\epsilon' \to \epsilon$, we can represent this requirement as:

$$-\frac{du_0(1 - c(\epsilon))}{d\ell}\frac{dc(\epsilon)}{d\epsilon} = \frac{du(\epsilon, H^{-1}(\epsilon))}{d\psi}\frac{dH^{-1}(\epsilon)}{d\epsilon}.$$

Under appropriate continuity assumptions, we can solve this differential equation for the equilibrium $c(\epsilon)$. In doing so, it is natural (but not necessary) to set the initial conditions for the solution to select the separating equilibrium which minimizes signaling costs, that is, the equilibrium in which a male of type 0, being doomed to an equilibrium match with the least desirable female, chooses a zero investment level. Rege [14] establishes the existence of a separating equilibrium via a similar method in a closely related model, using an evolutionary stability criterion to select the minimum-cost separating equilibrium.

Is the efficient minimum-cost equilibrium efficient? To focus attention on the issues, assume that the economy is as symmetric as possible, in that males' and females' utility functions u and v are identical and that the distributions F and G are identical. In one sense, the answer is obviously no. The males' consumption is purely wasteful. Payoffs from a match depend only on the characteristics of the agents in that match. One could then obviously generate a superior outcome by retaining the pattern of matches, but specifying zero production for workers. However, it is not clear that this is an appropriate comparison, since it is not obvious how the same pattern of matches can be achieved without the help of the consumption signal.

We might then compare the minimum-cost separating equilibrium (hereafter referred to simply as the separating equilibrium) to the cost-minimizing pooling equilibrium, in which no signals are sent and males and females are randomly matched. It is clear that the separating equilibrium does not Pareto dominate the pooling equilibrium. The male with the smallest value of ϵ bears no cost in either case, but receives a random draw from the set of females in the pooling equilibrium while being confined to the least attractive female in the separating equilibrium. However, males with higher characteristics potentially fare better in the separating equilibrium, where they are assured matches with desirable females. Still, these preferred matches come only at the cost of expensive signals.

Is it possible that the pooling equilibrium Pareto dominates the separating equilibrium? More precisely, is it possible that for all ϵ and ψ,

$$u_0(1 - c(\epsilon)) + u(\epsilon, H^{-1}(\epsilon)) < u_0(1) + \int u(\epsilon, \psi)dG(\psi)$$

$$u(H(\psi), \psi) < \int u(\epsilon, \psi)dF(\epsilon)\,?$$

The left side of each expression is the agent's utility in the separating equilibrium, while the right side is the expected utility from the pooling equilibrium. It is a familiar result in the signaling literature that the answer may be "yes." For example, the penchant for existing equilibrium refinements to select separating equilibria, even when they are so counterproductive as to doom every agent to a lower payoff than a pooling equilibrium, provided one motivate for the undefeated equilibrium concept of Mailath, Okuno-Fujiwara, and Postlewaite [11]. When the separating equilibrium is Pareto dominated, the preferred partners purchased by males' equilibrium signals come at such a cost that the males would prefer to simply choose females blindly. Unfortunately for the females, the separating equilibrium precludes the opportunity of such blind choice.

As a second source of insight, we might ask whether aggregate, measured as the sum of males' and females' utilities (retaining our assumption of identical utility functions), is higher in the separating or pooling equilibrium. To provide some justification for summing utilities, we might think of this as a calculation of the *ex ante* utility, conducted behind the veil of ignorance that prevails before workers learn their types. For example, such a calculation may be relevant to a parent assessing the expected utility of a child. The separating equilibrium fares better in this regard if

$$\int \left(u_0(1 - c(\epsilon)) + u(\epsilon, H^{-1}(\epsilon)) \right) dF(\epsilon) > \int \int u(\epsilon, \psi)dF(\epsilon)dG(\psi)$$

$$\int u(H(\psi), \psi) dF(\epsilon) > \int \int u(\epsilon, \psi) dF(\epsilon) dG(\psi).$$

A necessary condition for the signaling equilibrium to fare better is

$$\int \left(u(\epsilon, H^{-1}(\epsilon)) \right) dF(\epsilon) > \int \int u(\epsilon, \psi) dF(\epsilon) dG(\psi),$$

which is to say that the utility function u must be supermodular. Intuitively, there must be complementarities in the types of males and females. Matching two high productivity agents and two low productivity agents must give a larger aggregate utility than forming two high/low pairs. If these complementarities are sufficiently strong as to outweigh the signaling costs, then the separating equilibrium will dominate the pooling equilibrium. Rege [14] presents an example.

A difficulty with many signaling models is that the incentive constraints, and hence equilibrium strategies, do not depend upon the distribution of types in the signaling population. In a conventional model in which workers signal their types to firms, a high-type worker spends just as much to separate himself from a low-type worker who appears in the population with probability .5 as he does from a low-type worker who appears in the population with probability $.5 \times 10^{-10}$. But the equilibrium becomes very different if the probability of the low type declines from $.5 \times 10^{-10}$ to zero. In the current model, a change in the distribution of workers alters the separating-equilibrium distribution of matches with firms. This in turn alters the incentives to misrepresent one's type and hence the equilibrium strategies. The result is a signaling model that more faithfully reflects our intuition concerning the behavior of equilibrium signals.

The dependence of equilibrium strategies on the distribution of male characteristics in the conspicuous consumption model is another manifestation of what appear to be relative consumption effects. Workers will appear to have a preference for consuming less leisure when their compatriots consume less leisure.

4 POLICY

Why are these issues important, and why are they important topics for further research? Our examples show that the relative consumption effects can give rise to inefficiencies. Moreover, the questions of when and how an outcome will be inefficient depend upon fine details of utility functions and market interactions. Whereas an instrumental approach to relative consumption effects insulates us from the arbitrariness of simply building such considerations into the utility function, we must still be much more precise about utility functions and market interactions than is the case with more conventional economic models.

These problems become more pressing when one moves beyond the simple question of whether market outcomes will be efficient for assessing the effects of policy interventions, whether to relieve inefficiencies or to address equity or other policy concerns. Consider, for example, the imposition of an income tax. In a standard economic model, the income tax appears as a reduction in the wage rate. The effects of this tax can then be discerned by examining the comparative statics of individual decisions in response to a decreased wage rate. Evaluating the effects of the tax hinge upon how one trades off the distorted individual labor-supply decisions against the public goods funded by the tax.

The response of the joint consumption economy to the income tax is more complicated. The obvious measure of income in this economy is c. We will think of the tax as requiring a proportion of good c to be paid to the government, leaving the rest to enter the utility function. The tax thus drives a wedge between the value of c produced by a male and the effective amount of c the male can bring to market. Again, we know that the outcome will be inefficient, and that an evaluation of the tax will hinge upon how this inefficiency is balanced against the value of the resulting public goods. Now, however, the individual responses to the consumption tax incorporate two factors. The first is the familiar observation that the tax alters the marginal return to investing in c and hence the males' choices of c. In principle, this effect is captured by examining the comparative statics of the males' utility maximization problem, though doing so required knowledge of how the characteristics ϵ and ψ fit into this utility function. An econometrician who estimates a conventional utility function, with ℓ and c as arguments, will not correctly identify this effect. In addition, there is a second effect that arises through the matching process. As males' investments adjust, so does the effective pricing schedule identifying the relationship between bids $g(c, \epsilon)$ and values of ψ. Even with a correct specification of utility, an analysis that fails to take the structure of the market into account will miss this "market reaction" to the income tax.

Does this market reaction capture anything other than the statement that any policy intervention induces direct effects and general equilibrium effects? The latter also appear in standard models, but are ignored because they are thought to be relatively insignificant. Notice, however, that we can construct economic models that are sufficiently simple as to exactly capture the general equilibrium effects of a tax. Effects arising out of relative consumption raise new complications even in such simple economies.

Second, whether one can safely ignore general equilibrium effects when evaluating policy interventions is an empirical question. The possibility of relative consumption effects gives us one more reason to believe that such considerations may not be small, and should not be ignored without evidence that they are unimportant.

Finally, the general equilibrium effects appearing in the joint consumption economy are qualitatively different from those arising in a standard model of competitive equilibrium. In particular, there is a sense in which markets are thin in the joint consumption economy, in that each agent defines a commodity that is offered on the market only by that agent. It is also clear that prices have only a limited ability to balance markets in the economy. We thus again have much less reason to believe that general equilibrium effects can be ignored.

Consider, in contrast, the one-sided payoff economy. Once again, the income tax induces an individual reaction and a market reaction that will typically be omitted under a standard analysis. In general, the equilibrium in this economy induces inefficiently high investments in the good c. Taxing these investments can then push the economy closer to an efficient outcome. (Corneo [6] comes to a similar conclusion.) The tax in this economy functions much like the transfer to the firm in the allocated surplus economy. There is then the chance that the tax can be Pareto improving. Unfortunately, this efficiency gain hinges upon a specification of utility and a market structure that ensures a quite specific division of the gains from trade, leaving no reason to expect the tax to push investment decisions toward efficiency in general.

The conspicuous consumption economy similarly represents a case in which the income tax can effect Pareto improvements. The consumption good c serves no purpose other than to convey information in this economy. Provided that after-tax consumption is an unambiguous signal of pre-tax investment, the incentive constraints defining a separating equilibrium can be expressed entirely in terms of pre-tax investments. The tax then has no effect on behavior, allowing the public good collected by the tax to be a pure gain. For example, luxury taxes may thus be viewed as an attempt to avoid inefficiencies by taxing goods that are especially likely to serve as signals rather than simply as devices to introduce progressivity into the tax structure.

The ability to tax signals without introducing distortions depends upon the ability of post-tax consumption to be as useful a signal as pre-tax consumption. If consumption is perfectly observable, this may well be the case. More realistically, we expect consumption to be observable only with some noise. One can form an approximate but not precise idea of the value of one's neighbor's house, car, jewelry, and vacation spending. If the imposition of a tax, by compressing the range of after-tax expenditures, makes distinctions in these levels less obvious, then the tax may reduce the ability of signaling to produce an assortative matching. If a random matching is preferred, this is an additional bonus for the tax. If the assortative matching is preferred, then the tax again raises its revenue only at the cost of a distortion.

These examples indicate that once behavioral interdependencies are allowed into our economic model, even such straightforward questions as whether distortionary taxes improve or dissipate welfare are open to question. The answer depends upon the nature of the interdependencies and the market in which these effects find expression. Without further study, none of our conventional welfare conclusions can be taken for granted.

5   CONCLUSION

Relative consumption effects can be both important and subtle. Both the efficiency implications of market interactions and the effects of policy interventions depend critically on the details of how individuals in the market interact to produce utilities. There is complexity aplenty here that awaits analysis.

The examples in this chapter have explored relative consumption effects that arise out of instrumental concerns for status. However, the set of possible sources of relative consumption effects is much richer. For example, behavioral interdependencies may arise out of informational concerns, as agents glean information about their environment from the choices of others, leading to information-based relative consumption effects (Samuelson [15]).

More importantly, matters become more complicated once we bring evolution into the picture. Think of evolution not as a metaphor for a dynamic process but more literally as the biological process that shaped us, including our preferences. Evolution is always eager to economize on the resources required to achieve her ends. If our preferences have been shaped in an environment in which either status-based or information-based relative consumption effects are important, then Nature may have found it convenient to economize on our reasoning resources by simply building such effects into our utility functions. We can then expect relative consumption effects to be intrinsic as well as instrumental.

These considerations suggest that conventional economic models miss not only the complexity of interactions between the agents, but also the complexities of the individual foundations of these agents' behavior. Studying the economy as an evolving complex system will require work on both types of complexity.

ACKNOWLEDGMENTS

Financial support from the National Science Foundation is gratefully acknowledged.

REFERENCES

[1] Aronson, Elliott. *The Social Animal.* New York: W. H. Freeman and Company, 1995.

[2] Brock, William A., and Steven N. Durlauf. "Interactions-Based Models." Working Paper 9910R, SSRI, University of Wisconsin, Madison, WI, 2000.

[3] Cialdini, Robert B. *Influence: Science and Practice.* Boston: Scott, Foresman and Company, 1988.

[4] Cole, Hal L., George J. Mailath, and Andrew Postlewaite. "Efficient Noncontractible Investments in Large Economies." *J. Econ. Theory* **101** (2001): 333–373.

[5] Cook, Philip J., and Robert H. Frank. *The Winner-Take-All Society*. New York: Penguin Books, 1995.

[6] Corneo, Giacomo. "The Efficient Side of Progressive Income Taxation." Working Paper 364, CESifo, Munich, Germany, 2000.

[7] Frank, Robert H. *Choosing the Right Pond*. Oxford: Oxford University Press, 1985.

[8] Frank, Robert H. *Luxury Fever*. New York: Free Press, 1999.

[9] Gale, David, and Lloyd Shapley. "College Admissions and the Stability of Marriage." *Am. Math. Monthly* **69** (1962): 9–15.

[10] Hirsch, Fred. *Social Limits to Growth*. Cambridge: Harvard University Press, 1976.

[11] Mailath, George J., Masahiro Okuno-Fujiwara, and Andrew Postlewaite. "Belief-Based Refinements in Signalling Games." *J. Econ. Theory* **60** (1993): 241–276.

[12] Manski, Charles F. "Identification Problems in the Social Sciences." In *Sociological Methodology*, edited by P. Marsden, vol. 23. Basil Blackwell, 1993.

[13] Postlewaite, Andrew. "The Social Basis of Interdependent Preferences." *Eu. Econ. Rev.* **42** (1998): 779–800.

[14] Rege, Mari. "Why Do People Care About Social Status?" Mimeo, Case Western Reserve University, Cleveland, OH, 2001.

[15] Samuelson, Larry. "Information-Based Relative Consumption Effects." *Econometrica* **72** (2004): 93–118.

The Diffusion of Innovations in Social Networks

H. Peyton Young

We consider processes in which new technologies and forms of behavior are transmitted through social or geographic networks. Agents adopt an innovation based on a combination of its inherent payoff and its local popularity (the number of neighbors who have adopted them) subject to some random error. We characterize the long-run dynamics of such processes in terms of the *geometry* of the network, but without placing *a priori* restrictions on the network structure. When agents interact in sufficiently small, close-knit groups, the expected waiting time until almost everyone is playing the stochastically stable equilibrium is bounded above independently of the number of agents and independently of the initial state.

1   INTRODUCTION

New ideas and ways of doing things do not necessarily take hold all at once, but often spread gradually through social networks. In a classic study, Coleman,

The Economy as an Evolving Complex System III,
edited by Lawrence E. Blume and Steven N. Durlauf, Oxford University Press   267

Katz, and Menzel [12] showed how doctors' willingness to prescribe the new antibiotic tetracycline diffused through professional contacts. A similar pattern has been documented in the adoption of family planning methods, new agricultural practices, and a variety of other innovations [32, 33, 34, ?]. In the first stage a few innovators adopt, then people in contact with the innovators adopt, then people in contact with those people adopt, and so forth until eventually the innovation spreads throughout the society.

A similar process can be used to describe the diffusion of certain norms of behavior. For example, if people are more likely to jaywalk when they see others in the neighborhood jaywalking, the actions of a few "innovators" may cause jaywalking to become common practice in a given area. This general kind of mechanism has been suggested to explain a variety of social pathologies, including criminality, having children out of wedlock, and dropping out of high school [1, 13, 19]. While such behaviors are not actually innovations, the process by which they spread has similar dynamic properties, namely, the propensity to adopt a behavior increases with the number (or proportion) of some reference group that has adopted it.

A traditional concern in the innovation literature has been to identify the characteristics associated with innovators, that is, people who are the first in their area to adopt. One may then ask how many innovators are needed, and how they need to be dispersed, in order to propel the adoption process [32, 36]. Implicit in some of this literature is the notion that innovation is essentially a one-way process: once an agent has adopted an innovation, he sticks with it. Yet the same feedback mechanisms that cause innovations to be adopted also cause them to be abandoned. For example, an innovation may die out before the critical threshold or tipping point is reached; indeed, this may happen even after the tipping point is reached due to random events that reverse the adoption process. Moreover there appear to be historical cases in which this actually did happen.[1] Thus, if we want to know how long it takes, in expectation, for a "new" behavior to replace an old one, we must analyze the balance of forces pushing the adoption process forward on the one hand, and those pushing it back on the other.

In this chapter we study this problem using an approach pioneered by Blume [6] and Ellison [17].[2] The model treats local feedback effects as a stochastic process: the probability that a given person adopts one of two possible actions in a given time period is assumed to be an increasing function of the number of his or her neighbors who have adopted it. We wish to characterize the waiting time until one of the actions (the "innovation") diffuses in society as a whole.

---

[1] Diamond [14] discusses instances in which fundamental innovations, such as spears, bone hooks, bows and arrows, pottery, etc., were adopted and later lost by some civilizations, especially those that were small and isolated, as in Polynesia.

[2] For related work on local interaction models see Anderlini and Ianni [2], Berninghaus and Schwalbe [3], Blume [5], Brock and Durlauf [9], Goyal and Janssen [21, 22], Durlauf [15], and Blume and Durlauf [7, 8].

Ellison [17] showed that, when agents are located around a "ring" and they interact with their near neighbors, the expected waiting time is bounded above independently of the number of agents. In this chapter we introduce a structural criterion, called *close-knittedness*, that can be used to analyze this phenomenon in much more general situations. Roughly speaking, a group is "close-knit" if its members have a relatively large fraction of their interactions with each other as opposed to outsiders.[3] We show that when agents have a logistic response function to their neighbors' choices, and they interact in small, close-knit groups, the expected waiting time for diffusion to occur is bounded above independently of the number of agents and independently of the initial state.

2 THE MODEL

A social network will be represented by a graph Γ consisting of a finite set V of vertices, together with a set E of edges. Each vertex i represents an *agent* in the system. A directed edge (i, j) from i to j indicates that i is influenced by j's actions. The *strength* of the interaction is given by a nonnegative weight w_{ij}. The interaction is *symmetric* if $w_{ij} = w_{ji}$, in which case we represent the mutual influence between i and j by an undirected edge $\{i, j\}$. A natural example occurs when the degree of influence is determined by geographic proximity, that is, w_{ij} is inversely related to the distance between i and j. In what follows we shall focus on the symmetric case; asymmetric interactions present certain technical complications that require separate treatment.

Assume that each agent has two available choices, A and B. The *state* of the process at any given time t is a vector $\mathbf{x}^t \in \{A, B\}^V$, where x_i^t denotes i's choice at time t. The utility to an agent of choosing A or B is assumed to have both an individual and a social component. The *individual component* of payoff $v_i(x_i)$ results from the agent's idiosyncratic preferences for A or B irrespective of other agents. The *social component* of payoff results from the externalities created by the choices of other agents. These externalities may arise from a variety of factors, including demonstration effects, increasing returns, or simply a desire to conform.

A general framework for capturing these effects is to suppose that social payoff takes the form $\Sigma w_{ij} u(x_i, x_j)$, where the sum is taken over all edges $\{i, j\} \in E$. The function $u(x_i, x_j)$ can be interpreted as the payoff function of a two-person game in which each player has the strategies A and B. The weight w_{ij} may be interpreted either as the "importance" that i attaches to j's actions, or as the probability that i plays agent j in a given time period. The total payoff

---

[3]The relationship between network structure and the dynamics of contagion processes has been examined in other settings by Goyal and Janssen [21], Chwe [11], and Morris [30]. In these cases (as in ours) the network structure is assumed to be fixed. For models in which the network structure is endogenous see Jackson and Watts [23].

to agent i in state $\mathbf{x}$ is

$$U_i(\mathbf{x}) = \sum_{\{i,j\} \in E} w_{ij} u(x_i, x_j) + v_i(x_i). \qquad (1)$$

To be concrete, imagine that A is an IBM computer and B is a MAC. People have different tastes for IBMs versus MACs, which are captured by the functions v_i. The network externality from interacting with other people with computers is a common effect that is reflected in the function u. Its impact on a given individual i depends on the agents with whom i interacts and the importance (or frequency) of the interaction, which is captured by the weight w_{ij}.

Notice that we may interpret $U_i(\mathbf{x})$ as the payoff function of an n-person game, where n is the number of vertices in Γ and each player has exactly two strategies, A and B. This is the *spatial game* on Γ induced by the payoff functions u and $v_i, 1 \le i \le n$.[4] The number and form of the equilibria of the spatial game depend crucially on the topological structure of the graph, as we shall see in a moment. Our principal interest, however, is in the dynamics of the process by which agents adjust their behaviors, both in and out of equilibrium.

To analyze this problem we employ a model due to Blume [6], which is based on the concept of an Ising model in statistical mechanics [25]. Assume that each individual updates his strategy at random times that are governed by a Poisson arrival process. Without any serious loss of generality we may suppose that each person updates once, on average, per unit time interval. (All of the results go through if instead we assume that individuals have different rates of updating that are bounded above and below by fixed positive numbers.) These updating processes are assumed to be independent among the individuals, so the probability is negligible that more than one person updates at any given time.

When an individual updates, the probability of choosing a given action is assumed to be a logistic function of the payoff difference between the two actions. That is, if $\mathbf{x}_{-i}$ represents the current choices of the other agents, then the probability that i chooses A is

$$P\{i \text{ chooses } A | \mathbf{x}_{-i}\} = \frac{e^{\beta[U_i(A, \mathbf{x}_{-i}) - U_i(B, \mathbf{x}_{-i})]}}{[1 + e^{\beta[U_i(A, \mathbf{x}_{-i}) - U_i(B, \mathbf{x}_{-i})]}]}. \qquad (2)$$

The probability of choosing B is, of course, one minus this quantity. The parameter $\beta \ge 0$ measures the sensitivity of the agent's response to payoff differences: the larger β is, the more likely it is that the agent chooses the action with the higher payoff. The case $\beta = \infty$ corresponds to the *strict best response function*, in which the unique action with highest utility is chosen with probability one. (If both actions have equal utility, each is chosen with probability one-half.) The functional form (2) is standard in the discrete choice literature [26]; it has

---

[4]Blume [6] considered the case where the graph is a finite-dimensional lattice and called the corresponding object a *lattice game*.

also been used to model subjects' empirical choice behaviors in laboratory situations [10, 27, 28, 29].

In what follows it will be useful to write the payoff function $u(\cdot, \cdot)$ in matrix form as follows:

$$
\begin{array}{c c c}
 & A & B \\
A & a,a & c,d \\
B & d,c & b,b\,.
\end{array}
\tag{3}
$$

In other words, when one's "partner" chooses B, the externality from also choosing B is b, whereas the externality from choosing A is c, and so forth. We shall assume that there are increasing returns from conformity. This means that matching the partner's choice is better than not matching ($b > c$ and $a > d$). For simplicity we assume that the increasing returns aspect is the same for all pairs of agents who interact. Heterogeneity is captured by differences in the importance weights w_{ij}, and also by differences in the idiosyncratic preferences for A and B, that is, by differences in the functions $v_i(\cdot)$.

The long-run behavior of this stochastic process can be analyzed using a potential function. For each state $\mathbf{x}$, let $w_{AA}(\mathbf{x})$ be the sum of the weights on all edges $\{i, j\}$ such that $x_i = x_j = A$. Similarly, let $w_{BB}(\mathbf{x})$ be the sum of the weights on all edges $\{i, j\}$ such that $x_i = x_j = B$. Finally, let $v(\mathbf{x}) = \Sigma v_i(x_i)$ be the sum of the idiosyncratic payoffs in state $\mathbf{x}$. Define the *potential* of state $\mathbf{x}$ to be

$$
\rho(\mathbf{x}) = (a - d)w_{AA}(\mathbf{A}) + (b - c)w_{BB}(\mathbf{x}) + v(\mathbf{A})\,.
\tag{4}
$$

We can think of $w_{AA}(\mathbf{x})$ and $w_{BB}(\mathbf{x})$ as rough measures of the "areas" of the A-region and the B-region respectively. The potential is, therefore, a linear combination of the area of the A-region, the area of the B-region, and the idiosyncratic payoffs from choosing A and B. The long-run relative frequency of each state $\mathbf{x}$ is given by the Gibbs distribution

$$
\mu^{\beta}(\mathbf{x}) = \frac{e^{\beta\rho(\mathbf{x})}}{\sum_{y \in \Xi} e^{\beta\rho(\mathbf{y})}}\,.
\tag{5}
$$

It follows that the log of the likelihood ratio between any two states is just a linear function of their difference in potential. When β is sufficiently large (there is little noise in the adjustment process), the long-run distribution will be concentrated almost entirely on the states with high potential. Such states are said to be *stochastically stable* [18].

3 ANALYSIS OF THE POTENTIAL FUNCTION

The potential function has a simple interpretation in terms of the spatial game. For any agent i, the *neighborhood* of i, $N_i = \{j : \{i, j\} \in E\}$ is the set of agents

j that are linked to i by an edge. Suppose that the current state is $\mathbf{x}$, and that i changes strategy from x_i to x_i'. Without loss of generality we can assume that $x_i = B$ and $x_i' = A$. Then the change in i's payoff is

$$
\begin{aligned}
U_i(A, \mathbf{x}_{-i}) &- U_i(B, \mathbf{x}_{-i}) \\
&= (a-d)\Sigma_{w_{ij}} - (b-c)\Sigma_{j \in N_i : x+j=B} w_{ij} + v_i(A) - v_i(B) \\
&= \rho(A, \mathbf{x}_i) - \rho(B, \mathbf{x}_i).
\end{aligned}
\tag{6}
$$

In other words, the change in i's payoff equals the change in potential. It follows that every pure Nash equilibrium of the spatial game is a local maximum of the potential function; conversely, every local maximum of the potential function corresponds to a pure Nash equilibrium of the game. Typically these equilibria correspond to "patchy" distributions of As and Bs that are locally stable; depending on the geometry of the situation there may be a great many of them.

It is important to recognize that the states that globally maximize potential do not necessarily maximize social welfare. To illustrate, consider our earlier example in which each person can buy a computer of type A or B. Assume that, in the absence of externalities, everyone would prefer A because it is easier to use. Let us also assume, however, that B networks more efficiently with other computers, and this externality is enough to overcome A's greater ease of use. Suppose, for example, that the payoffs are as follows:

$$
\begin{array}{ccc}
\text{network externality}(u) & & \text{idiosyncratic payoff}(v) \\
A & & B \\
\begin{array}{c} A \\ B \end{array}
\begin{array}{cc} 1,1 & 0,0 \\ 0,0 & 4,4 \end{array}
& &
\begin{array}{c} v(A) = 8 \\ v(B) = 0 \end{array}
\end{array}
\tag{7}
$$

Let $n_A(\mathbf{x})$ be the number of agents who choose A in state $\mathbf{x}$. Then the potential function takes the form

$$
\rho(\mathbf{x}) = w_{AA}(\mathbf{x}) + 4w_{BB}(\mathbf{x}) + 8n_A(\mathbf{x}),
\tag{8}
$$

whereas the welfare function is

$$
\omega(\mathbf{x}) = 2w_{AA}(\mathbf{x}) + 8w_{BB}(\mathbf{x}) + 8n_A(\mathbf{x}).
\tag{9}
$$

It is clear that the all-B state maximizes social welfare, whereas the all-A state maximizes potential. Thus, in the long run, the process results (with high probability) in a state where most people have adopted the less favorable technology.[5]

---

[5]If everyone is indifferent between A and B, that is, $v(x)$ is a constant, the potential function takes the form $(a-d)w_{AA}(\mathbf{x}) + (b-c)w_{BB}(\mathbf{x}) + K$. This is maximized in the all-A state when $a-d > b-c$, and in the all-B state when $b-c > a-d$, that is, the process selects the risk dominant equilibrium. An analogous result holds in many other evolutionary learning models [4, 24, 37, 39].

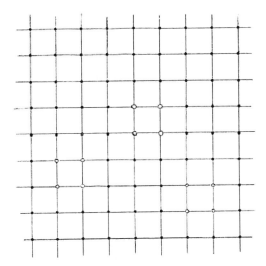

FIGURE 1   Small enclaves of A's (hollow nodes) surrounded by Bs (solid nodes).

4   THE UNRAVELLING PROBLEM

We turn now to the question of how long it takes for the process to come close to the stochastically stable state, starting from an arbitrary initial state. To illustrate the nature of the problem, consider the following example. The agents are located at the vertices of a square grid, which is embedded on the surface of a torus. Thus everyone has exactly four neighbors, and the weights on all edges are one (see fig. 1). Assume that the idiosyncratic payoffs from choosing A or B are zero; all that matters are the payoffs from externalities, which are given by the following payoff matrix

$$
\begin{array}{ccc}
 & A & B \\
A & 3,3 & 0,0 \\
B & 0,0 & 2,2 \,.
\end{array}
\tag{10}
$$

The corresponding potential function is $\rho(\mathbf{x}) = 3w_{AA}(\mathbf{x}) + 2w_{BB}(\mathbf{x})$. Thus, the all-$A$ state, $\mathbf{A}$, maximizes potential as well as social welfare.

Suppose that the process begins in the all-B state, $\mathbf{B}$. Let $\varepsilon = e^{-\beta}$. In a unit time interval, each agent updates once in expectation. Conditional on updating, an agent surrounded by Bs will switch to A with probability $e^0/(e^0+e^8) \sim \epsilon^{8\beta}$. If an agent does switch to A, then in the next time interval each of his four neighbors will switch to A with a probability approximately equal to ϵ^3. Eventually, small patches of As will form that are surrounded by Bs. If each such patch forms a rectangle (an "enclave"), then the process is at a Nash equilibrium: no one's payoff increases by switching. But this does not necessarily mean that the process has reached a tipping point from which A spreads rapidly. Indeed, if the A-enclaves are sufficiently small, they are more likely to revert back to B before they expand. This is the "unravelling problem." It can only be overcome once a sufficiently large A-enclave forms, which may take quite some time.

There is a simple geometric criterion which measures the vulnerability of a set to unravelling. Consider any two nonempty subsets of vertices S and S', not necessarily disjoint. Define the *internal degree of S' in S, $d(S', S)$,* to be the number of edges $\{i, j\}$ such that $i \in S'$ and $j \in S$. The *degree* of i, d_i, is the total number of edges that involve i. The vertex is *isolated* if $d_i = 0$. Let Γ be a graph with no isolated vertices. For every nonempty subset of vertices S in Γ, we say that S is *r-close-knit* if the ratio of the internal degree to the total degree is at least r for every nonempty subset of S:

$$\min_{S' \subseteq S} \frac{d(S', S)}{\sum_{i \in S'} d_i} \geq r. \tag{11}$$

This requires, in particular, that every member of S have at least r of its interactions with other members of S. Such a set is said to be *r-cohesive* [30]. In general, however, r-close-knittedness is more demanding than r-cohesiveness. Consider, for example, a 2×2 enclave: each member has half of its interactions with other members of the enclave. Then it is 1/2-cohesive, but it is only 1/4-close-knit, because it has four internal edges while the sum of the degrees of its members is 16. While each vertex taken individually passes muster, the boundary is too large relative to the size of the set.

Not only must the boundary of the whole set be reasonably small for the set to be close-knit, so must every portion of the boundary. In other words, eq. (11) requires that the ratio of internal to total degree must be at least r for *every* subset, or else the set may begin to unravel at the weakest part of the boundary. This possibility is illustrated in figure 2: the ratio $d(S, S)/\sum_{i \in S} d_i$ for the set S of A's is .4125, but the ratio $d(S', S)/\sum_{i \in S'} d_i$ for the dog-leg S' consisting of four A's at the bottom is only .375. The set S is most vulnerable to unravelling in this region of the graph.

Given a positive real number $r < 1/2$ and a positive integer k, we say that a graph Γ is (r, k)-*close-knit* if every person belongs to some group of size at most k that is at least r-close-knit. A family $\mathcal{F}$ of graphs is *close-knit* if for every $0 < r < 1/2$ there exists an integer k (possibly depending on r) such that every graph in the family is (r, k)-close-knit.

As an example, consider the class of all polygons. In a polygon, the degree of every vertex is two. Each subset S of k consecutive vertices contains $k - 1$ edges, so $d(S, S)/\sum_{i \in S} d_i = (k - 1)/2k$. It is straightforward to check that, in fact, $d(S', S)/\sum_{i \in S'} d_i \geq (k - 1)/2k$ for every nonempty subset S' of S, hence every subset of k consecutive vertices is $(1/2 - 1/2k)$-close-knit. Since every vertex is contained in such a set, the class of polygons is close-knit. For a square lattice

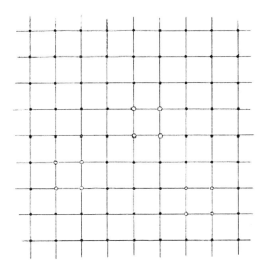

FIGURE 2   Set of A's (hollow nodes) containing a weak dog-leg.

embedded on the surface of a torus, it can be verified that every subsquare of side h is $(1/2 - 1/2h, h^2)$-close-knit. It follows that the family of square lattices is close-knit.

5   A THEOREM ON WAITING TIMES

In this section we show that if a graph comes from a close-knit family, then we can bound the waiting time until the process comes close to a state having maximum potential, and this bound holds uniformly no matter how large the graphs are. Since we need to compare graphs of different sizes, we shall assume henceforth that agents have neutral idiosyncratic preferences ($v(\mathbf{x})$ is constant) and that all edge-weights are unity. There is no loss of generality in assuming that $v(\mathbf{x}) = 0$. The externalities are described by a 2×2 game Γ with payoffs

$$
\begin{array}{ccc}
 & A & B \\
A & a,a & c,d \\
B & d,c & b,b\,.
\end{array}
\tag{12}
$$

Thus the potential function is

$$\rho(\mathbf{x}) = (a - d)w_{AA}(\mathbf{x}) + (b - c)w_{BB}(\mathbf{x})\,, \tag{13}$$

and potential is maximized at the risk-dominant equilibrium.

Let β be the response parameter, and let $\mathbf{x}^0$ be the initial state. Given a small $\delta > 0$, let $T(\Gamma, \beta, G, \delta, \mathbf{x}^0)$ denote the expected value of the first time t such that, starting from the initial state $\mathbf{x}^0$, the probability is at least $1 - \delta$ that at least $1 - \delta$ of the population is using the risk-dominant equilibrium at t and all times thereafter. The δ-inertia of the process defined by Γ, β, G is the longest such time over all possible initial states:

$$T(\Gamma, \beta, G, \delta) = \max_{\mathbf{x}^0} T(\Gamma, \beta, G, \delta, \mathbf{x}^0). \tag{14}$$

The following result generalizes Ellison [17], who proved that the waiting time is bounded for an essentially one-dimensional process in which the agents are located around a ring.[6]

Theorem. *Let $\mathcal{F}$ be a close-knit family of graphs, and let G be a symmetric 2×2 game with a risk dominant equilibrium. Given any small $\delta > 0$, there exists a β_δ such that, for every $\beta \geq \beta_\delta$, the expected waiting time $T(\Gamma, \beta, G, \delta)$ until the probability is at least $1 - \delta$ that at least $1 - \delta$ of the population is using the risk dominant equilibrium is uniformly bounded above for all graphs in $\mathcal{F}$.*

Proof. Let $\mathcal{F}$ and G be as in the statement of the theorem. Without loss of generality we can assume that $a - d > b - c$, that is, A is the risk dominant equilibrium. Let $r^* = (b - c)/((a - d) + (b - c)) < 1/2$ and fix $r \in (r^*, 1/2)$. Since $\mathcal{F}$ is close-knit, there exists an integer k such that every graph in $\mathcal{F}$ is (r, k)-close-knit. The parameters r and k will remain fixed throughout the proof. We are going to show that, given any $\delta \in (0, 1)$, there exists β_δ such that for each $\beta \geq \beta_\delta$, the δ-inertia of the process is bounded above for all $\Gamma \in \mathcal{F}$. ∎

Choose $\Gamma \in \mathcal{F}$ having vertex set V, and let S be an r-close-knit subset of size k. The adaptive process on G will be denoted by $P^{\Gamma, \beta}$. Now consider the following modification of $P^{\Gamma, \beta}$: whenever agents in S update, they do so according to the log-linear response process with parameter β, but the agents in $\overline{S}$, the complement of S, always choose B. Denote this *restricted process* by $P^{\Gamma, S, \beta}$. States of the restricted process will be denoted by $\mathbf{y}$, and states of the *unrestricted process* $P^{\Gamma, \beta}$ will be denoted by $\mathbf{x}$. Let Ξ_S denote the set of restricted states, and Ξ the set of all states.

Let $A(\mathbf{x})$ denote the number of edges in which the players at both ends choose actionx A in state $\mathbf{x}$; similarly let $B(\mathbf{x})$ denote the number of edges in which both players choose action B. By assumption, every agent is indifferent between A and B when there are no externalities, so we can drop the term $v(\mathbf{x})$ and write the potential function as

$$\rho(\mathbf{x}) = (a - d)A(\mathbf{x}) + (b - c)B(\mathbf{x}). \tag{15}$$

---

[6]Ellison used a somewhat different stochastic adjustment model in which agents deviate from best reply with a fixed probability ε. In our model they deviate with a probability that depends on the resulting loss in utility.

By eq. (5) we know that the stationary distribution $\mu^{\Gamma,\beta}(\mathbf{x})$ of $P^{\Gamma,\beta}$ satisfies $\mu^{\Gamma,\beta}(\mathbf{x}) \propto e^{\beta\rho(\mathbf{x})}$ for all $\mathbf{x} \in \Xi$. Similarly it can be shown that the stationary distribution $\mu^{\Gamma,S,\beta}(\mathbf{y})$ of $P^{\Gamma,S,\beta}$ satisfies $\mu^{\Gamma,S,\beta}(\mathbf{y}) \propto e^{\beta\rho(\mathbf{y})}$ for all $\mathbf{y} \in \Xi_S$.

Let $\mathbf{A}_S$ denote the state in Ξ_S such that everyone in i chooses action A, and everyone in $\overline{S}$ chooses action B. We claim that $\mathbf{A}_S$ uniquely maximizes $\rho(\mathbf{y})$ among all restricted states $\mathbf{y}$. To see this, consider any restricted state $\mathbf{y}$ and let $S' = \{i \in S : y_i = B\}$. Then

$$\rho(\mathbf{y}) = (a - d)d(S - S', S - S') + (b - c)[d(S', S') + e(S', \overline{S}) + d(\overline{S}, \overline{S})],$$

and

$$\rho(\mathbf{A}_S) = (a - d)d(S, S) + (b - c)d(\overline{S}, \overline{S}).$$

It follows that

$$\rho(\mathbf{A}_S) - \rho(\mathbf{y}) = (a - d)d(S', S) - (b - c)[d(S', S') + d(S', \overline{S})]$$
$$= (a - d)d(S', S) - (b - c)[d(S', S') + d(S', V) - d(S', S)].$$

Thus $\rho(\mathbf{A}_S) - \rho(\mathbf{y}) > 0$ if and only if

$$[(a - d) + (b - c)]d(S', S) > (b - c)[d(S', V) + d(S', S')]. \tag{16}$$

However, the latter holds because by assumption

$$\frac{d(S', S)}{\sum_{i \in S'} d_i} = \frac{d(S', S)}{[d(S', V) + d(S', S')]} > r^* = \frac{(b - c)}{[(a - d) + (b - c)]}. \tag{17}$$

(Note that $d(S', V) + d(S', S') > 0$, because by assumption there are no isolated vertices in the graph.) Thus $\mathbf{y} = \mathbf{A}_S$ uniquely maximizes $\rho(\mathbf{y})$ as claimed. It follows that $\mu^{\Gamma,S,\beta}$ puts arbitrarily high probability on the state $\mathbf{A}_S$ whenever β is sufficiently large.

Now fix $\delta \in (0, 1)$. It follows from the preceding discussion that there exists a finite value $\beta(\Gamma, S, \delta)$ such that $\mu^{\Gamma,S,\beta}(\mathbf{A}_S) \geq 1 - \delta^2/2$ for all $\beta \geq \beta(\Gamma, S, \delta)$. Fix such a value β. Consider the restricted process $P^{\Gamma,S,\beta}$ starting in the initial state $\mathbf{y}^0$, and let the random variable $\mathbf{y}^\tau$ denote the state of this process at time τ. The probability that $\mathbf{y}^\tau$ is in any given state $\mathbf{y}$ approaches the long-run probability of $\mathbf{y}$, $\mu^{\Gamma,S,\beta}(\mathbf{y})$, as τ goes to infinity. (This follows from the fact that the embedded finite chain is irreducible and aperiodic.) In particular, $\lim_{\tau \to \infty} Pr[\mathbf{y}^\tau = \mathbf{A}_S] = \mu^{\Gamma,S,\beta}(\mathbf{A}_S)$. Hence, there is a finite time $\tau(\Gamma, S, \delta, \beta)$ such that, from any initial state $\mathbf{y}^0$,

$$\forall \beta \geq \beta(\Gamma, S, \delta), \forall \tau \geq \tau(\Gamma, S, \delta, \beta), \qquad P[\mathbf{y}^\tau = \mathbf{A}_S] \geq 1 - \delta^2. \tag{18}$$

Observe now that the continuous process $P^{\Gamma,S,\beta}$ depends on Γ and S only through the configuration of internal edges that link vertices of S to other vertices of S, and on the configuration of external edges that link vertices of S to vertices outside of S. Since S is of size k, there is a finite number of internal edges and a finite number of ways in which they can be configured. Since S is of size k and r-close-knit, there is a finite number of external edges, and a finite number of ways in which they can be configured vis-à-vis vertices outside of S. Thus, for a given r and k, there is a finite number of distinct processes $P^{\Gamma,S,\beta}$ up to isomorphism. In particular, we can find $\beta(r,k,\delta)$ and $\tau(r,k,\delta,\beta)$ such that, among all graphs Γ in $\mathcal{F}$ and all r-close-knit subsets S with k vertices, the following holds independently of the initial state:

$$\forall \beta \geq \beta(r,k,\delta), \forall \tau \geq \tau(r,k,\delta,\beta), \qquad P[\mathbf{y}^\tau = \mathbf{A}_S] = 1 - \delta^2. \qquad (19)$$

For the remainder of the discussion, we shall fix r, k, and δ as in the theorem. Let us also fix $\beta^* \geq \beta(r,k,\delta)$ and $\tau^* \geq \tau(r,k,\delta,\beta^*)$. (In effect, $\beta(r,k,\delta)$ is the value β_δ claimed in the theorem.)

Let Γ be a graph in $\mathcal{F}$ with n vertices, and let S be an r-close-knit subset in Γ of size k. We shall couple the unrestricted process P^{Γ,β^*} and the restricted process P^{Γ,S,β^*} as follows. Create two disjoint isomorphic copies of the graph Γ, say Γ_1 and Γ_2, where the ith vertex in Γ_1 corresponds to the ith vertex in Γ_2. We will define a single process that mimics P^{Γ,β^*} on Γ_1, and mimics P^{Γ,S,β^*} on Γ_2. For each state $\mathbf{x}$ of the unrestricted process P^{Γ,β^*}, let $q_i(A|\mathbf{x})$ denote the probability that i chooses A when i updates, given that the current state is $\mathbf{x}$. Similarly, for each state $\mathbf{y}$ of the restricted process P^{Γ,S,β^*}, let $q'_i(A|\mathbf{y})$ denote the probability that i chooses A when i updates, given that the current state is $\mathbf{y}$. Note that $q'_i(A|\mathbf{y}) = 0$ for all $i \in \overline{S}$.

The coupled process operates as follows. The *state* at time τ is a pair $(\mathbf{x}^\tau, \mathbf{y}^\tau)$ where x_i^τ is the choice (A or B) at the ith vertex in Γ_1, and y_i^τ is the choice (A or B) at the ith vertex in Γ_2. Each matched pair of vertices in the two graphs is governed by a single Poisson process with unit expectation, and these processes are independent among the n matched pairs. Thus, whenever the ith agent in Γ_1 updates, the ith agent in Γ_2 updates, and vice versa. Let Θ be a random variable that is distributed uniformly on the interval $[0,1]$. Suppose that the ith pair of individuals updates at time τ. Draw a value of Θ at random, and denote its realization by θ. The ith individual in Γ_1 chooses A if $\theta \leq q_i(A|\mathbf{x}^\tau)$ and chooses B if $\theta > q_i(A|\mathbf{x}^\tau)$. Similarly, the ith individual in Γ_2 chooses A if $\theta \leq q'_i(A|\mathbf{y}^\tau)$ and chooses B if $\theta > q'_i(A|\mathbf{y}^\tau)$.

For every two states $\mathbf{x}$ and $\mathbf{y}$ on Γ_1 and Γ_2 respectively, write $\mathbf{x} \geq_A \mathbf{y}$ if $y_i = A$ implies $x_i = A$ for all i. In other words, if A appears at the ith vertex in $\mathbf{y}$ then A appears at the ith vertex in $\mathbf{x}$. It is evident that $\mathbf{x} \geq_A \mathbf{y}$ implies $q_i(A|\mathbf{x}) = q'_i(A|\mathbf{y})$ for all i. By construction of the process, if i chooses A in $\mathbf{y}^\tau$ then necessarily i chooses A in $\mathbf{x}^\tau$. Hence, if $\mathbf{x}^\tau \geq_A \mathbf{y}^\tau$ at some time τ, then $\mathbf{x}^{\tau'} \geq_A \mathbf{y}^{\tau'}$ at all subsequent times $\tau' = \tau$.

Now let the coupled process begin in the initial state $\mathbf{x}^0$ on Γ_1 and $\mathbf{y}^0$ on Γ_2, where $x_i^0 = y_i^0$ for all $i \in S$, and $y_i^0 = B$ for all $i \in \overline{S}$. Obviously we have $\mathbf{x}^0 \geq_A \mathbf{y}^0$ initially, hence we have $\mathbf{x}^\tau \geq_A \mathbf{y}^\tau$ for all $\tau = 0$. From eq. (17) and the choice of τ^* we know that

$$\forall \tau \geq \tau^*, \qquad P[\mathbf{y}_i^\tau = A \text{ for all } i \in S] \geq 1 - \delta^2, \qquad (20)$$

hence

$$\forall \tau \geq \tau^*, \qquad P[\mathbf{x}_i^\tau = A \text{ for all } i \in S] \geq 1 - \delta^2, \qquad (21)$$

This holds for every r-close-knit set S in Γ. Since every vertex i is, by hypothesis, contained in such an S, it follows that

$$\forall \tau \geq \tau^*, \qquad \forall i \quad P[\mathbf{x}_i^\tau = A] \geq 1 - \delta^2, \qquad (22)$$

Letting α^τ be the *proportion* of individuals in Γ_1 playing action A at time τ, it follows that

$$\forall \tau \geq \tau^*, \qquad E[\alpha^\tau] \geq 1 - \delta^2. \qquad (23)$$

We claim that this implies

$$\forall \tau \geq \tau^*, \qquad P[\alpha^\tau = 1 - \delta] \geq 1 - \delta. \qquad (24)$$

If this were false, the probability would be greater than δ that more than δ of the individuals at time τ were playing B. But this would imply that $E[\alpha^\tau] < 1 - \delta^2$, contradicting eq. (23). Thus eq. (24) holds for all graphs Γ in the family $\mathcal{F}$, which concludes the proof of the theorem.

6 ACKNOWLEDGMENTS

This research was supported by National Science Foundation Grant SES 9818975. The chapter benefited from constructive comments by Larry Blume, Steven Durlauf, Dean Foster, Stephen Morris, and participants at the workshop on the Economy as an Evolving Complex System held at the Santa Fe Institute, November, 2001.

REFERENCES

[1] Akerlof, George A. "Social Distance and Social Decisions." *Econometrica* **65** (1997): 1005–1027.
[2] Anderlini, Luc, and Antonella Ianni. "Path Dependence and Learning from Neighbors." *Games & Econ. Behav.* **13** (1996): 141–177.
[3] Berninghaus, S., and U. Schwalbe. "Conventions, Local Interaction, and Automata Networks." *J. Evol. Econ.* **6** (1996): 297–312.
[4] Blume, Larry. "How Noise Matters." Mimeo, Department of Economics, Cornell University, Ithaca, NY, 1995.
[5] Blume, Larry. "The Statistical Mechanics of Best-Response Strategy Revision." *Games & Econ. Behav.* **11** (1995): 111–145.

[6] Blume, Larry. "The Statistical Mechanics of Strategic Interaction." *Games & Econ. Behav.* **4** (1993): 387–424.

[7] Blume, Larry, and Steven N. Durlauf. "Equilibrium Concepts for Models with Social Interactions." Mimeo, Cornell University, Ithaca, NY, 1999.

[8] Blume, Larry, and Steven N. Durlauf. "The Interactions Based Approach to Socioeconomic Behavior." In *Social Dynamics*, edited by Steven N. Durlauf and H. Peyton Young. Washington, D.C.: The Brookings Institution, 2000.

[9] Brock, William A., and Steven N. Durlauf. "Discrete Choice with Social Interactions." *Rev. Econ. Stud.* **68** (2001): 235–260.

[10] Camerer, Colin, and Teck-Hua Ho. "Experience-Weighted Attraction Learning in Normal Form Games." *Econometrica* **67** (1999): 827–874.

[11] Chwe, Michael. "Communication and Coordination in Social Networks." *Rev. Econ. Stud.* **67** (2000): 1–16.

[12] Coleman, James S., Elihu Katz, and Herbert Menzel. *Medical Innovation: A Diffusion Study.* New York: Bobbs Merrill, 1996.

[13] Crane, Jonathan. "The Epidemic Theory of Ghettos and Neighborhood Effects on Dropping Out and Teenage Childbearing." *Amer. J. Sociol.* **96** (1991): 1226–1259.

[14] Diamond, Jared. *Guns, Germs, and Steel.* New York: Norton, 1997.

[15] Durlauf, Steven N. "Statistical Mechanical Approaches to Socioeconomic Behavior." In *The Economy as a Complex Evolving System*, edited by W. Brian Arthur, Steven N. Durlauf, and David Lane, vol. 2. Redwood City, CA: Addison-Wesley, 1997.

[16] Ellison, Glenn. "Basins of Attraction, Long-Run Stochastic Stability, and the Speed of Step-by-Step Evolution." *Rev. Econ. Stud.* **67** (2000): 17–45.

[17] Ellison, Glenn. "Learning, Social Interaction, and Coordination." *Econometrica* **61** (1993): 1047–1071.

[18] Foster, Dean P. and H. Peyton Young. "Stochastic Evolutionary Game Dynamics." *Theor. Pop. Biol.* **38** (1990): 219–232.

[19] Glaeser, Edward L., Bruce Sacerdote, and Jose A. Scheinkman. "Crime and Social Interactions." *Quart. J. Econ.* **11** (1996): 507–548.

[20] Glaeser, Edward L., and Jose A. Scheinkman. "Measuring Social Interactions." In *Social Dynamics*, edited by Steven N. Durlauf and H. Peyton Young. Washington, D.C.: The Brookings Institution, 2000.

[21] Goyal, Sanjeev, and Maarten Janssen. "Interaction Structure and Social Change." *J. Inst. Theor. Econ.* **152** (1996): 472–495.

[22] Goyal, Sanjeev, and Maarten Janssen. "Non-Exclusive Conventions and Social Coordination." *J. Econ. Theory* **77** (1997): 34–57.

[23] Jackson, Matthew O., and Alison Watts. "The Evolution of Social and Economic Networks." Mimeo, California Institute of Technology and Vanderbilt University, 1998.

[24] Kandori, Michihiro, George Mailath, and Rafael Rob. "Learning, Mutation, and Long-Run Equilibria in Games." *Econometrica* **61** (1993): 29–56.

[25] Liggett, Thomas. *Interacting Particle Systems*. New York; Springer Verlag, 1985.

[26] McFadden, Daniel. "Conditional Logit Analysis of Qualitative Choice Behavior." In *Frontiers in Econometrics*, edited by Paul Zarembka. New York: Academic Press, 1974.

[27] McKelvey, Richard, and Thomas Palfrey. "Quantal Response Equilibria for Normal Form Games." *Games & Econ. Behav.* **10** (1995): 6–38.

[28] Mookherjee, Dilip, and Barry Sopher. "Learning and Decision Costs in Experimental Constant-Sum Games." *Games & Econ. Behav.* **19** (1997): 97–132.

[29] Mookherjee, Dilip, and Barry Sopher. "Learning Behavior in an Experimental Matching Pennies Game." *Games & Econ. Behav.* **7** (1994): 62–91.

[30] Morris, Stephen. "Contagion." *Rev. Econ. Stud.* **67** (2000): 57–78.

[31] Pagano and A. Nicita, eds. *The Evolution of Economic Diversity*. London: Routledge, 2001.

[32] Rogers, Everett M. *Diffusion of Innovations*. 3d ed. New York: Free Press, 1983.

[33] Rogers, Everett M., and D. L. Kincaid. *Communication Networks: A New Paradigm for Research*. New York: Free Press, 1981.

[34] Rogers, Everett M, and F. F. Shoemaker. *Communication of Innovations: A Cross-Cultural Approach*. New York: Free Press, 1971.

[35] Valente, Thomas W. "Social Network Thresholds in the Diffusion of Information." *Social Networks* **18** (1996): 69–89.

[36] Valente, Thomas W. *Network Models of the Diffusion of Innovations*. Creskill, NJ: Hampton Press, 1995.

[37] van Damme, Eric, and Jörgen Weibull. "Evolution with Endogenous Mistake Probabilities." *J. of Econ. Theor.* **106** (2002): 296–315.

[38] Young, H. Peyton. *Individual Strategy and Social Structure: An Evolutionary Theory of Institutions*. Princeton: Princeton University Press, 1998.

[39] Young, H. Peyton. "The Evolution of Conventions." *Econometrica* **61** (1993): 57–94.

Dynamic Properties of Local Interaction Models

Timothy G. Conley
Giorgio Topa

This chapter analyzes a local interaction model of urban unemployment defined at the level of individual agents. Census tract level data are used to estimate the model parameters by matching empirical moments of the spatial distribution of unemployment in the Los Angeles Standard Metropolitan Statistical Area (SMSA) with their simulated counterparts.

1 INTRODUCTION

Local interaction models in economics can be defined as models in which agents' preferences, information, choices, or outcomes are affected by other agents' behavior "directly," rather than being mediated by markets. A common assumption in these models is that individuals interact "locally," with a set of neighbors defined by a social or economic distance metric.

The relevance of local interactions has increasingly been recognized by economists in a variety of contexts. Glaeser et al. [35] explain the very high

The Economy as an Evolving Complex System III,
edited by Lawrence E. Blume and Steven N. Durlauf, Oxford University Press   283

variance of crime rates across U.S. cities through a model in which agents' propensity to engage in criminal activities is influenced by neighbors' choices. Case and Katz [19] explore the role of neighborhood effects on several behavioral outcomes, such as criminal activity, drug and alcohol use, childbearing out of wedlock, schooling, church attendance. Crane [26] also looks at neighborhood influences on several social pathologies, focusing on nonlinearities and threshold effects. Katz et al. [46] and Ludwig et al. [52] use the Moving to Opportunity Program (MTO) as a natural experiment to evaluate the magnitude of neighborhood effects. Bertrand et al. [12] find that local social networks have a significant impact on individual welfare participation. Weinberg et al. [66] find significant neighborhood effects in hours worked using detailed panel data from the National Longitudinal Survey of Youty (NLSY).[1]

In studies concerning education, there is a long tradition starting with the Coleman report [20] of studying possible peer influences and neighborhood effects on educational outcomes: Aaronson [1] exploits data on siblings who grew up in different communities; Hanushek et al. [40] use very detailed data on Texan schools to estimate peer effects in student achievement; Zax and Rees [69] use a Wisconsin Longitudinal Study to estimate the impact of peer influences during school years on subsequent earnings. Sacerdote [63] uses a natural experiment (randomized assignment of roommates at Dartmouth college) to find evidence of peer effects in a variety of outcomes.

At a theoretical level, several authors have analyzed the role of local interactions and externalities in models of endogenous growth, income inequality, and neighborhood formation: Benabou [10, 11], Durlauf [28, 29], Fernandez and Rogerson [31]. These models share a common assumption that human capital accumulation is affected by choices and characteristics of local community members. There exists also a rich theoretical literature that considers local interactions in models of information cascades, such as Banerjee [6] and Bikhchandani et al. [13]; models of learning from neighbors [4], Gale and Rosenthal [32], Morris [58]; the emergence of conformity and social norms (Young [68], Munshi and Myaux [59]); and models of interdependent preferences as in Becker [7], Bell [9], and Kockesen et al. [47]. Brock and Durlauf [15] use random field theory to study generalized logistic models in which each agent's random utility of a given choice is affected by her contacts' outcomes.

In more applied work, knowledge spillovers, input-output linkages, and other economies of agglomeration have been used in the new economic geography literature to explain the observed patterns of spatial concentration of firms in a given industry (see Rauch [61], Audretsch and Feldman [3], and Ellison and Glaeser [30]), the observed growth rates in cities (as in Glaeser et al. [34]), or the presence of temporal "lumping" in the process that determines the spread of a given industry from one country to another [60]. Evidence of local information

---

[1] Jencks and Mayer [45] present a survey of empirical work on neighborhood effects. Ioannides and Datcher [43] and Brock and Durlauf [15] also give excellent surveys of the existing literature.

exchanges and knowledge spillovers determining the adoption and diffusion of new social norms has been reported by Munshi and Myaux [59], Jaffe et al. [44], and Kohler [48].

Finally, the importance of informal contacts and information networks in the job search process has been empirically documented in a growing economics and sociology literature. An early study of the Chicago labor market by Rees and Schultz [62] finds that informal sources such as referrals from current employees accounts for about half of all white collar hires and for about four-fifths of blue collar hires. Granovetter [36, 37] finds that roughly 56% of all new jobs are found through neighbors, friends, relatives, or business acquaintances. Corcoran et al. [25] confirm this basic finding and report, in addition, that informal hiring channels are more prevalent among black workers, as well as younger and less educated workers.

The use of informal channels such as referrals can be rationalized as a means to reduce the uncertainty regarding the quality of a prospective employee. Montgomery [56] studies a model in which employers find it optimal to use referrals from current employees to reduce the adverse selection problem in hiring: firms are assumed not to perfectly observe a worker's type at the moment of hiring, although the type is subsequently revealed. Further, it is assumed that there exists assortative matching in social networks, so that a high quality worker is more likely to refer someone like herself.[2]

Focusing more closely on the information exchange among workers, Calvo-Armengol and Jackson [18] analyze an explicit network model of job search in which agents receive random offers and decide whether to use them themselves or pass them on to their unemployed contacts, depending on their own employment status and current wage. The model generates very interesting implications that are consistent with the data: for example, positive correlations of unemployment and wages across agents both in a cross section and over time; long run inequality in expected unemployment rates and wages across groups; dependence duration in unemployment spells; decreasing marginal value of additional employed contacts.

It is worth noting that local interactions have been the subject of numerous studies in social sciences other than economics. Sociologists have theorized, long before economists, that individuals do not exist as isolated entities but are embedded into networks of relations that provide opportunities and constraints, such as information flows, the reduction of transaction costs, the provision and enforcement of norms. Burt [17] is an excellent introduction to social network theory. Coleman [21] is the first (to our knowledge) to have introduced the notion of social capital. Geographers and regional scientists have also used the idea that agents are more likely to trade, compete, or exchange information with other agents who reside "close" to them in some metric than with individuals far

---

[2]Montgomery [57] also shows how assortative matching within social networks combined with the presence of informal hiring channels can bring about persistent and widening income inequality, and polarization.

away, to explain patterns of spatial agglomeration, regional differentiation and inequality, or clustering. Curry [27] contains a fascinating collection of papers on these themes that are based on stochastic models of local interactions and derive the equilibrium spatial distributions of various outcome variables.

In this chapter, we focus on the study of local interactions in the context of urban unemployment. The main empirical motivation is the observed high variance and clustering in unemployment outcomes across neighborhoods within metropolitan areas. For example, using Chicago Census data, Topa [65] finds high levels of spatial correlation of unemployment: both in 1980 and in 1990, Census tracts with high levels of unemployment tended to be clustered together in geographically contiguous areas, rather than being spread around in a random fashion. The change in unemployment rates between 1980 and 1990 was also spatially correlated. This geographic "lumping" is consistent with the presence of local interactions and information spillovers. Positive spatial correlations are also present when other socioeconomic distance metrics are employed (see Conley-Topa [24].)

We study a "reduced-form" model in which agents' employment probabilities depend on the employment status of their neighbors. Such a role for neighbors' employment status could arise from an underlying exchange of information about job opportunities within social networks. This could occur, for example, in a model where useful tips or referrals are transmitted by currently employed agents to their unemployed contacts, in the expectation of receiving similar leads when unemployed. Such information exchanges might be viewed as informal mutual insurance arrangements that are sustainable even in the presence of limited commitment.[3] Our model is defined at the level of individual agents arranged on a set of locations with an explicit distance metric. Agents are heterogeneous with respect to race/ethnicity and education levels. We also allow the employment status of neighbors from an agent's own racial/ethnic group to have a different impact on her employment chances than the employment status of neighbors who belong to other groups. Individual networks are based on physical distance between agents, in the sense that social ties are more likely between agents that are physically close, although long-distance ties may also arise with small but strictly positive probability.[4]

Formally, the model generates a first-order Markov process over a very large but finite state space, where the state of the system at each point in time is a configuration of individual employment outcomes. It is straightforward to show that a stationary distribution exists and is unique, for a given distribution of

---

[3]Limited enforcement contracts of this sort have been analyzed by Thomas and Worrall [64] in the context of long-term wage contracts, and by Ligon, Thomas, and Worrall [51] in the context of informal credit in developing economies.

[4]In principle other distance metrics may also be used, based on travel time, ethnicity, occupations etc. (see Conley and Topa [24]).

individual characteristics (that are assumed to be fixed over time).[5] Because of the local positive feedback generated by the information exchange, the stationary distribution of unemployment is characterized by positive spatial correlations, that are bounded above by a quantity decreasing in the distance between agents.

This model is closely related to contact processes that are studied in the interacting particle systems literature.[6] These are typically continuous time Markov processes defined on infinite integer lattices in $\mathcal{Z}^d$, where particles can be in one of two states at each instant. The transition rates between states are affected by the state of a finite set of nearest neighbors on the lattice. For the contact process, there exists a critical value of a parameter governing the strength of interactions between neighbors such that nondegenerate distributions over the set of configurations only exist for parameter values above this threshold.

Model properties can vary according to the graph structure connecting agents. For example, when agents are connected on tree structures, the contact process has two distinct critical values: an intermediate phase appears where the process survives globally, but dies out locally (see Liggett [49]). The graph structure is also important in our context: in particular, the number of connections held by each agent and the lengths of agents' links affect the spatial properties of the stationary distribution of unemployment. Therefore, in our empirical application, we attempt to construct a network structure that is as realistic as possible, drawing heavily from the existing sociological literature on social networks (see Marsden [54, 55]).

We use the stationary distribution implied by our model for estimation. An alternative strategy would be to estimate the model parameters using data on individual transitions in and out of unemployment—this is perhaps more intuitive given that the process is a Markov chain. Unfortunately, this is not feasible because of limitations in the available data. Individual transitions can be estimated from the current population survey (CPS) or better still from longitudinal datasets such as the NLSY. However, these data sources lack detailed geographic information on the location of agents: this is problematic because in our model the transitions into employment depend on the state of the agent's social contacts. In the absence of detailed spatial information then, we cannot estimate all the transition rates that are necessary to estimate the model parameters. Therefore, we use census data on the cross-sectional distribution of unemployment across census tracts.

There are drawbacks to using this approach. First, in the absence of social interactions, not all the model parameters can be identified from the stationary

---

[5]In a static framework, Brock-Durlauf [15] and Glaeser-Scheinkman [33] analyze local interactions models in which multiple equilibria are possible, depending on the strength of the "social multiplier" brought about by the local interactions. Estimation of the model parameters is problematic in this case, although Brock-Durlauf [16] and Bisin et al. [14] present estimators that are consistent and efficient even in the presence of multiple equilibria.

[6]The contact process was first introduced by Harris [41]. See Liggett [49, 50] for a very rigorous and thorough introduction to interacting particle systems.

distribution, since the latter is fully defined from the *ratio* of entry and exit rates into unemployment. We use individual transition data from the CPS to calibrate the parameters that are not identified from the stationary distribution. More specifically, we use monthly transitions from employed to unemployed to calibrate the entry rate into unemployment, which does not depend on social interactions in our model. Second, no closed form solution exists for the likelihood function implied by the stationary distribution of our model. Therefore, we use simulation methods for estimation. In particular, the structural parameters of our model are estimated by matching several empirical moments of the cross-sectional distribution of unemployment in the Los Angeles metropolitan area with their simulated counterparts generated by the model.

This chapter's main contributions are an investigation of two aspects of this model's empirical performance. First we attempt to evaluate how well the distribution of agents' unemployment spells from our estimated model compares to CPS data on in-progress unemployment spells.[7] This is important in order to assess the goodness of fit of our model in a dimension that is not used in the estimation. It is also important in a broader research agenda that aims at studying the effects of local shocks not only on unemployment rates over different locations, but also on unemployment durations.

The second aspect we investigate is whether local interactions are really required to explain observed levels of cross-sectional clustering. In particular, we look at agents with heterogeneous employment transition rates but independent transitions and ask whether their sorting across locations is sufficient to explain observed clustering. It is plausible that, for example, agents with different races or education levels would have differing transition rates. It is also plausible that individuals sort into different neighborhoods on the basis of their neighbors' characteristics or because they have similar preferences over different consumption bundles (see Becker and Murphy [8]). Such sorting of individuals with different transition rates may induce positive spatial correlation of unemployment even in the absence of any local information spillovers. We allow agents to be heterogeneous with respect to race/ethnicity and education, and we replicate the spatial patterns of these covariates in Los Angeles in our model simulations.[8][9] We then compare cross-sectional clustering patterns in the data to those generated by our framework both with and without the presence of dependence across agents.

The rest of this chapter is organized as follows. Section 2 describes the model. Section 3 describes the estimation strategy, the details of the calibration of a subset of parameters, and the evaluation exercise. Section 4 reports the results

---

[7] As we will discuss in section 3, the data provide information on the length of in-progress unemployment spells for respondents who are currently unemployed, sampled at a given point in time. We replicate this sampling scheme in our simulations.

[8] In previous work, these two covariates seem to contribute the most to explaining the degree of spatial dependence present in unemployment data. See Conley-Topa [24].

[9] Other possible identification strategies involve the use of information about local community boundaries, see Topa [65].

of the estimation of the model parameters, with and without local interactions. Finally, we offer some conclusions in section 5.

2   MODEL

Our model is an extension of the information exchange model in Topa [65]. There is a finite set of agents M in the model, residing in a finite set of locations $s \in S \subset \Re^2$. A subset M_s of agents resides at each location s; and they remain at these locations over time. Agents are allowed to be heterogeneous in race/ethnicity and education. We allow three racial/ethnic groups corresponding to a partition of the population into African American, with indicator A_i; Hispanic with indicator H_i; and white (includes Asian and all others) with indicator W_i. An indicator X_i of high/low education status further characterizes each agent and corresponds to college education status. Time flows discretely from 0 to ∞ in the model. The state of agent i at time t, $y_{i,t}$, is her employment status: $y_{i,t} \in \{1,0\}$, where 1 represents the employed state and 0 the unemployed state. Therefore, the state of the system at each point in time is a configuration of employment states $y_t \in \mathcal{Y} \equiv \{1,0\}^M$.

The configuration of agents and their characteristics are calibrated to 1990 census data for the Los Angeles primary metropolitan statistical area (PMSA), which coincides with Los Angeles County. The set S contains 1622 locations determined by the latitude and longitude coordinates for centroids of 1622 of the 1643 census tracts in this PMSA.[10] The number of agents of each race/ethnicity at location s corresponds to the population of adults (16+ years of age) of that race/ethnicity in the 1990 census divided by 100, rounded up. So, for example, tract number 2317, in South Central Los Angeles had 5921 adult residents: 63 whites, 1788 African Americans, and 4070 Hispanics. In our model, the corresponding location has 60 agents: 1 white, 18 African American, and 41 Hispanic. The distribution of X_i across agents is separately calibrated within each tract—level race/ethnicity group. For each racial/ethnic group in each tract, the fraction of agents with $X_i = 1$ is set equal to the reported proportion of those with college attainment in the 1990 census, if it can be expressed using the available integer ratios. If available integer ratios could not match the proportion exactly, we randomized between the two closest integer ratios to the census data proportion so that the expected proportion of college-educated agents matched the census data proportion.[11] This calibration resulted in a total of 69,832 agents. The number of agents across tracts ranges from 8 to a maximum of 203, with a median of 39.

---

[10]We dropped 21 of the 1643 census tracts in the Los Angeles PMSA due to their very low populations.

[11]For example, if 21 of the 63 whites in tract 2317 had college educations, then the 1 white agent in the corresponding model location would have been randomly assigned $X = 1$ with probability 1/3 and $X = 0$ with probability 2/3.

Our specification for agents' information networks is based on their locations. Each agent i is randomly assigned links to five other agents based upon the following algorithm. The set S of all locations is partitioned into three subsets: the agent's own location s_i, the four nearest neighbors of s_i, and the complement of all locations in S other than s_i and its four nearest neighbors. Links are drawn in two steps, the first of which is to randomly select among these subsets of S with probabilities 65%, 34%, and 1%, respectively. Then an agent from the selected subset is drawn with a uniform probability and linked with agent i. Links are drawn without replacement and considered to be unidirectional, so each agent has exactly five links, and when agent i is linked with agent j, j will not always be linked with i. We use the notation N_i to refer to the set of five agents linked to agent i. Agents' employment transitions are assumed to depend only upon the states of the first-order neighbors in N_i.

The motivation for this choice of network structure comes from a rich sociology literature on social networks. Evidence from the General Social Survey strongly suggests that individual networks used to discuss important matters rarely exceed five contacts (see Marsden [54, 55]). Further, in a study of Toronto inhabitants in the 1980s, Wellman [67] finds that a surprisingly high fraction of interactions took place among people who lived less than five miles apart. We use his findings to roughly calibrate the parameters used in our network algorithm. Finally, allowing agents to draw contacts from locations far away with small probability is motivated by Granovetter [38], who documents the existence and importance of weak ties.

The evolution of the system is ruled by the following conditional transition probabilities for the state of each agent i, given the configuration of the system in the previous period. In keeping with our interpretation of social interactions as reflecting information about new job opportunities, we specify probabilities for transitions into unemployment as depending only on agents' characteristics, race/ethnicity, and education:

$$Pr(y_{i,t+1} = 0 | y_{i,t} = 1 \, ; A_i, H_i, X_i)$$
$$= \Lambda[(\alpha_{1A} + \alpha_{2A} X_i)A_i + (\alpha_{1H} + \alpha_{2H} X_i)H_i$$
$$+ (\alpha_{1W} + \alpha_{2W} X_i)W_i] . \tag{1}$$

where $\Lambda(\cdot) = \exp(\cdot)/(1 + \exp(\cdot))$. In contrast, the probability that an unemployed agent finds a job depends both on own characteristics and on information flows concerning job opportunities that she receives from her currently employed social contacts at time t. Formally, information received by agent i in location s is assumed to be a function of the number of employed individuals in her set of neighbors N_i. We will distinguish the number of employed individuals of an individual's own race/ethnicity from those of the other two groups using the notation $I_{i,t}^{\text{Own}}$ and $I_{i,t}^{\text{Other}}$. This allows us to investigate the possibility that information flow may depend on race/ethnicity. The precise definitions of $I_{i,t}^{\text{Own}}$ and

$I_{i,t}^{\text{Other}}$ when agent i is African American are:

$$I_{i,t}^{\text{Own}} \equiv \sum_{j \in N_i} y_{jt} \times A_j \text{ and } I_{i,t}^{\text{Other}} \equiv \sum_{j \in N_i} y_{jt} \times (1 - A_j). \qquad (2)$$

The values of $I_{i,t}^{\text{Own}}$ and $I_{i,t}^{\text{Other}}$ are analogously defined for members of the remaining two racial/ethnic partitions. We define the transition probabilities into employment for African Americans as:[12]

$$Pr(y_{i,t+1} = 1 | y_{i,t} = 0 \,; A_i = 1, X_i) \qquad (3)$$
$$= \Lambda[\beta_A + \gamma_A X_i + \lambda_A^{\text{Own}}(I_{i,t}^{\text{Own}})^\sigma + \lambda_A^{\text{Other}}(I_{i,t}^{\text{Other}})^\sigma]. \qquad (4)$$

The transitions for the other two racial/ethnicity groups are parameterized analogously with group-specific $\beta, \gamma, \lambda^{\text{Own}}$, and λ^{Other}, with the only common parameter across groups being σ. This parameter is also the only deviation from the typical logistic functional form as $I_{i,t}^{\text{Own}}$ is allowed to enter into the logit index only after being raised to the power σ. We use this power function to allow for additional flexibility (beyond that in the logit functional form) in fitting nonlinear effects of information as there is evidence that such nonlinear information effects may be important. For example, Bandiera and Rasul [5] study farmer networks and the adoption of new crops in Mozambique, and find that the informational value of an additional contact is decreasing in the number of contacts. This concavity is also found by Calvo-Armengol and Jackson [18] in simulations of their theoretical model.[13]

The model defined above generates a first-order Markov process y_t with state space $\mathcal{Y}$ of configurations over the set of locations. It can be shown that a stationary distribution exists and is unique for any choice of agents' characteristics. The stationary distribution of unemployment is characterized by positive spatial correlations that are bounded above by a quantity decreasing in the distance between agents. However, it is hard to characterize the invariant distribution analytically: that is why one uses simulation-based estimation methods, such as Simulated Method of Moments or an indirect inference methodology.

3   EMPIRICAL METHODOLOGY

We use a mix of calibration and estimation in our analysis. We estimate the model parameters using its implications for the stationary distribution of cross-sectional

---

[12]These transition probabilities implicitly assume that labor demand in the city is perfectly elastic. When labor demand is less than perfectly elastic, the total number of vacancies should affect the probability of exiting unemployment. So for example, if a group is largely unemployed, this makes it easier for another group to find jobs (abstracting from skill differentials, job types, etc.). We thank Ken Arrow for pointing this out to us.

[13]For example, for σ close to zero $I_{i,t}$ simply becomes an indicator for whether any of i's contacts are currently employed.

tract-level unemployment rates. Using only the information in the stationary distribution, the model's α and γ parameters are not separately identified for given values of λ and σ. In particular, these parameters are not separately identified for the natural base case with no social interactions for any racial/ethnic group, $\lambda^{\mathrm{Own}} = \lambda^{\mathrm{Other}} = 0$. Therefore, we use individual spell data to calibrate the α parameters for each of the six race and education combinations. We maintain this calibration of α parameters when we allow for social interactions to be present, even though we conjecture that these parameters may be identified due to the model's nonlinearity of the model and the addition of a continuous regressor. Calibrating the α parameters in both models is motivated by a desire to limit the number of parameters estimated with the cross-sectional distribution and to better isolate the marginal contribution of the social interaction terms.

ONE TO ZERO TRANSITION CALIBRATION

We calibrate the model parameters $(\alpha_{1A}, \alpha_{2A}, \alpha_{1H}, \alpha_{2H}, \alpha_{1W}, \alpha_{2W})$ using individual transition data from the CPS. Each household in the CPS is interviewed once per month during two sets of four consecutive months, usually during the third week of the month.[14] The data contains an indicator of whether the respondent was employed or unemployed during the week prior to each interview.[15] We treat months as though they have exactly four weeks and proceed as though each pair of consecutive months provides data on an individual's employment state at week t and week $t + 4$. We calibrate a weekly transition rate from employment to unemployment from this data, ignoring potential quick transitions back to employment between t and $t + 4$. In effect, we assume that no unemployment to employment transitions occur between t and $t + 4$. With this imposed, letting δ denote the weekly employed to unemployed transition probability, the conditional probability of an individual being unemployed in week $t + 4$, given she was employed at t, is

$$\delta + \delta(1 - \delta) + \delta(1 - \delta)^2 + \delta(1 - \delta)^3 . \tag{5}$$

We separately calibrate δ for all six race/ethnicity and college education combinations so that expression (5) equals the sample frequency of unemployed individuals at $t + 4$ who were employed at t.

---

[14]Each month, CPS field representatives attempt to collect data from the sample units during the week of the 19th.

[15]The precise wording of the employment question is: "Last week, did you do any work for either pay or profit? Did you have a job either full- or part-time? Include any job from which you were temporarily absent." If the respondent answers "Yes" to either, she is counted as *employed*. The precise wording of the unemployment question is: "Last week, were you on layoff from a job? Have you been doing anything to find work during the last four weeks?" If the respondent answers "Yes" to both, she is counted as *unemployed*.

ESTIMATION OF GAMMA AND SIGMA PARAMETERS

After calibrating α, we use a simulation method to estimate the remaining parameters. We estimate two specifications: the full parametrization of zero to one transition rates with local interactions in eq. (3), and for comparison, a restricted version of that model without local interactions present (λ parameters set to zero). For the specification with local interactions, the vector of model parameters θ_0 is defined as $\theta_0 \equiv [\beta_A, \gamma_A \lambda_A^{\text{Own}}, \gamma_A^{\text{Other}}, \beta_H, \gamma_H, \lambda_H^{\text{Own}}, \lambda_H^{\text{Other}}, \beta_W, \gamma_W, \lambda_W^{\text{Own}}, \lambda_W^{\text{Other}}, \sigma]$ and is assumed to be in the interior of some compact parameter space $\Theta \subset \Re^{13}$.

For each candidate parameter value, we use simulations to determine a vector of cross-sectional moments for tract-level unemployment rates by racial/ethnic groups: $\psi(\theta)$.[16] There are three sets of moments in the vector $\psi(\theta)$, one for each group: African Americans, Hispanics, and whites. For each group, the moments are: the expected value of the tract-level unemployment rate; the variance of the tract-level unemployment rate; and the average covariances of tract-level unemployment rates between tracts whose centroids are between .25 to 1.75, 2.25 to 3.75, and 5.25 to 6.75 km apart. Thus there is a total of 15 elements in $\psi(\theta)$.

θ_0 is estimated by minimizing the (quadratic form or chi-squared) distance between the simulated moments $\psi(\theta)$ and their sample analogs: $\widehat{\psi}$.[17] The estimator $\widehat{\theta}$ is defined as:

$$\widehat{\theta} = \arg \min_{\Theta} (\widehat{\psi} - \psi(\theta))^{\top} \Omega^{-1} (\widehat{\psi} - \psi(\theta)), \tag{6}$$

where Ω is an estimate of the asymptotic covariance matrix of the empirical moment conditions.[18] The restricted specification without local interactions is estimated in the same fashion, using the same 15 moments. The logit index specification for 0 to 1 transitions is restricted by omitting the I^{Own} and I^{Other}

---

[16] For a given value of θ, the model is simulated starting from a configuration with all agents employed for 100 periods, to attempt to reach the stationary distribution. Then, a simulated configuration of employment y is sampled and simulated moments $\psi(\theta)$ are computed for that θ. We use a simulated annealing algorithm to minimize the objective criterion over Θ. This algorithm is particularly robust to the possible presence of multiple local optima and/or discontinuities in the objective function. We thank Bill Goffe for kindly providing the Matlab SIMANN code to us.

[17] It is difficult to formally show that the model parameters θ are identified as the solution to the limiting form of this criterion function given our choice of moments ψ. However, Conley and Topa [23] examine the question of local identification for a similar local interaction model (albeit a simpler one), defined at the level of individual agents, when the data used for estimation are only available at the level of spatial aggregates, such as tracts or zip codes: this is exactly the situation we face in this paper. Numerical simulations are strongly suggestive that local identification is attained in this case. Therefore, we are confident that local identification is preserved in the present setup.

[18] Ω is a nonparametric estimate constructed via the method in Conley [22], which is analogous to Bartlett (Newey-West) covariance matrix estimators for time series. The estimate is a weighted sum of cross products of tract-level observations with a weight function that declines linearly from one at distance 0 km to zero at distance 20 km.

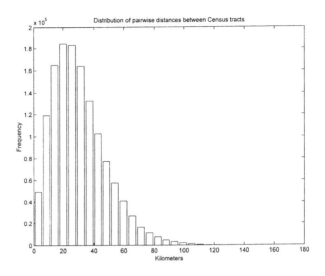

FIGURE 1   Distribution of pairwise distances between census tracts.

terms for all racial/ethnic groups from equation (3). Thus the σ and λ parameters vanish leaving only 6 parameters to estimate: $[\beta_A, \gamma_A, \beta_H, \gamma_H, \beta_W, \gamma_W]$.

EVALUATION BASED ON INDIVIDUALS' EMPLOYMENT SPELLS

We use data from the 1988–1990 March files of the CPS for individuals in the Los Angeles PMSA to investigate the empirical plausibility of our models' estimated spell distributions.[19] In particular we compare the distributions of in-progress unemployment spells for agents in each racial/ethnic group from our model with spells for observations from the corresponding racial/ethnic group in the CPS.

4   RESULTS

Table 1 reports summary statistics. There is a large Hispanic presence in Los Angeles, accounting for about one third of the population over 16 years of age. Hispanics tend to have the highest median unemployment rate (by census tract), and the lowest percentage of adults (25 years and older) with at least a college degree.

---

[19]We use three separate waves of the CPS in order to have a sufficient number of currently unemployed persons in our sample. The total sample size is 14,490 observations: out of these, a total of 389 were unemployed at the time of the interview. The overall unemployment rate in the Los Angeles area was roughly the same (around 5.3%) during this period, suggesting that business cycle conditions were fairly stable.

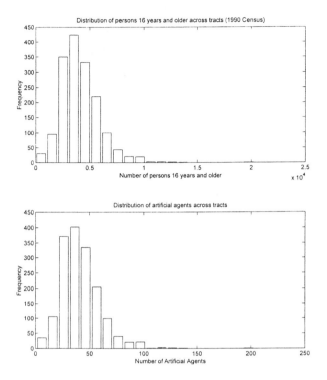

FIGURE 2 Comparison of persons and agents by tract.

Conversely, whites have the lowest median unemployment rate and the highest education levels.[20] Figure 3 reports non-parametric estimates of the spatial auto-correlation function (ACF) for total unemployment, as well as for unemployment conditional on race. There is a substantial amount of spatial correlation in the data. Interestingly, the correlation is much lower once one conditions on race: this is consistent with our findings for the city of Chicago reported in Conley and Topa [24]. Table 2 presents our results for the model without local interactions. Column A reports our calibrated transition probabilities from employment (1) to unemployment (0), for our six racial/ethnic group and college education category combinations. Column B reports the corresponding estimates of 95% confidence intervals for the transition back to employment, 0 to 1. For comparison with estimates for the full specification with interactions, we also present these results in terms of parameters in the logit indices in eq. (1) and eq. (3)

---

[20]Notice that the average unemployment rate is 7.5%, which is higher that the average unemployment rate for individuals reported in the CPS. This is because we are taking the average over tract-level unemployment rates.

TABLE 1   Summary statistics by census tract, Los Angeles County, 1990 census.

	Mean	Median	Std. Dev.	Min. Value	Max. Value
Number of Persons 16 Years and Older	4123.2	3890	1812.5	2	20294
Percentage Asians & Non-Hispanic Whites	57.77	67.46	31.06	0.00	100.00
Percentage Blacks	11.66	2.84	20.57	0.00	94.65
Percentage Hispanics	32.13	23.60	26.26	0.00	100.00
Unemployment Rate (Total)	7.49	6.42	4.74	0.00	47.07
Unemployment Rate (Asians & N.H. Whites)	5.75	4.60	5.31	0.00	59.09
Unemployment Rate (Blacks)	9.42	6.43	12.67	0.00	100.00
Unemployment Rate (Hispanics)	8.07	7.93	5.52	0.00	50.57
Percent with at least College Degree (Total)	22.10	18.33	16.31	0.00	100.00
Percent with at least College Degree (Asians & N.H. Whites)	28.15	25.43	16.04	0.00	100.00
Percent with at least College Degree (Blacks)	24.14	18.16	24.23	0.00	100.00
Percent with at least College Degree (Hispanics)	11.90	7.10	12.88	0.00	100.00

$N = 1,643$ Census Tracts, Los Angeles County (Los Angeles PMSA)

with its λ parameters set to zero. Column C reports the calibrated parameter values for the intercept and coefficient on education for each racial/ethnic group in the logit index for the 0 to 1 transition, eq. (1). Similarly, Column D presents estimated intercepts and slopes for the logit index in the 0 to 1 transition, eq. (3). Column E reports standard errors.

The model without local interactions performs quite badly in terms of producing sensible transition rates back to employment. For whites for example, the probability of finding a job within a week is almost one for persons without college, whereas it is close to zero for persons with college. So the model implies that whites who have attended college, experience especially long unemployment spells, which is clearly at odds with the empirical evidence in labor economics. We conjecture that the reason for this result is that the model tries to fit the observed spatial correlation patterns in unemployment by imposing long unemployment histories on college educated agents, who are characterized by positive spatial sorting. Finally, the test of the over-identifying restrictions yields a resounding rejection of the model, with a p-value practically equal to zero.s

Table 3 presents our results for the model with local interactions. For ease of comparison, column A repeats calibrated parameters in the logit index for the 1 to 0 transitions, eq. (1). Column B reports the estimated parameter values for

TABLE 2   Estimates for model without local interactions.

		A Calibrated 1 to 0 Probabilities*	B 95% CI for 0 to 1 Probabilities**	C Calibrated 1 to 0 Index Parameters
African American	No College	1.67	51.0530 − 95.7462	
	College	0.28	2.1781 − 97.0038	
Hispanic	No College	0.57	15.4947 − 17.3246	
	College	0.29	0.0000 − 100.0000	
White	No College	0.44	99.8030 − 99.9511	
	College	0.35	0.4592 − 6.9287	
African American	Intercept			−4.078
	Education			−1.802
Hispanic	Intercept			−5.157
	Education			−0.672
White	Intercept			−5.421
	Education			−0.218

∗ Weekly Probabilities of Entering Unemployment, in Percentage Points.
∗∗ Weekly Probabilities of Exiting Unemployment, in Percentage Points.

TABLE 2   cont'd.

		D Estimated 0 to 1 Index Parameters	E S.E. for the Estimated 0 to 1 Index Parameters
African American	No College		
	College		
Hispanic	No College		
	College		
White	No College		
	College		
African American	Intercept	1.578	0.784
	Education	−1.742	1.074
Hispanic	Intercept	−1.630	0.034
	Education	1.316	8.665
White	Intercept	6.925	0.356
	Education	−10.913	0.354

TABLE 3   Estimates for model with local interactions.

		A Calibrated 1 to 0 Index Parameters	B Estimated 0 to 1 Index Parameters	C S.E. for the Estimated 0 to 1 Index Parameters
African American	Intercept	−4.078	−4.106	1.980
	Education	−1.802	1.745	12.596
	Own Race Info	·	0.081	0.828
	Other Race Info	·	1.524	1.063
Hispanic	Intercept	−5.157	−3.995	0.095
	Education	−0.672	0.133	0.888
	Own Race Info	·	0.085	0.015
	Other Race Info	·	1.009	0.063
White	Intercept	−5.421	−5.711	0.163
	Education	−0.218	5.370	29.175
	Own Race Info	·	0.561	0.057
	Own Race Info	·	1.274	0.113
Nonlinearity Parameter Sigma		·	0.812	0.016

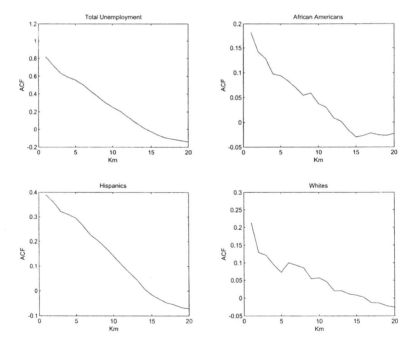

FIGURE 3   Autocorrelations of unemployment.

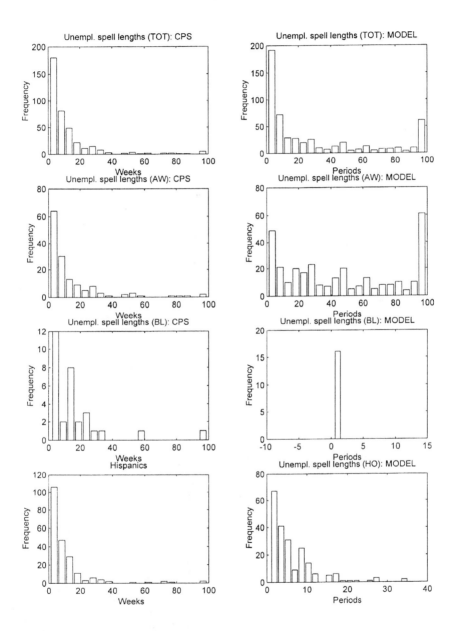

FIGURE 4   Unemployment spells, models WITHOUT interactions.

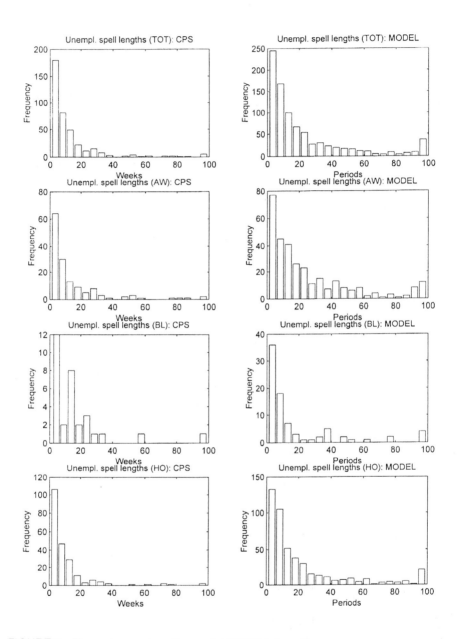

FIGURE 5   Unemployment spells, model WITH interactions

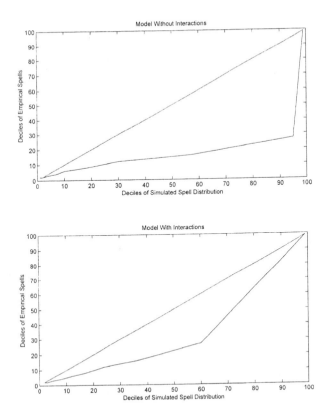

FIGURE 6   Empirical vs. simulated spells.

the terms in the logit index for the 0 to 1 transition, eq. (3). Column C again reports standard errors. With respect to the model without interactions, the estimates now imply reasonable transition probabilities back into employment, with a positive effect of education and of information, both from one's own group and from others. However, the estimates of $(\lambda_i^{\text{Own}}, \lambda_i^{\text{Other}})$, $i = A, H, W$, indicate that agents are affected more by information received by members of different groups than by information from one's own group: for African Americans and Hispanics this may suggest that members of these groups benefit more from interactions with whites than with members of their own group, but the result is implausible for whites. We conjecture that one explanation might be the possibility that inter-group social ties tend to be "weak," whereas intra-group ties tend to be "strong": Granovetter [38] has argued that weak ties are more effective at transmitting useful information than strong ones. Finally, the estimated σ is about 0.8, indicating the presence of strong concavity in the effectiveness of additional contacts. This is consistent with independent findings in Bandiera and Rasul [5]. A note of caution is introduced by the test of the over-identifying restrictions: while the test statistic is significantly lower than that for the model without interactions (702.9 vs. 974.5, respectively), the model with interactions is still overwhelmingly rejected.

Table 4 illustrates the marginal benefit of allowing for local interactions in terms of matching the estimated spatial correlations. A comparison of columns C and D reveals that the model with interactions performs much better than that without interactions in fitting the observed spatial correlation patterns. Therefore, there is a strong indication that sorting without local interactions is not sufficient to explain the unconditional spatial correlations of unemployment.

Finally, table 5 and figures 4–6 provide a measure of how well these local interactions models can fit the distribution of in-progress spells measured with CPS data. As is quite clear from a visual inspection of figures 4 and 5, again the model with interactions performs much better in terms of fitting the observed distribution. Figure 6 confirms this impression by comparing the deciles of the empirical distribution (not conditioning on race) with those from the simulated distribution, for both models. In table 5, we make this comparison more rigorous by comparing the simulated proportions of spells falling within four separate ranges with the 95% confidence intervals for the actual proportions. While the model without interactions is able to match only four out of the sixteen proportions under consideration, the model with interactions can match ten out of sixteen.

The model with interactions still generates spells that tend to be longer than the empirical ones: in particular, the right tail is fatter for the distribution of simulated spells. This is suggestive of duration dependence, and is consistent with the theoretical implications of the search model with network effects analyzed by Calvo-Armengol and Jackson [18]. They find that the presence of information networks alone is able to generate duration dependence in unemployment spells, even in the absence of unobserved heterogeneity.

5   SUMMARY AND CONCLUSIONS

In this chapter we have studied a model of local interactions, defined at the level of individual agents, in the context of urban unemployment. Our objective was, on the one hand, to investigate whether or not local interactions are really required to explain observed spatial patterns of unemployment. On the other, we wanted to evaluate the plausibility of the model with respect to a dimension of the data not used in the estimation, namely the distribution of in-progress individual unemployment spells. With respect to the first objective, the results show that indeed the model with interactions performs much better than the one without in two areas: first, it is better able to replicate the spatial correlation

TABLE 4   Spatial correlations of unemployment rates (totals and by race).

	Tract Distance Range	A Empirical Empirical Correlation	B S.E. for Empirical Correlation	C Model Correlation without Interactions	D Model Correlation With Interactions
Total	.25 to 1.75 km	0.535	0.035	0.395	0.410
	2.25 to 3.75 km	0.400	0.033	0.276	0.207
	5.25 to 6.75 km	0.282	0.024	0.167	0.068
African Americans	.25 to 1.75 km	0.123	0.027	0.016	0.156
	2.25 to 3.75 km	0.080	0.013	0.011	0.108
	5.25 to 6.75 km	0.029	0.010	0.007	0.048
Hispanics	.25 to 1.75 km	0.249	0.032	0.143	0.306
	2.25 to 3.75 km	0.208	0.022	0.107	0.207
	5.25 to 6.75 km	0.148	0.016	0.069	0.114
Whites	.25 to 1.75 km	0.158	0.033	0.023	0.130
	2.25 to 3.75 km	0.118	0.020	0.017	0.097
	5.25 to 6.75 km	0.077	0.014	0.012	0.054

TABLE 5   In progress unemployment spell distribution comparison.

	Spell Length Range	A 95% CI for Actual Proportion	B Model Proportion Without Interactions	C Model Proportion With Interactions
Total	4 Weeks or Less	0.4004 - 0.4993	0.2992	0.2569
	5 to 9 Weeks	0.1536 - 0.2320	0.1615	0.1783
	10 to 18 Weeks	0.1465 - 0.2237	0.1325	0.1858
	19+ Weeks	0.1347 - 0.2098	0.4027	0.3668
African Americans	4 Weeks or Less	0.1580 - 0.4871	1.0000	0.3655
	5 to 9 Weeks	0.0110 - 0.2470	0.0000	0.1928
	10 to 18 Weeks	0.1305 - 0.4501	0.0000	0.1526
	19+ Weeks	0.1040 - 0.4121	0.0000	0.2851
Hispanics	4 Weeks or Less	0.4077 - 0.5412	0.4955	0.2638
	5 to 9 Weeks	0.1591 - 0.2688	0.3042	0.2012
	10 to 18 Weeks	0.1340 - 0.2381	0.1461	0.1794
	19+ Weeks	0.0813 - 0.1699	0.0512	0.3414
Whites	4 Weeks or Less	0.3565 - 0.5185	0.1359	0.2196
	5 to 9 Weeks	0.1117 - 0.2355	0.0754	0.1433
	10 to 18 Weeks	0.1058 - 0.2275	0.1300	0.2031
	19+ Weeks	0.1543 - 0.2901	0.6538	0.4227

patterns present in the data; and second, it is able to do so while still producing meaningful individual transition rates back into employment.

With respect to the second exercise, again the model with interactions performs much better than the model which only takes into account sorting along observed characteristics, although the former still tends to generate too many very long spells relative to the empirical distribution. This is quite interesting on various dimensions. First, it is consistent with a set of theoretical results in Calvo-Armengol and Jackson [18], who show that network interactions in job search are sufficient to generate duration dependence in unemployment. Second, it suggests that one cannot just fit cross-sectional moments to provide a plausible model of unemployment, but rather must develop a richer model in order to better capture the duration dimension as well. This is, in our opinion, an important avenue for future research.

ACKNOWLEDGMENTS

The authors are grateful to Ken Arrow, Alberto Bisin, Steven Durlauf, Hiroyuki Kasahara, Chuck Manski, Philip Merrigan, participants at the Santa Fe Institute conference on the Economy as an Evolving System III, and various seminar audiences for helpful comments. Ryo Nakajima and Adeline Delavande provided excellent research assistance. Conley gratefully acknowledges financial support from the NSF. Topa gratefully acknowledges financial support from the NSF and from the C.V. Starr Center for Applied Economics at NYU. The authors are, of course, responsible for all errors.

REFERENCES

[1] Aaronson, Daniel. "Using Sibling Data to Estimate the Impact of Neighborhoods on Children's Educational Outcomes." Working Paper, Federal Reserve Bank of Chicago, Chicago, IL, 1996.

[2] Akerlof, George A. "Social Distance and Social Decisions." *Econometrica* **65** (1997): 1005–1027.

[3] Audretsch, David B., and Maryann P. Feldman. "R&D Spillovers and the Geography of Innovation and Production." *Am. Econ. Rev.* **86** (1996): 630–640.

[4] Bala. Venkatesh, and sanjeev Goyal. "Learning from Neighbors." *Rev. Econ. Stud.* **65** (1998): 595–622.

[5] Bandiera, Oriana, and Imran Rasul. "Complementarities, Social Networks and Technology Adoption in Northern Mozambique." Unpublished manuscript, London School of Economics, London, England, 2002.

[6] Banerjee, Abhijit V. "A Simple Model of Herd Behavior." *Quart. J. Econ.* **107** (1992): 797–817.

[7] Becker, Gary S. *Accounting for Tastes*. Cambridge, MA: Harvard University Press, 1996.

[8] Becker, Gary S., and Kevin M. Murphy. "The Sorting of Individuals into Categories when Tastes and Productivity Depend on the Composition of Members." Unpublished manuscript, University of Chicago, Chicago, IL, 1994.

[9] Bell, Ann. "Dynamically Interdependent Preferences in a General Equilibrium Environment." Unpublished manuscript, Vanderbilt University, Nashville, TN, 1995.

[10] Benabou, Roland. "Equity and Effciency in Human Capital Investment: The Local Connection." *Rev. Econ. Stud.* **63** (1996): 237–264.

[11] Benabou, Roland. "Workings of a City: Location, Education, and Production." *Quart. J. Econ.* **108** (1993): 619–652.

[12] Bertrand, Marianne, Erzo F. P. Luttmer, and Sedhil Mullainathan. "Network Effects and Welfare Cultures." Unpublished manuscript, University of Chicago, Chicago, IL, 1999.

[13] Bikhchandani, Sushil, David Hirshleifer, and Ivo Welch. "A Theory of Fads, Fashion, Custom, and Cultural Change as Informational Cascades." *J. Pol. Econ.* **100** (1992): 992–1026.

[14] Bisin, Alberto, Andrea Moro, and Giorgio Topa. "The Empirical Content of Models with Multiple Equilibria." Unpublished manuscript, New York University, New York, 2003.

[15] Brock, William A., and Steven N. Durlauf. "Discrete Choice with Social Interactions." *Rev. Econ. Stud.* **68** (2001): 235–260.

[16] Brock, William A., and Steven N. Durlauf. "Interactions-Based Models." In *Handbook of Econometrics*, edited by James J. Heckman and Edward Leamer, 3297–3380, vol. V. Amsterdam: North Holland, 2001.

[17] Burt, Ronald S. *Structural Holes: The Social Structure of Competition*. Cambridge, MA: Harvard University Press, 1992.

[18] Calvo-Armengol A., and M. O. Jackson. "Social Networks in Determining Employment and Wages: Patterns, Dynamics and Inequality." Mimeo, California Institute of Technology, 2002.

[19] Case, Anne C., and Lawrence F. Katz. "The Company You Keep: The Effects of Family and Neighborhood on Disadvantaged Youths." Working Paper 3705, National Bureau of Economic Research, 1991.

[20] Coleman, James S., E. Campbell, J. Hobson, J. McPartland, A. Mood, F. Weinfeld, and R. York. *Equality of Educational Opportunity*. Washington DC: U.S. Government Printing Offce, 1966.

[21] Coleman, James S. "Social Capital in the Creation of Human Capital." *Am. J. Sociol.* **94** (1988): S95–S120.

[22] Conley, Timothy G. "GMM Estimation with Cross Sectional Dependence." *J. App. Econ.* **92** (1999): 1–45.

[23] Conley, Timothy G., and G. Topa. "Identification of Local Interaction Models with Imperfect Location Data." *J. App. Econ* **18(5)** (2003): 605–618.

[24] Conley, Timothy G., and G. Topa. "Socio-Economic Distance and Spatial Patterns in Unemployment." *J. App. Econ* **17(4)** (2002): 303–327.

[25] Corcoran, Mary, Linda Datcher, and Greg Duncan. "Information and Influence Networks in Labor Markets." In *Five Thousand American Families: Patterns of Economic Progress*, edited by Greg Duncan and James Morgan, vol. 7, 1–37. Ann Arbor, MI: Institute for Social Research, 1980.

[26] Crane, Jonathan. "The Epidemic Theory of Ghettos and Neighborhood Effects on Dropping Out and Teenage Childbearing." *Am. J. Sociol.* **96(5)** (1991): 1226–1259.

[27] Curry, Leslie. *The Random Spatial Economy and Its Evolution.* Brookfield, VT: Ashgate, 1998.

[28] Durlauf, Steven N. "Neighborhood Feedbacks, Endogenous Stratification, and Income Inequality." In *Dynamic Disequilibrium Modelling: Proceedings of the Ninth International Symposium on Economic Theory and Econometrics*, edited by W. Barnett, G. Gandolfo, and C. Hillinger. Cambridge University Press, 1996.

[29] Durlauf, Steven N. "A Theory of Persistent Income Inequality." *J. Econ. Growth* **1** (1996): 75–93.

[30] Ellison, Glenn, and Edward L. Glaeser. "Geographic Concentration in U .S. Manufacturing Industries: A Dartboard Approach." *J. Pol. Econ.* **105** (1997): 889–927.

[31] Fernandez, Raquel, and Richard Rogerson. "Income Distribution, Communities, and the Quality of Public Education." *Quart. J. Econ.* **111** (1996): 135–164.

[32] Gale, Douglas, and Robert Rosenthal. "Experimentation, Imitation, and Strategic Stability." *J. Econ. Theory* **84** (1999): 1–40.

[33] Glaeser, Edward L., and José A. Scheinkman. "Measuring Social Interactions." In *Social Dynamics*, edited by Durlauf and Young, 83–102. Cambridge, MA: MIT Press, 2001.

[34] Glaeser, Edward L., H. D. Kallal, J. A. Scheinkman, and A. Shleifer. "Growth in Cities." *J. Pol. Econ.* **100** (1992): 1126–1152.

[35] Glaeser, Edward L., Bruce Sacerdote, and José A. Scheinkman. "Crime and Social Interactions." *Quart. J. Econ.* **111** (1996): 507–548.

[36] Granovetter, Mark S. *Getting a Job: A Study of Contacts and Careers.* Cambridge, MA: Harvard University Press, 1995.

[37] Granovetter, Mark S. *Getting A Job: A Study of Contacts and Careers.* Chicago, IL: The University of Chicago Press, 1974.

[38] Granovetter, Mark S. "The Strength of Weak Ties." *Am. J. Sociol.* **78(6)** (1973): 1360–1380.

[39] Hall, P., N. I. Fisher, and B. Hoffman. "On the Non-Parametric Estimation of Covariance Functions." Unpublished manuscript, Australian National University, Canberra, Australia, 1992.

[40] Hanushek, Eric, John F. Kain, Jacob Markman, and Steven Rivken. "Do Peers Affect Student Achievement?" Unpublished manuscript, University of Rochester, Rochester, NY, 2000.

[41] Harris, Theodore E. Contact Interactions on a Lattice." *Annals of Probability* **2** (1974): 969–988.

[42] Hunter, Albert. *Symbolic Communities: The Persistence and Change of Chicago's Local Communities.* Chicago: The University of Chicago Press, 1974.

[43] Ioannides, Yannis M., and Linda Datcher Loury. "Job Information Networks, Neighborhood Effects and Inequality." Unpublished manuscript, Dept. of Economics, Tufts University, Medford, MA, 1999.

[44] Jaffe, Adam B., Manuel Trajtenberg, and Rebecca Henderson. "Geographic Localization of Knowledge Spillovers as Evidenced by Patent Citations." *Quart. J. Econ.* **108** (1993): 577–598.

[45] Jencks, Christopher, and Susan E. Mayer. "The Social Consequences of Growing Up in a Poor Neighborhood." In *Inner-City Poverty in the United States*, edited by L. Lynn and M. McGeary, 111–186. Washington, DC: National Academy Press, 1990.

[46] Katz, Lawrence F., Jeffrey Kling, and Jeffrey Liebman. "Moving To Opportunity in Boston: Early Impacts of a Housing Mobility Program." Unpublished manuscript, Harvard University, Boston, MA, 1999.

[47] Kockesen, Levent, Efe Ok, and Rajiv Sethi. "Evolution of Interdependent Preferences in Aggregative Games." *Games & Economic Behavior* (forthcoming).

[48] Kohler, Hans-Peter. ""Fertility and Social Interaction: An Economic Approach." Unpublished Ph.D. diss., UC Berkeley, CA, 1997.

[49] Liggett, Thomas M. *Stochastic Interacting Systems: Contact, Voter and Exclusion Processes.* New York: Springer Verlag, 1999.

[50] Liggett, Thomas M. *Interacting Particle Systems.* New York: Springer Verlag, 1985.

[51] Ligon, Ethan, Jonathan P. Thomas, and Tim Worrall. "Mutual Insurance with Limited Commitment: Theory and Evidence from Village Economies." Unpublished manuscript, UC Berkeley, CA, 1999.

[52] Ludwig, Jens, Greg J. Duncan, and Paul Hirschfield. "Urban Poverty and Juvenile Crime: Evidence from a Randomized Housing-Mobility Experiment." Unpublished manuscript, Georgetown University, Washington, DC, 1999.

[53] Manski, Charles F. "Identification of Endogenous Social Effects: the Reflection Problem." *Rev. Econ. Stud.* **60** (1993): 531–542.

[54] Marsden, Peter V. "Core Discussion Networks of Americans." *Am. Soc. Rev.* **52** (1987): 122–131.

[55] Marsden, Peter V. "Homogeneity in Confiding Relations." *Soc. Net.* **10** (1988): 57–76.

[56] Montgomery, James D. "Social Networks and Labor-Market Outcomes: Toward an Economic Analysis." *The Am. Econ. Rev.* **81(5)** (1991): 1408–1418.

[57] Montgomery, James D. "Social Networks and Persistent Inequality in the Labor Market." Unpublished manuscript, Northwestern University, Chicago, IL, 1992.

[58] Morris, Stephen. "Contagion." CARESS Working Paper 97-01, University of Pennsylvania, Philadelphia, PA, 1997.

[59] Munshi, Kaivan, and Jacques Myaux. "Social Change and Individual Decisions: With an Application to the Demographic Transition." Unpublished manuscript, University of Pennsylvania, Philadelphia, PA, 2002.

[60] Puga, Diego, and Anthony J. Venables. "The Spread of Industry: Spatial Agglomeration in Economic Development." Discussion Paper no. 1354, Centre for Economic Policy Research, London, 1996.

[61] Rauch, James E. "Does History Matter Only When It Matters Little? The Case of City-Industry Location." *Quart. J. Econ.* **108** (1993): 843–867.

[62] Rees, Albert, and George P. Schultz. *Workers and Wages in an Urban Labor Market.* Chicago: University of Chicago Press, 1970.

[63] Sacerdote, Bruce. "Peer Effects with Random Assignment: Results for Dartmouth Roommates." *Quart. J. Econ.* **116(2)** (2001): 681–704.

[64] Thomas, Jonathan P., and Tim Worrall. "Self-Enforcing Wage Contracts." *Rev. Econ. Stud.* **55** (1988): 541–554.

[65] Topa, Giorgio. "Social Interactions, Local Spillovers, and Unemployment." *Rev. Econ. Stud.* **68** (2001): 261–295.

[66] Weinberg, Bruce, Patricia Reagan, and Jeffrey Yankow. "Do Neighborhoods Affect Hours Worked: Evidence from Longitudinal Data?" Working Paper, Department of Economics, Ohio State University, 2000. To appear in *J. Labor Econ..*

[67] Wellman, Barry. "Are Personal Communities Local? A Dumptarian Reconsideration." *Social Networks* **18** (1996): 347–354.

[68] Young, H. Peyton. "The Dynamics of Conformity." In *Social Dynamics*, edited by S. N. Durlauf and H. P. Young. Cambridge, MA: MIT Press, 2001.

[69] Zax, Jeffrey S., and Daniel I. Rees. "Environment, Ability, Effort, and Earnings." Unpublished manuscript, University of Colorado–Boulder, 1999.

Useful Knowledge as an Evolving System: The View from Economic History

Joel Mokyr

Some of the material in this chapter is adapted from my book *The Gifts of Athena: Historical Origins of the Knowledge Economy*, Princeton University Press, 2002.

1 INTRODUCTION

"Knowledge" has become fashionable again. Books and articles with the word, preferably paired with "economy" and "growth" are coming out in droves. In his collection *Essays in the Theory of Risk Bearing* [2], Ken Arrow used the term extensively, long before the return of *knowledge* to respectability. I studied these papers while in graduate school, and find myself returning to them often. They represent the kinds of models that are most useful to economic historians, who can be squarely classified as consumers rather than producers of theory. Arrow's work has inspired an entire generation of empirical economists concerned with the role of technology in the modern economy, and provided the theoretical underpinnings that inspired a great deal of the new growth economics and a great deal of the work of those economic historians—a number of them at Stanford—who realized the importance of technological change as the central feature of economic change in modern history.

What we learned from Arrow above all is that the market for knowledge does not work as well and in the same way as the markets for most other commodities. There is an inherent riskiness against which insurance cannot be obtained, and a public good property that makes it impossible to design first-best allocative mechanisms. Competitive economies will not get the production and diffusion of new knowledge quite right, no matter what. Despite an enormous amount of research, technology and knowledge have remained a slippery topic for economists.

Yet the historian needs to tell his tale. And the big story is that in the past centuries, useful knowledge has become a dominant factor in history. It was not always thus: in the more remote past, economies could and did grow with only minimal and slow changes in technology. Even in the more recent past, institutional changes have contributed to the process of economic growth. All the same, it is surely true that we are richer today because we know more than past societies. The process of *modern* growth is different from the kind of growth experienced in Europe and the Orient before 1800 in that it is sustained. Whereas in the premodern past, growth spurts would always run into negative feedback, no such ceiling seems to have been limiting the economic expansion of the past two centuries. Even the horrors of two world wars were, in the long run, unable to slow down the expansion of those economies—primarily, but not exclusively "western"—that were able to get their institutional foundations in order. At least for those, economic growth seems, to put it somewhat crudely, to have lost its concavity.

The enigma of modern growth has led to a great deal of modeling and speculation amongst economists interested in the topic. One important theme in the literature has been that the Malthusian models that provided much of the negative feedback before 1800, have been short-circuited by the desire and ability of a growing number of individuals to reduce their fertility [27, 48]. Another has been institutional change, which has reduced opportunistic behavior and uncertainty. What has not been stressed enough is that the new technology was made possible by ever increasing "useful knowledge" as Kuznets called it.[1] The sources of this growth in knowledge, surprisingly, have not been fully analyzed. The "new growth economics" has realized that new technology is created by inputs, such as the resources devoted to research and development and investment in human capital. Although we have learned a great deal from this literature, its contribution to the understanding of the mechanism of growth of useful knowledge is tantamount to opening a black box, finding a smaller black box inside it and calling out "Eureka!"

---

[1] Elsewhere, he seems to have preferred the term "tested knowledge" but given the ambiguity of what constitutes an "acceptable" test, I shall refrain from using that term [43, p. 87].

How does the kind of "useful knowledge" that Kuznets [43] and Machlup [49] wrote about a generation ago emerge and develop? Why does it occur in one society and not another, at one time, and why does it take the form it does? There are two different approaches we can take. One is to bite the bullet and attack the highly imperfect market for knowledge despite the many difficulties it poses, and try to analyze the supply and demand for new technology.[2] The underlying assumption here is that people who discover new knowledge are in it primarily for the money, and that technology is "produced" by a rational economic system. In this model, the limits of the resources on which society can draw to produce this knowledge are not fully specified, and so the exact production function that determines the relation between the inputs and the output of new knowledge is still left in the middle. It ignores other motives that historically have driven the growth of useful knowledge such as curiosity ambition, an altruistic drive to serve humanity, and religion. The other approach is to concentrate on the historical process of new knowledge creation and to examine the details of how new knowledge is created by various combinations of luck, trial and error, inference, and experiment. An explicit consideration of the incentives and economic mechanisms involved can be incorporated in this story, but they do not drive the outcome.

The historical route comes less naturally to the economist, but it might be one worth experimenting with once more.[3] In what follows, I will define some of the terms with more precision, and then propose an evolutionary framework to analyze them, stressing both the advantages and shortcomings of applying an evolutionary framework to the economic history of useful knowledge. The argument that an evolutionary framework is a natural way to approach the "history" of complex phenomena seems to be enjoying a renewed popularity, although many of the applications of "evolution" to the history of useful knowledge use rather informal and at times careless formulations [3].

2 USEFUL KNOWLEDGE

Technology and production are about harnessing natural phenomena and regularities for our material welfare. It seems, therefore, natural to define useful knowledge in those terms, and leave out other forms of knowledge such as economic, legal, social, and institutional knowledge. The confusion implied by this terminological choice is minor: some of the "useful" knowledge here is really not applicable directly to production, whereas organizational knowledge or familiarity with institutions is, of course, of great importance. There are obvious gray

---

[2]This approach characterizes the research that economic historians have carried out in the traditions established by Zvi Griliches. See, for example, Khan and Sokoloff [37, 38].

[3]The work of Richard Nelson, starting with Nelson and Winter [60] and culminating in Nelson [57, 58] and Nelson and Nelson [59] has inspired much of what is to follow.

areas such as psychology. But when we ask questions about technology in the strict sense above, this shortcut may be acceptable.

A number of remarks on the concept *useful knowledge* follow:

1. The useful knowledge of a society is defined as the union of the knowledge of the individuals in that society and whatever is stored in storage devices. Density can then be defined as the ratio of the size of *shared* knowledge (weighted by the number of people sharing it) to total knowledge.

2. The knowledge set is partitioned into two subsets which are distinct. One is *propositional* or Ω-knowledge which describes and catalogues natural phenomena and the relationships between them. The other is *prescriptive* or λ-knowledge which contains instructions that can be executed.[4]

3. Propositional knowledge Ω contains what we today would call *science* (formalized knowledge), but it contains a great deal more, including geographical knowledge, artisanal and agricultural knowledge, and any other natural regularity and phenomenon that can be exploited in some way.[5] Some fields of knowledge, such as engineering science and applied mechanics are somewhere between science and artisanal knowledge [67].

4. Prescriptive knowledge λ consists of a monstrous book of blueprints, whether codified or tacit, of techniques that society could carry out if it wanted. Only a small proportion of those techniques are actually ever executed. Each element of λ consists of a set of instructions, much like a recipe. These recipes can be codified as they are in cookbooks or engineering manuals, or they can be implicit and tacit.

5. Each technique in λ has an *epistemic base* or support in Ω. This base contains the knowledge of the natural regularities that are harnessed for this technique to be possible, and can be wide or narrow. The wider it is, the more that is understood about how and why the technique works. The size of the base is bounded from below by a degenerate support: the very least a society must know about a technique is that it works (the catalog of all elements in λ is part of Ω). If nothing else is known, we may call these *singleton techniques* (because their epistemic base consists of one element). For each technique we can describe a minimum epistemic base without which it could not exist. As the epistemic base widens, society knows more about the natural processes at

---

[4]The partitioning of useful knowledge in this way is commonly carried out by epistemologists [71]. Michael Polanyi [63, p. 175] points out that the differences boil down to observing that Ω can be "right or wrong" whereas "action can only be successful or unsuccessful." He also notes that the distinction is recognized by patent law which will patent inventions (additions to λ) but not discoveries (additions to Ω), though some new techniques, of course, are not patentable. In some way, the dichotomy between Ω and λ is symmetric to Ryle's [70], (see also Loasby [47]) distinction between knowledge "that" and knowledge "how."

[5]Examples include an intuitive grasp of the *six engines* of classical antiquity (the lever, wheel, wedge, screw, pulley, and balance), as well as the lubricating qualities of oil, the direction of the trade winds, the response of crops to fertilizers, and that the offspring of two animals with some salient characteristic was more likely to display this characteristic.

work, which has major implications about the rate of technological progress. The epistemic base is not bound from above, because we can always know "more" about the natural processes at work around us.

6. The width of the epistemic base determines the ability of an economy to improve upon an existing technique, extend its applications, economize its production process, and adapt it to new circumstances. Inventions based on narrow epistemic bases have low adaptability and tend to lead to technological stasis fairly soon after their emergence.

7. There is no requirement for the epistemic base of any technique used historically to be *true*. Indeed, *true* can only mean here conforms to the Ω knowledge of 2001. Considerable chunks of past technology were used with some success based on elements of Ω we no longer accept, such as Ptolemaic astronomy. As long as it can serve as the basis for some kind of action, "knowledge" here really is "believing."

8. Knowledge can, however, be defined as "tight" or "untight." Tightness has two dimensions: confidence and consensus. The tighter a piece of knowledge is, the stronger the belief people have that a piece of knowledge is true, and the less likely it is that many people hold views inconsistent with it. Flat Earth Society members and those who believe that AIDS can be transmitted by mosquito bites may be few in numbers, but many Americans still do not believe in the Darwinian theory of evolution and believe in the possibility of predicting human affairs from looking at the stars.

9. There is a historically important connection between the tightness of Ω knowledge and that of λ knowledge. Tightness of Ω depends on persuasion and on rhetorical conventions (such as mathematical proof, the interpretation of experimental and statistical data, and confidence in experts and authorities), but the tightness of techniques is often easily verified if the efficacy of the technique is easily observable. However, in those techniques in which the efficacy of the technique is hard to verify (or may have unintended side effects), its tightness will be higher, the tighter the knowledge that serves as its epistemic base. Conversely, if a technique based on an untight piece of Ω knowledge can be shown to work, this success will increase confidence in the Ω knowledge supporting it.

10. Knowledge is distributed and shared, that is, individuals specialize in what they know. Access to knowledge possessed by others is, therefore, an important variable determining the technological capabilities of a society. *Access costs* are the costs paid by a person acquiring knowledge from a source, and depend on the technology, institutions, and culture of knowledge transfer. For instance, the invention of the printing press, the emergence of "open science" in the seventeenth century, and the development of "search engines" such as

technical encyclopedias and manuals in the eighteenth century are examples of access-cost-reducing developments.[6]

11. There is an important difference between an epistemic base, the propositional knowledge necessary to create an *invention* (i.e., write a new "program" contained in λ), and the knowledge needed to execute these instructions by a firm or household activating the technique, a concept often referred to in the business literature as "competence." Normally, it is not possible to write a complete set of instructions. They are written in code, and the codebook itself is tacit, or the code to decipher the codebook is, and so on [19]. Often, many of the codifiable instructions are not included. The relation between competence and epistemic base is quite complex and can only be touched upon briefly here. More complex Ω-knowledge may of course require more skills and human capital on the part of the operators, but it could equally be used to economize on those skills by frontloading the knowledge in the equipment or instructions, breaking them down into simple steps, where the increased knowledge is concentrated in the design and the coordination.

3   AN EVOLUTIONARY APPROACH TO USEFUL KNOWLEDGE

The notion that useful knowledge evolves over time in a manner in some ways analogous to phylogenetic processes has been suggested many times. The idea goes back to the 1950s through the work of Karl Popper and Donald Campbell and has ripened into a field now known as evolutionary epistemology.[7] Originally, the notion was to apply Darwinian models of "blind variation *cum* selective retention" to science, but the analogies with technology were too obvious to be ignored and were soon made explicit in the work of historians of technology such as Edward Constant [18], Walter Vincenti [77], Brian Cragg [20], George Basalla [3], and John Ziman [84]. Applying a methodology from one field to another in a mad scramble for isomorphisms, shoehorning concepts into uses for which they were not intended seems a bad research strategy. If we are to find any use for an evolutionary approach to the history of useful knowledge, it needs to develop its own framework. Evolutionary theory as a mode of historical explanation is larger than the biology that spawned it.

It is striking, however, to what extent the analogy with technology and machines has been attractive to biologists and natural scientists. What has prompted the analogy is not only the fanciful notion that the difference between a machine and a living being is one of degree [52], but because many biologists and systems theorists have noted that the evolutionary dynamics of living be-

---

[6]For a more detailed discussion of the historical and conceptual problem of access costs, see Mokyr [55].

[7]For surveys, see Wuketits [83]; Bradie [7]; Hahlweg and Hooker [29].

ings is similar to that of technology.[8] In what follows, I will try to demonstrate that something can be learned from this analogy, but that the differences between Darwinian systems and systems of knowledge are as instructive. Models of cultural evolution such as Cavalli-Sforza and Feldman [13] (see also Cavalli-Sforza [12]), and Boyd and Richerson [5] pursue this question in much greater detail and deal with a wider array of cultural phenomena. Here I will try to focus on "useful knowledge" and technology only.

Central to any evolutionary approach to knowledge is the choice of the unit of analysis. The difficulty in isolating the correct unit of knowledge or culture has derailed much of Richard Dawkins's idea of *memes* as an analog of genes. Despite recent attempts to revive "memetics" as a serious science, the definition of the "unit" remains the Achilles heel of the Dawkinsian program [4, 6, 42]. I propose to overcome this difficulty by taking the Nelson-Winter concept of the technique as the fundamental unit of technology. Each element of λ is a separate unit or recipe, containing a set of instructions on how to produce a good or service. Such a definition has its share of ambiguities, but it is immune to the objections launched against memes.[9] Although techniques are obviously related to other techniques in similar ways that different species are (as complements, rivals, or unrelated), they can be meaningfully distinguished from one another.

An evolutionary model consists of three components: structure, dynamics and heritability, and variation cum selection.[10] The odd thing is that for a model to be "evolutionary," there is no absolute need for it to *evolve*, that is, to change constantly over time. One can imagine a system that for all practical purposes has reached a stationary state in which all innovations are suppressed and in which the environment is constant. Such a system would not be an interesting one to study (except perhaps in order to examine the historical process that led to a dead end), but would still qualify as evolutionary.

3.1 STRUCTURE

An evolutionary framework of the type that will prove useful here rests on the distinction between an underlying basis that constrains but does not wholly determine a unit that is the manifested entity. This duality is not part of the classical Darwinian setup. But modern Darwinism is unthinkable without Mendel, and

---

[8]Examples include biologists (Stebbins [72, p. 432]; Vermeij [74, p. 144]; Mayr [51, p. 256]; Vogel [78, p. 298f]) as well as complexity theorists (such as Cohen and Stewart [17, p. 330] and Kauffman [36, p. 202]) have been sympathetic to an analogy between natural history and technological history.

[9]The most serious of these objections is that there is no guarantee that ideas or memes are replicated identically from mind to mind even if they generate the same phenotypical performance, because language and other mediating tools come in between [6, p. 155]. Lists of instructions on how to produce, however, can in principle be codified, and although some component of it remains tacit and is thus vulnerable to the same critique, the teaching process creates built-in incentive to replicate the content accurately.

[10]This classification differs a bit from the classic tripartite definitions suggested by Lewontin [46] and Maynard Smith [50].

what Mendelian genetics added to Darwinian theory was the distinction between the appearance and traits of a unit of analysis, and the *underlying information* that brings this phenotype about and is shared with other entities. Evolutionary systems are systems of information and some of that information does something and creates a "manifest entity." In biology, the underlying structure is the genotype consisting of DNA and the manifested entity is the living specimen, that is, the phenotype. There is a mapping from genotype to phenotype, and while it is not wholly determinate, it is easy to see how the genotype constrains what the phenotype *cannot* be. A giraffe is limited by its genes from looking like a hippopotamus. In the history of knowledge, these classes correspond very roughly to our earlier distinction between propositional knowledge and prescriptive knowledge. The distinction between information ("knowing") and applying it ("doing") seems useful in a world of technology. Propositional knowledge cannot rule in any techniques, but it can rule out a lot. Societies that do not have advanced physics are constrained away from building nuclear reactors or MRI machines. All the same, the underlying epistemic base does not determine the exact shape of the technique, and a lot is left to the environment (taken widely as consisting not only of the physical and institutional parameters, but also relative prices, factor costs, and the existence of other techniques, whether substitutes or complements).

A great deal of the underlying Ω knowledge is inactive or "dormant": the vast majority of all useful propositional knowledge is noncoding or "junk" in the sense that it does not apply directly to production. Perhaps some dormant segments of useful knowledge, such as advances in paleontology or improved understanding about the distances of other galaxies or the properties of black holes are at first glance dormant forever, but many dormant sections of Ω can become active given a change in the environment.[11]

It is important to realize the limitations of the analogy. The minimum epistemic base of many techniques, as noted, can be quite slender or even close to a singleton. When such techniques emerge, often by accident or by arduous processes of trial and error, they are limited in their expandability and adaptability.[12] It is the overall narrowness of the epistemic bases of pre-1800 techniques that imposed the concavity of technological progress functions. Their expansion

---

[11]Most scientific (let alone other forms of) knowledge has no applications and does not affect production technology right away, although it may be "stored" and in rare cases called into action when there is a change in the environment or when another complementary invention comes along. By *environment* here, I mean not only the physical environment in which the technique operates but also the development of complementary or rival techniques which may lead to the activation of previously dormant knowledge. Indeed, such processes are what constitute "adaptation" in all evolutionary processes.

[12]Vincenti's [77] use of Laudan's [44] framework of the selection and solution of technological problems, akin to Landes's notion of "challenge and response," followed by choice between rival solutions, provides one way to look at the connection between knowledge and technique; the knowledge provides the tools to solve the problem, while the technique embodies the solution. Other mechanisms can be imagined. There are very few limitations on the knowledge underlying a technique: it can vary from the list provided by Vincenti (ranging

after 1800 is discussed elsewhere [53, 56] and this is not the place to discuss them. There is no obvious isomorph to the variable width of the epistemic base in evolutionary biology: a trait either has a base in the DNA, in which case it might exist, or it does not. Yet does that invalidate an evolutionary approach? It could be argued that the fairly narrow parameters of evolutionary biology are a special case, and that cultural evolution can be and usually is far more flexible than that of living beings.

The existence of a minimum epistemic base is a necessary condition for a technique to emerge, but it does not describe anything like a sufficient condition. A great deal of technological history happens inside the envelope of propositional knowledge: some simple mechanical devices such as the wheelbarrow or barbed wire were perfectly feasible long before they emerged, and required only limited epistemic bases. It stands to reason that they did not emerge earlier simply because they did not occur to anyone. Even when the ideas were there, there could be a variety of technical and institutional barriers to the emergence of the new element in λ, and even more barriers in its actual execution.

There is another widely discussed difference between Darwinian biology and the evolution of useful knowledge. Whereas the genetic base of a species is entirely embedded in the DNA of a living specimen and vanishes as soon as the species goes extinct, underlying useful knowledge can survive even if the techniques it implies are no longer in use. In other words, in all living beings the composition of the gene pool depends on the selection of the phenotypes because the genes cannot exist outside the living beings which are the "vehicles" or "carriers" of the genetic information. In this respect, useful knowledge is quite different because, unlike DNA information, it is exosomatic, that is, it can be stored in storage devices—primarily human minds who can retain knowledge of a technique even if they do not execute it. Indeed, a technique can in some sense be "extinct" (not used or known by anyone) and yet still survive (e.g., explained in old engineering textbooks or history of technology articles or survive embodied in an artifact). All the same, the analogy has some merit because the tacit component of knowledge is irretrievably lost unless a way is found to codify and store it. It is also conceivable that the epistemic base that has supported a technique vanishes but the technique itself survives. The connection between Ω and λ is thus different from that between genotype and phenotype, and they coevolve in dynamic patterns that could become quite complex. The setup of this structure is illustrated in figure 1.

3.2 DYNAMICS

Evolutionary models are historical in the sense that they are designed to explain existing outcomes on the basis of their past. The historical element that provides evolution in living beings with its inertia is heritability. Evolutionary units need

---

from "fundamental design concepts and operational principles" to "design instrumentalities") to pure personal experience ("I tried it and it works, but I don't know how").

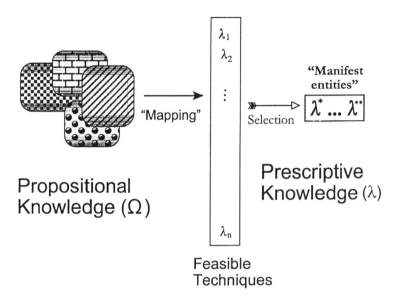

FIGURE 1   Propositional and prescriptive knowledge.

to replicate. Each living specimen's genotype is a linear combination of his/her parents' genotypes plus a small error term (a mutation).[13] It was once believed that such error could be fairly large and create "hopeful monsters," but the evidence for the viability of such radical departures is weak [15]. Similarly, in the history of useful knowledge, innovation is predominantly "local" and thus constrained by history since it is limited by the cumulative knowledge of the past. This is equally true for Ω and λ knowledge: both have an internal dynamic in which change is made possible by cumulative past change, which produces both the challenges and the opportunities for further progress. While there is no *a priori* limitation on how large an innovation can be, and some radical departures (macroinventions) can be discerned, they are rare. The vast bulk of accretions to useful knowledge are small and local.

What makes biology evolutionary is that the carriers of genetic information are subject to wear and tear and have finite lives, so they have to transmit this information over time through reproduction. During reproduction, the potential for germline change is released, either through linear combinations with exist-

---

[13]It seems plausible, for instance, to think of it as a Markov chain in which the state in t is dependent entirely on the state in $t-1$ plus some transition probabilities, and earlier history does not matter since it is entirely encapsulated in the state at t. *Extinction* might then be thought of as an absorbing barrier, but as long as the underlying knowledge (or some crucial component of it) has not been lost, the technique can be regenerated.

ing information (in the case of biparental reproduction) or through mutation. In models of cultural evolution, the transmission over time works differently. The underlying propositional knowledge, as noted, can exist and evolve on its own without being "expressed" in an underlying technique.[14] Propositional knowledge is "expressed" by the techniques it generates, and its manifest entity is observable when the prescriptive knowledge is actually carried out.

How and why do techniques *replicate*? It might well be that the set of instructions that tell a farmer how to grow wheat on a field "reproduces" when he carries out the same instructions the next year, but unlike Samuel Butler's famous chicken, which was nothing but the way for an egg to make another egg, techniques require people to reproduce. Most times this simply happens through human memory: if you know how drive a truck from Chicago to Des Moines today, you can do it again next week. The successful long-term reproduction of a technique, however, requires a mode of transmission between humans such as imitation or training. The concept of a "generation" is clearly arbitrary here, though the same can be said of many forms of life: is the cutting made from a perennial plant a separate entity or the same specimen? Of course, much of what biologists do (such as taxonomy) seems less useful to the historian of technology, since phylogenetic lineages have no obvious analog in the evolution of useful knowledge (or better put, their complexity is such that such trees are not a very useful tool). None of these differences, as Cavalli-Sforza and Feldman [13, p. 14] stress, should stop us from observing the selection and acceptance of a trait over time and the evolution of the distribution of the frequency of a technique in the population.

Evolutionary processes are both inertial and path dependent. No species can change too much at one time, though neither biologists nor cultural evolutionists will agree easily on how much is too much. Given enough time, however, small differences can be bifurcating and lead to quite different outcomes in the long run. Path dependence means that the final outcome depends on the exact itinerary taken [21, 22, 23]. This implies that there is a great deal of contingency in determining the final outcome of the historical process [54]. Consider two disjoint environments that develop separate trajectories. Some fairly minor difference far back in history could determine whether mammals would develop as marsupials or placentals, and unless these environments came into direct contact, their histories could remain different. There was nothing *inevitable* about the appear-

---

[14]The underlying structure of technological phenotypes lives and reproduces independently of the living specimen. If a particular element in Ω in Ω (say, water starts boiling when heated) maps into a technique (say, this is how you prepare a cup of tea), that knowledge will be passed on and reproduce itself whether tea is drunk in this society or not. The selfish or unselfish "gene" of knowledge does not need its carrier, though the carrier needs the gene. It is still true, however, that when a child is taught to make a cup of tea, the implicit knowledge that water boils when heated is "carried" in these instructions, so the child does not have to know many details about water boiling. The argument I am making is that "heated water will boil" and "how to make tea" are different kinds of knowledge, but the difference is not on the order of "an elephant" and "the genes that make an elephant."

ance of zebras or cockroaches, although there are certain morphological traits such as wings and eyes that have appeared more than once independently and can, therefore, be said to reflect some kind of evolutionary logic. Evolutionary logic, moreover, rules out a large number of imaginable life forms that violate some obvious constraint. All the same, the evolutionary logic cannot be extended to declare some observed outcomes as *inexorable*. There certainly was nothing *ex ante* inevitable about the appearance of intelligent life on this planet although it may not be quite as much of a fluke as Stephen Jay Gould supposes [82], it surely was not nearly as pre-ordained as believed by Wright [82].

Something similar could be argued for the development of technology. An interesting question is whether modern technology as it evolved in the past two centuries can be assessed as dictated by some kind of evolutionary logic [54]. The answer depends on whether we take the epistemic base as given: given an Ω set, the likelihood of a particular set of techniques implied by it evolving is fairly high, even if the particular form it takes is, of course, still up for grabs. But how "probable" was the emergence of the components of propositional knowledge that supported modern technology? And how probable were the institutions and metarules which supported the emergence of this Ω knowledge?

3.3   SELECTION

Natural selection is the key to any evolutionary model. Given superfecundity and variability, selection can impart adaptive properties to the units of evolution. As has long been realized, cultural selection of any kind does not work exclusively through the mechanics of differential survival and reproduction of specimens or memes, but through conscious decisions made by agents. Fitness, in the sense of a likelihood of being selected, is still a meaningful concept, however, and much of the story to be told in technological selection does mirror our notions of natural selection. But again, literal adherence to the biological model can be misleading: in the living world, selection occurs on phenotypes, the living specimens. Whether *selfish genes* manipulate the organisms or not, the selection process on the organisms determines whether the underlying information structure survives or not. If the organisms survive and reproduce, the DNA they carry is retained. If they do not, and the species goes extinct, both genotype and phenotype are gone.

In the evolution of useful knowledge, there is a *dual* process of selection which is considerably more complex. We need to consider separately the selection on prescriptive knowledge and propositional knowledge. Technological selection on λ knowledge is relatively straightforward. Evolutionary logic dictates that for selection to occur, there has to be variability among these entities. In the world of technology, variability and diversity are ubiquitous. History, geography, and culture have conspired to create an enormous amount of technological variability. So have human creativity and human folly. For instance, there are many ways to drive from Cincinnati to Kansas City, and among those, certain specific routes are selected and others are not. One would conjecture that drivers would settle on the shortest, fastest or cheapest route, but the outcome will depend on what the agent knows and likes, as well as on road conditions that could change. We can be reasonably sure, all the same, that the chosen route does not lead through Philadelphia. Many of these choices of techniques are trivial, of course, and the area above the isoquant is not very interesting. After a choice has been made and a technique has been executed, the outcome is evaluated by a set of selection criteria that determine whether this particular technique will be actually used again or not, in a manner comparable to the way in which natural selection criteria pick living specimens and "decides" (so to speak) which will be selected for survival and reproduction, and thus continue to exist in the gene pool.

Here "tightness" is central to the story. Some techniques are tight, in the sense that we can evaluate their characteristics easily. Choosing between a dot-matrix and a laser printer, or between surgery with or without anesthesia is a no-brainer. But in many cases, firms and households have difficulty evaluating the effects of techniques, and fitness becomes to some extent contingent. In a few documentable cases, techniques that were ineffective (as it seems to us) were selected and retained, to a point that still baffles historians.[15] Economists tend to think of a selection environment consistent with rationality (even if techniques are untight) but it is clear that historically, selection is influenced by other factors such as politics, aesthetics, and ideology, and hence fitness itself is highly contingent.[16] All the same, choices are made, and some techniques are retained for selection, others are not.

Selection on Ω knowledge is more complex. As noted, unlike what happens in living beings, the retention of the underlying information is not a byproduct of the survival of the "manifest entities." There is no selfish knowledge. When a technique is selected, it means someone is using it. However, when a unit of Ω is selected, it is unclear what this means. To be included in Ω at all, a piece of useful knowledge must be in existence either in someone's mind or a storage device from which it can be retrieved. It is, therefore, unclear what precisely would be meant by superfecundity, unless there is some physical constraint on the amount of knowledge that society can carry as a whole. Only if there is some form of congestion of knowledge or storage cost will society shed some pieces of knowledge as it acquires and selects better ones. Through most of human history before the age of the gigabyte, such congestion was a reality: books were hugely expensive before the invention of printing, and while their

---

[15]Hall [31], for instance, poses the difficulty that artillery in the early modern period employed guns in which the aspect ratio (the ratio between length and caliber) was far larger than optimal, and that the cannon (a piece of artillery of approximately optimal aspect ratio) took centuries to become dominant despite the rather obvious way in which the optimal ratio could be measured through experimental methods.

[16]Contingency can be compounded when selection is frequency dependent so that prior choices become a factor in fitness. In technical selection this occurs not only in the widely discussed cases of network externalities, but also when techniques are untight and agents engage in imitation as an information cost saving device.

price fell with the advent of printing, they were still quite costly by the time of the Industrial Revolution. Other forms of storage outside of human memory, such as drawings, models, and artifacts in museums, were all expensive. Some selection may, therefore, have even occurred at that level. But when storage costs fell, congestion became less of a problem, and thus the issue of selection became moot. Libraries are full of old science and engineering books, as well as books on alchemy, astrology, quack medicine, and other forms of superseded knowledge about the regularities of the natural world, and the knowledge in them can be retrieved whether their manifest entities are expressed or not. Yet in our own time, the improved ability to store knowledge is matched by the growth in our capacity to generate new knowledge, and even now we must dispose of some knowledge that seems redundant, so selections are made. Perhaps the concept of selection which, at its most abstract level has a binary interpretation (either a unit is selected or it is not) should be replaced by a continuous variable of accessibility, measured by the costs of finding and retrieving knowledge that has been preserved. This variable would become infinite for knowledge that has been permanently deleted.

Evolutionary epistemology has suggested a different definition: Selection may be viewed as the process in which some people choose to *believe* certain theories and regularities about natural phenomena and reject others. Yet this interpretation of selection on Ω knowledge is also problematic. For one thing, it is not identical to the previous definition. While of course certain views of nature are incompatible with each other so that some theories are rejected if others are accepted, the discarded theories and beliefs do not necessarily become extinct in the technical sense of being inaccessible. Thus the humoral theory of disease is still understood today, but no longer serves as a source for prescriptive techniques in modern medicine. Scientific theories that are *accepted* will normally be the ones that are mapped onto the techniques in use, whereas the ones that are rejected will be dormant, known only to historians of knowledge or stored in library books. Accepting the work of Lavoisier meant that one had to abandon phlogiston theory but not necessarily destroy any trace of it.

Moreover, here, too, selection may not mean a binary variable of either accepting or rejecting a piece of knowledge. Untight knowledge means, basically, that a person may have a subjective probability distribution on whether the knowledge is "true." What matters here is whether a person will "act" on that knowledge, that is, whether he or she will select a technique based on knowledge that is untight. Rational choice implies that the person will select a technique depending on the cost functions associated with type I and type II errors. It is quite possible, in other words, to "select" a technique even if the preponderance of the evidence is that the epistemic base on which it rests is false, much like a technological Pascal's wager.

The stringency of the selective pressures could also vary. A high-pressure intellectual environment forces choices between incompatible views. In a low-pressure intellectual environment many "species" of Ω knowledge could coexist in one mind even if by some logical standard they were mutually inconsistent. People might believe that even if there are natural laws, they could somehow generate exceptions (such as magic or miracles). The selection criteria on Ω are culturally contingent, and it is easy to envisage a cultural climate in which the question "but is it true?" can be routinely answered by "sometimes" or "maybe" or "if God wills it." [17] Furthermore, the selection criterion "is it elegant" might have to compete with such criteria as "is it elegant?" or "is it morally improving?" or "is it consistent with our traditions?" Science, to be sure, is largely consensual, and glaring inconsistencies are frowned upon. People have to choose between incompatible or incommensurate theories and will do so if they can, in some sense, rank them [24].

Selection of propositional knowledge by this definition is determined by the rhetorical conventions accepted in society that persuade people that something is true or at least tested. Such rhetorical conventions vary from "Aristotle said" to "the experiment demonstrates" to "the estimated coefficient is 2.3 times its standard error." These standards are invariably socially set within paradigms: what constitutes logical proof? What is the acceptable power of a statistical test? Do we always insist on double blindness when testing a new compound? How many times need an experiment be replicated before the consensus deems it sound?

Much of the tightness of knowledge is a function of social relations such as "who is an authority" on a subject, who appoints those authorities, and how often do nonexperts question authority. If a piece of knowledge is not very tight, as Durlauf shows, choosing between competing pieces of knowledge may well become a function of imitation, persuasion, and fashion. [18] How and why such choices take place is, of course, the central issue in the history of science with opinions varying between scholars as to what extent evolutionary success is correlated with some measure of progress or truth [33, 39].

There is one other dynamic element that differs to a degree between biological and technological selection systems. In living systems, the selection process is myopic: the dynamic properties that the investigator discerns are not observed by

---

[17] An example is the Jain belief of *syadvada*, which can be summarized to say that "the world of appearances may or may not be real, or both may and may not be real, or may be indescribable, or may be real and indescribable, or unreal and indescribable, or in the end may be real *and* unreal *and* indescribable." Cited by Kaplan [35, p. 45], emph. added.

[18] One example to illustrate this principle: A Scottish physician by the name of John Brown (1735–88) revolutionized the medicine of his age with Brownianism, a system which postulated that all diseases were the result of over or underexcitement of the neuromuscular system by the environment. Brown was no enthusiast for bleeding, and instead treated all his patients with mixtures of opium, alcohol, and highly seasoned foods. His popularity was international: Benjamin Rush brought his system to America, and in 1802 his controversial views elicited a riot among medical students in Göttingen, requiring troops to quell it. A medical revolutionary in an age of radical changes, his influence is a good example of the difficulty which contemporaries had selecting amongst alternative techniques and the enormous possibilities for failure in this area (Brown was asserted to have killed more people than the French Revolution and the Napoleonic Wars combined).

the system; selection takes place exclusively by the criteria of *present* fitness, not using the criterion of the fitness implications of the future development implied by the choice made. This myopia can, of course, lead to disastrous long-term consequences.[19] In technological systems, because the choices are made by intelligent, forward looking agents rather than by the mechanical processes of survival and reproductive success, it is conceivable that selection is not wholly myopic but instead may, in some cases, select (or reject) a technique for its potential rather than for its immediate consequences. Such assessments of the future are, however, very hazardous to make, and people can and will differ about the dangers of slippery technological slopes. Yet many of the current debates on techniques such as genetically modified organisms or nuclear power must be understood in this way.

4 EVOLUTION AND THE ECONOMIC HISTORY OF TECHNOLOGY

What lessons can economic historians learn from such an evolutionary story and how can they best apply them? First and foremost, it suggests that they have been ignoring the history of science and technology at their peril. The dual structure of the model suggests that the intellectual origins of technological progress are not peripheral to the enterprise but are at the very basis of it. What has confused scholars, in my view, is that they have taken too narrow a view of science as a proxy for what I have called Ω knowledge. Such an approach inevitably truncates what really might have mattered: an accumulation of pragmatic knowledge of mundane natural regularities and better access to it, which both increases the epistemic base of techniques and increases the likelihood of projecting from that base onto the set of techniques. In the early stages of the Industrial Revolution, the practical knowledge collected by engineers like John Smeaton, ironmasters like Darby and Cort, potters like Josiah Wedgwood, or clockmakers like John Harrison was economically more valuable than the science of Cavendish, Lavoisier, or Dalton.

Invention in a world of very narrow epistemic bases, could be thought of as much like a random mutation in a purely Weismannian world of undirected innovations. Invention in such a world is serendipitous or the result of inefficient and clumsy trial and error processes. When it occurs, the likelihood of much further progress is low. This is not to say that there are no systematic differences

---

[19]Selection could misfire when a trait leads to what Allen and Lesser [1] call *positive feedback traps*, that is, selection of a trait because of its success in satisfying the fitness criterion but trapping it at a low level. Their example is the peacock's tail, which helps each peacock in the reproductive game and thus conveys a selective advantage despite the uselessness of the tail in survival related functions. The same was true for the extinct Irish Elk: its enormous antlers gave its bearers a putative advantage in mating, but they were apparently useless as a defensive tool, and helped in the demise of the species.

between different societies in their rates of technological change, much as there are differences between environments in their mutagenicity. But the inventions that occur and the needs of society are largely uncorrelated. The only mechanism that gives it direction is the selection on λ. Such a process could provide technological progress over a long period, but sustained growth would be limited by the narrow epistemic bases of techniques in use.

To be more exact, imagine a parameter ρ which measures the correlation between the probability of an invention occurring and the "needs" of the system. In a purely Darwinian system $\rho = 0$; mutations are undirected, and the directionality of the system is imparted entirely by selection. In such a world, technological change is not produced by directed research and development, and much of the modern theory of endogenous growth does not apply. No historical system in which ρ was zero ever quite existed, but before 1750 in most areas it was quite close to it. Change was produced by "tinkering," and nature, too, is often regarded as making changes that way [34].

The other extreme possibility, equally imaginary, is a world in which $\rho = 1$, and the system produces whatever knowledge it needs through research and development. In such a world, technological knowledge is just another commodity, which is produced in the system through a production function. As the epistemic base became wider after 1800, ρ increased and the process of invention became more directed, the searches more efficient, and the likelihood of expanding and adapting a technique to changing circumstances became more likely. Yet the serendipitous and accidental component in invention remained high even if it declined over time.

The higher the level of ρ, the more we can speak of technological change as being "induced," that is, sensitive to signals that the economy sends [69]. Yet it is also clear that inducement here can mean different things. First, responses to exogenous stimuli can be built into the software of a technique in the form of conditional instructions. This flexibility is comparable to what biologists call phenotypic plasticity, or what Williams [79] has called a facultative response (if x then do y). Second, society can search over its entire catalog of λ's and replace techniques in use by others when there is a change in the environment. This is simple substitution, and closest conceptually to the adaptive nature of natural selection. Third, at a higher level we can find what biologists refer to as genetic assimilation (a term due to Conrad Waddington).[20] The idea is that the *activation* of existing genetic information is sensitive to environmental stimuli, and natural selection favors organisms in which the activation of "dormant" information is feasible. One can imagine a world in which an external shock, from a change in relative prices to a natural disaster, will cause society to search over its existing Ω set looking for existing knowledge that will form the basis of a new technique that has now become attractive. This phenomenon is closest

---

[20]Waddington argued that mutations are predominantly *neutral* and do not affect the selection criteria one way or another, but may become useful when the environment changes and calls for adaptation (see also Stebbins, [72, p. 76]).

to induced invention. Fourth, society can channel its research agenda to expand those segments of Ω that are more likely to map eventually into a technique it desires, so that not only the technique is induced but also the Ω knowledge on which it rests. While these four mechanisms differ in detail, they all point to the fact that wider epistemic bases of techniques in use mean higher adaptability and flexibility both for the techniques in use and indirectly for the people using them.

It is at this point that evolutionary dynamics can help us understand some crucial aspect of economic history. The coevolution of the Ω set (what people knew) and the λ set (what they did) in the later eighteenth and early nineteenth centuries in Europe produced a positive feedback loop that ignited a chain of technological innovations we often refer to as the Industrial Revolution and which eventually led to the emergence of modern economic growth. In the terms used by system theorists, there was a state transition, and technology went from a state in which negative feedback dominated to one of positive feedback producing what Kaufmann has called a *supercritical* state. Instead of eventually burning itself out and asymptoting away, as it had done in the past, technological progress continued apace and embarked on a trajectory in which it eventually spun out of control. The continuous back and forth interaction between propositional and prescriptive knowledge created what Geerat Vermeij [75, 76] has called *escalation*. By its very nature, this divergence phenomenon was not an economy-wide phenomenon: it differed in degree and in timing from industry to industry and from technique to technique. During the first Industrial Revolution it was confined to a few sectors, and its impact on the aggregate economy was not decisive. But as the epistemic base was built up, by the growth of science, engineering, and the accumulation of a growing base of empirical knowledge about what worked, coupled to declining access costs, the phase transition took place in the decades between 1815 and 1860.

Both of these mechanisms provide an explicit way in which the two types of knowledge interact in a positive feedback relation, creating a coevolutionary dynamic in which all bets are off. Much like genotype and phenotype, Ω and λ inhabit different geographies. When this happens, and the attractors in Ω and λ do not match up nicely, feedback can have a creative effect and both parts of the structure can change in unpredictable ways [17, pp. 420–421]. The interaction between λ and Ω is something economic historians can readily trace, even if data here takes the form of anecdotes.

The feedback from λ back to Ω is, of course, very different in nature than the feedback from phenotype to genotype which (according to the Weismannian orthodoxy) cannot occur within a single organism and depends on populational processes that alter relative gene frequencies. In the context here, escalation is created by the processes by which techniques enhance the Ω knowledge base on which they rest, which creates ever better techniques and so forth. This works through two basic mechanisms. One of these is Rosenberg's [68] famous concept of *focusing devices*. When a technique is known to work, but nobody is quite sure why and how it does so, the puzzle will stimulate and focus the attention of scientists or natural philosophers on the subject, in part out of pure curiosity, and in part out of a desire to adapt and extend the technique further.[21] The second is Derek Price's [64] idea of *artificial revelation*. Price argued that science (and for that matter all knowledge of natural phenomena) is far more constrained by the technology of observation, measurement, and processing than is commonly realized, and that a great deal of progress in propositional knowledge was due to the emergence of certain instruments and tools that simply extended our ability to watch, experiment, and compute. A relatively minor invention may set off the emergence of a new area of propositional knowledge that eventually leads to large-scale technological advances.

5   KNOWLEDGE AND TECHNOLOGICAL CHANGE AFTER 1750

The phase transition that occurred in the technological universe of the West after 1750 thus depended on a mutual relationship between Ω and λ. Historians have not emphasized this enough, in part because they have tended to look only at formal science, which was a small (if rapidly growing) subset of Ω. A few examples below drive this home. Consider first the well-documented and understood case of steampower. One might consider the minimum epistemic base of an atmospheric engine to be the realization that the surface of the earth is really at the bottom of an atmospheric ocean. This knowledge emerged when Evangelista Torricelli invented the barometer in the 1640s, leading to widespread attempts to measure atmospheric pressure, the most famous of which were Pascal's experiments at the Puy de Dôme. Many people began wondering how this pressure could be exploited, among them the great Dutch physicist and mathematician Christiaan Huygens and the Englishman Robert Hooke. A model of a steam engine was first constructed by Denis Papin (a student and protegé of Huygens's) and the real thing followed in the form of Thomas Newcomen's famous 1712 Dudley Castle engine. The improvements introduced by Smeaton, Watt, Trevithick, Woolf, and others in the late eighteenth century relied mostly on empirical extensions of this knowledge basis, and while they improved the engine, its efficiency was constrained by their failure to understand the basic laws that regulated that efficiency.[22] The scientific part of the epistemic base was inspired by the engine, and expanded a great deal between 1824 and 1850,

---

[21]The infusion of practical knowledge about industry into academic research in the electric industry became sufficiently important for one historian [40] to suggest that we could term what emerged *industry-based science* as much as *science-based industry*.

[22]As late as the 1830s, the understanding of steam power was still as a vapor-pressure engine rather than a heat engine. The influential engineering books by Farey [25] and François-Marie Pambour [61], were still based on the standard assumption of steam in this way. See Woolrich [81] and Kroes [41].

as physicists in France, Britain, and Germany worked out the fundamental laws they called thermodynamics.[23] This epistemic base led in its turn to fundamental improvements in the utilization of steam power when William Rankine made the insights of thermodynamics available to engineers [14].[24] Once these laws were understood, it became clearer how to design internal combustion engines. In 1876, N. A. Otto filed a patent for an internal combustion engine based on the four-stroke principle. Without the constant growth of the epistemic base, the steam engine would have ended up like another source of energy, water and wind power, raising productivity for a while, but eventually running into diminishing returns. To be sure, no simple linear progression should be imagined here.[25] Yet it is striking that in the following decades, the engine invented by the eponymous Rudolf Diesel was designed in the light of thermodynamic principles, trying to maximize fuel efficiency.[26]

The history of chemicals before 1900 shows a similar image of a gradually widening epistemic base interacting with technology. Most of the breakthroughs before the chemical revolution were largely serendipitous, and relative to the hopes that many had in the early eighteenth century regarding the potential of chemical philosophy to produce a high return in agriculture and industry, the results before the late 1780s were disappointing [28]. A number of breakthroughs took place (Leblanc's soda making process of 1787 and Berthollet's discovery of chlorine bleaching), but without the corresponding changes in Ω, this movement would have leveled off. The chemical revolution of Lavoisier and Dalton relied in

---

[23]The first enunciation of the principles at work here—efficiency was a function of the differences in temperature—were laid out by a French engineer, Sadi Carnot, in 1824 after observing the differences in efficiency between a high pressure Woolf engine and an older model. The next big step was made by an Englishman, James P. Joule who showed the conversion rates from work to heat and back. Joule's work and that of Carnot were then reconciled by a German, R. J. E. Clausius (the discoverer of entropy), and by 1850 a new branch of science dubbed by William Thomson (later Lord Kelvin) "thermodynamics" had emerged [9, 10].

[24]Rankine, the author of *Manual of the Steam Engine* [65], made thermodynamics accessible to engineers and Scottish steam engines made good use of the Carnot principle that the efficiency of a steam engine depends on the temperature range over which the engine operates. His study of the unresolved issues of the effects of expansion led to his recommendation to apply steam-jacketing to heat the cylinder (a technique previously tried but then abandoned). One of Rankine's students, John Elder, developed the two-cylinder compound marine engine in the 1850s, which sealed the eventual victory of steam over sailing ships.

[25]N.A. Otto insisted that he was unaware of the paper written a few years earlier by Alphonse Beau de Rochas, which proved theoretically that the Carnot principles applied to all heat engines, and that the most efficient system would be a four-stroke cycle.

[26]Diesel built his engine based on the idea that the temperature of air inside a combustion chamber could be raised sufficiently by compression to ignite the fuel, thus converting all of the energy from combustion into work. He was not a tinkerer, however, but a trained engineer, working with state of the art scientific techniques. He started off searching for an engine incorporating the theoretical Carnot cycle, in which maximum efficiency is obtained by isothermal expansion so that no energy is wasted, and a cheap, crude fuel can be used to boot (originally Diesel used coal dust in his engines). Isothermal expansion turned out to be impossible, and the central feature of Diesel engines today has remained compression-induced combustion, which Diesel had at first considered to be incidental [8].

part the refinement of chemical laboratory technology in the second half of the eighteenth century.[27] A few years after the new chemistry was announced by the publication of Lavoisier's landmark *Traité élémentaire de Chimie* [45], Alessandro Volta invented his famous *pile* or battery, which was to have dramatic effects on the growth of chemistry. Volta's battery was soon produced in industrial quantities by William Cruickshank. Electrolysis became the tool by which chemists, led by William Nicholson, Humphry Davy, and Michael Faraday, filled in the gaps in the contours outlined by Lavoisier, isolating and discovering elements. The effects on industry were already noticeable before the advance of organic chemistry in the 1830s. In the 1820s the French chemist Michel Eugéne Chevreul became interested in the nature of fatty acids and isolated such substances as cholesterol, glycerol, and stearic acid. He discovered that fats are combinations of glycerol and fatty acids, easily separated by saponification (hydrolysis), which immediately improved the manufacture of soap.[28] A few decades later came the development of soil chemistry, a classic instance of the widening of the epistemic base of an existing technique, which led to the fine tuning of fertilization and eventually to the development of chemical fertilizers.

Mineral exploration provides another example of the positive feedback between λ and Ω knowledge. The Industrial Revolution was not the beginning of the widespread use of coal in Britain, and much of the growth of the Tudor and Stuart economies can be attributed to the adoption of coal as the fuel of choice in manufacturing.[29] Yet throughout the eighteenth century mining entrepreneurs were, in Flinn's words, forced to rely on surface observation and folklore [26, p. 40]. William Smith's association with Somerset coalminers focused his attention on the basic issue in geology namely that it had to be knowledge in three dimensions and that he needed a key to understanding the strata. This key was supplied by his insight that geological strata could be identified by the fossils found in them, and that collecting enough data would make a geological map possible. Decades of collecting this information yielded Smith's "Map that Changed the World" [80], one of the more palpable increments in the Ω set

---

[27]Much of the late eighteenth century chemical revolution was made possible by new instruments such as Volta's eudiometer, a glass container with two electrodes intended to measure the content of air, used by Cavendish to show the nature of water as a compound. The famous "Memoir on Heat" coauthored by Lavoisier and Laplace was made possible by the calorimeter, designed by Laplace who, in addition to his mathematical skills, was an expert in the design of experimental instruments [62, pp. 136–137].

[28]Clow and Clow in their classic account [16, p. 126] assess that his work "placed soap-making on a sure quantitative basis and technics was placed under one of its greatest debts to chemistry." His better understanding of fatty substances led to the development of stearic candles, which he patented in 1825 together with another French chemist, Gay-Lussac. His work on dyes and the optical nature of colors was also of substantial importance.

[29]In his excellent survey of the issue, John Harris [32] points out that the switch from charcoal to coal-based fuels in the iron industry in the second half of the eighteenth century is often believed to be the first such transition whereas in fact it was "virtually the last." Industries such as soap-boiling, brewing, and glassmaking had switched to coal centuries earlier, and home-heating (the largest use for fuel) had become dependent on coal much earlier as well.

during the Industrial Revolution.[30] Smith became a valuable consultant to mineowners and geology increasingly informed the search for minerals. After that, geology can be seen to coevolve with the techniques of exploration, although it took many decades to become fully integrated with it. The widening epistemic base of mineral exploration and mining technology surely were the reason that the many warnings that Britain was exhausting its coal supplies turned out to be false alarms. From the late eighteenth century, too, boring techniques were improved and became a highly skilled craft performed by specialists. In other areas related to mining, too, propositional knowledge aided and abetted the actual techniques. In 1815, Humphry Davy, the most prominent scientist in Britain in his time, invented the famous *miner's friend*, a lamp that reduced the risk of explosions due to exposure to open flames.

A good example of Derek Price's principle of artificial revelation is the development of the microscope. The invention of the modern compound microscope by Joseph J. Lister (father of the famous surgeon) in 1830 serves as another good example. Lister was an amateur optician, whose revolutionary method of grinding lenses greatly improved image resolution by eliminating chromatic and spherical aberrations. The invention was used to construct a theoretical basis for combining lenses and it reduced the average image distortion by a huge proportion, from 19 to 3 percent. Lister was the first human being ever to see a red blood cell [66]. His invention changed microscopy from an amusing diversion to a serious scientific endeavor and eventually allowed Pasteur, Koch, and their disciples to refute spontaneous generation and to establish the germ theory, one of the most revolutionary changes in useful knowledge in human history, and one which has been mapped into a large number of new techniques in medicine, both preventive and clinical. Another example of techniques aiding in scientific discovery is the spillover from the synthetic chemical industry to the growing understanding of cell biology through the technique of staining pioneered by the young Paul Ehrlich in the 1880s [73].

Bacteriology and chemistry depended on formal science, but most of the interesting action was in the less formal segment of Ω. Many of the advances in textiles, pottery, glass, paper, clock and instrument making, and food processing depended on minor discoveries of how to manipulate materials and machines. In metallurgy, the interaction between the nonscience part of Ω knowledge and techniques played a major role in some of the great breakthroughs of the era. The epochal invention of the Industrial Revolution was Cort's puddling and rolling technique (1785), which owed little to formal metallurgy or chemistry but a great deal to pragmatic knowledge about natural phenomena.[31] Cort realized fullwell the importance of turning pig iron into wrought or bar iron by removing

---

[30]The geological map, produced in 1815, was 8 feet by 6 feet, hand-painted and showed the "delineation of the strata" in Britain, with the "collieries and mines"—clearly this knowledge was meant to be exploited.

[31]See Hall [30, p. 101]; in a famous letter, Joseph Black wrote to James Watt that Cort was "a plain Englishman, without Science."

what contemporaries thought of as "plumbago" (a term taken from phlogiston theory and equivalent to a substance we would call today carbon). The problem was to generate enough heat to keep the molten iron liquid and to prevent it from crystallizing before all the carbon had been removed. Cort knew that reverberating furnaces using coke generated higher temperatures. He also realized that by rolling the hot metal between grooved rollers, its composition would become more homogenous. How and why he mapped this prior knowledge into his famous invention will never be exactly known, but the fact that so many other ironmasters were following similar tracks indicates that they were all drawing from a common knowledge pool.

Two generations later, the Bessemer steelmaking process of 1856 was invented by a man who, by his own admission had "very limited knowledge of iron metallurgy" [11, p. 19]. His knowledge was limited to the point where the typical Bessemer blast, in his own words was "a revelation to me, as I had in no way anticipated such results." Yet the epistemic base was by no means empty: Bessemer knew enough chemistry to recognize eventually that the reason why his process succeeded and similar experiments by others had failed was that the pig iron he had used was, by accident, singularly free of phosphorus and that by adding carbon at the right time, he would get the correct mixture of carbon and iron, that is, steel. He did not know enough, however, to come up with a technique that would rid iron of the phosphorus; this took another twenty years, when the basic process was discovered. The epistemic base at the time was, however, larger than Bessemer's knowledge. This is demonstrated by the recognition, by an experienced metallurgist named Robert Mushet, that Bessemer steel suffered from excess oxygen, which could be remedied by the addition of a decarburizer consisting of a mixture of manganese, carbon, and iron. The Bessemer and related microinventions led, in the words of Donald Cardwell [9, p. 292] to "the establishment of metallurgy as a study on the border of science and technology"—the arrow of causation clearly going from λ to Ω.

6   CONCLUSIONS

The idea of useful knowledge as an evolving entity should be not juxtaposed with knowledge as an economic entity. The two concepts are not at odds with one another but are different ways to look at the same phenomenon. Evolutionary models, however, produce somewhat different insights. One of these, which I discussed above, is that the coevolution of Ω and λ knowledge can produce a better way of looking at the technological "takeoff" of the past two centuries as a mutually reinforcing positive feedback effect and a liberation from the homeostatic constraints of the more remote past in which technology was never able to raise economic performance in a sustained way.

Such models, however, raise other issues as well, none of which can be dealt with here. One of them was pointed out by Ziman [84]: selectionist models stress that what matters to history is that very rare events get amplified and ultimately determine the outcome. The challenge to historians then becomes to try to understand which rare events take on that function, and under what circumstances they get selected. But this way of thinking does perhaps help to remind us that in the emergence of useful knowledge and modern technology, a small number of persons made crucially important contributions. This is not a plea to return to the nineteenth century "hero" model of invention. Had Galileo or Newton or Planck never been born, their insights would in all likelihood have been generated by colleagues. But this knowledge was all the same created by a small, mechanically and technically minded elite. The culture, the institutions, the incentives, the research agendas, and the instruments at the disposal of these vital few were only slightly less contingent. So was the existence of mechanics, craftsmen, and engineers who could carry out their instructions, read their blueprints, and provide the parts and materials they specified with sufficient precision. The idea of a tiny but crucial sliver of the labor force driving history by adding materially to the useful knowledge that the rest of the workers were relying upon seems apposite. In 1666, Robert Hooke noted that the new found world of making inquiries in "the nature and causes of things" in order to produce something of use for themselves or mankind, must be conquered "by a Cortesian army, well disciplined and regulated, though their numbers be but small."

No more than for biology can this kind of thinking yield exact predictions or even very tight explanations. In fact, the indeterminacy of history through layers of contingency is a reminder that, whatever the differences between phylogenetic development and the history of technological change, both imply that whatever happened did not have to happen. Historical explanation is thus advised that some modicum of modesty is apposite, and that attempts to make the rise of the West seem natural or inevitable or even over determined are much like attempts to explain the emergence of intelligent life on the planet. There was nothing ineluctable about it, much less can we explain why it happened *when* it did. Homo sapiens could not have evolved before the Cretaceous extinction of the dinosaurs, but there is no reason why it could not have happened in the middle of the Tertiary, for instance, during the period known as Oligocene. An evolutionary perspective reminds us of a truism that too much neoclassical belief might obscure: "Very few things happen at the right time, and the rest do not happen at all."[32]

ACKNOWLEDGMENTS

The comments of Wolfram Latsch, Tim Lewens, and Peter Murmann on a preliminary version are acknowledged.

---

[32]The statement is from Mark Twain's "acknowledgments" to *A Horse's Tale* and attributed by him—in jest—to Herodotus. He adds mischievously that "the conscientious historian will correct these defects."

REFERENCES

[1] Allen, Peter M., and M. Lesser. "Evolutionary Human Systems: Learning, Ignorance and Subjectivity." In *Evolutionary Theories of Economic and Technological Change: Present Status and Future Prospects*, edited by P. P. Saviotti and J. S. Metcalfe. London: Harwood Publishing, 1991.

[2] Arrow, Kenneth J. *Essays in the Theory of Risk-Bearing*. Chicago, IL: Markham, 1971.

[3] Basalla, George. *The Evolution of Technology*. Cambridge, MA: Cambridge University Press, 1988.

[4] Bloch, Maurice. "A Well-Disposed Social Anthropologist's Problem with Memes." In *Darwinizing Culture: The Status of Memetics as a Science*, edited by Robert Aunger, 189–204. Cambridge, MA: Cambridge University Press, 2000.

[5] Boyd, Robert, and Peter J. Richerson. *Culture and the Evolutionary Process*. Chicago, IL: University of Chicago Press, 1985.

[6] Boyd, Robert, and Peter J. Richerson. "Memes: Universal Acid or a Better Mousetrap?" In *Darwinizing Culture: The Status of Memetics as a Science*, edited by Robert Aunger, 143–162. Cambridge, MA: Cambridge University Press, 2000.

[7] Bradie, Michael. "Assessing Evolutionary Epistemology." *Biol. & Phil.* **1(4)** (1986): 401–459.

[8] Bryant, Lynwood. "Rudolf Diesel and his Rational Engine." *Sci. Am.* **221** (1969): 108–117.

[9] Cardwell, Donald S. L. *The Fontana History of Technology*. London: Fontana Press, 1994.

[10] Cardwell, Donald S. L. *From Watt to Clausius: The Rise of Thermodynamics in the Early Industrial Age*. Ithaca: Cornell University Press, 1971.

[11] Carr, J. C., and W. Taplin. *A History of the British Steel Industry*. Oxford: Basil Blackwell, 1962.

[12] Cavalli-Sforza, Luigi L. "Cultural Evolution." *Am. Zool.* **26** (1986): 845–855.

[13] Cavalli-Sforza, Luigi L., and W. M. Feldman. *Cultural Transmission and Evolution: A Quantitative Approach*. Princeton: Princeton University Press, 1981.

[14] Channell, David F. "The Harmony of Theory and Practice: the Engineering Science of W. J. M. Rankine." *Tech. & Culture* **23(1)** (1982): 39–52.

[15] Charlesworth, Brian, and A. R. Templeton. "Hopeful Monsters Cannot Fly." *Paleobiology* **8(4)** (1982): 469–474.

[16] Clow, Archibald, and Nan L. Clow. *The Chemical Revolution: A Contribution to Social Technology*. London: Batchworth, 1952. (Reproduced by Gordon and Breach in 1992.)

[17] Cohen, Jack, and Ian Stewart. *The Collapse of Chaos*. New York: Penguin, 1994.

[18] Constant, Edward. W. *The Origins of the Turbojet Revolution*. Baltimore, MD: Johns Hopkins Press, 1980.

[19] Cowan, Robin, and Dominique Foray. "The Economics of Codification and the Diffusion of Knowledge." *Ind. & Corp. Change* **6(3)** (1997): 595–622.

[20] Cragg, C. Brian. "Evolution of the Steam Engine." In *Issues in Evolutionary Epistemology*, edited by Kai Hahlweg and C. A. Hooker, 313–356. Albany: SUNY Press, 1989.

[21] David, Paul A. "Path Dependence and the Quest for Historical Economics." Discussion Papers in Economic and Social History, No. 20 (November), University of Oxford, 1997.

[22] David, Paul A. "Path-Dependence in Economic Processes: Implications for Policy Analysis in Dynamical System Contexts." In *International Journal of Industrial Organization*. Special Issue on Path-Dependence. 1996.

[23] David, Paul A. "Why Are Institutions the 'Carriers of History'?: Notes on Path-Dependence and the Evolution of Conventions, Organizations and Institutions." *Struct. Change & Econ. Dyn.* **5(2)** (1994): 205–220.

[24] Durlauf, Steven N. "Reflections on How Economic Reasoning can Contribute to the Study of Science." Working Paper 97-05-043, Santa Fe Institute, Santa Fe, NM, 1997.

[25] Farley, John. *A Treatise on the Steam Engine, Historical, Practical, and Descriptive*. London: Longman, Rees, Orme, Brown, and Green, 1827.

[26] Flinn, Michael W. *The History of the British Coal Industry, 1700–1830*. Oxford: Oxford University Press, 1984.

[27] Galor, Oded, and David Weil. "Population, Technology, and Growth." *Am. Econ. Rev.* **90(4)** (2000): 806–828.

[28] Golinski, Jan. *Science as Public Culture: Chemistry and Enlightenment in Britain, 1760–1820*. Cambridge: Cambridge University Press, 1992.

[29] Hahlweg, Kai, and C. A. Hooker. "Evolutionary Epistemology and Philosophy of Science." In *Issues in Evolutionary Epistemology*, edited by Kai Hahlweg and C.A. Hooker, 21–100. Albany: SUNY Press, 1989.

[30] Hall, A. Rupert. "On Knowing and Knowing How To ..." *Hist. & Tech.* **3** (1978): 91–104.

[31] Hall, Bert S. "The Long and the Short of It: The Search for Ideal Proportions in Artillery in Early Modern Europe." Paper read before the Society for the History of Technology Annual Meeting, San Jose, California, October, 2001.

[32] Harris, John R. *The British Iron Industry, 1700–1850*. Houndsmill and London: MacMillan Education Ltd., 1988.

[33] Hull, David L. *Science as a Process*. Chicago, IL: University of Chicago Press, 1988.

[34] Jacob, François. "Evolution and Tinkering." *Science* **196(4295)** (1977): 116–166.

[35] Kaplan Robert. *The Nothing That Is*. Oxford: Oxford University Press, 1999.

[36] Kauffman, Stuart A. *At Home in the Universe: The Search for the Laws of Self-Organization and Complexity*. New York: Oxford University Press, 1995.

[37] Khan, B. Zorina, and Kenneth L. Sokoloff. "The Early Development of Intellectual Property Institutions in the United States." *J. Econ. Perspectives* **15(2)** (2001): 115.

[38] Khan, B. Zorina, and Kenneth L. Sokoloff. "Patent Institutions, Industrial Organization, and Early Technological Change: Britain and the United States, 1790–1850." In *Technological Revolutions in Europe*, edited by Maxine Berg and Kristin Bruland, 292–313. Cheltenham: Edward Elgar, 1998.

[39] Kitcher, Philip. *The Advancement of Science: Science without Legend, Objectivity without Illusions*. New York: Oxford University Press, 1993.

[40] König, Wolfgang. "Sciencebased Industry or Industrybased Science? Electrical Engineering in Germany before World War I." *Tech. & Culture* **37(1)** (1996): 70–101.

[41] Kroes, Peter. "On the Role of Designing Theories: Pambour's Theory of the Steam Engine." In *Technological Development and Science in the Industrial Age*, edited by Peter Kroes and Martijn Bakker, 69–98. Dordrecht: Kluwer, 1992.

[42] Kuper, Adam. "If Memes are the Answer, What is the Question?" In *Darwinizing Culture: The Status of Memetics as a Science*, edited by Robert Aunger, 175–188. Cambridge, MA: Cambridge University Press, 2000.

[43] Kuznets, Simon. *Economic Growth and Structure*. New York: W.W. Norton, 1965.

[44] Laudan, Rachel. "Cognitive Change in Technology and Science." In *The Nature of Knowledge: Are Models of Scientific Change Relevant?*, edited by Rachel Laudan. Dordrecht: Kluwer, 1984.

[45] Lavoisier. "Tabelle der einfachen Körper." *Traité élémentaire de Chimie*. 1793.

[46] Lewontin, Richard C. "The Units of Selection." *Ann. Rev. Ecol. & Sys.* **1** (1970): 118.

[47] Loasby, Brian J. *Knowledge, Institutions, and Evolution in Economics*. London: Routledge, 1999.

[48] Lucas, Robert E. *The Industrial Revolution: Past and Future*. Unpublished manuscript, 1998.

[49] Machlup, Fritz. *Knowledge: Its Creation, Distribution and Economic Significance*, 3 volumes. Princeton University Press, Princeton, NJ: 1980–1984.

[50] Maynard Smith, John. *The Problems of Biology*. Oxford: Oxford University Press, 1986.

[51] Mayr, Ernst. *Toward a New Philosophy of Biology*. Cambridge, MA: The Belknap Press, 1988.

[52] Mazlish, Bruce. *The Fourth Discontinuity: The Coevolution of Humans and Machines*. New Haven: Yale University Press, 1993.

[53] Mokyr, Joel. *The Gifts of Athena: Historical Origins of the Knowledge Economy.* Princeton: Princeton University Press, 2002.

[54] Mokyr, Joel. "King Kong and Cold Fusion: Counterfactual Analysis and the History of Technology." In *Counterfactual Analysis in History and the Social Sciences,* edited by Philip Tetlock, Ned Lebow, and Geoffrey Parker. 2001.

[55] Mokyr, Joel. "Long-Term Economic Growth and the History of Technology." In *Handbook of Economic Growth,* edited by Philippe Aghion and Steven Durlauf. 2004.

[56] Mokyr, Joel. "The Intellectual Origins of Modern Economic Growth." *J. Econ. Hist.* (2005).

[57] Nelson, Richard R. "Knowledge and Innovation Systems." In *Knowledge Management in the Learning Society.* Paris: OECD, 2000.

[58] Nelson, Richard R. "Selection Criteria and Selection Processes in Cultural Evolution Theories." In *Technological Innovation as an Evolutionary Process,* edited by John Ziman, 66–74. Cambridge: Cambridge University Press, 2000.

[59] Nelson, Katherine, and Richard Nelson. "On the Nature and Evolution of Human Knowhow." *Research Policy* **31(5)** (2002): 719–733.

[60] Nelson, Richard R., and Sidney Winter. *An Evolutionary Theory of Economic Change.* Cambridge, MA: The Belknap Press, 1982.

[61] Pambour, François-Marie. *Théorie de la Machine à Vapeur.* Paris: Bachelier, 1839.

[62] Poirier, Jean-Pierre. *Lavoisier: Chemist, Biologist, Economist.* Philadelphia: University of Pennsylvania Press, 1998.

[63] Polanyi, Michael. *Personal Knowledge: Towards a Post-Critical Philosophy.* Chicago, IL: Chicago University Press, 1962.

[64] Price, Derek J. de Solla. "Notes Towards a Philosophy of the Science/Technology Interaction," In *The Nature of Knowledge: Are Models of Scientific Change Relevant?,* edited by Rachel Laudan. Dordrecht: Kluwer, 1984.

[65] Rankine. *Manual of the Steam Engine.* London: R. Griffin, 1859.

[66] Reiser, Stanley Joel. *Medicine and the Reign of Technology.* Cambridge, MA: Cambridge University Press, 1978.

[67] Rosenberg, Nathan. "Engineering Knowledge." Unpublished manuscript, Stanford University, 2001.

[68] Rosenberg, Nathan. *Perspectives on Technology.* Cambridge, MA: Cambridge University Press, 1976.

[69] Ruttan, Vernon W. *Technology, Growth, and Development: An Induced Innovation Perspective.* New York: Oxford University Press, 2001.

[70] Ryle, Gilbert. *The Concept of Mind.* Chicago, IL: University of Chicago Press, 1949.

[71] Scheffler, Israel. *Conditions of Knowledge.* Chicago, IL: Scott, Foresman and Co., 1965.

[72] Stebbins, G. Ledyard. *Darwin to DNA, Molecules to Humanity*. San Francisco: W.H. Freeman, 1982.

[73] Travis, Anthony. "Science as Receptor of Technology: Paul Ehrlich and the Synthetic Dyestuff Industry." *Science in Context* **3(2)** (1989): 383–408.

[74] Vermeij, Geerat J. "Economics, Volcanoes, and Phanerozoic Revolutions." *Paleobiology* **21(3)** (1995): 125–152.

[75] Vermeij, Geerat J. *Evolution and Escalation: An Ecological History of Life*. Princeton: Princeton University Press, 1987.

[76] Vermeij, Geerat J. "The Evolutionary Interaction Among Species: Selection, Escalation, and Coevolution." *Ann. Rev. Ecol. Sys.* **25** (1994): 219–236.

[77] Vincenti, Walter G. *What Engineers Know and How They Know It*. Baltimore: Johns Hopkins Press, 1990.

[78] Vogel, Steven. *Cats' Paws and Catapults: Mechanical Worlds of Nature and People*. New York: Norton 1998.

[79] Williams, George C. *Adaptation and Natural Selection*. Princeton: Princeton University Press, 1966.

[80] Winchester, Simon. *The Map that Changed the World*. New York: Harper Collins, 2001.

[81] Woolrich, A. P. "John Farey and his *Treatise on the Steam Engine* of 1827." *Hist. Tech.* **22** (2000): 63–106.

[82] Wright, Robert. *Nonzero: The Logic of Human Destiny*. New York: Vintage Books, 2000.

[83] Wuketits, Franz. *Evolutionary Epistemology and Its Implications for Humankind*. Albany: SUNY Press, 1990.

[84] Ziman, John. "Selectionism and Complexity." In *Technological Innovation as an Evolutionary Process*, edited by John Ziman, 41–51. Cambridge, MA: Cambridge University Press, 2000.

Prosocial Emotions

Samuel Bowles
Herbert Gintis

Adherence to social norms is underwritten not only by the cognitively mediated pursuit of self-interest, but also by emotions. Shame, guilt, pride, regret, joy, and other visceral reactions play a central role in sustaining cooperative relations, including successful transactions in the absence of complete contracting. We consider a public goods game where agents maximize a utility function that captures five distinct motives: material payoffs to oneself, one's valuation of the payoffs to others, which depend both on one's altruism and one's degree of reciprocity, and one's sense of guilt or shame in response to one's own and others' actions. We present evidence suggesting that such emotions play a role in the public goods game, and we develop an analytical model showing that reciprocity, shame, and guilt increase the level of cooperation in the group. Finally, we provide an explanation of the long-term evolutionary success of prosocial emotions in terms of both the individual and group-level benefits they confer.

The Economy as an Evolving Complex System III,
edited by Lawrence E. Blume and Steven N. Durlauf, Oxford University Press

Let's not forget that the little emotions are the great captains of our lives and we obey them without realizing it.
>   —Vincent Van Gogh in a letter to his brother Theo

The heart has reasons that Reason knows nothing about.
>   —Blaise Pascal, *Pensées* (1670)

How selfish soever man may be supposed, there are evidently some principles in his nature, which interest him in the fortunes of others, and render their happiness necessary to him, though he derives nothing from it, except the pleasure of seeing it...
Our imagination therefore attaches the idea of shame to all violations of faith.
>   —Adam Smith, *The Theory of Moral Sentiments* (1759)

1   INTRODUCTION

Social interactions in modern economies are typically quasi-contractual. Some aspects of what is being transacted are regulated by complete and readily-enforceable contracts, while others are not. Transactions concerning credit, employment, information, and other goods and services where quality is difficult to monitor provide examples of quasi-contractual exchanges. Where contracting is absent or incomplete, the optimality properties of decentralized market allocations no longer hold. But where the invisible hand fails, the handshake may succeed. Kenneth Arrow [4, p.22], whom we honor with this essay and this volume, wrote

> In the absence of trust... opportunities for mutually beneficial cooperation would have to be foregone... norms of social behavior, including ethical and moral codes [may be]... reactions of society to compensate for market failures.

As in many other areas, Arrow's insight long predates the recent recognition of the economic importance of norms. Surprisingly little progress has been made in the intervening years in understanding how norms affect behavior and why some norms that impose costs on their adherents, such as forgoing opportunities to lie, cheat, and steal even when the prospect of discovery is vanishingly small, might have been successful by the test of either genetic or cultural evolution. This lack of progress, we think, may be traced to two shortcomings of the way behavioral scientists have addressed the problem.

The first is the common representation of seemingly unselfish acts as reflecting the farsighted pursuit of self interest. The second is the neglect of emotions as important influences on behavior. An explanation of the adherence to social norms with wide acceptance in biology [67], evolutionary psychology [22], political science [6, 66], and economics [36] is that individually costly behaviors that confer benefits on others are sustained by the repeated nature of interactions that allow for punishment of norm violators. We have explained elsewhere why we believe these explanations to be insufficient. In brief, they fail to explain compelling evidence of adherence to norms in both experimental and real world situations that are clearly nonrepeated. Moreover, in interactions among more than a few individuals, it is very difficult to sustain high levels of adherence to social norms if errors in play or in the perceptions of others' play occur [12, 15].

A second reason for our limited success in understanding social norms is the remarkable neglect of emotions in the study of behavior. It may seem odd that an approach once said to be based on the "calculus of pleasure and pain" would pay so little attention to feelings. But in the standard economic model, people act to bring about valued consequences. The process by which the individual arrives at the action is cognitive, not affective. Visceral reactions such as joy, shame, fear, and disgust thus play no role in the process of decision making, however much their anticipation may influence the evaluation of the consequences of an action. The neglect of the behavioral consequences of emotions is not limited to economics, but extends to psychology and neuroscience as well, where cognitive aspects of behavior is a major line of research, while the causes of emotions receive far more attention than their behavioral consequences.[1]

The interpretation we would like to advance here is that *adherence to social norms is underwritten by emotions, not only by the expectation of future reciprocation.* The experience of shame, guilt, pride, regret, joy, and other visceral reactions plays a central role in sustaining cooperative relations, including successful transactions in the absence of complete contracting. An example will illustrate our view and its potential relevance to economic policy making.

Parents are sometimes late in picking up their children at day care centers. In Haifa, at six randomly chosen centers, a fine was imposed for lateness while in a control group of centers no fine was imposed [39]. The expectation was that punctuality would improve at the first group of centers. But parents responded to the fine by even greater tardiness. The fraction picking up their children late more than doubled. Even more striking was the fact that when, after 16 weeks, the fining policy was rescinded, their enhanced tardiness persisted, showing no tendency to return to the *status quo ante.* Over the entire 20 weeks of the experiment, there were no changes in the degree of lateness at the day care centers in the control group. The authors of the study, Uri Gneezy and Aldo Rustichini, reason that the fine was a contextual cue, unintentionally providing information about the appropriate behavior. The effect was to convert lateness from the violation of an obligation which might have occasioned the feeling of guilt,

---

[1] This situation is being rectified. In psychology, see Zajonic [72], Damasio [23], Greene [40], Moll [56], Rilling [60], Cohen [21], and in economics see Lowenstein [54], Laibson [52], and Bosman and Van Winden [10].

to a choice with a price that many were willing to pay. They titled their study "A Fine is a Price" and concluded that imposing a fine labeled the interaction as a market-like situation, one in which parents were more than willing to buy lateness. Revoking the fine did not restore the initial framing, but rather just lowered the price of lateness to zero.

The fact that monetary incentives for punctuality instead induced even greater tardiness is both counter to the predictions of the standard behavioral model in economics and suggests an alternative approach in which social norms and the activation of emotions when norms are violated play a central role in behavior. We define a behavior as *prosocial* if its exercise increases the average payoff to members of the group. One of the most important emotions contributing to prosocial behavior is *shame*, the feeling of discomfort at having done something wrong not only by one's own norms but also in the eyes of those whose opinions matter to you.[2]

Prosocial emotions function like the basic emotion, "pain," in providing guides for action that bypass the explicit cognitive optimizing process that lies at the core of the standard behavioral model in economics. Antonio [23, p. 173] calls these "somatic markers," that is, bodily responses that "forces attention on the negative outcome to which a given action may lead and functions as an automated alarm signal which says: Beware of danger ahead if you choose the option that leads to this outcome.... The automated signal protects you against future losses." Emotions thus contribute to the decision-making process, not simply by clouding reason, but in beneficial ways as well. Damasio continues: "suffering puts us on notice.... It increases the probability that individuals will heed pain signals and act to avert their source or correct their consequences." (p. 264)

To explore the role of guilt and shame in inducing prosocial behaviors we will consider a particular interaction having the structure of a public goods game. We assume individuals maximize a utility function that captures five distinct motives: one's individual material payoffs, how much one values the payoffs to others, which depend both on ones' altruism and one's degree of reciprocity, and one's sense of guilt or shame in response to one's own and others' actions. To this end, we will amend and extend a utility function derived from the work of Geanakoplos [37], Falk and Fischbacher [30], Levine [53], and Sethi and Somanathan [63].

The shame term in the utility function captures the idea that individuals may experience discomfort based on their beliefs about the extent to which it is socially acceptable to take self-interested actions at the expense of others. The sense of shame is not exogenously given, but rather is influenced by how others respond to one's actions. Thus an individual taking an action that generates a material payoff to himself while inflicting costs on others may provoke punishment by fellow group members resulting in a reduction in payoffs to the

---

[2]Shame differs from guilt in that while both involve the violation of a norm, the former but not the latter is necessarily induced by others knowing about the violation and making their displeasure known to the violator.

miscreant. But in addition to the payoff reduction, he also may experience a level of shame that depends, in addition to the action he took, on the extent to which other group members expressed their disapproval by inflicting punishment upon him.

In the public good setting, contributing too little to the public account may evoke shame if a person feels that he has appropriated "too much" to himself. Because shame is socially induced, being punished when one has contributed little triggers the feeling of having taken too much. In this case, the effect of punishment on behavior may not operate by changing the incentives facing the individual, that is, by making it clear that his payoffs will be reduced by the expected punishments in future rounds. Rather it evokes a different evaluation by the individual of the act of taking too much, namely, shame. This is the view expressed by Elster [28, p. 67] "material sanctions themselves are best understood as vehicles of the emotion of contempt, which is the direct trigger of shame." Thus, self-interested actions, *per se*, may induce guilt, but not shame. If one contributes little and is not punished, one comes to consider these actions as unshameful. If, by contrast, one is punished when one has contributed generously, the emotional reaction may be spite toward the members of one's group.

The interpretation of behavior advanced here may be contrasted with a related and complementary modification of the canonical behavioral model in economics, namely, the assumption of bounded rationality [65]. In our interpretation, agents may be deviating from the predictions of the standard model not because they are incapable of doing the cognitive operations required by the model but because they do not feel like doing (and acting on) these calculations. Indeed their feelings may cause them to act in ways inconsistent with the standard model even when they have flawlessly done the required calculations.

In section 2, we present experimental evidence consistent with the view that punishment not only reduces material payoffs but also recruits emotions of shame toward the modification of behavior in prosocial directions. In section 3, we model the process by which an emotion such as shame may affect behavior in a simple three-person public goods game. In section 4, we generalize to an n-person public goods game. In section 5, we ask how behaviorally important emotions such as shame might have evolved. We conclude with some implications for economic theory and policy.

2   THE MORAL RESPONSE TO PUNISHMENT: EXPERIMENTAL EVIDENCE

Strong reciprocity is the predisposition to cooperate with others and punish non-cooperators, even when this behavior cannot be justified in terms of self-interest, however broadly conceived. An extensive body of evidence suggests that a considerable fraction of the population, in many different societies, and under many different social conditions, including complete anonymity, are strong reciprocators. We here review laboratory evidence concerning the public goods game. For additional evidence, including the results of dictator, ultimatum, common pool resource, and trust games, see Güth and Tietz [42], Roth [61], Camerer and Thaler [19], and Henrich et al. [46]

The public goods game consists of n subjects under conditions of strict anonymity. Each subject is given w "points," redeemable at the end of the experimental session for real money. Each subject then places some number of points in a "common account," and keeps the rest. The experimenter then gives each subject a fraction $q \in (1/n, 1)$ times the total amount in the common account. Contributing is thus an altruistic act, because it increases the average payoff to the group ($q > 1/n$) at the expense of the individual ($q < 1$).

Contributing nothing to the common account is a dominant strategy in the public goods game if subjects are self-interested. Public goods experiments, however, show that only a fraction of subjects conform to the self-interested model. Rather, subjects begin by contributing, on average, about half of their endowment to the common account.

If the game is continued over several rounds, however, contributions tend to fall. In a meta-study of twelve public goods experiments, Fehr and Schmidt [32] found that in the early rounds, average and median contribution levels ranged from 40% to 60% of the endowment, in the final period (usually round ten) 73% of all individuals ($N = 1042$) contributed nothing, and many of the remaining players contributed close to zero. The explanation for the decay of cooperation offered by subjects when debriefed after the experiment is that cooperative subjects became angry at others who contributed less than themselves, and retaliated against free-riding low contributors in the only way available to them—by lowering their own contributions. Experimental evidence supports this interpretation. When subjects are allowed to punish noncontributors, they do so at a cost to themselves [24, 57, 62, 69, 70, 71].

Fehr and Gächter [31], for instance, set up a ten-round public goods game with $n = 4$ and costly punishment, employing three different methods of assigning members to groups. Under the *Partner* treatment, the four subjects remained in the same group for all ten periods. Under the *Stranger* treatment, the subjects were randomly reassigned after each round. Finally, under the *Perfect Stranger* treatment the subjects were randomly reassigned and assured that they would never meet another subject more than once (in this case, the number of rounds had to be reduced from ten to six to accommodate the size of the subject pool). Subjects earned an average of about \$35 for an experimental session.

Fehr and Gächter [31] performed their experiment for ten rounds with punishment and ten rounds without. Their results are illustrated in figure 1. We see that when costly punishment is permitted, cooperation does not deteriorate, and in the Partner treatment, despite strict anonymity, cooperation increases almost to full cooperation, even on the final round. When punishment is not permitted, however, the same subjects experience the deterioration of cooperation found in previous public goods games.

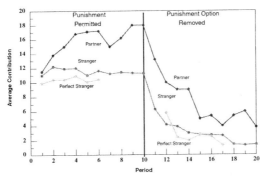

FIGURE 1   Average contributions over time in the partner, stranger, and perfect stranger treatments when the punishment condition is played first (adapted from Fehr and Gächter [31]).

The contrast between the Partner effect and the two Stranger effects is worth noting. In the latter case, punishment prevented the deterioration of cooperation, whereas in the former case, punishment led to an increase in participation over time, until near full cooperation was achieved. This result suggests that subjects are motivated by the personal desire to punish free riders (the Stranger treatment), but are even more strongly motivated when there is an identifiable group, to which they belong, whose cooperative effort is impaired by free riding (the Partner treatment). Thus, the more strongly manifested the prosociality of strong reciprocity, the more coherent and permanent the group in question.

The frequency with which subjects paid to punish other group members raises serious doubts about the adequacy of the standard behavioral model, for in the perfect stranger treatment (or in the final periods of other treatments) the dominant strategy is to contribute nothing and to refrain from punishing. Indeed, strategically, punishment is identical to the contribution to the public good. Both are forms of altruism—a benefit conferred on others at a cost to oneself. The fact that subjects avidly punish low contributors, and display considerable negative affect when asked why they do so, suggests that they are responding emotionally—specifically, they are acting on feelings of anger.

In this chapter we focus on the response of the punishees, which appears no less prompted by emotions. Unlike punishing behavior, which cannot be motivated by payoff gains, a positive response to the experience of being punished could be explained by the desire to avoid further reductions in payoffs due to being punished in subsequent rounds. But as we will see, in many experimental settings, this motivation explains only part of the response. We will first present one of our own experiments conducted with Jeffrey Carpenter [13] and then comment on the results of two remarkable experiments by others.

By implementing the Stranger Treatment, in which subjects are randomly reassigned to a new group at the beginning of each round of play, we deliberately created an experimental environment in which cooperation would be difficult to sustain. We also make punishing shirkers quite costly to punishers: the cost of inflicting a penalty of two experimental "points" is one point for the punisher. Suppose there are n players. Each player receives w points at the beginning of each round, and player i contributes a_i to the public good. These contributions are revealed to the other players, who then can punish by purchasing as much punishment as they want at a cost of one point per sanction. Let μ_{ij} be the expenditure on sanctions assigned by player i to player j (we assume $\mu_{ii} = 0$). Then the payoff to player i is given by

$$\pi_i = w - a_i + q \sum_{j=1}^{n} a_j - \sum_{j=1}^{n} \mu_{ij} - 2 \sum_{j=1}^{n} \mu_{ji}. \tag{1}$$

The first two terms $(w - a_i)$ represent the amount i keeps for himself, the third term is the amount he receives from the common pool, the fourth term is the amount he spends on punishing others, and the final term is the amount he is punished by others.

To study the effect of group size and the degree of harm caused by shirking, we used two group sizes (four and eight) and two values of q (0.3 and 0.70), allowing us to compare across our treatment variables to look for similarities in behavior based on the payoff losses that shirkers inflict on other group members. Our underlying behavioral assumptions concerning reciprocity imply that an agent's punishment of another agent would vary both with the other agent's shirking rate and the harm caused by a unit of shirking, the latter depending on the size of the group and the marginal per-person return on contribution to the public account. There are two ways to measure the harm done by a shirking group member. The first, which we term the *private cost of shirking*, is the reduction in each agent's payoffs associated with an act of shirking by individual i, or $q(w - a_i)$. By contrast, z_i, the *social cost* of shirking by member i takes account of the costs borne by every group member other than the shirker, or $z_i = (n-1)q(w - a_i)$.

We conducted twelve sessions, three per treatment, with 172 participants. The number of participants, and therefore groups, per treatment vary due to no-shows. All subjects were recruited by e-mail from the general student population and none had ever participated in a public goods experiment before. Each subject was given a five dollar show-up fee upon arrival and then was seated at a partially isolated computer terminal so that decisions were made in privacy. Each session took approximately 45 minutes from sign-in to payments, and subjects earned $20.58 on average, including the show-up fee.

Each session lasted ten periods. In each period (a) subjects were randomly reassigned to a group, given an endowment of $w = 25$ points, and allowed to contribute, anonymously, any fraction of the endowment to a public account, the remainder going to the subject's private account; (b) the total group contribution, the subject's gross earnings, and the contributions of other group members (presented in random order) were then revealed to each subject, who was then permitted to assign sanctions to others. Finally, payoffs were calculated according to (1), and subjects were informed of their net payoffs for the period. They were then again randomly reassigned to groups and the process continued.

Our experimental results confirmed the following:

Hypothesis 1: Punishing occurs whenever shirking occurs. Punishment occurs in all periods and under all treatment conditions when $a_i < w$ for some i. Indeed, 89% of our subjects exercised the punishment option at least once, and in no treatment was the fraction punishing less than 80%.

Hypothesis 2: The level of punishment directed toward player i increases with the cost imposed on individual punishers, $q(w - a_i)$.

Hypothesis 3: Shirkers respond to punishment. Punishment in one round leads shirkers to increase their contributions in subsequent rounds.

Hypothesis 4: Punishment fosters contributions. The level of contributions does not decay when costly punishment is permitted.

Hypothesis 5: Altruism does not explain punishment. We will explain this result below.

Because we are interested in how behavior changes over time as players learn more about the consequences of their actions, we used the panel nature of our data to estimate a number of the implied learning models. It is possible that those punishing low contributors sought to modify the behavior of the shirkers in order to raise the payoffs of others. But were this the case, subjects would both contribute more in larger groups (because for a given q, more benefits to others are distributed in large groups) and punish more in large groups (because if successful in inducing the free rider to contribute more, it would generate more aggregate benefits). The fact that group size *per se* has no effect on either punishment or contributions suggests that altruism toward other group members is not what is generating the high levels of punishment of free riders.

A further test is the following. If our subjects correctly estimated the responsiveness of those punished in subsequent periods, we can then calculate the degree of altruism which would have made punishment a best response given these beliefs. Could plausible levels of altruism explain the punishing behavior? The answer is no: in the smaller of our groups punishment actually lowers average benefits (the cost of the punishment is not made up by the subsequent higher contributions of those punished) so even if the punisher cared as much about others' payoffs as his own, punishment would not "pay." We conclude that motives other than a concern of the payoffs of others motivate punishment.

While we think it likely that anger at low contributors was an important motive for punishment, the role of emotions is more clearly revealed in the responses of the targets of punishment. Subjects responded to punishment in the following way. Those giving less than the mean ("shirkers"), when punished, contributed more, and the effect of punishment on contribution was larger the farther away from the mean. Those contributing more than the mean ("good citizens") also responded to punishment but in the opposite direction: good citizens did not revert to the mean unless they were punished, in which case they strongly reduced their contributions. These results are all statistically significant at conventional levels.

Is the shirkers' positive response to punishment a best response defined over the payoffs of the game? Or, by contrast, does shirking still pay even when the expected costs of punishment are considered? Our estimates indicated that shirkers are punished by sanctions reducing their payoffs by 0.5 points for each point not contributed to the group project (this punishment response to shirking appears not to vary across groups). The act of shirking deprives the shirker of the returns from the public project, so (differentiating (1) with respect to a_i) we see that the net benefit of shirking in the absence of punishment is just $1 - q$. Comparing the benefits of shirking $(1 - q)$ with the cost (0.5), we find that for the two low-q groups shirking pays quite well $(0.70-0.5)$, while for the high q groups it does not $(0.3-0.5)$. Of course we do not know that the subjects correctly estimated the effect of shirking on the likelihood of being punished, but the econometric estimate of the cost is quite precise $(t = 12)$ and it seems plausible that at least in the later rounds of the experiment subjects had an approximate idea of the punishment costs of shirking.

The conclusion is that *responding positively to punishment is not a best response defined over the payoffs of the game.* Our interpretation, which we develop in the next section, is that punishment signaled social disapproval, which evoked an emotion of shame in the shirkers and they responded positively so as to relieve that uncomfortable feeling. A reasonable interpretation of good citizens' behavior is that group members respond spitefully to being punished only when it is clear they are contributing well above the norm.

This interpretation is consistent with the results of a remarkable public goods with punishment experiment implemented in 18 rural communities in Zimbabwe by Barr [7]. The game was structured along the above lines, except for the punishment stage, in which there was no option to reduce the payoffs to others. Rather, following the contribution stage, Barr's assistant stood beside each player in turn and said "Player number __, Mr/Mrs __, contributed __. Does anyone have anything to say about that?" followed by an opportunity for all group members to criticize or praise the player. A quarter of the participants were criticized for contributing too little ("stingy," "mean," "Now I know why I never get offered food when I drop by your house!") Five percent were criticized for giving too much ("stupid," "careless with money"). Those who made low contributions and were criticized made larger contributions in subsequent rounds. Moreover, those who contributed low amounts and escaped criticism, but had witnessed the criticism of others who had contributed similar amounts, increased their contributions by *even more than those directly criticized*. As in our experiments, those who had contributed large amounts and were criticized reduced their contributions in subsequent rounds. Where low contributors escaped criticism entirely, contributions fell in subsequent rounds.

A second experiment with both monetary and nonmonetary punishment [55] yielded similar results with the interesting twist that the response to being awarded "punishment points" was significantly greater when they carried no monetary penalty than when they resulted in payoff reductions of the players. This was true in both a stranger and a partner treatment, but more so in the latter.

We proceed now to a model of public-goods-type interactions among individuals with social preferences.

3 RECIPROCITY, SHAME, AND PUNISHMENT WITH TWO AGENTS

Consider two agents who play a one-shot public goods game, and who (a) are *self-interested* and thus care about their own material payoffs; (b) are generically *altruistic or spiteful* and thus place some weight, positive, negative, or zero, on the payoffs of the other player, independent of their beliefs about the others' types or their past behavior; (c) are *strong reciprocators* and thus, depending on the other's type, value their payoffs (positively or negatively); (d) have contribution norms, indicating to what extent it is ethical to contribute, and if they violate their own norms, they experience *guilt*; and finally (e) experience *shame* if they violate their own contribution norm and are publicly sanctioned for this behavior. The altruism and strong reciprocity of these individuals may lead them to value the payoffs of the other, and thus to contribute on other's behalf. The strong reciprocity motive may lead the individual to engage in costly punishment if the other contributes little (reducing his payoff). Finally, guilt feelings may lead individuals to contribute, as will shame, if punishment of non-contributors is anticipated.

We assume each agent starts with a personal account equal to one unit. Each agent contributes $a_i \in [0, 1]$, and then each receives $q(a_1 + a_2)$, where $q \in (1/2, 1)$. Thus, the agents do best when each cooperates ($a_i = 1$), but each has an incentive to defect ($a_i = 0$), no matter what the other does. The two-person public goods game in the absence of punishment thus would be a prisoner's dilemma. But at the end of this *production period* there is a second period, which we call the *punishment period*, in which the agents are informed of the contribution of the other agents, and each agent $i = 1, 2$ may impose a penalty μ_{ij} on the other agent $(j \neq i)$ at a cost $c(\mu_{ij})$. For illustrative purposes, we will assume $c(\mu) = \gamma \mu^2 / 2$. The material payoffs to the agents are thus given by

$$\pi_i = 1 - a_i + q(a_1 + a_2) - \mu_{ji} \quad i = 1, 2, \tag{2}$$

plus the cost to i of punishing j, which is $\gamma \mu_{ij}^2 / 2$, where $j \neq i$. We have not included this last expression in is material payoff for reasons explained below (in fact, simulations show that this choice does not affect the general behavior of the model). In eq. (2), the first two terms give the amount remaining in the agent's private account after contributing, the third term is the agent's share of the total reward from cooperation, and the fourth term is the punishment inflicted upon the agent.

We assume each player i suffers a psychic cost $\beta_i(a_i^* - a_i)^2$ when he contributes a_i and his *contribution norm* is a_i^*. The parameter β_i thus measures the strength of the player's *guilt* at not living up to his ideals. It may seem odd that the agent is guilty if he contributes *more* than his ideal. But if that which he retains $(1 - a_i)$ is directed to other "worthy" purposes about which he also has norms (e.g., his own family's well-being), then the symmetry of guilt around a_i^* makes sense.

We represent the weight that agent i places on the material payoff π_j of agent $j \neq i$ by

$$\delta_{ij} = \alpha_i + \lambda_i(a_j - a_i^*), \tag{3}$$

and for convenience we define $\delta_{ii} = 0$. The parameter α_i reflects the agent's *unconditional altruism* motive toward the other players. We assume $\alpha_i \geq 0$ (benevolence) in this illustrative model, but in general $\alpha_i < 0$ (spite) is also possible. The parameter $\lambda_i \geq 0$ is the agent's *reciprocity* motive. Note that when $\lambda_i > 0$, i is more favorably inclined toward j, the larger is js contribution compared to is contribution norm a_i^*.

We include the shame, s_i, experienced by agent i by including negatively in the utility function the psychic costs of being punished in the utility function:

$$s_i = \sigma_i(a_i^* - a_i)\mu_{ji}, \tag{4}$$

where $j \neq i$. Thus, punishment triggers shame, and σ_i is a measure of the susceptibility of agent i to feeling shame. Note that the shame term is positive only if one has contributed less than one's contribution norm. Otherwise, this term represents spite, since in this case when an agent is punished, lowering his contribution increases his utility.

Thus, the objective functions of the two agents are given by

$$u_i = \pi_i + \delta_{ij}\pi_j - \frac{\beta_i(a_i^* - a_i)^2 - \gamma \mu_{ij}^2}{2 - \sigma_i(a_i^* - a_i)\mu_{ji}} \tag{5}$$

where $j \neq i$. Note that each agent i must choose a_i, and then choose μ_{ij} as a function of the level of contribution a_j chosen by the other agent. The first-order condition for $\mu_{ij}(j \neq i)$ is given by

$$\frac{\partial u_i}{\partial \mu_{ij}} = -\gamma \mu_{ij} - \delta_{ij} = 0\,, \tag{6}$$

where $j \neq i$. This requires that the agent choose a level of punishment that equates the marginal cost of punishment (the first term) to the marginal benefit of punishment, namely the valuation placed on reducing the payoff of the other (the second term). This has the solution

$$\mu_{ij} = \begin{cases} -\delta_{ij}/\gamma & a_i^* > a_j + \frac{\alpha_i}{\lambda_i}\,, \\ 0 & \text{otherwise}\,. \end{cases} \tag{7}$$

where $j \neq i$. Where punishment is positive, this is clearly increasing in the degree of reciprocity and decreasing in the level of altruism.[3] Finally, as noted above, we do not apply δ_{ij} to js cost of punishing i, because we consider it implausible that i will increase his contribution because he cares about j and he realizes that j will have to punish him if he contributes too little.

We assume that each player i, in selecting a contribution level a_i, knows the other's utility function, thus knowing eq. (7), anticipates the effect of shirking on the punishment one may expect to receive from another player j. The first-order condition for a_i, $\partial u_i/\partial a_i = 0$, is then given by

$$\frac{\partial u_i}{\partial a_i} = -1 + q + \frac{\lambda_j}{\gamma} + \delta_{ij}q + 2\beta_i(a_i^* - a_i) + \sigma_i\left(\mu_{ji} + (a_i^* - a_i)\frac{\lambda_j}{\gamma}\right) = 0. \tag{8}$$

Note that $1-q$ is the marginal cost of contributing, λ_j/γ is the marginal reduction in punishment associated with contributing more, $\delta_{ij}q$ is the valuation of the marginal effect of contributing on the payoffs of the other agent, $2\beta_i(a_i^* - a_i)$ is the marginal reduction in guilt, and the last two terms are the reduction in shame occasioned by the lesser violation of one's norm (the penultimate term), and the reduced punishment (the final term).

Equation (8) gives the best response function

$$a_i = \frac{\gamma(q(1 + \delta_{ij}) + 2\beta_i a_i^* - 1) + \sigma_i(\lambda_j(a_j^* + a_i^*) - \alpha_j) + \lambda_j}{2(\beta_i\gamma + \lambda_j\sigma_i)}. \tag{9}$$

For positive levels of reciprocity, the best response of each individual is increasing in the contribution of the other. Comparative static analysis of each shows that for $a_i^* > a_i$, $da_i/d\sigma_i$ and $da_i/d\beta_i$ are both positive, so an increase in either guilt or shame shifts the relevant function upwards. Figure 2 presents the best response functions for the two individuals, their intersection giving a Nash equilibrium. The shifts in the best response functions in figure 2 illustrate the effect on the

---

[3]Special cases not included in this solution are: if $\lambda_i = 0, \alpha_i \geq 0$, then $\mu_{ij} = 0$, and if $\lambda_i = 0, \alpha_i < 0$, then $\mu_{ij} = -\alpha_i/\gamma$. We will assume that if $\lambda_i = 0$ then the agent is purely selfish, so $\alpha_i = 0$ also holds.

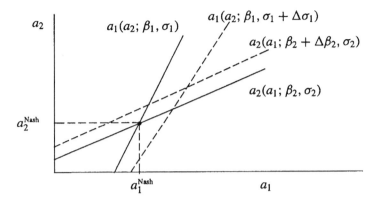

FIGURE 2   Comparative Statics. The best response functions (9) determine the Nash equilibrium contribution levels (a_1^{Nash} and a_2^{Nash}), which are both displaced upward by an increase in 1's level of shame and or 2's level of guilt.

Nash equilibrium of an increase in shame by individual 1 and an increase in guilt by individual 2. The effects of both, singly and together, are to increase the equilibrium contributions of both individuals.

Solving the resulting set of best response functions to get a Nash equilibrium is straightforward, and the equilibrium is unique. The expression for the solution is complicated, however, and we will not list it here.

We can also give some comparative static results for particular ranges of the parameters. First, suppose the two agents have the same behavioral attributes, so $\alpha_1 = \alpha_2$, $\lambda_1 = \lambda_2$, $\beta_1 = \beta_2$, $\sigma_1 = \sigma_2$, and $\alpha_1^* = a_2^*$. Furthermore, suppose $\gamma = 2$, $q = 0.75$, $a_1^* = 0.7$, $\alpha_1 = 0.01$, $\lambda_1 = 0.2$, $\beta_1 = 0.5$, and $\sigma_1 = 0.5$. Then we find $a_1 = a_2 = 0.55$, and each agent punishes the other a small amount, $\mu_{ij} = 0.01$. For the comparative statics, let us first vary σ_1 from 0 to 30. We find that the equilibrium contribution increases from 0.54 to about 0.66. The reason for this small effect of shame is that the guilt parameter $\beta_1 = 0.5$ is rather large. If we reduce this to $\beta_1 = 0.20$, then the equilibrium contribution increases from 0.15 to 0.65 when we vary σ_1 from 0 to 30. The central point is that simulations show that an increase in shame leads to an increase in cooperation, and to a decline in the amount of punishment meted out.

The guilt parameter behaves similarly. If we increase β_i from 0.17 to 2, equilibrium contribution increases from 0 to 0.64, and equilibrium punishment declines from 0.045 to 0.

We can similarly show that increasing the altruism parameter α_1, the reciprocity parameter λ_1, or the contribution norm a_1^* leads to an increase in the amount of cooperation.

TABLE 1   Simulation parameters.

Symbol	Value	Meaning
α_1, α_2	0.01	Unconditional Altruism Coefficient
β_1, β_2	0.05	Guilt Coefficient
γ	2.00	Cost of Punishment
γ_1, γ_2	0.20	Conditional Altruism Coefficient
ω_1, ω_2	0.50	Shame Coefficient
a_1^*, a_2^*	0.7	Contribution Norm
q	0.75	Per Agent Share of Common Account

Second, suppose one player is as before, but the second is perfectly self-interested, with $\alpha_2 = \lambda_2 = \beta_2 = \sigma_2 = a_2^* = 0$. In this case, player 2 never punishes, first-order condition for player 1 is given by

$$\frac{\partial u_1}{\partial a_1} = -1 + q(1 + \delta_{12}) + 2\beta_1(a_1^* - a_1) = 0, \tag{10}$$

while for player 2 we have

$$\frac{\partial u_2}{\partial a_2} = -1 + q + \frac{\lambda_1}{\gamma}. \tag{11}$$

Thus if $\lambda_1/\gamma > 1 - q$, the punishment cost of shirking exceeds the net gain from shirking, so player 2 will set a_2 to the value that equates μ_{12} to 0 (since, by definition, μ_{12} cannot be negative). This gives

$$a_2 = a_1^* - \frac{\alpha_1}{\lambda_1}, \tag{12}$$

and

$$a_1 = a_1^* - \frac{1-q}{2\beta_1}. \tag{13}$$

In this case, which occurs when the cost of punishing, γ, is low and the intensity of reciprocation, λ_1 is high, the Nash equilibrium is relatively efficient, since no punishment actually occurs. Nevertheless, the agents do not attain their contribution norms, and the outcome could be far from optimal if the reciprocator's contribution norm is low.

Conversely, if $\lambda_1/\gamma < 1 - q$, player 2 will set $a_2 = 0$, so

$$a_1 = a_1^* \left(1 - \frac{q\lambda_1}{2\beta_1}\right) - \frac{1 - q(1 + \alpha_1)}{2\beta_1}. \tag{14}$$

The level of punishment of the self-interested player is given by

$$\mu_{12} = \frac{\lambda_1 a_1^* - \alpha_1}{\gamma},$$

which is bounded above by $(1 - q)a_1^*$. Thus, there can be extensive punishment in this case, although it does not induce the selfish type to cooperate. Also, it is clear that the level of punishment is increasing in the reciprocator's contribution norm, a_1^*, the intensity of reciprocation, λ_1, and is decreasing in the reciprocator's level of altruism, α_1, and the cost of punishment, γ.

We can also show, using this asymmetric model, that if agent 2 moves from being purely self-interested to experiencing shame, the average level of contribution of the agents will increase and the amount of punishment will decline. So let us now suppose that $\sigma_2 > 0$, $\alpha_2^* = a_1^*$, and $1 - q > \lambda_1/\gamma$, so agent 2 contributes nothing when $\sigma_2 = 0$. We also assume $a_1^* > \alpha_1/\lambda_1$, without which no punishment can occur. In this case, the equilibrium value of a_2 is

$$a_2 = \max\left\{\frac{\sigma_2(2\lambda_1 a_1^* - \alpha_1) + \lambda_1 - (1 - q)\gamma}{2\lambda_1\sigma_2}, 0\right\}.$$

For sufficiently small σ_2, this expression is zero, as we would expect. But a_2 is increasing in σ_2, and is positive for sufficiently large σ_2. The amount of punishment is

$$\mu_{12} = \frac{\lambda_1(a_1^* - a_2) - \alpha_1}{\gamma},$$

so clearly punishment declines as agent 2's shame level increases. Finally, we have

$$a_1 = a_1^* - \frac{(1 - q) - q(\alpha_1 - \lambda_1(a_2 - a_1^*))}{2\beta_1},$$

which is clearly increasing in a_2. Hence, when agent 2's shame level increases, both players contribute more and the level of punishment declines.

We now develop a more general model of cooperation in a public goods game in which individuals have the same structure of preferences as in the previous section.

4   A GENERAL MODEL OF RECIPROCITY, SHAME, AND PUNISHMENT

Consider a group with members $i = 1, \ldots, n$, each of whom has an endowment w_i and can make a contribution $a_i \in [0, w_i]$ that yields a payoff $f(a_1, \ldots, a_n)$ to each member of the group, where f is increasing in each of its arguments, but $\partial f/\partial a_i < 1$, so a member does best contributing nothing, everything else being equal. As above, at the end of this *production period* there is a second period, which we call the *punishment period*, in which each member i of the group is informed of the vector of endowments $(w_1, \ldots, w_n)$ and contributions $(a_1, \ldots, a_n)$, in light of which each may impose a penalty μ_{ij} on each member $j \neq i$ at a cost $c_i(\mu_{ij})$ to himself. For notational convenience, we assume $\mu_{ii} = 0$

and $c_i(0) = 0$. We define the *material payoff* to member i as

$$\pi_i = w_i - a_i + f(a_1, \ldots, a_n) - \sum \mu_{ji}. \tag{15}$$

For the reason described in the previous section, we have not included the cost to i of punishing others in the expression for π_i.

Agent is assessment of js type is a function of a_j. Generalizing the two-person model, the weight δ_{ij} that i places on js material payoff is given by eq. (3), the disutility of shame is given by eq. (4), and the psychic cost of guilt is $\beta_i(a_i^* - a_i)^2$. The utility of member i is then given by

$$u_i = \pi_i + \sum \delta_{ij}\pi_j - \sum c_i(\mu_{ij}) - \beta_i(a_i^* - a_i)^2 - \sigma_i(a_i^* - a_i)\sum \mu_{ji}, \tag{16}$$

the first-order condition for $\mu_{ij}, j \neq i$, is given by

$$\frac{\partial u_i}{\partial \mu_{ij}} = -\frac{\partial c_i}{\partial \mu_{ij}} - \delta_{ij} \leq 0, \tag{17}$$

and equality holds if $\mu_{ij} > 0$. Assuming equality in the first-order condition, and totally differentiating with respect to a_j, we have

$$\frac{\partial^2 u_i}{\partial \mu_{ij}^2}\frac{d\mu_{ij}}{da_j} + \frac{\partial^2 u_i}{\partial \mu_{ij}\partial a_j} = 0.$$

The first double partial is negative by the second-order condition, and $\partial^2 u_i/\partial \mu_{ij}\,\partial a_j = -\lambda_i < 0$. Hence $d\mu_{ij}/da_j < 0$, which means that when js contribution increases, i punishes j less (or at least not more).

The first-order condition for a_i is given by

$$\frac{\partial u_i}{\partial a_i} = -1 + \frac{\partial f}{\partial a_i}(1 + \sum \delta_{ij}) + 2\beta_i(a_i^* - a_i)$$

$$+\sigma_i \sum \mu_{ji} - \sum(\delta_{ij} + \sigma_i(a_i^* - a_i))\frac{\partial \mu_{ji}}{\partial a_i} = 0. \tag{18}$$

Totally differentiating the first-order conditions with respect to σ_i, we get

$$\mathbf{J}\begin{bmatrix} \frac{da_1}{d\sigma_i} \\ \vdots \\ \frac{da_1}{d\sigma_i} \end{bmatrix} = -\begin{bmatrix} \frac{\partial^2 u}{\partial a_1 \partial \sigma_i} \\ \vdots \\ \frac{\partial^2 u}{\partial a_1 \partial \sigma_i} \end{bmatrix}.$$

However, we have

$$\frac{\partial^2 u_i}{\partial a_i \partial \sigma_i} = -(a_i^* - a_i)\sum_{j \neq i}\frac{\partial \mu_{ji}}{\partial a_i},$$

and

$$\frac{\partial^2 u_i}{\partial a_j \partial \sigma_i} = 0, \qquad \text{for } j \neq i.$$

Thus

$$
\begin{bmatrix} \frac{da_1}{d\sigma_i} \\ \vdots \\ \frac{da_1}{d\sigma_i} \end{bmatrix} = -\mathbf{J}^{-1} \begin{bmatrix} 0 \\ \vdots \\ (a_i^* - a_i)\sum_{j \neq i}\frac{\partial\mu_{ji}}{\partial\sigma_i} \\ \vdots \\ 0 \end{bmatrix}.
$$

If we solve for $da_i/d\sigma_i$ using Cramer's rule, and using the fact that the second-order condition for a maximum requires that the determinant of $\mathbf{J}$ and that of the ith principal minor must have opposite signs, we conclude that $da_i/da_i^* > 0$ when $a_i^* > a_i$; (i.e., *if an agent is contributing less than his contribution norm, an increase in the strength of shame will induce the agent to contribute more*). It is precisely in this sense that shame is a prosocial emotion. The same reasoning shows that an individual who is contributing more than he thinks morally warranted (perhaps to avoid being punished), and is punished anyway, will respond by *reducing* his contribution when the shame-spite factor σ_i is increased.

Totally differentiating the first-order conditions with respect to α_i^*, we get

$$
\mathbf{J} \begin{bmatrix} \frac{da_1}{da_i^*} \\ \vdots \\ \frac{da_1}{da_i^*} \end{bmatrix} = - \begin{bmatrix} \frac{\partial^2 u}{\partial a_1 \partial a_i^*} \\ \vdots \\ \frac{\partial^2 u}{\partial a_1 \partial a_i^*} \end{bmatrix}
$$

where $\mathbf{J}$ is the Hessian matrix associated with the optimization. However, we have

$$
\frac{\partial^2 u_i}{\partial a_i \partial a_i^*} = 2\beta_i - \sigma_i \sum \frac{\partial\mu_{ji}}{\partial a_i},
$$

and

$$
\frac{\partial^2 u_i}{\partial a_j \partial a_i^*} = 0, \qquad \text{for } j \neq i.
$$

Thus

$$
\begin{bmatrix} \frac{da_1}{da_i^*} \\ \vdots \\ \frac{da_1}{da_i^*} \end{bmatrix} = -\mathbf{J}^{-1} \begin{bmatrix} 0 \\ \vdots \\ 2\beta_i - \sigma_i \sum \frac{\partial\mu_{ji}}{\partial a_i} \\ \vdots \\ 0 \end{bmatrix}.
$$

If we solve for da_i/da_i^* using Cramer's rule, and using the fact that the second-order condition for a maximum requires that the determinant of $\mathbf{J}$ and that of the ith principal minor must have opposite signs, we conclude that $da_i/da_i^* > 0$; in other words, *if an agent raises his contribution norm, his contribution increases*.

5   THE BIOECONOMICS OF PROSOCIAL EMOTIONS

The Adam Smith of *The Theory of Moral Sentiments* is, of course, much less well known and less studied than the Adam Smith of *The Wealth of Nations*. Generations of economists have puzzled that the same Scottish philosopher whose analysis of sympathy is perhaps the greatest analysis of emotion in the English language before William James [49], could also give us an even more famous discourse based on the idea that "It is not from the benevolence of the butcher, the brewer, or the baker that we expect our dinner, but from their regard to their own interest." In fact, we now know from laboratory experiments that subjects in market-like situations behave like the Adam Smith of *The Wealth of Nations*, while their behavior in strategic interactions resembles more the Adam Smith of *The Theory of Moral Sentiments*. Perhaps this is the distinction Smith had in mind in writing his two great books.

Economic theorists have long assumed that individuals act to maximize their private gain. While arguments in favor of this assumption are rarely systematically presented, the informal argument is that other types of behavior should be driven from the scene by the relentless success of the self-interested types. This argument may be plausible when profit-oriented firms are the object of analysis [1], but why should it hold when subjective utility is the object of our strivings?

To answer this question, arguments from biology have conveniently stepped in to fill the breech [43, 67, 68]. Evolution ensures that only the self-interested survive. What appears to be altruism—personal sacrifice on behalf of others—is really just self-interest at the genetic level. Richard Dawkins [25], for instance, writes "We are survival machines—robot vehicles blindly programmed to preserve the selfish molecules known as genes.... This gene selfishness will usually give rise to selfishness in individual behavior." Similarly, in a famous work devoted exclusively to human sociality, R. D. Alexander [2] asserts that "ethics, morality, human conduct, and the human psyche are to be understood only if societies are seen as collections of individuals seeking their own self-interest." (p. 3).

The empirical evidence shows that humans systematically deviate from the model of the self-interested actor, and we think the evidence is strong that prosocial emotions account for much of this behavior. But, alternative descriptions of behavior would be more compelling if we understood how prosocial emotions might have evolved, culturally, genetically, or both. The puzzle here is that prosocial emotions are at least *prima facie* altruistic, benefiting others at a cost to oneself, so that under simple payoff-monotonic replicator dynamics, in which the selfishly favorable trait tends to increase in frequency, prosociality should atrophy. This question is, of course, the subject of active research these days among economists and other decision theorists [23, 27, 28, 34, 35]. We will not propose a definitive answer, but rather suggest some fruitful lines of research and the reasoning on which they are based.

5.1   THE INTERNALIZATION OF NORMS

One does not feel shame merely because one is thought ill of by one's social group. Indeed, if one has acted honorably according to one's own values, and one is nevertheless punished, one feels spiteful rather than shameful. This is indicated in our model by the fact that the sign of the shame term depends on whether $a^* > a$, in which case one feels shame when punished, and hence acts to increase one's contribution a, or $a^* > a$, in which case one feels spite, and hence acts to decrease one's contribution a. The parameter a^* is thus a personal attribute that is absolutely central to how one reacts emotionally to group sanctions. What sort of entity is a^*?

Parameter a^* is an *internalized norm*. In general, a *norm* is a rule sanctioned by a group and followed by its members [5, 9, 12, 16, 29, 33, 45, 50, 51]. Generally, then, norms are *constraints* that one must obey in maximizing one's welfare (e.g., the norm of honesty in commercial transactions), presumably because violating the norm would be more costly than obeying it.

An *internalized* norm is a norm that one has accepted, not as a constraint, but rather as an *argument of one's objective function*. We strive to conform to internalized norms not only because we will be punished if we do not conform, but because we actively *wish* to conform. For instance, consider the norm of "helping individuals in distress." I may help an individual in distress because I will be rewarded by my social group for doing so, or I will be punished for not doing so. If the norm is internalized, however, I help because I personally and genuinely want to (or at least believe I should want to), and if I did not help, I would feel *guilt*. Moreover, if I were discovered not helping, I would feel *shame*. In the latter case, I have "internalized" the norm of helping people in distress. Abraham Lincoln captured the idea of internalized norms when he wrote "when I do good, I feel good. When I do bad, I feel bad. That is my religion."

Sociological theory treats the internalization of norms as a central element in the analysis of prosocial behavior [26, 41, 58]. Norms are trasmitted from parents (*vertical transmission*), influential elders and institutional practices (*oblique transmission*), and one's peers (*horizontal transmission*) [14, 20]. The psychological mechanisms that account for internalization are doubtless complex, and the phenomenon is probably unique to our species. The fully informed, self-interested optimizer of standard economic theory would not internalize a norm, since doing so places value on the norm above and beyond the extrinsic social benefit of conforming to it and social cost of violating it, so the optimizer will conform more closely to the norm than he would if he treated it simply as a constraint. So why does internalization exist?

The answer may be that human society is so complex and the benefits and costs of conforming to or violating its many norms so difficult to assess, that full-scale optimization using norms as constraints is excessively, and even perhaps fatally, error-prone [8, 44]. The internalization of norms eliminates many of the cost/benefit calculations and replaces them with simple moral and prudential guidelines for action. Individuals who internalize norms may, therefore, have higher payoffs than those who do not, so the psychological mechanisms of internalization are evolutionarily selected.

There are two important implications of norm internalization for the economic analysis of social cooperation. The first is that when an agent internalizes a norm, it remains an argument in his utility function in social settings other than those accounting for the evolutionary success of the norm. This explains why an individual who has a norm of "rejecting low offers," which serves him well in daily life by helping build a reputation for hard bargaining, will continue to embrace this norm in a one-shot ultimatum game. Norm internalization thus may help explain the otherwise anomalous behavior exhibited in laboratory bargaining settings.

The second important implication of norm internalization is that it can explain *altruistic* behavior, in which the individual behaves in a way that is personally costly but that benefits the group—as, for instance, punishing noncontributors in a public goods game. The connection between altruism and internalization was first proposed by Herbert Simon [64], who suggested that if internalization (Simon called it "docility," in its root meaning of "easy to mold or shape") is, in general, fitness enhancing, then social institutions could add to the set of norms transmitted vertically and obliquely, some that in fact are fitness reducing for the individual, though group beneficial. Gintis [38] provides a gene-culture coevolution model demonstrating the plausibility of Simon's theory.[4]

Empirically, all societies indeed promote a combination of self-regarding and altruistic norms. All known cultures foster norms that enhance personal fitness, such as prudence, personal hygiene, and control of emotions, but also promote norms that subordinate the individual to group welfare, fostering such behaviors as unconditional bravery, honesty, fairness, and willingness to cooperate, to refrain from overexploiting a common pool resource, to vote and otherwise participate in the political life of the community, to act on behalf of one's ethnic or religious group, and to identify with the goals of an organization of which one is a member, such as a business firm or a residential community [18]. The central tenets of virtually all of the world's great religions also exhibit this tendency of combining personally fitness-enhancing norms and altruistic norms, as well as denying that there is any essential difference between the two.

One important social norm is "reward those who obey social norms and punish those who do not." This norm is clearly altruistic, and is subject to internalization. Those who internalize this norm in the public goods game are precisely those with high λs.

---

[4]The central problem any such model must handle is why those who internalize both the fitness-enhancing norms and the altruistic norms are not out-competed by those who internalize only the fitness-enhancing norms. An analysis of genotype-phenotype interaction explains why this "unraveling" of altruistic behavior need not occur.

5.2   PAIN

Pain is one of the six so-called "basic" emotions, the others being pleasure, anger, fear, surprise, and disgust. Shame is one of the seven so-called "social" emotions, of which the others are love, guilt, embarrassment, pride, envy, and jealousy [27, 59]. Shame has a similar role in regulating social behavior as does pain in regulating behavior in general, so we shall begin with an analysis of the role of pain in behavior. Basic and social emotions are expressed in all human societies, although their expression is affected by cultural conditions. For instance, one may be angered by an immoral act, or disgusted by an unusual foodstuff, but what counts as an immoral act or a disgusting foodstuff is, at least to some extent, culturally specific.

Complex organisms have the ability to learn to avoid damage. The measure of damage is pain, a highly aversive sensation the organism will attempt to avoid in the future. Yet an organism with complete information, an unlimited capacity to process information, and with a fitness-maximizing way of discounting future costs and benefits would have no use for pain. Such an agent would be able to assess the costs of any damage to itself, would calculate an optimal response to such damage, and would prepare optimally for future occurrences of this damage. The aversive stimulus—pain—would then be *strongly distorting of optimal behavior*, because pain will lead the agent to assuasive and avoidance behavior *in addition to* responding constructively to the damage. Since pain clearly does have adaptive value, it follows that modeling pain *presupposes* that the agent experiencing pain must have incomplete information and/or a limited capacity to process information, and/or an excessively high rate of discounting future benefits and costs.

5.3   SHAME

Pain is a pre-social emotion. Shame is a social emotion: a distress that is experienced when one is devalued in the eyes of one's consociates because of a value that one has violated or a behavioral norm that one has not lived up to.

Does shame serve a purpose similar to that of pain? If being socially devalued has fitness costs, and if the amount of shame is closely correlated with the level of these fitness costs, then the answer is affirmative. Shame, like pain, is an aversive stimulus that leads the agent experiencing it to repair the situation that led to the stimulus, and to avoid such situations in the future. Shame, like pain, replaces an involved optimization process with a simple message: whatever you did, undo it if possible, and do not do it again.

Since shame is evolutionarily selected and is costly to use, it very likely confers a selective advantage on those who experience it. Two types of selective advantage are at work here. First, shame may raise the fitness of an agent who has incomplete information (e.g., as to how fitness-reducing a particular antisocial action is), limited or imperfect information-processing capacity, and/or a tendency to undervalue costs and benefits that accrue in the future. Probably all three conditions conspire to react suboptimally to social disapprobation in the absence of shame, and shame brings us closer to the optimum. Of course the role of shame in alerting us to negative consequences in the future presupposes that society is organized to impose those costs on rule violators. The emotion of shame may have coevolved with the emotions motivating punishment of antisocial actions (the reciprocity motive in our model).

The second selective advantage to those experiencing shame arises through the effects of group competition. Where the emotion of shame is common, punishment of antisocial actions will be particularly effective and, as a result, seldom used. Thus, groups in which shame is common can sustain high levels of group cooperation at limited cost and will be more likely to spread through interdemic group selection [11, 17]. Shame thus serves as a means of economizing on costly within-group punishment.

6 CONCLUSION

The experimental evidence and reasoning presented here suggest that there is something fundamentally wrong with the behavioral assumptions underlying the canonical approach to economic policy and constitution-making. This approach assumes that agents will maximize a pre-given objective function subject to whatever costs and benefits are defined by the policy or law. However, when agents consider the policy-making body to be valid and legitimate, they will avoid violating the rules on principle, and not only because they will be rewarded for obeying, or punished for transgressing the rules. Albert Hirschman [47, p. 10] described the situation this way:

> *Economists often propose to deal with unethical or antisocial behavior by raising the cost of that behavior rather than proclaiming standards and imposing prohibitions and sanctions. The reason is probably that they think of citizens as consumers with unchanging or arbitrarily changing tastes in matters of civic as well as commodity-oriented behavior. A principal purpose of publicly proclaimed laws and regulations is to stigmatize antisocial behavior and thereby to influence citizens' values and behavior codes.*

Hirschman believes that penalties imposed on miscreants affect behavior in two ways: first, they alter the payoff consequences of various actions; and second, they affect the preferences that actors use in evaluating the consequences of their actions. His point is that economists are remiss in focusing entirely on the first. This narrow focus is nowhere more clear than in much of modern public economics, which seeks to design policies such that agents' given (selfish) preferences lead them individually to act in ways that implement a socially valued outcome as a Nash equilibrium.

Hirschman is arguing against a venerable tradition, not only in economics, but in political philosophy as well, one dating back before Smith wrote his *Theory of Moral Sentiments*. In 1754, David Hume [48] advised "that, in contriving any system of government. . . every man ought to be supposed to be a knave and to have no other end, in all his actions, than his private interest." But he was appealing to prudence, not to realism. His next sentence reads: "it is strange that a maxim should be true in politics which is false in fact." However if, as Hume realized, individuals are not uniformly selfish, but rather are sometimes given to the honorable sentiments about which Smith wrote, then prudence might recommend an alternative dictum: policy makers and constitution builders should know that populations are heterogeneous and the individuals making them up are both versatile and plastic, and that good policies and constitutions are those that support socially valued outcomes not only by harnessing selfish motives to socially valued ends, but also by evoking, cultivating, and empowering publicly spirited motives. It is not as tidy as Hume's dictum, and implementing it requires the analysis of the emergent properties of rather complex interactions among heterogeneous agents, but both realism and prudence may be claimed for it.

ACKNOWLEDGMENTS

We dedicate this chapter to Kenneth Arrow, both as a scientist and a friend, for whom we have the deepest admiration, and from whom we have drawn the most profound inspiration. Presented at the workshop, The Economy as a Complex Evolving System III, in honor of Kenneth Arrow, Santa Fe Institute, November 16–18, 2001. Thanks to Kenneth Arrow, John Geanakoplos, Charles Manski, Giorgio Topa, Peyton Young, and other workshop participants for helpful comments, to George Cowan for the van Gogh quote, to the John D. and Catherine T. MacArthur Foundation for financial support.

REFERENCES

[1] Alchian, Armen. "Uncertainty, Evolution, and Economic Theory." *J. Pol. Econ.* **58** (1950): 211–221.

[2] Alexander, R. D. *The Biology of Moral Systems*. New York: Aldine, 1987.

[3] Andreoni, James. "Cooperation in Public Goods Experiments: Kindness or Confusion." *Am. Econ. Rev.* **85(4)** (1995): 891–904.

[4] Arrow, Kenneth J. "Political and Economic Evaluation of Social Effects and Externalities." In *Frontiers of Quantitative Economics*, edited by M. D. Intriligator, 3–23. Amsterdam: North Holland, 1971.

[5] Axelrod, Robert. "An Evolutionary Approach to Norms." *Am. Pol. Sci. Rev.* **80** (1986): 1095–1111.

[6] Axelrod, Robert, and William D. Hamilton. "The Evolution of Cooperation." *Science* **211** (1981): 1390–1396.

[7] Barr, Abigail. "Social Dilemmas, Shame Based Sanctions, and Shamelessness: Experimental Results from Rural Zimbabwe." Paper presented at third Tokyo International Conference on African Development, held August 2003, in Tokyo, Japan. October 2003. ⟨http://www.comminit.com/st2003/sld-900.html⟩

[8] Benabou, Roland, and Jean Tirole. "Self Confidence and Personal Motivation." *Quart. J. Econ.* **117(3)** (2002): 871–915.

[9] Binmore, Ken, and Larry Samuelson. "An Economist's Perspective on the Evolution of Norms." *J. Inst. Theoret. Econ.* (1994): 45–63.

[10] Bosman, Ronald, and Frans van Winden. "Emotional Hazard in a Power-to-Take Experiment." *Econ. J.* **112** (2002): 147–169.

[11] Bowles, Samuel, and Herbert Gintis. "The Evolution of Strong Reciprocity: Cooperation in Heterogeneous Populations." *Theor. Pop. Biol.* **65** (2004): 17–28.

[12] Bowles, Samuel, and Herbert Gintis. "The Origins of Human Cooperation." In *The Genetic and Cultural Origins of Cooperation*, edited by Peter Hammerstein. Cambridge, MA: MIT Press, 2003.

[13] Bowles, Samuel, and Herbert Gintis. "Social Capital and Community Governance." *Econ. J.* **112(483)** (2002): 419–436.

[14] Boyd, Robert, and Peter J. Richerson. *Culture and the Evolutionary Process.* Chicago, IL: University of Chicago Press, 1985.

[15] Boyd, Robert, and Peter J. Richerson. "The Evolution of Reciprocity in Sizable Groups." *J. Theoret. Biol.* **132** (1988): 337–356.

[16] Boyd, Robert, and Peter J. Richerson. "The Evolution of Norms: An Anthropological View." *J. Inst. Theoret. Econ.* **150(1)** (1994): 72–87.

[17] Boyd, Robert, Herbert Gintis, Samuel Bowles, and Peter J. Richerson. "Altruistic Punishment in Large Groups Evolves by Interdemic Group Selection." *PNAS* **100** (2003): 3531–3535.

[18] Brown, Donald E. *Human Universals.* New York: McGraw-Hill, 1991.

[19] Camerer, Colin, and Richard Thaler. "Ultimatums, Dictators, and Manners." *J. Econ. Pers.* **9(2)** (1995): 209–219.

[20] Cavalli-Sforza, Luigi L., and Marcus W. Feldman. *Cultural Transmission and Evolution*. Princeton, NJ: Princeton University Press, 1981.

[21] Cohen, Jonathan D. "Reward and Decision." *Neuron* **36** (2002): 193–198.

[22] Cosmides, Leda, and John Tooby. "Cognitive Adaptations for Social Exchange." In *The Adapted Mind: Evolutionary Psychology and the Generation of Culture*, Jerome H. Barkow, Leda Cosmides, and John Tooby, 163–228. New York: Oxford University Press, 1992.

[23] Damasio, Antonio R. *Descartes' Error: Emotion, Reason, and the Human Brain.* New York: Avon Books, 1994.

[24] Dawes, Robyn M., John M. Orbell, and J. C. Van de Kragt. "Organizing Groups for Collective Action." *Am. Pol. Sci. Rev.* **80** (1986): 1171–1185.

[25] Dawkins, Richard. *The Selfish Gene*, 2d ed. Oxford: Oxford University Press, 1989.

[26] Durkheim, Emile. *Suicide, A Study in Sociology.* New York: Free Press, 1951.

[27] Ekman, Paul. "An Argument for Basic Emotions." *Cog. & Emotion* **6** (1992): 169–200.

[28] Elster, Jon. "Emotions and Economic Theory." *J. Econ. Pers.* **36** (1998): 47–74.

[29] Elster, Jon. "Social Norms and Economic Theory." *J. Econ. Pers.* **3(4)** (1989): 99–117.

[30] Falk, Armin, and Urs Fischbacher. "Modeling Strong Reciprocity." In *Interest: On the Foundations of Cooperation in Economic Life.* Cambridge, MA: MIT Press, 2005.

[31] Fehr, Ernst, and Simon Gächter. "Cooperation and Punishment." *Am. Econ. Rev.* **90(4)** (2000): 980–994.

[32] Fehr, Ernst, and Klaus M. Schmidt. "A Theory of Fairness, Competition, and Cooperation." *Quart. J. Econ.* **114** (1999): 817–868.

[33] Frank, Robert. "Social Forces in the Workplace." In *Social Norms and Economic Institutions*, edited by Kenneth Koford and Jeffrey Miller, 151–179. Ann Arbor, MI: University of Michigan Press, 1991.

[34] Frank, Robert H. "If *Homo Economicus* Could Choose His Own Utility Function, Would He Want One with a Conscience?" *Am. Econ. Rev.* **77(4)** (1987): 593–604.

[35] Frank, Robert H. *Passions Within Reason: The Strategic Role of the Emotions.* New York: Norton, 1988.

[36] Fudenberg, Drew, and Eric Maskin. "The Folk Theorem in Repeated Games with Discounting or with Incomplete Information." *Econometrica* **54(3)** (1986): 533–554.

[37] Geanakoplos, John, David Pearce, and Ennio Stacchetti. "Psychological Games and Sequential Rationality." *Games & Econ. Behav.* **1** (1989): 60–79.

[38] Gintis, Herbert. "The Hitchhiker's Guide to Altruism: Gene—Culture, Coevolution, and the Internalization of Norms." *J. Theoret. Biol.* **220(4)** (2003): 407–418.

[39] Gneezy, Uri, and Aldo Rustichini. "A Fine is a Price." *J. Legal Stud.* **29** (2000): 1–17.

[40] Greene, Joshua D. "An fMRI Investigation of Emotional Engagement in Moral Judgement." *Science* **293** (2001): 2105–2108.

[41] Grusec, Joan E., and Leon Kuczynski. *Parenting and Children's Internalization of Values: A Handbook of Contemporary Theory.* New York: John Wiley & Sons, 1997.

[42] Güth, Werner, and Reinhard Tietz. "Ultimatum Bargaining Behavior: A Survey and Comparison of Experimental Results." *J. Econ. Psychol.* **11** (1990): 417–449.

[43] Hamilton, W. D. "The Genetical Evolution of Social Behavior." *J. Theoret. Biol.* **37** (1964): 1–16, 17–52.

[44] Heiner, Ronald, A. "Imperfect Choice and Rule-Governed Behavior." In *Markets and Democracy: Participation Accountability and Efficiency,* edited by Samuel Bowles, Herbert Gintis, and B. Gustafsson. Cambridge, UK: Cambridge University Press, 1993.

[45] Henrich, Joseph, and Robert Boyd. "Why People Punish Defectors: Weak Conformist Transmission can Stabilize Costly Enforcement of Norms in Co-operative Dilemmas." *J. Theoret. Biol.* **208** (2001): 79–89.

[46] Henrich, Joe, Robert Boyd, Samuel Bowles, Colin Camerer, Ernst Fehr, and Herbert Gintis. *Foundations of Human Sociality.* Oxford: Oxford University Press, 2004.

[47] Hirschman, Albert. "Against Parsimony." *Econ. Phil.* **1** (1985): 7–21.

[48] Hume, David. *Essays: Moral, Political, and Literary.* London: Longmans, Green, 1898 [1754].

[49] James, William. "What is an Emotion?" *Mind* **9** (1884): 188–205.

[50] Jordan, J. S. "Bayesian Learning in Normal Form Games." *Games & Econ. Behav.* **3** (1991): 60–81.

[51] Kandori, Michihiro. "Social Norms and Community Enforcement." *Rev. Econ. Stud.* **57** (1992): 63–80.

[52] Laibson, David. "A Cue-Theory of Consumption." *Quart. J. Econ.* **66(1)** (2001): 81–120.

[53] Levine, David K. "Modeling Altruism and Spitefulness in Experiments." *Rev. Econ. Dyn.* **1(3)** (1998): 593–622.

[54] Loewenstein, George F. "Out of Control: Visceral Influences on Behavior." *Org. Behav. & Hum. Dec. Proc.* **65** (1996): 272–292.

[55] Masclet, David, Charles Noussair, Steven Tucker, and Marie-Claire Villeval. "Monetary and Non-Monetary Punishment in the Voluntary Contributions Mechanism." *Am. Econ. Rev.* **93(1)** (2003): 366–380.

[56] Moll, Jorge. "The Neural Correlates of Moral Sensitivity: A Functional Magnetic Resonance Imaging Investigation of Basic and Moral Emotions." *J. Neurosci.* **22(7)** (2002): 2730–2736.

[57] Ostrom, Elinor, James Walker, and Roy Gardner. "Covenants with and Without a Sword: Self-Governance Is Possible." *Am. Pol. Sci. Rev.* **86(2)** (1992): 404–417.

[58] Parsons, Talcott. *Sociological Theory and Modern Society.* New York: Free Press, 1967.

[59] Plutchik, R. *Emotion: A Psychoevolutionary Synthesis.* New York: Harper & Row, 1980.

[60] Rilling, James K. "A Neural Basis for Social Cooperation." *Neuron* **35** (2002): 395–405.

[61] Roth, Alvin. "Bargaining Experiments." In *The Handbook of Experimental Economics*, edited by John Kagel and Alvin Roth. Princeton, NJ: Princeton University Press, 1995.

[62] Sato, Kaori. "Distribution and the Cost of Maintaining Common Property Resources." *J. Exper. Soc. Psychol.* **23** (1987): 19–31.

[63] Sethi, Rajiv, and E. Somanathan. "Preference Evolution and Reciprocity." *J. Econ. Theor.* **97** (2001): 273–297.

[64] Simon, Herbert. "A Mechanism for Social Selection and Successful Altruism." *Science* **250** (1990): 1665–1668.

[65] Simon, Herbert. *Models of Bounded Rationality.* Cambridge, MA: MIT Press, 1982.

[66] Taylor, Michael. *Anarchy and Cooperation.* London: John Wiley & Sons, 1976.

[67] Trivers, R. L. "The Evolution of Reciprocal Altruism." *Quart. Rev. Biol.* **46** (1971): 35–57.

[68] Williams, G. C. *Adaptation and Natural Selection: A Critique of Some Current Evolutionary Thought.* Princeton, NJ: Princeton University Press, 1966.

[69] Yamagishi, Toshio. "Group Size and the Provision of a Sanctioning System in a Social Dilemma." In *Social Dilemma: Theoretical Issues and Research Findings*, edited by W. B. G. Liebrand, David M. Messick, and H. A. M. Wilke, 267–287. Oxford: Pergamon Press, 1992.

[70] Yamagishi, Toshio. "The Provision of a Sanctioning System in the United States and Japan." *Soc. Psychol. Quart.* **51(3)** (1988): 265–271.

[71] Yamagishi, Toshio. "Seriousness of Social Dilemmas and the Provision of a Sanctioning System." *Soc. Psychol. Quart.* **51(1)** (1988): 32–42.

[72] Zajonc, R. B. "Feeling and Thinking: Preferences Need No Inferences." *Am. Psychol.* **35(2)** (1980): 151–175.

Index

A

Aaronson, D., 282
Abreu, D., 216
access costs, 311
additive process, 104
adoption, 31
agent-based models, 16–26
agglomeration, 282
aggregate
    choice probabilities, 180–182
    distribution, 111, 112
    endowment, 61, 62
    expectations equations, 6
    inflation expectations, 24–26
    price change, 124
Akiva, B., 194
Alexander, R. D., 355
allocated surplus economy, 255, 256
alternative error assumptions, 188–190
altruism, 344, 345, 347, 350, 355
Amaro de Matos, J., 184
ambiguity, 34, 40, 46, 47
American Stock Exchange (AMEX), 74
analysis of patterns, 2

analysis of social interaction, 3
annihilation rate, 149
arbitrage, 60
arms race game, 206
Arrow securities economy, 51, 57, 59, 60, 63, 61
Arrow, K., 174, 196, 307
artificial revelation, 325, 329
asset markets, 49
asset prices, 64
assortative matching, 253
asymptotic
    bias, 18
    depth, 146
    equality, 82
atmospheric engine, 325, 326
augmented Dickey-Fuller test, 12
autocorrelation function, 294
average price impact function, 135, 158

B

Bak, P., 140
Baliga, S., 215
Bandiera, O., 289

Banerjee, A. Y., 282
Barr, A., 346
Bayesian decision theory, 37
Bayesian investor, 58
Bayesian learning, 53, 54
Bayesian updating, 50, 53
Becker, G. S., 282
behavior choice, 191–195
behavior preferences motivated by expected utility, 56–58
behavioral anonymity, 241
behavioral independence, 242
behavioral interdependence, 241
belief restrictions, 50, 51
belief-based expected utility (BBEU) representation, 55–56, 57
Bell, A., 282
Benabou, R., 282
Bertrand, M., 282
Bessemer steelmaking response, 329
bid-ask spread, 133, 135
Bikhchandani, S., 282
binary action example, 209–216, 221
binary choice, 184, 198
bioeconomics of prosocial emotions, 355–359
Blume, Lawrence E., 1, 49, 266, 268
Boissevain, C. H., 104
Bollerslev, T., 140
boundary conditions, 139
bounded marginals, 227
bounded rationality, 341
Bowles, Samuel, 337
Brock, William A., 173, 183, 282
Brunnermeir, M., 216
bunching, 182
Burdzy, K., 216
Burt, R. S., 283

C
Calvo-Armengol, A., 283, 289, 300
Campbell, D., 312
Carlsson, H., 232, 233
Carroll, Christopher D., 5, 7
Case, A. C., 282
Cavalli-Sforza, L. L., 313, 317

Center for Research and Security Prices (CRSP) database, 75
central limit theorem, 75, 77, 79, 184
chemicals, history and epistemic base, 326, 327
Chicago labor market, 283
Ciccone, A., 216
close-knittedness, 267, 272, 274–276
clustering, 284
coherency condition, 54, 56–58
cohesiveness, 272
Cole, H. L., 256
Coleman, J. S., 265, 282, 283
collective efficacy, 176
common source model, 5, 16
competence, 312
competitive equilibrium, 241, 246
complete information analysis, 228
complete information games, 206
complexity, 46, 242
concave market impact functions, 135
conformity, 179, 282
Conley, Timothy G., 281
conservation law, 161
conspicuous consumption economy, 256–259, 261
consumption, 246
contextual effects, 185, 186
contingent decision problems, 54–56
contingent preference structure, 54, 55
continuous double auction, 133, 136, 137
Cooper, R., 208, 221, 228
cooperative equilibria, 182–184
Corcoran, M., 283
correct beliefs, 64
correlated effects, 243
correlated heterogeneity, 216
correlations in the volatility, 77, 78
Cort's puddling and rolling technique, 328
cost-minimizing pooling equilibrium, 258
Costain, J., 216
Cournot duopoly, 246
Crane, J., 282
critical phenomena, 71
critical point phenomena, 70
cross-correlations, 84, 85

cross-section variability, 21, 22
cross-sectional clustering, 286
crossing limit order, 137, 138
cultural selection, 318
cumulative distribution function, 157
current population survey (CRS), 285, 286, 290, 292
Curtin, R. T., 21

D

Damasio, A. R., 340
Daniels, Marcus G., 133, 137
Darwinian system, 313
data collapse, 71
Davis, H., 103, 104
Dawkins, R., 313, 355
decision theory, 60
decisionmakers, 31, 32, 51, 55
    rational expectations of, 35
decisionmaking, 35–37
    in social interactions, 174
Delong, J. b., 51
demand storage, 134
density function, 122
depth fluctuations, 166
depth profile, 136, 147–150
Dickey-Fuller test, 12
detrended fluctuation analysis (DFA), 84
differentiability, 253
diffusion, 107
dimensional analysis, 136, 141–145, 147
dimensional reduction, 142
dimensional scaling formula, 145
direct effect, 231
discount factors, 63
discreteness parameters, 142
distribution of stock returns, 102
distribution of talent, 112
distribution of wealth, 102
Doblin-Gnedenko result, 123
dominated actions, 36
Domowitz, I., 140
Durbin-Watson statistic, 20
Durlauf, Steven N., 1, 173, 183, 282
dynamic games, 209
dynamic interpretation, 213

dynamical statistical model, 133
dynamics, 313
    of choice, 38, 39
    of information accumulation, 32, 33
    of wealth, 61–64

E

Easley, David, 49
econometric analysis, 184, 191, 192
economic fluctuations, 67
economic history, 307
    of technology, 322
econophysics, 90
education, 282, 288
effective limit orders, 138
effective market orders, 138
efficiency, 250, 251
efficient equilibrium, 254, 256
Eliezer, D., 140
Ellis, R., 183
Ellison, G., 266, 267, 274
Elster, Jon, 341
emotions, moral response to punishment, 341–347
endogenous effects, 185, 186, 243, 244
endogenous group membership, and linear-in-means model, 192–194
endogenous growth, 282
endowment, 60–62
epidemiology
    of expectations, 8–16
    of inflation expectations, 9–13
    of macroeconomic expectations, 5
epistemic base, 310–312, 314, 315, 322, 324–326, 328
equilibrium
    analysis, 241, 242
    market phases, 86, 87
    matching function, 254, 257
    phase, 67
    prices, 59, 60
equity, 259
erogeneity, 206
escalation, 324
evolutionary analysis, 241
evolutionary dynamics, 324
evolutionary epistemology, 320

excess demand function, 135
exogenous contextual effects, 243
exogenous effects, 243
expected utility, 55–58

F
facultative response, 323
Farmer, J. Doyne, 133
Farmer networks, 289
Fehr, E., 342
Feldman, W. M., 313, 317
Fernandez, R., 282
filling orders, 133
financial earthquakes, 68, 69, 83
first-order Markov process, 284, 289
fitness, 318
focusing devices, 324
Frank, R. H., 251
Frankel, D., 216, 230
future beliefs, 56–57

G
Gabaix, Xavier, 67
Gächter, S., 342
Gale, D., 282
Gautreaux program, 175
general equilibrium effects, 260, 261
general equilibrium model, 51
genetic assimilation, 323
geometric discounting, 52
Gillemot, László, 133
Gintis, Herbert, 337, 357
Glaeser, E. L., 281
global conservation relations, 161
global games, 206, 215, 232
global heterogeneity sufficient condition, 227
Gneezy, U., 339
Gopikrishnan, Parameswaran, 67
Granovetter, M. S., 174, 283, 288, 299
granularity parameter ϵ, 147–156
group choice, 191–195
group competition, 359
group membership, 191–194, 195
guilt, 337, 340, 347–350

H
Hanushek, E., 282
Harsanyi, J., 208, 232
Heckman, J., 193
heritability, 313, 315
Herrendorf, B., 216
heterogeneity, 206, 216, 227
  generating uniqueness, 205–238
  in λ, 17–20
  in interaction games, 205–229, 231–238
  independent, 215
Hirsch, F., 246
Hirschman, Albert, 359
homogeneous multiplicative wealth accumulation process, 106–108
household survey expectations, 7
Hume, D., 360
Hurwicz, L., 37

I
identification problems
  in social interactions models, 185–189
  for binary choice models, 198
  parametric, 190
  self-selection correction in, 192, 193
iid
  beliefs, 62
  economy, 62, 63
  order flow, 169
income inequality, 282
income tax, 260, 261
incomplete information
  case, 206
  games, 205
  interpretation, 213
  related literature, 215, 216
incomplete knowledge, 44
independent interval approximation, 164–166
indirect inference methodology, 289
individual outcomes, and neighborhoods, 175
Industrial Revolution, 324, 327, 328
inefficiency, 254, 255
inflation expectations
  agent-based models of, 16–26

inflation expectations (cont'd)
    aggregate, 24–26
    cross-section variability of, 22, 23
    matching standard deviations, 20–23
    social transmission of, 23–26
inflation
    estimating, 13–16
    forecasts, 18
    transitory shock, 11
    unit root, 12
inflation rate, 11, 13
information accumulation, 32–35
information
    assumption, 32
    cascades, 282
    exchange model, 287
    flows, 283
innovation, 31, 316
    adoption rate, 41, 46
    choosing, 37–40
    in social networks, 265
    time path of adoption, 38, 41
innovators, 266
inside quotes, 136
instantaneous price impact, 150, 157
institutional change, 308
instrumental dependencies, 244
integration behaviors, nested choice approach to, 194, 195
inter-equilibrium multiplier effect, 231
interacting particle system, 285
interaction games, heterogeneity and uniqueness in, 205–229, 231–238
interdependent preferences, 282
internalization of norms, 356, 357
internalized norm, 356
intra-equilibrium multiplier effect, 229, 231
intra-equilibrium notion, 208
intrinsic interdependencies, 244
inventions, 312, 322, 323
inverse cubic law, 73
investor naïvité, 58
investor's wealth, 115, 122
Ioannides, Y., 192
Ising model, 268

J
Jackson, M. O., 283, 289, 300
job search process, 283
John, A., 208, 221, 228
joint consumption economy, 248–251
    with one-sided payoffs, 252–255

K
Katz, E., 266
Katz, L. F., 282
Keynes, J. M., 6
knowledge
    economy, 307
    λ, 311, 316, 324, 325, 327–329
    Ω, 311, 314, 319–321, 322, 324, 325, 327–329
    shared, 311
    tightness of, 311, 319, 321
    See also useful knowledge
knowledge system, vs. Darwinian systems, 313
Kockesen, L., 282
Kogan, I. I., 140
Krishnamurthy, Supriya, 133
Kuznets, S., 308, 309

L
λ knowledge, 311, 316, 324, 325, 327–329
learned behavior, 345
learning, 1
    by doing, 32
    from neighbors, 282
learning rule, belief based, 50, 55
Lee, L.-F., 192, 193
Levy, Moshe, 101
Lévy distribution, 122
    of stock returns, 101, 113–115
    truncated, 74, 114
Lévy price-change distribution, 122, 124
Lévy probability density function, deviation at 0, 125
Lévy probability distribution, 113
Lévy return distribution, $\alpha - L$, 115–117
limit order book, 136, 138, 142, 157
limit uniqueness property, 229

limiting stationary wealth distribution, 107

linear-in-means models and endogenous group membership, 192–194

liquidity, 134, 136, 150
  for limit orders, 157
  for market orders, 150–153

local heterogeneity, 229, 231, 232
  sufficient condition, 227

local interaction games, 205–206

local interaction interpretation, 213

local interaction models, dynamic properties of, 281–294, 300, 302

logarithmic prices, 139

London Stock Exchange, 135, 153, 168, 169

Lori, Giulia, 133

Los Angeles Standard Metropolitan Statistical Area (SMSA), 281

M

Machlup, F., 309

macroeconomic expectations
  agent-based models of, 16–26
  epidemiology of, 5
  inflation, 9–13
  SIR model, 8, 9

Mailath, G. J., 256

Malthusian models, 308

Mandelbrot, B. B., 73, 74, 113, 114

Mankiw, N. G., 7, 10, 15, 26

Manski, Charles F., 31, 32, 184, 185, 192, 193, 243

Mantegna, R. N., 115, 116

marginal utilities, 62, 63

market
  efficiency, 101, 102, 108–112, 121
  inefficiency, 112, 121
  orders, 136, 150–153
  phases, 86, 87

marketable limit order, 137

Markov process, 284, 289

Maslov, S., 140

matching, 136

Matia, K., 73, 74

Matsui, A., 216

Matsuyama, K., 216

McFadden, D., 194

McKelvey, D., 215

mean-field approach, 136

memory errors, 23

Mendelson, H., 140

Mendelian genetics, 314

Menzel, H., 266

mid-price diffusion, 157

mineral exploration, 327, 328

minimum-cost equilibrium, 257

missing market, 255

Mokyr, Joel, 307

Monte Carlo simulations, 107, 111

Montgomery, J. D., 283

moral response to punishment, 341–347

Morris, Stephen, 205, 216, 230, 282

Moving to Opportunity Demonstration, 175

multinomial choice model, 198

multinomial logit approach to social interactions, 178–184

multinomial logit property for the individual choices, 184

multinormal approach to social interactions, properties of, 180–182

multiplicity, 206

Myatt, D., 215

N

Nash, J., 208

Nash equilibrium, 250, 270, 350

National Association of Securities Dealers Automated Quotation (NASDAQ), 74

natural selection, 318

nature of beliefs, 49

neighborhood formation, 282

Nelson-Winter concept, 313

nested choice approach to integration behaviors and group memberships, 194

network effects, 300

network structure, 288

New York Stock Exchange (NYSE), 74, 168

news media, 6, 9, 11, 13
  affect on models, 170

news media (cont'd)
  and professional forecasters, 14
noise traders, 51
non-homogeneous multiplicative processes, 108–112
noncooperative equilibria, 182
nondimensional scale parameter, 143
norms, internalization of, 356, 357

O

observability of past actions and outcomes, 33
Ω knowledge, 311, 314, 316, 322, 324, 325, 327–329
  selection on, 319–321
one-sided payoff economy, 252–255, 261
order flow rates, 142, 168
order placement, 139, 140, 169
order size, 143, 145
order-density master equation, 161–164
out-of-equilibrium market phases, 67, 86, 87
outcome distributions, 33, 34
outliers, 67, 68, 73

P

pain, 358
Palfrey, T., 215
parametric identification for the multinomial choice model, 190
Pareto, V., 69, 70, 72, 103, 104
Pareto
  constant, 125
  density function, 123
  law, 110, 122, 126
  optimal allocations, 61
  probability density function, 107
Pareto distribution, 103–105, 107, 108
  and market efficiency, 121
  vs. aggregate distribution, 111, 112
Pareto wealth distribution, 101, 102, 106, 113, 122, 127
  $\alpha - W$, 118–120
  and Lévy distribution of stock returns, 113–115
Paris Bourse, 169
Partner effect, 342, 343

pattern identification, 2
Pauzner, A., 216, 230
payoffs, 267, 273
  and emotions, 337
  and punishment, 345, 346
  functions, 52, 54, 61, 218, 268, 269
  material, 348
pecuniary externality, 246
percolation problem, 70
Perez, J ., 184
perfect rationality, 134
perscriptive knowledge, 310, 324
persistence, 134
phenotypic plasticity, 323
Plerou, Vasiliki, 67
Poisson distribution, 138
policy interventions, 259
pooling equilibrium, 258
Popper, K., 312
positional good, 246
Postlewaite, A., 244, 256
potential function, 269, 270
poverty traps, 175
power laws, 69, 82
  See also Pareto wealth distribution
power-law scale invariance, 90
prescriptive knowledge, 310, 314, 324
  selection in, 318
price, 136, 140, 142
  diffusion and volatility, 155–157
  fluctuations, 79, 80
  impact function, 133, 134, 135, 150–153, 170
  volatility, 133
price formation
  random order placement model, 133
Price, D., 325, 329
price-change distribution, 123
prior information, 32
private values game, 210
probability and time to fill, 157
probability density function, 116, 124
probability density of the spread, 153–155
productivity, 248, 253
Project on Human Development in Chicago Neighborhoods, 176

properties of markets, 133
propositional knowledge, 310, 312, 314,
    315, 317, 324
  selection in, 318
  selection of, 321
prosocial emotions, 337, 341–347
  bioeconomics of, 355–359
  defined, 340
public goods game, 340–342
  with two agents, 347–352
  Zimbabwe, 346, 347
publicity multiplier, 208
punishment
  general model of, 352–354
  with two agents, 347–352
purification, 208, 232

Q
quantal response equilibria, 206, 215

R
race/ethnicity, 288, 291, 292, 294
random field theory, 282
random matching, 205, 206, 209, 216
random mixing, 25
random order placement model, 133, 140
  description of, 137–139
Rasul, I., 289
rate of decay, 166
rate of return, 116
rational behavior, 49
rational expectations, 6, 35, 36, 49, 50,
    51, 63, 64
rationality, 49
reciprocity
  future, 339
  general model of, 352–354
  motive, 337, 348
  with two agents, 347–352
Rees, A., 283
Rees, D. I., 282
reference group, 35
Rege, M., 257
regularity condition, 32
Reis, R., 7, 10, 15, 26
relative consumption, 244–246, 262
  benchmark model, 245, 246

relative consumption (cont'd)
  effects, 251
relative economic position, 242–244
return distribution, 113
  scaling of, 77, 78
  universality of, 76, 77
returns and share volume traded, 81,
    82
risk-dominant equilibrium, 273, 274
Roberts, J. M., 7, 15
Rogerson, R., 282
Rosenberg, N., 324
Rosenthal, R., 282
Rustichini, A., 339

S
Sacerdote, B., 282
Samuelson, Larry, 241
Sandroni, A., 51
scale invariance, 71, 82
scale-invariant distribution, 69, 70
scaling
  first discovery of, 69
  laws, 71, 73
  of return distributions, 77, 78
Schmidt, K. M., 342
Schultz, G. P, 283
selection, 49
  problem, 32
self-consistent, 179, 190, 195, 197
  beliefs, 185
  equilibria, 189, 197
self-interest, 347
self-selection correction, 192, 193
separating equilibrium, 257–258
serial correlation properties, 20
shame, 337, 340, 341, 346, 356, 358, 359
  general model of, 352–354
  with two agents, 347–352
shares, 142
share volume traded, 80
  and returns, 81, 82
  time correlations in, 81
Shin, Hyun Song, 205
shirkers, 344–346, 349, 351
Shleifer, A., 51
signaling costs, 257, 259

Simon, Herbert, 357
Simulated Method of Moments, 289
single-crossing condition, 253
singleton techniques, 310
SIR model, 8, 9
Sjöström, T., 215
Slanina, F., 140
slow decaying, 78
Smith, A., 355
Smith, D. Eric, 133
smooth symmetric model, 221
smoothing process, 107
Snyder, C., 103
social capital, 283
social interactions, 173, 267
    in predetermined groups, 175
    modeling, 176–178
    observe in census data, 285
social interacting multinormal approach,
    178–184
social interaction models, identification
    problems in, 185–189
social learning, 31
    from private experiences, 32–40
social multiplier, 208
social network theory, 283
social networks, 285
    innovation in, 265
social norms, 338, 339
social transmission of inflation expec-
    tations, 23–26
social transmission of information, 24,
    25
social utility, 181, 182
social welfare, 270, 271
Souleles, N., 7, 17
spatial agglomeration, 284
spatial game, 268, 269
speed-of-adjustment parameter, 19
spillovers, 282, 283
spontaneous decay process, 144
spread, 136, 153–155
stable matching, 249
standard deviation, 20–23
Stanley, H. Eugene, 67, 115, 116
stationarity assumption, 32

stationarity of outcome distributions,
    34
stationary distribution of unemployment,
    289
statistical physics, 67
statistical regularity plus outliers, 68
status, 244
steady-state
    behavior, 138
    wealth distribution, 112
stochastic multiplicative processes, 104–
    108
stochastic stability, 269
stock price fluctuations, 73, 75–82
Stranger effects, 342–344
strategic complementarities, 206, 208,
    224, 229
strategic multipliers, 228, 229, 231, 232
strategic uncertainty, 225
strict best response function, 268
strong reciprocity, 341, 343, 347
structure, 313
subjective beliefs, 52
subjective expected utility (SEU), 50–
    54
    maximizer effect on equilibrium prices,
        49, 56–60, 64
    rationality, 51, 56
    representation, 54, 55
substitution, 323
Summers, L., 51
summing utilities, 258
supercritical state, 324
Survey of Professional Forecasters (SPF),
    14, 19
    inflation forecasts, 19, 21

T
tails of the return distribution, 75, 78
Tang, L.-H., 140
technology, economic history of, 322
terminal information state, 35, 39, 40
theory of the firm, 72, 73
ticks, 136, 158
tick size, 139, 142, 143, 145, 147
    varying, 157, 158
tightness of knowledge, 311, 319, 321

time, 142
  deformation, 78
  scaling, 75
  separation, 52
time correlations in share volume traded,
    81
  and volatility, 83
time-invariant probability distribution,
    40
time-scale dynamics, 74
Topa, Giorgio, 281, 284
tractable boundary condition, 138
Trades and Quotes (TAQ) database, 74
trading activity, 78–80
trading frequency, 124
transition calibration, 290
transitory shock, 12
true probability, 51
truncated Lévy distribution, 74, 114
truncation, 116, 117, 121
two-player two-action coordination game,
    215, 233
two-sided investment-and-matching model,
    256

U
Ui, T., 215
unconditional altruism, 348
undefeated equilibrium, 258
undominated actions, 37
unemployment, 26
unemployment rate, 290, 291
uniform order placement process, 149
uniformly bounded marginals on differ-
    ences, 217
uniqueness from heterogeneity, 223–228
uniqueness from payoffs alone, 222
uniqueness in interaction games, 205–
    229, 231–238
unit root, 12
universality, 72
  of the distribution of returns, 76, 77
  first discovery of, 69
University of Michigan's Survey Research
    Center, 13
unravelling problem, 271–273
urban unemployment, 281, 284–286

Urry, L., 284
useful knowledge, 308, 309
  defined, 308–312
  evolutionary approach, 312–322
  selection in, 318–322
utilitarian social welfare, 45
utility functions, 60, 62
utility maximization, 195

V
Valentinyi, A., 216
valuation, 170
van Damme, E., 232, 233
variable trading frequency, 124
Vermeij, G., 324
volatility, 83, 84, 170
  and price diffusion, 155–157
  and time correlation, 83
  correlations in, 77, 78, 80

W
waiting times, 273–277
Wald, A., 37
Waldman, R., 51
Waldmann, R., 216
Wallace, C., 215
Wang, J., 140
warring exponentials, 90
wealth
  accumulation, 110
  dynamics, 61–64
  flows, 51
  inequality, 102
  in United Kingdom, 119–120
  in United States, 119
wealth distribution, 105, 107, 112
Weinberg, B., 282
welfare analysis, 44–46
Wellman, B., 288
white noise, 11
Wisconsin Longitudinal Study, 282
Wolff, E., 125

Y
Young, H. Peyton, 265

Z
Zabel, J., 192
Zax, J. S., 282
zero-intelligence model, 170
zero-intelligence random behavior, 135